Second Edition

Women and Men Communicating

Second Edition

Women and Men Communicating

Challenges and Changes

Laurie P. Arliss
Ithaca College

Deborah J. Borisoff
New York University

WAVELAND PRESS, INC.
Long Grove, Illinois

For information about this book, contact:
Waveland Press, Inc.
4180 IL Route 83, Suite 101
Long Grove, IL 60047-9580
(847) 634-0081
info@waveland.com
www.waveland.com

Cover photo: Private Collection/Diana Ong/SuperStock

ISBN 1-57766-168-0

Printed in the United States of America

8 7 6 5 4 3 2

About the Contributors

Julie Adams (Ph.D., Pacific University) holds a doctorate in clinical psychology and a master's in journalism from Columbia University. She also completed a postdoctoral fellowship at the University of Washington Medical School and conducted research at Yale University's substance abuse treatment unit. She was an administrator for the Johns Hopkins Center for Talented Youth. She taught in the Psychology Department at Seattle University for four years.

Brenda J. Allen (Ph.D., Howard University) is associate chair and associate professor in the Department of Communication at the University of Colorado in Boulder. Her primary area of teaching and research is organizational communication, with an emphasis on workplace diversity and socially constructed aspects of identity (race, ethnicity, gender, sexual orientation, class). Her work has been published in *Management Communication Quarterly, the Journal of Applied Communication Research, Communication Theory, Communication Studies, the Southern Journal of Communication, and Sex Roles.* She has written chapters for *Rethinking Organizational and Managerial Communication from Feminist Perspectives* and *Our Voices: Essays in Culture, Ethnicity, and Communication.*

Laurie P. Arliss (Ph.D., State University of New York at Buffalo) is Professor of Speech Communication at Ithaca College in Ithaca, New York. Gender issues are central in all of her teaching and research interests. Her books include *Gender Communication* and *Contemporary Family Communication*. She has also published journal articles and book chapters on related topics such as nonverbal communication, communication in sibling dyads, and spousal interaction. She has acted as communication consultant to a variety of educational, civic, and business organizations; has served as Editor of the *Speech*

Communication Annual; and was selected as the first John F. Wilson Fellow, an honor presented by the New York State Communication Association.

Deborah J. Borisoff (Ph.D., New York University) is Professor and Director for New York University's Speech and Interpersonal Communication Program in the Department of Culture and Communication. She has coauthored or coedited nine books on communication as well as numerous journal articles and book chapters. Recent books include *The Power to Communicate: Gender Differences as Barriers, Conflict Management: A Communication Skills Approach*, and *Listening in Everyday Life: A Personal and Professional Approach*. In addition, she has served as a communication consultant to government agencies, corporations, and educational institutions both here and abroad. She is a past president of the New York State Communication Association and the Eastern Communication Association. Dr. Borisoff was recently named Distinguished Research Fellow and Distinguished Teaching Fellow by the Eastern Communication Association. In 1998, ECA awarded her the Donald H. Ecroyd and Caroline Drummond Ecroyd Teaching Excellence Award.

Judi Brownell (Ph.D., Syracuse University) is Professor of Communication and Associate Dean for Academic Affairs at the School of Hotel Administration at Cornell University. She teaches courses in organizational and managerial communication and has designed and conducted training seminars for a wide range of hospitality, educational, and other work organizations. She is author of several business and communication texts, including *Listening: Principles, Attitudes, and Skills*. She has published over seventy articles in communication and management journals. She is a past president of the International Listening Association and has been inducted into the International Listening Association Hall of Fame.

Carma L. Bylund (Ph.D. Candidate, Northwestern University) is a graduate student whose primary interests are family communication and health communication. Her scholarly interests include the examination of the functions of family stories and the creation of a teaching website about genograms for family communication students. Her publications include two pedagogical articles in *Teaching Ideas for the Basic Communication Course II*.

James W. Chesebro (Ph.D., University of Minnesota) is Professor in the Department of Communication at Indiana State University. He is past president of the National Communication Association and Eastern Communication Association. He is author of *Analyzing Media, Computer-Mediated Communication, Public Policy Decision-Making, Orientations to Public Communication* and coeditor of the third edition of *Methods of Rhetorical Criticism*. He has published articles in journals such as the *Quarterly Journal of Speech, Critical Studies in Mass Communication, Communication Monographs, Communication Education, Text and Performance Quarterly,* and *Journal of Applied Communication Research*. He has received outstanding research and service awards from the National Communication Association, Eastern Communication Association, and the Kenneth Burke Society.

Pamela Cooper (Ph.D., Purdue University) is Professor of Communication Studies at Northwestern University. Her teaching and research interests center around gender and communication, classroom communication, and intercultural communication. She has written and published extensively in all three areas. Her publications include the coauthored texts *Communication for the Classroom Teacher, Communication Between the Sexes, The Power of Story: Storytelling in Education, Roots and Routes: Intercultural Communication,* and *Making Connections: Readings in Relational Communication.*

Roberta A. Davilla (Ph.D., Ohio University) is Associate Professor of Communication Studies at the University of Northern Iowa. She specializes in family communication, interpersonal communication, and instructional development and has published articles, book chapters, and instructor's manuals in these areas. Also, she incorporates service learning components into many of her classroom assignments. She serves on a number of editorial boards and has most recently been the editor of the *Iowa Journal of Communication.* She is presently studying adolescent friendship development.

Kathleen M. Galvin (Ph.D., Northwestern University) is Professor of Communication Studies at Northwestern University where she was awarded the prestigious "Excellence in Teaching Award." She presently serves as Associate Dean of the School of Speech. Galvin is a well-known scholar who has published widely in the areas of instructional communication and family communication. She is the author of nine books, including *Family Communication: Cohesion and Change* (Allyn & Bacon, 5th ed., 1999). Her distance learning package on family communication is distributed through PBS. Galvin has presented more than 250 workshops in family communication for professional and community groups.

Joyce Hauser (Ph.D., Union Institute) is Associate Professor in the Department of Culture and Communication at New York University. She is author of a book and many articles that focus on mediation as a possible alternative to legal action and communication as a family issue. She served as a mediator and arbitrator for the Victim Services Agency and the Institute of Mediation and Conflict Resolution. She also worked as CEO of Marketing Concepts and as a broadcast journalist with NBC radio. She was honored by the National Cancer Society as one of the Top Fifteen Women in America and was named Professor of the Year at New York University's School of Education.

Elaine Bass Jenks (Ph.D., The Pennsylvania State University) is Associate Professor of Communication Studies at West Chester University. Her major teaching and research interests are health communication and gender communication. Many of her scholarly presentations are concerned with interpersonal exchanges in health care settings. Her current research focuses on interpersonal communication between and among the blind, the sighted, and the visually impaired.

Amber E. Kinser (Ph.D., Purdue University) is Assistant Professor of Communication at East Tennessee State University, where she teaches graduate and undergraduate courses in family communication, gender, workplace diversity, interpersonal communication, and persuasion. Her research interests include interpretive and critical approaches to studying family interaction, sexuality and gender, and language and meaning. Her addresses, performances, and workshops have included topics such as gender equity in the classroom, affirming gender diversity in the workplace, talking with children about sexuality, and feminist parenting. She is currently director of the Women's Studies Program at East Tennessee State University.

Linda Costigan Lederman (Ph.D., Rutgers University) is Professor in the Department of Communication at Rutgers University. She specializes in communication and health issues with an emphasis on the role of experiential learning in socially situated interactions. She has written ten books and more than three dozen journal articles and book chapters. Her research has been funded by the U.S. Department of Education, Rutgers University Health Services, and the New Jersey Consortium on Alcohol and other Drug Prevention. She is a past president of the Eastern Communication Association and received the association's Distinguished Service Award and Distinguished Teaching Fellow award. She served as Editor of *Communication Quarterly.*

Anna Matias (M.S., Claremont University; M.S. Candidate, New York University) is a human resources professional with management, staffing, training, and organizational development experience. She has worked in the financial and management consulting industries, primarily for Fortune 500 companies. She holds a master's in business from the Peter Drucker School of Management at Claremont University and is currently studying speech and interpersonal communication at New York University.

Judy C. Pearson (Ph.D., Indiana University) is Associate Dean of Arts, Humanities, and Social Sciences and Professor of Communication at North Dakota State University in Fargo, North Dakota. She has published forty-seven articles, seventeen chapters in books and monographs, and twenty-three books. Her research has been popularized on television and radio and in magazines and newspapers. She has presented over 200 convention papers and served as guest speaker at 61 colleges and universities. She is a past president of the World Communication Association and the Central States Communication Association.

Steven M. Ralston (Ph.D., Indiana University) is Associate Professor of Communication at East Tennessee State University, where he also serves as the Director of the Speech Division, Director of the Oral Communication Proficiency Program, and the Assistant Director of the Teaching and Learning Center. His research on employment interviewing has appeared in numerous scholarly journals, including the *Journal of Applied Communication Research, Communication Education,* the *Journal of Business Communication,* and the *Journal of Business and Technical Communication.* He currently serves as the Associate Editor of the *Journal of Business Communication.*

William K. Rawlins (Ph.D., Temple University) is Professor and Director of Graduate Studies in the Department of Communication at Purdue University. He teaches courses in interpersonal communication, dialogue and experience, interpretive and ethnographic inquiry, Gregory Bateson and communication theory, and communication in friendships across the life course. He received Purdue's W. Charles Redding Award for Excellence in Teaching in the years 1994–1995, 1995–1996, and 1996–1997. His book, *Friendship Matters: Communication, Dialectics, and the Life Course,* was selected as an Outstanding Academic Book by the editors of *Choice,* and received the Gerald R. Miller Book Award from the Interpersonal and Small Group Interaction Division of NCA.

Marcia Rock (Ph.D., New York University) is Director of the Broadcast Journalism Program at New York University. She is coauthor of *Waiting for Primetime: The Women of Television News.* As an independent producer, she has won two Emmy awards and numerous other awards for her documentaries on Irish American history, the conflict in Northern Ireland, women's issues, and artistic legacies. Recent works include *Back from Beyond: Women, Abuse, and Drugs* and *Daughters of Troubles: Belfast Stories,* which won the AWRT Grand Award for documentaries.

Cheri J. Simonds (Ph.D., University of Oklahoma) is Assistant Professor and Director of the Basic Communication Course at Illinois State University. She has coauthored a book titled *Communication in the Classroom* and has published several articles on gender representation in communication textbooks, teacher clarity, challenge behavior in the college classroom, and the classroom assessment.

Sheila Stainback (M.S. Candidate, Columbia University) is a veteran, Emmy–award-winning anchorwoman and television journalist at Court TV Network. She teaches broadcast journalism at New York University and is the Associate Director of the Journalism, Race, and Ethnicity Workshop at Columbia University. She has written and spoken on multicultural issues in television news, and her work has been published in the *Columbia Journalism Review, The Communicator,* and *Essence Magazine.* She has worked at CNBC, the Fox News Channel, and television stations in Baltimore, Chicago, and Miami.

Lea P. Stewart (Ph.D., Purdue University) is Professor in the Department of Communication at Rutgers University. She specializes in communication and gender, communication ethics, and organizational communication. She has written or edited eight books, published 38 book chapters and journal articles, and codesigned a variety of simulations and games for instructional use. Her books include *Communication and Gender* and *Communication and Human Behavior.* Her scholarly work has appeared in such journals as *Communication Monographs, Journal of Communication, Academy of Management Journal,* and *Communication Education.*

David A. Victor (Ph.D., University of Michigan) is Professor of Management at the Eastern Michigan University College of Business, where he teaches graduate and undergraduate courses on international business communication, managerial communication, and international management. He is author of *International Business Communication* and coauthor of *Conflict Management: A Communication Skills Approach.* He has published several scholarly articles in international management and business communication journals and received several grants from the U.S. Department of Education in the area of international business. He was the first Distinguished Visiting Foreign Professor at Mexico's Instituto Technologico y de Superiores de Monterrey.

Contents

Preface

Until recently, many early works on gender and communication regarded men and women, masculinity and femininity, male and female as polar opposites. It was assumed that growing up male or female in North American culture implied learning divergent communication styles. Attitudes toward relationships, toward the world of work, and toward participating in the family were presumed to be distinct. Even the sex-trait and sex-role stereotypes and behavioral expectations deemed appropriate for women and men were regarded as different. Notice the terms used in the last few sentences: "divergent," "distinct," "different." Why has this oppositional orientation persisted?

Thinking in bipolar terms reflects a legacy of Western thought. One set of opposites that has endured for centuries is male and female. Most particularly, however, the Industrial Revolution became one marker that both physically as well as psychically etched distinct spheres for women and men in society. Men belonged in the world of work; they were expected to provide for the family. Women belonged in the home; they were supposed to act as caretakers for the family's emotional needs. Over time, these expectations have been altered considerably. Educational opportunities have opened to women as well as to men. Economic realities meant that for the majority of women, working outside of the home was no longer viewed as a frill, or "just a second income." Whether single or married, women's incomes became essential for their survival; moreover, the boundaries between "typical" careers for women and for men became blurred. Nurturing was no longer exclusively connected to femininity; the law has made it possible for men to take a leave of absence to care for a child or family member.

In addition to expanding opportunities for women and men, how we define, identify, and evaluate gendered behavior has undergone intense scrutiny simultaneously. There has been a resistance to perpetuating the idea that one's biological sex is sufficient to limit, prescribe, and explain behavior. Standpoint theorists urge us to consider how one's biological sex alone is not sufficient to explain behavior. We need to look beyond biological sex and consider how race, education, class, culture, and sexual orientation, for example, also exert enormous influence on communication. Thus, we no longer can assume that all women and all men communicate in the same way. Instead, researchers from diverse fields suggest that we should refrain from viewing gender in terms of opposites, and instead consider the many ways in which the sexes behave similarly. Undergirding these perspectives is the notion that what we embrace as gendered behavior is not merely a biological imperative; rather, it is a product of one's culture and, to this extent, it is constructed.

This transformation in how we regard gendered behavior, however, may be easier to prescribe than actually to realize. How we reconceptualize and develop ourselves, our relationships with others, and our roles as professionals reflect still some potent traditional stereotypes. These challenges provide the rationale for writing a second edition of this book. We have retained three overarching sections that consider the self (part one), personal relationships (part two), and the professional realm (part three). Original chapters have been updated and new chapters on masculinities, race, and the employment interview have been added. Additionally, several discussion or research questions have been added at the end of each chapter.

Part one looks at the ways women and men communicate and how this behavior is manifested. Judy Pearson and Roberta Davilla, in chapter 1, consider what we mean by gender and what it means to be a man or a woman in our culture. The effect of gender on expectations for intimate relationships is addressed by Deborah Borisoff in chapter 2. Traditional notions of masculinity are challenged by James Chesebro. In chapter 3, he considers multiple perspectives on masculine identity for men in general and for gay men in particular. Gender differences are not limited to North American culture. How these differences exist cross-culturally is discussed in chapter 4 by David Victor. In chapter 5, Linda Costigan Lederman examines gender differences in intrapersonal communication.

Part two of the book considers gender and communication in the context of personal relationships. Developing cross-sex friendships is considered in chapter 6 by William Rawlins. Laurie Arliss traces communication in romantic relationships in chapter 7. Kathleen Galvin and Carma Bylund (chapter 8) and Joyce Hauser (chapter 9) look at gender and communication within the frameworks of first-marriage families and stepfamilies.

In part three, we move from the realm of personal relationships to the world of education and of work. Lea Stewart provides an overview of gender issues in corporate communication in chapter 10. However, even before one enters the workplace, gender stereotypes may exert an influence, as explained by Steven Ralston and Amber Kinser in chapter 11 on the employment interview. Chapter 12, by Brenda Allen, considers how assumptions about race and gender may influence how communication is interpreted in professional contexts. Many of the assumptions about what types of careers are possible for women and for men stem from experiences in the classroom—the focus of chapter 13 by Cheri Simonds and Pamela Cooper. The final four chapters of the book scrutinize gender differences in distinct fields—selected because they reflect large numbers of both women and men. Anna Matias examines the difficulties women, especially, face in their efforts to enter the legal field (chapter 14). Elaine Bass Jenks explores gendered communication in health care settings (chapter 15). In chapter 16, Judi Brownell presents the impact of women's and men's communication in the hospitality industry. In the final chapter, Marcia Rock, Sheila Stainback, and Julie Adams reveal the difficulties that women, primarily, confront in the broadcasting industry (chapter 17).

The contributing authors represent some of the leading scholars in the area of gender studies and related fields. We invite you to listen to their voices.

Deborah J. Borisoff
Laurie P. Arliss

PART I

Understanding Why Men and Women Communicate Differently

CHAPTER 1

The Gender Construct
Understanding Why Men and Women Communicate Differently

Judy Pearson
Roberta Davilla

POINTS TO BE ADDRESSED

- The difference between sex and gender
- The process of gender identification
- Differences between male and female development
- Differences between male and female ways of knowing
- Differences between male and female ways of being

Now, more than ever before, men and women recognize the need to understand the differences that separate them. We have always relied on male–female relationships in the private world of the family, but legal and social changes now demand that we feel comfortable in a wide range of public male–female associations. The difficulty of relating to another individual is logically complicated when that individual is perceived as "different," but understanding the sources of difference can provide both enlightenment and comfort. In this book, the urgency of understanding male–female communication is addressed by communication scholars. Each chapter focuses on an important aspect of gender communication or examines gender issues in an important setting. The authors attempt to characterize the unique challenges inherent in male–female interaction at a time of great change.

Prior to examining specific aspects of interaction between men and women, it is useful to consider the important process by which we come to know ourselves as gendered individuals in a world where gender matters. While researchers in the physical sciences continue to seek answers to biological questions, researchers in the social sciences work to clarify the social, moral, and linguistic dimensions of gender differences. In this introduction, we explain the difference between biological sex and its socially constructed correlate, gender. We discuss the development of gender identity, and explain how men and women emerge with unique ways of knowing and ways of being. We argue that male–female interaction is affected by the unique experiences of being male and being female in our society.

Although biological sex has probably always been of interest to researchers and educators, the focus on gender is relatively new. Before the mid-1970s, the term "sex" was used to refer to biological differences that existed between people. Research on "sex differences" simply categorized people on the basis of their biological differences. A variety of forces came together in the mid-1970s to encourage a reconceptualization of gender. One influence was the work of psychologists such as Bem (1974, 1975a, 1975b), and Spence, Helmreich, and Stapp (1974a, 1974b; Spence and Helmreich, 1978). Gilligan (1982) contributed to the debate with her landmark book, *In a Different Voice*, a few years later. Today researchers continue to investigate the influence of gender in a variety of contexts such as communication style (House, Dallinger, and Kilgallen, 1998), education (Borisoff and Hahn, 1995; Cawyer, Bystrom, Miller, Simonds, O'Brien, and Storey-Marin, 1994), small groups (Hawkins, 1995), organizations (Haslett, 1993), and intercultural communication (Uchida, 1997).

Bem's work is an exemplar of the new research and theory on gender. Before this time, people were categorized on masculinity and femininity measures as being more or less of each of these measures. In other words, masculinity was placed on one end of the continuum and femininity was placed on the other end, as illustrated in the figure below.

Masculinity ———————————————— Femininity

An individual, through a series of questions, would be categorized as either masculine or feminine or somewhere between the two extremes. We should observe, however, that the more masculine one indicated that he or she was, the less feminine he or she would be. An individual could not be rated high in both masculinity and femininity or low in both categories.

In private conversations, Bem (1974) has explained that she felt limited by this conceptualization of masculinity and femininity. She perceived herself as possessing a number of both masculine and feminine traits. In other words, she felt that she should score high on both masculinity and femininity.

Instead, when she was categorized, her score indicated that she was somewhere between masculinity and femininity and was thus viewed as neither feminine nor masculine.

Bem (1974) created a new way to measure and to conceive of sex roles in the Bem Sex Role Inventory. She suggested that masculinity and femininity are separate dimensions and that one might be high in masculinity and low in femininity (masculine), low in masculinity and high in femininity (feminine), high in masculinity and high in femininity (androgynous), or low in masculinity and low in femininity (undifferentiated). This view is depicted below.

	High in Femininity	
Androgynous		Feminine
High in Masculinity		Low in Masculinity
Masculine		Undifferentiated
	Low in Femininity	

Although the differences in Bem's conceptualization may appear to be fairly simplistic, her perspective radically altered the way women and men were categorized. In the past, women and men were viewed as different because of biological traits and they were categorized on masculinity–femininity scales in a unidimensional way. Bem suggests that people should be categorized based on the extent to which they have internalized societal standards for masculine and feminine behaviors. In addition, both biological males and biological females could be feminine, masculine, androgynous, or undifferentiated.

Sex and gender are thus not identical constructs. As Maya Angelou (1986: 67) so aptly wrote in *All God's Children Need Traveling Shoes,*

> I had long known that there were worlds of difference between males and men as there were between females and women. Genitalia indicated sex, but work, discipline, courage and love were needed for the creation of men and women.

Sociologists, psychologists, and communication researchers generally agree that sex refers to one's biological or physical self while gender refers to one's psychological, social, and interactive characteristics (see, for example, Bernard, 1971; Lipman-Blumen and Tickamyer, 1975; Pearson, 1975; Pearson and Cooks, 1994; Reeder, 1996; Stoller, 1968;).

Researchers in the physical sciences continue to be interested in biological sex. Social scientists are more likely to focus on gender or gender roles, because they have traditionally examined our social lives. Nonetheless, a relationship exists between sex and gender. Indeed, women are more likely than men to behave in a feminine way, while men are more likely than women to behave in a masculine manner.

To what extent does one's biological sex influence that individual's social and psychological gender? MacCorquodale (1989) explains,

> . . . the relative weight given by a belief system to social versus biological factors results in an ideology that maximizes or minimizes sex differences. Within both feminist and traditional systems of belief, there is a division between those who believe the influences of biology are indirect and mediated by society (social constructionists) and those who believe that direct effects of biology endow each gender with certain essential characteristics (biological essentialism). (Sayers, 1982: 95)

Although the nature vs. nurture argument continues to be debated in some quarters (and across disciplines), an even more complicated discussion now ensues. The newer argument concerns the tolerance and fluidity with which an individual can comfortably move among gender identifications. Stable gender identity is not a universally accepted experience. Researchers (Imperato-McGuinley, Peterson, Gautier, and Sturla, 1979; Money and Ehrhardt, 1972) vary in their views about how gender identity becomes fixed. Money and Ehrhardt assert that gender identity is formed during a child's first three years. Imperato-McGuinley and her colleagues, on the other side, believe that gender remains flexible during childhood. Once the hormones during puberty "take hold," gender identity becomes established.

Imperato-McGuinley et al. (1979) studied sexually incongruous children from rural Santo Domingo villages. The people exhibited an inherited deficiency known as DHT-deficiency and had ambiguous genitalia. Eighteen of the people had been raised as females. At puberty, these "females" experienced lowering of their voices and the growth of a penis and scrotum. The phenomenon was common enough to warrant the word that translated literally means "penis at twelve." Of the eighteen children raised as girls, only two experienced sex role confusion. The other sixteen were successful in assuming the male gender role and married and fathered children.

The researcher drew two conclusions from her study. The first was that gender identification is not unalterably fixed, but evolves throughout childhood. The second conclusion was that when the sex of rearing conflicts with the biologically based sex, the biological sex prevails. On the one hand, the study provides evidence for a more fluid understanding of gender identification. On the other, it supports biological determinism.

The new conceptualization of gender allows us to assert that, to some extent, our social interaction influences gender. Our communicative exchanges tell us what our roles are and encourage or discourage us from internalizing predispositions that relate to masculinity or femininity. Symbolic interactionists suggest that people develop through three stages (see, for example, Mead, 1977). The prepatory phase includes the stage in which infants imitate others by mirroring. In the play stage, the child responds simultaneously in a generalized way to several others. The child generalizes a composite role by considering all others' definitions of self. The person thus develops a unified role from which he or she sees the self. This perception is the overall way that other people see the individual. People unify their self-concepts by internalizing this composite view. This self-picture emerges from years of symbolically interacting or communicating with others.

The integrated self tends toward the behaviors others encourage and away from behaviors that others discourage. From birth, people are treated differently because of genitalia. Male and female babies are dressed in different kinds and colors of clothing. Parents respond differently to male and female infants (see, for example, Bell and Carver, 1980). Male and female babies are described with different adjectives: boys are strong, solid, and independent, while girls are loving, cute and sweet. People describe identical behavior on the part of infants differently if they are told the infant is a "boy" or a "girl" (see, for example, Condry and Condry, 1976). Preschool children observe commercials and cartoons on television, are read books, and play with toys in which "appropriate" sex roles are depicted. In many ways, people are treated differently because of their biological sex.

Because of such differences in treatment, it is not surprising that women and men develop differently. Gilligan (1982) helped to explain differences in the moral development of women and men through a psychological approach. Kohlberg's (1958; 1969; 1973; 1976; 1981) previous work in moral development relied on studying only male subjects. "Standard" stages of moral development were created, and females did not fit into the "norm." Kohlberg presumed that females were deviants and no research was done at that time to see if females morally developed through a differing process.

Gilligan (1982) attempted to correct this problem by studying women. She suggests that relationships and issues of dependence are experienced very differently by males and females. Through socialization and subsequent moral development, males rely on separation and individuation to establish their gender identity. Feminine identity does not depend on the achievement of separation from the mother or on the development of individuation. Because masculinity is defined by separation while femininity is defined through attachment, male gender identity is threatened by intimacy and female gender identity is threatened by separation.

To amplify this point, Gilligan (1982) cites Lever, who studied role-taking during conflict resolution. Lever observed children at play, and reported that when a dispute erupted, girls ended the game, while boys elaborated the rules for resolving disputes. Lever concluded that boys learn independence and the organizational skills necessary for coordinating activities with groups of people through play. By learning the socially approved rules of the game, boys are better able to deal directly with competition from both their friends and their enemies. However, girls learn cooperation, not competition. They play in smaller, more intimate pairs, usually in private places. When disagreements erupted while playing a game, girls were quick to end the game. The significance of maintaining the primary relationships was tantamount for girls. Their identities were fostered in cooperative relationships with others, rather than individual goal-achievement and rule-following.

The message that Gilligan underscores is that, presumably from socialization differences, women and men have different voices of experience. Neither is superior, but the male voice traditionally has been the voice heard. Standards based on male behaviors are created and females are therefore left out. When female experiences are questioned in the pursuit of knowledge, a problem of what to do with those experiences results.

Belenky, Clinchy, Goldberger, and Tarule (1986) similarly showed that women's ways of knowing and being are distinctive from men's. They conducted extensive interviews with women who were in a variety of education settings. The institutions from which the female students were selected ranged from a traditional Ivy League college to an "invisible college," a human service agency that assisted women in caring for their children. A goal of the study was to utilize Perry's epistemological framework and expand it. Perry (1970) had studied the intellectual and ethical development of undergraduate students at Harvard University. However, most of his subjects were males and the result was a useful design charting their epistemological development. Due to the proliferation of research on males' experiences, Belenky and her colleagues chose to study only women's experiences in terms of their relationships to various institutions.

These researchers grouped women's knowing perspectives into five categories: silence, a voiceless position that is subject to external approval; received knowledge, in which women gain externally generated knowledge but do not create knowledge of their own; subjective knowledge, which is knowledge created intuitively, personally, and privately; procedural knowledge, in which women are included in the learning and application of objective procedures for communicating knowledge; and constructed knowledge, in which women create their own knowledge, and the value of both subjective and objective knowledge is recognized (Belenky et al., 1986: 15).

In order to explain differences in ways of knowing, Belenky and her associates cite two stories related by two middle-aged women. The first woman recollected how, on the first day of a science class, the professor brought in a jar filled with beans and asked the class to tell him how many beans were in the jar. The class members shouted out many different guesses. The professor responded to their attempts by stating that they should never trust their own senses, and invited the class to go on a mysterious journey into the realms of scientific inquiry, with the professor as their guide. The young female first-year college student dropped the course later that day and never went near a science classroom again.

The second woman remembered, on her first day in a philosophy class, how a philosophy professor entered the room and placed a large cardboard cube on the desk. The professor asked the students what the object was. The students responded that the object was a cube. The professor pressed her students by asking what a cube was. The students stated that a cube contained six sides. The professor asked, "But how do you know?" She pointed out that it was impossible for anyone to see all six sides simultaneously. The cube existed because of intelligence, and the brain invented the sides that were not physically seen. Each student was able to invent the truth about cubes.

These examples illustrate the differences in ways of knowing. The first illustration envelops the silent and received knowledge perspectives; knowing can only be realized through an external source. The external source generates superior knowledge and the student/learner of this knowledge must seek approval of what is learned and what is "right." The science professor was the authority; he could teach his students the "truth." Students were to rely on his authority rather than recognizing and relying on their own knowledge. The second story illustrates subjective, procedural, and constructed knowledge. The students/learners in this situation were confirmed in their assessment of what they already knew in terms of their own experiences. The philosophy professor confirmed the students' individual, intuitive knowledge. They were all authorities and their "truths" were confirmed.

Women and men are treated differently, they develop differently, and their ways of knowing are discrete. These differences are apparent in our language. The importance of language was explained by Kramarae (1981): "Language is used in social contexts; used to construct and maintain social relationships between and among women and men" (vii). With her colleagues, Schulz and O'Barr, Kramarae adds,

> . . . it is only within the latter part of the twentieth century that the study of language implies for most scholars simultaneous concern with society. Language is, after all, spoken by people in social contexts as they communicate about human concerns. (1984: 9)

An increasing amount of research demonstrates that the symbols we use to communicate are man-made. The language that we use was created primarily by men, for men. The words we have available reflect male experience and they encourage male domination.

What are some obvious examples of man-made words? Let us consider the language of business. Although the business world may be viewed as an area that is open to both women and men, when one listens carefully, it appears to be primarily a "male club." Many business clichés, for example, come straight from sports—a decidedly male activity. If you want to be successful, you may have to "keep your eye on the ball," be a "boy wonder," "keep your head down," be a "team player," be a "pinch hitter," and "tackle the job." What do you avoid? You don't want to be in the "penalty box," "under fire," "under the gun," be in the "cellar," be a "disqualified player," have a "jock mentality," or be "caught with your pants down."

We can also build the argument that language is male-dominated when we deal with the so-called generic pronouns. When we talk about generic people using the singular, which pronoun do we choose? Until recently, it had been customary to use the male form to refer to both men and women: "he," "his," and "him" could refer to a male in some cases and to either a male or female in other cases. Rarely had "she" and "her" been used to refer to men, or to both women and men. We may question why these forms are not equally appropriate.

Kramarae (1981) observes that language does not serve all of its users equally well. Women are left out far more often than men, but both men and women may find that language limits the expression of their experience. Kramarae offers four theoretical frameworks from which to understand the relationship between gender, language, and social structure. Among these are the muted group framework, the reconstructed psychoanalysis framework, the speech styles framework, and the strategy framework.

The muted group theory is based on the notion that people who are dominant in a particular social hierarchy determine the communication system of that social group; people who are subordinate are "muted." The subordinate group is further rendered inarticulate because the dominant group creates language based on their own worldview. The subordinate group has different perceptions and the need for different language; however, no allowance has been made either for that differing perception or for the language that would correspond to it. Kramarae offers the basic assumptions of this theory, applying it to women and men.

1. Women perceive the world differently from men because of women's and men's different experiences and activities, rooted in the division of labor.
2. Because of their political dominance, the men's system of perception is dominant, impeding the free expression of the women's alternative models of the world.
3. In order to participate in society women must transform their own models in terms of the received male system of expression (3).

The reconstructed psychoanalysis approach is derived by Kramarae from the original theorizing of Freud and his reinterpreter Lacan. She explains that Lacan argues repeatedly that the unconscious is a language and thus psychoanalysis is linguistic analysis. Through the acquisition of language we are located (as female or as male) into a social structure. In learning our language we "learn dichotomous opposition: speech/silence, science/poetry, logic/intuition, author/reader—masculine/feminine." Kramarae notes that this approach "stresses symbolism over cognitive development" (66).

Lacan does not subscribe to a fixed reality in which words have a one-to-one correspondence with some concept within that reality. Instead, words have only a relationship to each other. Further, according to Kramarae, a "language code represents and authorizes social hierarchies, and the ideological superstructure (the system of ideas of the culture)" (67). The child's acquisition of a language thus renders him or her a social being within a particular ideological superstructure. Kramarae concludes:

> What I stress here is that language has, for Lacan, the central, all-informing role; the human is formed by language. The language code gives individuals their construction of reality, and their location in that reality, including their gender identity. (67–68)

The speech styles approach may be viewed as a more fluid or dynamic approach than is either the muted group theory or the reconstructed psychoanalysis theory to understanding gender. This theory suggests that women's and men's speech behavior is based on their perception of their social group. In other words, women and men communicate in ways that are distinctive because they are placed in different, and apparently relevant, social groups. Kramarae explains that this somewhat static approach to language and gender is made more dynamic by the addition of three emphases:

1. the ways that distinctive speech can be used by members of a group to create solidarity and to exclude members of out-groups from some interactions;
2. the ways that dominant group members use the distinctive features, actual or perceived, of the speech of subordinate groups as a focus for ridicule; and
3. the ways that speakers manipulate their speaking styles to emphasize or de-emphasize particular social identities (91).

The speech styles approach allows us to examine women and men as two linguistic groups, just as blacks, whites, and other subcultures have been placed into separate social groups. We can also consider both the convergence and divergence of members of the two social groups as they mirror the behavior of the other social group in cross-sexed interactions, or as they refuse to accommodate a speaker of the other social group. We can examine how women, as a subordinate group, can alter their linguistic usage to be viewed more positively by others. Finally, we can learn about women's challenges to male predominance in the linguistic arena (Kramarae, 1981: 91).

Mulac, Wiemann, Widenmann, and Gibson (1988) tested the convergence theory and found "greater differences in gender-linked language behavior in same-sex than in mixed-sex dyads" (315). Both women and men appeared to converge in their language when speaking to members of the opposite sex. These researchers claim that the behavioral convergence may be based on the sex-role stereotypes that exist in opposite sex interactions.

The strategy model is based on the idea that all communication is "strategic, a term broadly understood, based on Brown and Levinson's (1978) definition, as

> (a) innovative plans of action, which may *still* be (but need not be) and (b) routines—that is, previously constructed plans whose original rational origin is still preserved in their construction, despite their present automatic application as ready-made programs. (90)

Kramarae (1981: 119) explains the reasoning that leads to the strategic model:

1. Industrialized capitalism has sharpened a division between the labors of women and men, and a separation in the location of their activities. . . .
2. Authority (legitimate power, authorized power to command) is associated with the public sphere and men have clear monopoly of this. . . .

3. As a consequence of the division of labor, the separation of spheres, and the use of differential allocation of resources and legitimate power, women and men will use different strategies to influence others and shape events.

In order to understand fully why men and women communicate differently, it is important to remember the distinction between sex and gender and, accordingly, to realize that gender is socially constructed. Because the lessons we learn about ourselves and our world are often gender-specific lessons, women and men develop differently. As children and later as adults, females and males are treated differently, so it is hardly surprising that our ways of knowing and ways of being are distinct. Language perpetuates current societal constructions of women and men and encourages both differences and dominance. Students of communication need to be keenly aware of the influence of gender in male–female interaction. However, we must also realize that, because it is socially created, the gender construct can and does change. In a time of tremendous legal and social change, we must all be ready for the interpersonal challenges that lie ahead.

For Further Discussion

1. List the ways that you "construct" yourself every day as a male or female. For example, females often apply makeup, curl their hair, and wear clothing that enhances their figures, such as push-up bras. Males often shave their facial whiskers, wear heavy fragrances, and wear clothes that flaunt their muscles. How did you learn to "genderize" yourself? Do you give the same attention to your efforts each day, or are there times when you are less careful about constructing your femininity or masculinity? Why?
2. Describe the first time that you realized that you were a girl or a boy. At what age did you realize your sex? Did your realization accompany a particular behavior that was identified as being more appropriate for a girl or a boy? What effect did this experience have on your understanding of feminine and masculine behaviors? For example, one of the authors realized that spitting on the sidewalk was a taboo behavior when she was 5 years old. As a young girl, she often accompanied her farmer father and saw him spit on the ground. One day, she was in town with her mother and sister. While they were walking along, she spat on the sidewalk. Her horrified mother and sister made it very clear that spitting was not appropriate for girls. Spitting was interpreted, thus, as a "male only" behavior.
3. Consider the ways and the frequency with which you use the Internet. What sites do you visit? Are they geared toward more male or female interests? How do you know? Have you ever chatted with a person that you were not sure was a male or female? How did you find out? Why was knowing if you were communicating with a male or female

important to you? Reflect on the cues that you use when you interact face-to-face with a person who is sexually ambiguous to us. Are the cues that you use the same when you use the Internet? How does the medium affect your communication strategies?

REFERENCES

Angelou, M. 1986. *All God's Children Need Traveling Shoes.* New York: Random House.

Banks, T. L. 1988. Gender bias in the classroom. *Journal of Legal Education* 38: 137–146.

Belenky, M. F., B. M. Clinchy, N. R. Goldberger, and J. M. Tarule. 1986. *Women's Ways of Knowing: The Development of Self, Voice, and Mind.* New York: Basic Books.

Bell, N. J., and W. Carver. 1980. A reevaluation of gender label effects: Expectant mothers' responses to infants. *Child Development* 51: 925–927.

Bem, S. 1974. The measurement of psychological androgyny. *Journal of Consulting and Clinical Psychology* 42: 155–162.

———. 1975a. Androgyny vs. the tight little lives of fluffy women and chesty men. *Psychology Today* 9: 58–59.

———. 1975b. Sex-role adaptability: One consequence of psychological androgyny. *Journal of Personality and Social Psychology* 31: 634–643.

Bernard, J. 1971. *Women and the Public Interest. An Essay on Policy and Protest.* Chicago: Aldine-Atherton.

Borisoff, D., and D. F. Hahn. 1995. From research to pedagogy: Teaching gender and communication. *Communication Quarterly* 43: 381–393.

Brown, P., and S. Levinson. 1978. Universals in language usage: Politeness phenomenon. In E. N. Goody, ed., *Questions and Politeness: Strategies in Social Interaction.* Cambridge, England: Cambridge University Press.

Cawyer, C. S., Bystrom, D., Miller, J., Simonds, C., O'Brien, M., and J. Storey-Marin. 1994. Communicating gender equity: Representation and portrayal of women and men in introductory communication textbooks. *Communication Studies* 45: 325–331.

Condry, J., and S. Condry. 1976. Sex differences: A study of the eye of the beholder, *Child Development* 47: 812–819.

Fausto-Sterling, A. 1985. *Myths of Gender: Biological Theories about Women and Men.* New York: Basic Books, Inc.

Gilligan, C. 1982. *In a Different Voice: Psychological Theory and Women's Development.* Cambridge, MA: Harvard University Press.

Haslett, B. 1993. Gender, power, and communication in organizations. *Progress in Communication Sciences* 11: 145–177.

Hawkins, K. W. 1995. Effects of gender and communication content on leadership emergence in small task-oriented groups. *Small Group Research* 26: 234–249.

Hill, C. L. 1988. Sexual bias in the law school classroom: One student's perspective. *Journal of Legal Education* 38: 603–609.

House, A., J. M. Dallinger, and D. Kilgallen. 1998. Androgyny and rhetorical sensitivity: The connection of gender and communication style. *Communication Reports* 11: 11–20.

Imperato-McGuinley, J., R. Peterson, T. Gautier, and E. Sturla. 1979. Androgens and the evolution of male-gender identity among male pseudohermaphrodites with a 5-alpha-reductase deficiency. *New England Journal of Medicine,* 300: 1236–1237.

Kohlberg, L. 1958. *The Development of Modes of Thinking and Choices in Years 10 to 16.* Unpublished doctoral dissertation, University of Chicago, Chicago, IL.

———. 1969. Stage and sequence: The cognitive-development approach to socialization. In D. A. Goslin, ed., *Handbook of Socialization Theory and Research*. Chicago: Rand McNally.

———. 1973. Continuities and discontinuities in childhood and adult moral development revisited. In *Collected Papers on Moral Development and Moral Education*. Moral Education Research Foundation, Harvard University, Cambridge, MA.

———. 1976. Moral stages and moralization: The cognitive-developmental approach. In T. Lickona, ed., *Moral Development and Behavior: Theory, Research and Social Issues*. New York: Holt, Rinehart & Winston.

———. 1981. *The Philosophy of Moral Development*. San Francisco, CA. Harper & Row.

Kramarae, C. 1981. *Women and Men Speaking: Frameworks for Analysis*. Rowley, MA: Newbury House Publishers, Inc.

Kramarae C., M. Schulz, and W. M. O'Barr, eds. 1984. *Language and Power*. Beverly Hills, CA: Sage Publications, Inc.

LaFrance, M. 1985. The school of hard knocks: Nonverbal sexism in the classroom. *Theory into Practice* 24: 40–44.

Lipman-Blumen, J., and A. R. Tickamyer. 1975. Sex roles in transition: A ten-year perspective. *Annual Review of Sociology* 1: 297–338.

MacCorquodale, P. 1989. Gender and sexual behavior. In K. McKinney and S. Sprecher, eds., *Human Sexuality: The Societal and Interpersonal Context*. Norwood, NJ: Ablex, 91–112.

Mead, G. H. 1977. *Quoted in Sociology: Human Society* by Melvin De Fleur et al. Glenview, IL: Scott, Foresman, 138.

Money, J., and A. Ehrhardt. 1972. *Man Woman/Boy Girl*. Baltimore, MD: Johns Hopkins University.

Mulac, A., J. M. Wiemann, S. J. Widenmann, and T. W. Gibson. 1988. Male/female language differences and effects in same-sex and mixed-sex dyads: The gender-linked language effect. *Communication Monographs* 55: 315–335.

Pearson, J. C. 1975. *The Effects of Sex and Sexism on the Criticism of Classroom Speeches*. Unpublished doctoral dissertation, Indiana University.

Pearson, J. C., and L. Cooks. 1994, November. *Gender and power*. Paper presented at the Speech Communication Association convention, New Orleans, LA.

Perry, W. G. 1970. *Forms of Intellectual and Ethical Development in the College Years*. New York: Holt, Rinehart & Winston.

Reeder, H. M. 1996. A critical look at gender difference in communication research. *Communication Studies* 47: 318–330.

Sayers, J. 1982. *Biological Politics*. London: Tavistock.

Spence, J. T., and R. Helmreich. 1978. *Masculinity and Femininity: Their Psychological Dimensions, Correlates, and Antecedents*. Austin: University of Texas Press.

Spence, J. T., R. Helmreich, and J. Stapp. 1974a. The personal attributes questionnaire: A measure of sex-role stereotypes and masculinity-femininity. *JSAS Catalog of Selected Documents in Psychology* 4: 127.

———. 1974b. Ratings of self and peers on sex-role attributes and their relation to self-esteem and conceptions of masculinity and femininity. *Journal of Personality and Social Psychology* 32: 29–39.

Stoller, R. J. 1968. *Sex and Gender, on the Development of Masculinity and Femininity*. New York: Science House.

Uchida, A. 1997. Doing gender and building culture: Toward a model of women's intercultural communication. *Howard Journal of Communications* 8: 41–76.

CHAPTER 2

The Effect of Gender on Establishing and Maintaining Intimate Relationships

Deborah Borisoff

POINTS TO BE ADDRESSED

- Intimacy as a Dance Metaphor
- Background: The Need to Study Intimacy
- Intimate Relationships: Definitions, Traits, and Corresponding Fears
- How Perceived Differences in Gendered Communication Sustain Barriers to Intimacy: Changing the Feminine and Masculine Scripts

Over the past several decades, the study of personal relationships and, in particular, intimacy, has received considerable attention in both scholarly and popular arenas. Fundamental assumptions in many of these works are that intimacy has different meanings for women and men; that they do not value intimacy equally. Fundamental, as well, is the belief that if we can just get women and men to change their behavior, all will be right with their relationships. These assumptions are predicated on difference: that women and men inhabit different cultures, or, different "planets." Consequently, they are presumed to have learned different "scripts" that guide their behavior.[1] This chapter examines to what extent these scripts have been rewritten.[2]

INTIMACY: A METAPHOR IN MOTION

In his work on literary theory, Ulrich Weisstein (1968) contends that legendary themes and heroes endure because their conditions still resonate for us. "In every mind devoted to justice," he writes, "there is an Antigone. . . . These heroes are in us, and we in them; they partake of our lives, and we see ourselves reflected in their shapes. . . . Our myths and our legendary themes are our polyvalence: they are the indices of humanity, the ideal forms of the tragic destiny, the human condition" (131).

If these heroes reflect our lives, our relationships, an interesting image emerges when we look at Faust and Luste's struggle for intimacy. Faust, the protagonist in Paul Valery's play, embodies the intellect. Luste, the heroine, represents the heart. Despite their struggle for closeness, they remain unsure about their feelings and their relationship. Critic Kurt Weinberg (1976) observes, "They need one another as interpreters, and as refracting mirrors that reflect one upon another with a certain degree of distortion" (27). These characters never realize their love. They are unable to achieve the intimacy they so desperately want because they are grounded firmly in their impossibly rigidified male/female identities.

When Luste is apart from Faust and is aroused merely by thinking about him, she tries to intellectualize her feelings. The intellectual process, attempted by a woman who represents pure emotion, fails to illuminate and prevents her from understanding herself fully. In the case of Faust, every time he is with Luste, the physical stirrings she arouses in him make it impossible to sustain his intellectual prowess. Emotions imposed on a man who represents pure intellect interfere with his ability to complete the work that would define him.

Luste tries to employ Faust's intellect and fails. Faust attempts to express the emotions so much a part of Luste. He, too, fails. The image of the two protagonists as they interact throughout the play is that of a dance—one, however, that is out of step. Yet the message conveyed by the heroes' circumstance is relevant today: to remain in the purely mental plane of the intellect is frustrating. It does not illuminate. To remain in the emotional plane of pure feeling is debilitating, and similarly cannot illuminate without the seeds of understanding. While Faust brings Luste to the point of wanting to understand herself through his intellectual example, Luste, through her physical presence, brings Faust to the point of wanting to live.

The image of a dance not quite in sync pervades the image of intimate relationships. Harriet Goldhor Lerner (1989) entitles her book *The Dance of Intimacy*, yet the dance she describes is not at all in step. Lillian Rubin (1983), in her work *Intimate Strangers*, the title itself reflecting a contradiction, calls intimacy among married couples an "approach-avoidance dance" (65). Intimate relationships between couples, these writers suggest, are fraught with difficulties. Many of these difficulties are attributed to presumed differences that reinforce prescriptions for distinct traits and roles for women and men.

This chapter addresses some of these differences in the context of recent research on intimacy. First, it considers why intimacy as an area of inquiry is important. Next, significant aspects of intimate relationships along with the concomitant fears that are barriers to intimacy are examined. The third section explores how many of the barriers to forging intimate relationships stem from dividing practices that encourage women and men to define and express intimacy in distinct ways. It concludes by examining how many of the assumptions about differences have been challenged and changed. While Faust and Luste as literary figures may represent the epitomes of intellect and emotion, changes in our expectations for, and evaluations of, gendered communication suggest that these separate spheres no longer are mutually exclusive. As the boundaries for intimate communication and relationships expand, these changes will help blur the lines that separate man and woman, Faust and Luste.

The Need to Study Intimacy

Although the actual study of intimacy is rooted around the turn of the twentieth century, research was initially limited for two reasons. First, scholars found it difficult to locate enough suitable subjects willing to participate in longitudinal studies. Second, until the late 1960s and early 1970s, self-disclosure was not regarded as appropriate behavior—especially for men (Perlman and Fehr, 1987).

A major factor contributing to a marked interest in studying intimate relationships was the recognition that close relationships are positively linked to psychological and physical well-being. Klinger's (1977) work with college students, for example, revealed that the majority believed that personal relationships made their lives meaningful. Similarly, for older populations a positive correlation was found between intimate connections, psychological well-being, and physical health (Reis, 1984). Conversely, and not surprisingly, the absence of intimate bonds has been found to have negative consequences. A higher rate of suicide among men was attributed, in part, to the absence of close male bonds (Goldberg, 1976). Depression for women was ten times more likely when they lacked someone in whom they could confide (Brown and Harris, 1978). Finally, men's inability to identify and express their innermost feelings (a condition called Alexithymia, which means "without words") has been attributed to early conditioning and linked to stress-related illnesses (Levant, 1996).

While the benefits of intimate connections have not been disputed, the traits that characterize intimate relationships simultaneously arouse certain fears. The following section provides a general overview of these traits and indicates how the accompanying fears may generate barriers to closeness.

INTIMATE RELATIONSHIPS: DEFINITIONS, TRAITS, AND CORRESPONDING FEARS

Intimacy is rooted in the Latin word *intimus*, meaning "inner" or "innermost." Those who address this topic foreground different aspects of the term. Therefore, intimacy has been regarded as a *quality* (Cherlune, Robison, and Kommor, 1984), as a *process* (Hatfield, 1984), and as a *cultural norm* shaped by social expectations and behavioral constraints (Acitelli and Duck, 1987). Regardless of what they emphasize, each of these, along with subsequent researchers, allude to five factors that characterize intimate relationships (Canary and Dindia, 1998; Canary and Emmers-Sommer, 1997; Prager, 1995). As the following list of traits indicates, understanding the components of intimacy is easy. However, the attempt to achieve and sustain closeness is not as easy, and the process of doing so may arouse certain fears that are potential barriers.

1. ***Knowledge*** of the innermost being of one another which is achieved through self-disclosure and validation of the partner.

   Fear of Exposure: No one enjoys being regarded negatively. Yet many individuals equate disclosing fears and concerns with weakness—what Jourard (1971) terms being "psychologically naked" (39). Many, consequently, keep hidden those feelings that they believe may be construed as signs of weakness.

2. ***Interdependence***, whereby partners can rely on one another for the emotional and physical well-being of the relationship.

   Fear of Loss of One's Individuality: The impetus to maintain one's independence evokes powerful metaphors for those who regard mutual reliance as shading into the loss of one's own individuality (Rubin, 1983), as being swallowed up or engulfed by one's partner (Lerner, 1989), and ultimately, as literally disappearing (Hatfield, 1982).

3. ***Trust*** in the relationship and in one another.

   Fear of Betrayal: Knowledge is power. Disclosing intimate information can be potentially damaging if passed on to third parties. We become especially vulnerable when we open ourselves to another, particularly if we cannot trust fully that this information will be guarded.

4. ***Commitment*** to a relationship that is reciprocal.

   Fear of a Power Imbalance and Loss of Control: When individuals view themselves as more vested in a relationship, they may believe that equal expectations for sharing information and access to their partners are denied them. Conversely, individuals may conceal their most inner thoughts and feelings so as to not risk being viewed as less powerful or not in control. Exerting one's power can take many forms, for example, through control of money, sexual behavior, and emotional manipulation.

5. ***Communication*** that is open and supportive.

   Fear of Communication that Is Misunderstood, Misinterpreted, or Defensive: Each of the traits and fears listed above is enacted through verbal and nonverbal messages. How we employ words, gestures, and physical contact to express ourselves as speaker and listener is a most powerful reflection of a relationship's health. Individuals who feel they are unable to communicate fully and productively with their partners are, ultimately, silenced.

The five fears described above coincide, according to Desmond Morris (1971), with a tendency to equate tenderness with weakness, with vulnerability. The prospect of being hurt, or controlled, or silenced, may be so compelling that we may never achieve the closeness for which we so ardently strive. Some of these fears are general in nature and are not necessarily linked to traditional prescriptions for masculine and feminine behavior. However, other fears have been attributed to stereotyped beliefs about how women and men are expected to communicate. The following section considers some of the salient factors that traditionally have influenced how women and men develop, express, and evaluate intimate relationships; it considers, moreover, how altering our perspectives on gendered scripts may break down barriers to intimacy.

How Perceived Differences in Gendered Communication Sustain Barriers to Intimacy: Changing the Masculine and Feminine Scripts

In 1954, Theodore Reik suggested that gender has a significant effect on the connotative interpretation of language:

> Men and women speak different languages even when they use the same words. The misunderstandings between men and women are thus much less a result of linguistic and semantic differences, but of emotional divergences when the two sexes use identical expressions. (15)

Reik's observations have not been contradicted. In fact, Gilligan's (1982) longitudinal studies on women's moral voices reflect the problems that can emerge when women and men use similar words to encode experiences of self; of social relationships: "Because these languages share an overlapping moral vocabulary, they contain a propensity for systematic mistranslation, creating misunderstandings which impede communication and limit the potential for cooperation and care in relationships" (173).

Reik's and Gilligan's words are striking because they eloquently suggest several reasons why men and women so often experience difficulty developing and maintaining intimate relationships. While it would be easy to accept unquestioningly the aforementioned pronouncements, it is important to examine what forces in our culture sustain beliefs about masculinity and femininity, which in turn fuel divergent beliefs about women's and men's roles in romantic intimate relationships. It is important to consider, moreover, whether women's and men's communication reflects actual or perceived differences in the intimate relationships they forge. Finally, we need to look at how the research conducted and reported influences our understanding about intimate relationships. An examination of these three areas will hopefully reveal that much of the received wisdom we embrace as the truth is far more nuanced than we thought initially.

Dichotomizing Masculinity and Femininity: Implications for Attitudes about Intimacy

Looking at the world and at behavior in bipolar terms reflects a legacy that can be traced at least as far back as the Pythagorean Brotherhood of the fifth century B.C., which embodied their dualism in ten sets of opposites: good and bad, motion and rest, light and darkness, square and oblong, straight and curved, odd and even, right and left, the one and the many, the limited and the unlimited, and male and female (Wilden, 1987). This propensity to view the world in terms of opposites remains a powerful force, for included in this tradition is the tendency to divide and assign behavioral traits, roles, and norms according to sex—what Sandra Bem (1993) has called "gendered scripts" (see also Aires, 1996, 1998; Borisoff and Hahn, 1995; Borisoff and Merrill, 1998; Canary and Emmers-Sommer, 1997; Haste, 1994; Prager, 1995; Reis, 1998; Wood, 1992, 2001).

Despite the fact that much has been written identifying other attributes that ought to be equally valued and encouraged (e.g., empathy, cooperation, sensitivity, assertiveness), we persist in using bipolar terms to characterize men as "independent," "active," "strong," "competitive," and "intelligent." We continue to assess women as "passive," "weak," "emotional," and "other-centered." These gender traits are so pervasive that they cross international boundaries. In a comprehensive thirty-nation study, social psychologists John Williams and Deborah Best (1982) report that these traits are consistently gender-linked. A more recent Gallup poll survey of 1,000 adults in 22 countries suggests that these sex-trait stereotypes have not changed (Lewin, 1996).

The result of maintaining a dichotomous view of appropriate traits for women and men is that we simultaneously construct dichotomous expectations for their behavior. Attitudes about intimacy is one arena where this discrepancy becomes evident. Psychologist Karen Prager (1995) contends that men are encouraged to be action-oriented (agentic) and value independence; women, in contrast, are expected to seek "connections" with others (a communal orientation). She suggests, moreover, that these pursuits are not valued equally: "U.S. culture seems to laud masculine, agentic values more than feminine, communal ones, which may discourage men's intimacy. Cultural norms not only dictate that women and men pursue different values but also more or less privilege one set of values (agentic vs. communal)" (245).

These divergent values may have a profound effect on the desires and expectations each sex will have in defining, establishing, and maintaining intimate relationships with a member of the opposite sex. Rubin (1983) describes how women's desires to seek closeness and men's wish to remain independent often result in a push-pull situation. That is, as women strive to get close to the men they love, the men, for whom too much closeness signals suffocation, begin to retreat. This retreat creates the desire in women to "clasp" further, which results in greater distancing.

This pattern illustrates a basic contradiction. One of the positive characteristics of intimate relationships is interdependence and open communication; one of the major barriers to intimacy is the fear of losing one's individuality. If men have learned to place a high value on independence and authenticity, they will be reluctant to move toward the interdependence essential for positive intimate bonds. Women, too, may suffer from the motivation to connect. Harriet Lerner (1989) points out that women receive conflicting messages: they are supposed to develop the self, yet they are expected to subordinate the self to the needs of others. "We all," she adds, "by virtue of being female, have learned to please and protect relationships by silencing, sacrificing, and betraying the self" (126). As long as the masculine and feminine selves are perceived as diametrically opposed, the dance of intimacy that Lerner describes will remain problematic.

Recent studies suggest that this diametrical gap may be closing. Self-reports by men and women indicate that insofar as how they define intimacy, both sexes mention self-disclosure of personal feelings, warmth, appreciation, and shared activity as important to them (Helgeson, Shaver, and Dyer, 1987; Monsour, 1992; Reis, 1990, 1998). However, despite the contention that "men and women clearly define intimacy and closeness in much the same way" (Reis, 1998: 219), the extent to which definition shades into behavior suggests that a gender gap persists in how closeness is communicated and evaluated.

Self-Disclosure as a Synonym for Closeness: The Gender Effect

Self-disclosure—the ability to open up, to make oneself vulnerable, and to validate the ideas and feelings of others—is an important quality of intimate relationships; it is the trait most frequently studied. It is a quality, moreover, that laces men's and women's definitions of intimacy. The controversy about men's presumed inability to self-disclose, however, does not surround the desire to share feelings. Rather, the socially constructed norms that are linked to "appropriate" masculine and feminine behavior may exert a powerful influence in the following ways: how we *define* personal topics; how *willingly* we self-disclose, and the *contexts* in which we feel most comfortable communicating. In the following examination of these factors, it becomes evident that while traditional prescriptions have privileged women's ways of communicating as the norm, recent research suggests that we should broaden long-standing beliefs about self-disclosure (Aires, 1996, 1998; Bem, 1993; Borisoff and Hahn, 1995; Borisoff and Merrill, 1998; Canary and Emmers-Sommer, 1997; Dindia and Allen, 1992; Haste, 1994; Hatfield and Rapson, 1993; Reis, 1998; Wood and Inman, 1993). How we define personal topics is closely connected to our willingness to self-disclose. Thus these facets are discussed in conjunction with each other, while we explore the context of closeness separately.

How Personal Topics Are Defined/How Willingly We Self-Disclose. "Men and women differ little, if at all, in how much they are willing to reveal to one another," Rubin tells us (1983: 215). What it is that they reveal, however, may be another matter. The conventional wisdom has been that men more readily disclose views and attitudes; women are more likely to reveal fears and feelings (Aires, 1998; Rubin, 1983). This supposition has led writers, such as Elaine Hatfield and Richard Rapson, to conclude that "modern tradition dictates that women are expected to be the 'intimacy' experts" (1993: 158). This supposition has led other scholars to suggest that the topics men might discuss, such as money and work, aren't considered "personal" (Aires, 1987; Wood and Inman, 1993). To the extent that the majority of men are socialized to measure their self-worth in relation to their professional and monetary achievements, we may begin to view these issues as extremely personal, important, and relevant to their self-esteem. As long as topics other than one's deepest emotions are excluded from the realm of "personal," we may be denying ourselves the opportunity to experience fully the depth of men's feelings.

There is an additional dilemma for men who want to reveal their most inner feelings on topics that fall outside of stereotypical masculine subjects. Men may learn from the role models in their lives that emotional vulnerability is unacceptable behavior. Such knowledge follows them into their relationships with others as well. For example, Derlega and Chaikin (1976) found that women and men are regarded differently when they disclose personal problems. They report that in male–male and/or male–female dyads, when a male stimulus person disclosed a personal problem, he was viewed more negatively than when he remained silent (the image of the strong, silent type is evoked here). The opposite results were obtained when female stimulus persons were evaluated. What may be operating here is that "even when men and women behave in an identical manner they may be perceived differently. Listeners bend their perceptions in the direction of expectations" (Aires, 1998: 74). The imperative for men to conform to expected behaviors that are associated with the aforementioned masculine sex-trait stereotypes may exact a toll. It appears that even if men want to reveal their feelings and their emotions, the negative assessment of such behavior would discourage them from doing so.

Admittedly, Derlega and Chaikin (1976) conducted their study on research subjects rather than on actual partners. This raises the question of whether the same negative assessments of men's self-revelation would occur if actual couples had participated. Dindia and Allen's (1992) meta-analysis of over 200 studies spanning three decades (with nearly 24,000 participants in all), suggests that self-disclosure is positively correlated when subjects know one another.[3] While knowledge of one's partner may help diminish the self-disclosure gap between women and men, other factors also may influence men's willingness to self-disclose.

In their work on sex and gender differences in personal relationships, Daniel Canary and Tara Emmers-Sommer (1997) refer to a mid-1980s study on 30 dual- and single-career married couples by Rosenfeld and Welsh (1985). This study indicates that when both partners work, not only do they report similarities in their communication, but significantly the "husbands reported disclosing more than their wives, contrary to differences hypothesized by [the] researchers" (Canary and Emmers-Sommer, 1997: 54).[4] Additionally, this study also reveals that in traditional marriages where the husband works outside of the home and the wife does not, the wives reportedly self-disclose more frequently and deeply about more topics than do their husbands, leading Canary and Emmers-Sommer to suggest, "As more people enter dual-career marriages, we may see more similarity in communicative acts such as self-disclosure" (54).

The latter findings are significant. We might speculate that dual-career couples regard themselves as equals in the relationship with concomitant equal access to communication—an important trait of intimate relationships discussed earlier. To the extent that the dual-career couples reported heightened self-disclosure also may reflect that role similarity creates a common bond. Additionally, we might wonder if perceived lack of access to a range of relationships influenced the stay-at-home wives to report different levels and amounts of self-disclosure. Although it was not examined in the Rosenfeld and Welsh (1985) study, we might consider if similar findings would emerge if stay-at-home husbands, rather than stay-at-home wives, had participated in the study. Viewed in this way, it is possible that role, rather than gender, may have been a significant factor in fueling the behavior of the wives who did not work outside of the home.

Communicating Closeness in Context. Scholarly and popular works on intimacy as well as interpersonal communication texts that consider intimacy and self-disclosure predominantly connect revealing innermost feelings in the context of face-to-face interaction. Often these works recommend that partners make time to engage in "quality" interaction in settings where they are unlikely to experience interruptions. Such prescriptions, consequently, privilege talk as the arbiter for communicating closeness. However, how men and women learn to utilize and value talk may be influenced by sex-role stereotyping, which prepares them differently to regard and to display interaction in the context prescribed by the scholars and popular writers who address intimacy.

Early socialization processes guide children into different spheres. Girls, more than boys, are encouraged to associate play with indoor, quiet, and safe activities while boys are encouraged to engage in group activities outdoors. Much has been written to suggest that expectations about daughters' responsibilities in the home along with greater concern for their safety have resulted in "gender differences in children's geographies" (Valentine, 1997: 39; see also Bem, 1993; Graebner, 1982; Hahn and Borisoff, 2000; Maltz and Borker, 1982; Thorne, 1993). Not only do these expectations result in distinct "landscapes of contemporary childhood" for each sex (Thorne, 1993), more significantly, boys may learn to experience closeness through shared, competitive activity—a product of how they have been encouraged to play—while girls learn to feel closeness through shared conversation (Maltz and Borker, 1982; Rubin, 1983).

This last point has had enormous consequences on how masculine versus feminine styles of self-disclosure are interpreted. Although it was suggested earlier that women and men may be more similar than they are different in how they define and value intimacy, the perception that men are less adept at expressing their feelings persists. As long as the feminine style for communicating closeness is viewed as normative, masculine modes of expression along with the contexts in which they are comfortable expressing themselves will remain marginalized. Men will continue to be accused of failing "to take [intimacy] seriously enough to learn about it or develop techniques to aid in gaining a measure of it" (Hatfield and Rapson, 1993: 133).

The ability to uncouple talk from closeness may facilitate a revaluation of men's modes of communication. The "standard" feminine script for closeness ignores masculine ways for expressing closeness, which, research suggests, emerge from shared activities (Duck, 1988, 1991; Helgeson, Shaver, and Dyer, 1987; Reis, 1998; Swain, 1989; Wood and Inman, 1993). As long as closeness "is defined exclusively or primarily by typically feminine behaviors such as self-disclosure, it is pregiven that women will be found more skilled than men" (Wood and Inman, 1993: 285). "To persist in dismissing ways of interacting that men seem to prefer and to excel in," Wood and Inman conclude, "impoverishes understanding of human communication" (291).

Much as feminist scholarship has argued that women's styles of communication could contribute positively to the work sphere and could expand our notion of effective communication in that arena, arguably we might consider how men's modes of communication and the content of their communication could inform our understanding of effective communication in intimate interaction. Rather than urging men to conform to women's modes of expression (the "deficit" hypothesis in reverse), we must refrain from defining, accepting, and testing intimate bonds solely in terms of a feminine framework (Aires, 1996, 1998; Borisoff and Hahn, 1995; Prager, 1995; Reis, 1998; Wood and Inman, 1993). Rather than perpetuating the biological dividing practices that fuel valuing "expressive communication [as constituting] intimacy while joint activities are dismissed as impersonal" (Wood and Inman, 1993: 290), we may begin to examine how shared experiences affect closeness.

Recognizing how research processes may be complicit in maintaining the perception of gender differences allows us to dispel many of the long-held assumptions about women's and men's communication and intimacy. The final section examines several challenges to revisiting these processes.

How Research Influences Understanding about Intimate Relationships: A Revaluation

In a society that values seeing the world in terms of opposites, it is understandable how such an orientation will rely on dividing practices to demonstrate, to substantiate, to perpetuate, and ultimately, to privilege difference rather than similarity. The study of gender and intimacy is one area that is predicated on this process. Recently, several scholars have suggested we scrutinize aspects of research on gender that may accentuate more difference than is warranted. A brief consideration of four aspects, in particular, illustrates the need for caution.

The Impetus to Seek Differences in Research. In their recent work on gender, writers such as Elizabeth Aires (1987, 1996, 1998), Sandra Bem (1993), and Helen Haste (1994) observe the impetus to uncover difference rather than similarity in the research process. Because assumptions about women's and men's differences are so firmly entrenched in the cultural psyche (along with attendant social, political, and economic policies that have been enacted based on the assumption of difference), we resist findings that would challenge long-held beliefs.

This orientation undoubtedly has influenced the scholarly arena. What is deemed publishable, these researchers argue, is rooted in the impetus to foreground difference. Consequently, works that find no gender differences may never see the scholarly light of day. Aires (1998) posits a secondary result of this orientation: "[I]n studies that use multiple dependent variables, the lack of gender differences on many of these variables is rarely cited by later reviewers while only the few significant differences are highlighted" (69–70). Thus, what scholars choose to emphasize may perpetuate the patina of gender differences that distorts the full picture of women's and men's communication.

Who We Study Matters. The populations we choose to study is a second area of research that merits examination. Studies on gender in general, and on aspects of intimacy in particular, have tended to use biological sex to group subjects. Moreover, studies on college-age populations rely heavily on the cohorts readily available, that is, on white, middle-class, heterosexual women and men. Findings are then attributed according to sex, frequently ignoring the various standpoints stemming from class, education, race, sexual orientation, psychological factors, and culture, which influence communication values and behaviors.

Two examples illustrate how using the male–female divide may obscure other important factors. For example, Stella Ting-Toomey's (1991) cross-cultural study on expressions of intimacy in the United States, France, and Japan revealed that cultural values based on individualism versus collectivism may have a more significant effect on love commitment and disclosure maintenance than biological sex. Relatedly, the aforementioned meta-analysis of studies on self-disclosure by Dindia and Allen revealed few actual differences in men's and women's behavior, leading these researchers to conclude that sex differences in this instance were more a myth than a reality (1992: 118). Borisoff and Merrill (1998: 39) suggest this conclusion may be unwarranted because it ignores differences within those groups:

> As always, we need to be wary of totalizing notions of "men's" and "women's" behaviors which erase differences within those groups. For example, Gaines (1995) found that African-American men tended to be more emotionally expressive than were men of Caucasian backgrounds, suggesting that the "differences" between women and men . . . may reflect more complex constructions of ethnicity and other variables, such as sexuality, as well as gender.

Multiple Factors Influence Gender Studies. The factors researchers actually look at is a third area of concern in gender research. Much of the extant research focuses on a single behavior or on a selected number of behaviors. The conclusions uncovered often then are generalized to a variety of situations, contexts, and relationships. Often ignored are other contextual factors that may exert a powerful influence. For example, the process and content of self-disclosure studied at a particular moment in time may ignore how one's stage in life as well as one's stage in a relationship may affect what, and how willingly, one self-discloses (Aires, 1987, 1996, 1998; Duck, 1991; Prager, 1995; Reis, 1998). Similarly, perceived power may be a more significant factor in one's willingness to self-disclose than gender (Prager, 1995; Rosenfeld and Welsh, 1985; Wood, 1998).

Aries (1987) maintains that the propensity to generalize findings across contexts and situations may be inaccurate: "When researchers focus on a single behavior, or even a selected number of behaviors, the total impression conveyed at a particular moment by a speaker through all available channels becomes distorted. In most studies, the motives, intentions, and expectations of the communicators are not systematically studied" (170).

How Data Collection Influences Findings. This last point is related to the final aspect of research that merits our scrutiny. Part of the dilemma with gathering empirical evidence about self-disclosure is embedded in the way self-disclosure is studied. "When a researcher is privy to the information between subjects," Arliss (1991) warns, "it cannot be considered real self-disclosure between two relationship members" (71). To rectify this problem, she continues, "most researchers have opted to study either self-reports . . . or recorded laboratory conversations designed to promote self-disclosure" (71).

Difficult to tease out is the extent to which subjects in laboratory-type situations "perform" communication that conforms to the sex-role and sex-trait stereotypes associated with masculinity and femininity. To the extent that they may resort to gendered scripts, research subjects may be enacting what they construe as some idealized version of how they think they ought to, rather than how they actually, behave. Additionally, what they report as examples of "closeness" may be influenced by societal definitions of topics deemed personal. As long as prescriptions for closeness persist, it will remain difficult to expand the range of topics and behaviors that may more accurately reflect what is deeply personal and what is deeply felt.

SUMMARY AND CONCLUSION

This chapter examined the role intimacy plays in our lives, described characteristics of intimate relationships, and considered how the impetus to think in bipolar terms about the world, particularly about gender, has perpetuated assumptions about women's and men's communication. As the final section indicated, many of the presumed differences about intimacy are more a matter of perception and are linked to how gender is studied and how research findings are interpreted. These perceptions have important implications.

If we return to the case of Faust and Luste, the protagonists introduced at the beginning of this chapter, the heroes are destined never to achieve real intimacy. Faust, in despair, eventually dies by his own hand. Guided solely by intellect and reason, the hero finds the temptation of the emotional side insufficiently compelling to alter either his character or his destiny. To the extent that gender is constructed, it is important to challenge the attitudes and behaviors that have imprisoned us. Unlike the characters in Valery's play, who are prisoners of the artist's imagination, women and men no longer need to be constrained by gender scripts. Rigid adherence to self-imposed gender scripts makes us dance to a tune we may not like, and that may not be appropriate. No matter how well you waltz, you and your partner will be out of sync if you are dancing to the tune of a techno beat.

FOR FURTHER DISCUSSION

1. Generate a list or chart of personal topics you discuss with others. In preparing this material include:
   a) With whom do you discuss these topics?
   b) Where do you typically hold these discussions?
   Compare your list with others in a group or with individuals you interview for this assignment. Do any patterns emerge that might indicate similarities and/or differences that may be related to culture, to gender, to race, or, to sexual orientation?
2. Consider the following observation by Sherry Turkle (1995: 178) regarding the Internet and relationship formation:

   > Many of the institutions that used to bring people together . . . no longer work as before. Many people spend most of their day alone at the screen of a television or a computer. . . . And the computer is playing a central role. We correspond with each other through electronic mail and contribute to electronic bulletin boards and mailing lists; we

> join interest groups whose participants include people from all over the world. Our rootedness to place has attenuated. These shifts raise many questions: What will computer-mediated communication do to our commitment to other people? Will it satisfy our needs for connection and social participation, or will it further undermine fragile relationships? What kind of responsibility and accountability will we assume for our virtual actions? (From: *Life on the Screen: Identity in the Age of the Internet*, New York: Simon and Schuster.)

How do you respond to Turkle's observations regarding the kind and quality of relationships you have developed in virtual and in real space? What are the similarities and/or differences in these relationships? Under what circumstances is one arena preferable over another?

3. Herbert Blumer has suggested that our values are continually influenced by our interactions with others, leading him to conclude that group values continually change over time. Select early and recent articles and/or popular works that have addressed intimacy. To what extent have prescriptions for intimacy been transformed? To what extent do these transformations affect expectations for women; for men? (Herbert Blumer, The Nature of Symbolic Interactionism, in *Symbolic Interactionism: Perspectives and Method* [Englewood Cliffs, NJ: Prentice-Hall, 1969], 2–21).

4. In her review of studies on gay and lesbian couples, Karen Prager (see reference section) notes,

> The few studies that have assessed satisfaction in gay and lesbian relationships indicate that, . . . the developmental course and sources of satisfaction in these relationships are quite similar to those in heterosexual relationships. . . . Gay and lesbian couples report levels of satisfaction in their relationship that are similar to those for heterosexual couples. (250–251)

In light of these findings, how would you respond to works that continue to dichotomize masculinity and femininity?

5. Select examples from literature (i.e., popular romance novels, plays, poetry, etc.). To what extent are the depictions of romantic love similar or different for men and for women?

6. Sam Keen (see reference section) has suggested that it is primarily through sexual intercourse that men are able to achieve intimacy. He writes,

> It is not that men are only interested in sex, but that we have been so conditioned to curtail our natural needs for intimacy that only in sex do we have cultural permission to feel close to another human being. . . . Emotionally speaking men are stutterers who often use sexual language to express their forbidden desires for communication. (78)

Do you agree or disagree with this statement? Defend your position.

Endnotes

1 Included among the many writers who have addressed these issues in both academic and popular publications are: Aaron Beck, 1988; Sandra Bem, 1993; John Gray, 1992; Helen Haste, 1994; Elaine Hatfield and Richard Rapson, 1993; Shere Hite, 1987; Harriet Goldhor Lerner, 1989; Lillian Rubin, 1983; and Deborah Tannen, 1990.

2 Although the authors who write on intimate relationships acknowledge that there are many different kinds of intimate relationships (for example, married couples, parent-child, friendship ties, gay and lesbian couples), the majority of the research on intimacy has, to this point, been conducted on heterosexual couples who are married. Because part of the purpose of this chapter is to integrate the research on gender differences and human communication into the work on intimate relationships, it was considered most productive to utilize the predominant research. Therefore, this chapter focuses on intimacy and communication within heterosexual couples.

3 The studies reviewed by Dindia and Allen extended beyond romantic heterosexual partners and included friends, spouses, and parents' interaction with their children. Also noted in their report is that women more frequently are the recipients of self-disclosure than men; there is also the tendency for women to self-disclose more than men.

4 Because this study relied on self-reporting, it is difficult to determine if the husbands in dual-career relationships truly self-disclosed more than their wives, especially in light of the overwhelming evidence in the Dindia and Allen meta-analysis that women self-disclose more than men. It is possible that the men in the Rosenfeld and Welsh study *perceived* that they self-disclosed more than their wives. However, even if they did not actually self-disclose more, the perception that they did so is, in and of itself, telling.

References

Acitelli, L. F., and S. Duck 1987. Intimacy as the proverbial elephant. In D. Perlman and S. Duck, eds., *Intimate Relationships: Development, Dynamics and Deterioration.* Beverly Hills, CA: Sage, 297–308.

Aires, E. 1987. Gender and communication. In P. Shaver and C. Hendrick, eds., *Sex and Gender.* Beverly Hills, CA: Sage, 149–176.

———. 1996. *Men and Women in Interaction.* New York: Oxford University Press.

———. 1998. Gender differences in interaction. In D. J. Canary and K. Dindia, eds., *Sex Differences and Similarities in Communication.* Mahwah, NJ: Lawrence Erlbaum, 65–81.

Arliss, L. P. 1991. *Gender Communication.* Englewood Cliffs, NJ: Prentice-Hall.

Beck, A. T. 1988. *Love Is Never Enough.* New York: Harper.

Bem, S. L. 1993. *The Lenses of Gender: Transforming the Debate on Sexual Inequality.* New Haven, CT: Yale University Press.

Borisoff, D., and D. F. Hahn. Fall, 1995. From research to pedagogy: Teaching gender and communication. *Communication Quarterly* 43(4): 381–393.

Borisoff, D., and L. Merrill. 1998. *The Power to Communicate: Gender Differences as Barriers.* 3d ed. Prospect Heights, IL: Waveland Press.

Brown, G. W., and T. Harris. 1978. *Social Origins of Depression: A Study of Psychiatric Disorder in Women.* New York: The Free Press.

Canary, D. J., and K. Dindia, eds. 1998. *Sex Differences and Similarities in Communication.* Mahwah, NJ: Erlbaum.

Canary, D. J., and T. M. Emmers-Sommer. 1997. *Sex and Gender Differences in Personal Relationships.* New York: The Guilford Press.

Chelune, G. J., J. T. Robison, and M. J. Kommor. 1984. A cognitive model of intimate relationships. In V. J. Derlega, ed., *Communication, Intimacy, and Close Relationships.* Orlando, FL: Academic Press, 11–40.

Derlega, V. J. 1984. Self-disclosure and intimate relationships. In V. J. Derlega, ed., *Communication, Intimacy, and Close Relationships.* Orlando, FL: Academic Press, 1–9.

Derlega, V. J., and A. L. Chaikin. 1976. Norms affecting self-disclosure in men and women. *Journal of Consulting and Clinical Psychology* 44: 376–380.

Dindia, K., and M. Allen. 1992. Sex differences in self-disclosure: A meta-analysis. *Psychological Bulletin*, 112: 106–124.

Duck, S. 1988. *Relating to Others.* Chicago: Dorsey.

———. 1991. *Understanding Relationships.* New York: The Guilford Press.

Gaines, S. 1995. Relationships between members of cultural minorities. In J. T. Wood and S. W. Duck, eds., *Understanding Relationship Processes: Understudied Relationships.* Thousand Oaks, CA: Sage, 51–88.

Gilligan, C. 1982. *In a Different Voice: Psychological Theory and Women's Development.* Cambridge, MA: Harvard University Press.

Goldberg, H. 1976. *The Hazards of Being Male: Surviving the Myth of Masculine Privilege.* New York: Nash.

Graebner, A. 1982. Growing up female. In L. A. Samovar and R. E. Porter, eds., *Intercultural Communication: A Reader.* Belmont, CA: Wadsworth.

Gray, J. 1992. *Men Are from Mars, Women Are from Venus: A Practical Guide for Improving Communication and Getting What You Want in Your Relationships.* New York: HarperCollins.

Hahn, D. F., and D. Borisoff. Winter 2000. How do we keep women in their place if woman is place? *Qualitative Research Reports in Communication* 1(1): 14–17.

Haste, H. 1994. *The Sexual Metaphor: Men, Women, and the Thinking that Makes the Difference.* Cambridge, MA: Harvard University Press.

Hatfield, E. 1982. What do women and men want from love and sex? In E. R. Allgeier and N. B. McCormick, eds., *Gender Roles and Sexual Behavior.* Palo Alto, CA: Mayfield, 106–134.

———. 1984. The dangers of intimacy. In V. J. Derlega, ed., *Communication, Intimacy, and Close Relationships.* Orlando, FL: Academic Press, 207–220.

Hatfield, E., and R. Rapson. 1993. *Love, Sex, and Intimacy: Their Psychology, Biology, and History.* New York: HarperCollins.

Helgeson, V. S., P. Shaver, and M. Dyer. 1987. Prototypes of intimacy and distance in same-sex and opposite-sex relationships. *Journal of Social and Personal Relationships* 14: 195–233.

Hite, S. 1987. *Women and Love: A Cultural Revolution in Progress.* New York: Alfred A. Knopf.

Jourard, S. M. 1971. *The Transparent Self.* New York: Van Nostrand-Reinhold.

Keen, S. 1991. *The Fire in the Belly: On Being a Man.* New York: Bantam Books.

Klinger, E. 1977. *Meaning and Voice: Inner Experiences and Incentives in Peoples' Lives.* Minneapolis: University of Minnesota Press.

Lerner, H. G. 1989. *The Dance of Intimacy.* New York: Harper and Row.

Levant, R. F. 1996. Reconstructing masculinity: The genesis and remediation of normative male Alexithymia. Paper presented at the American Psychological Association annual convention, Toronto, August 9–13.

Lewin, T. 2 March 1996. Child care in conflict with job. *The New York Times*, 8.

Maltz, D. N., and R. A. Borker. 1982. A cultural approach to male-female miscommunications. In J. J. Gumperz, ed., *Language and Social Identity.* Cambridge, UK: Cambridge University Press, 196–216.

Monsour, M. 1992. Meanings of intimacy in cross- and same-sex friendships. *Journal of Social and Personal Relationships* 9: 277–296.

Morris, D. 1971. *Intimate Behaviors.* New York: Random House.

Perlman, D., and S. Duck, eds. 1987. *Intimate Relationships: Development, Dynamics, and Deterioration.* Beverly Hills, CA: Sage.

Perlman, D., and S. Fehr, eds. 1987. *Development of Intimate Relationships: Development, Dynamics, and Deterioration.* Newbury Park, CA: Sage.

Prager, K. J. 1995. *The Psychology of Intimacy.* New York: The Guilford Press.

Reik, T. 1954. Men and women speak different languages. *Psychoanalysis* 2: 3–15.

Reis, H. T. 1984. Social interaction and personal relationships. In S. Duck, ed., *Personal Relationships 5: Repairing Personal Relationships.* London: Academic Press, 21–45.

———. 1990. The role of intimacy in interpersonal relations. *Journal of Social and Clinical Psychology* 9: 15–30.

———. 1998. Gender differences in intimacy and related behaviors: Contexts and process. In D. J. Canary and K. Dindia, eds., *Sex Differences and Similarities in Communication.* Mahwah, NJ: Lawrence Erlbaum, 203–232.

Rosenfeld, L. B., and M. Welsh. 1985. Differences in self-disclosure in dual-career and single-career marriages. *Communication Monographs* 52: 253–263.

Rubin, L. B. 1983. *Intimate Strangers: Men and Women Together.* New York: Harper and Row.

Swain, S. 1989. Covert intimacy: Closeness in men's friendships. In B. J. Risman and P. Schwartz, eds., *Gender in Intimate Relationships.* Belmont, CA: Wadsworth, 71–86.

Tannen, D. 1990. *You Just Don't Understand: Women and Men in Conversation.* New York: William Morrow.

Thorne, B. 1993. *Gender Play: Girls and Boys in School.* New Brunswick, NJ: Rutgers University Press.

Ting-Toomey, S. 1991. Intimacy expressions in three cultures: France, Japan, and the United States. *International Journal of Intercultural Relations* 15(1): 29–46.

Valentine, G. March, 1997. "My son's a bit ditzy." "My wife's a bit soft": Gender, children and cultures of parenting. *Gender, Place and Culture* 4(1): 37–62.

Valery, P. 1941. Luste, or the crystal girl. Trans. David Paul. In J. Mathews, ed., *Paul Valery Plays, Vol. 3.* New York: Pantheon Books, 1960, 5–140.

Weinberg, K. 1976. *The Figure of Faust in Valery and Goethe.* Princeton, NJ: Princeton University Press.

Weisstein, U. 1968. *Comparative Literature and Literary Theory.* Trans. W. Riggan. Bloomington: Indiana University Press.

Wilden, A. 1987. *Man and Woman, War and Peace: A Strategist's Companion.* New York: Routledge and Kegan Paul.

Williams, J. E., and D. L. Best. 1982. *Measuring Sex Stereotypes: A Thirty Nation Study.* Beverly Hills, CA: Sage.

Wood, J. T. Spring, 1992. Gender and moral voice: Moving from woman's nature to standpoint epistemology. *Women's Studies in Communication* 15(1): 1–24.

———. 2001. *Gendered Lives: Communication, Gender, and Culture.* 4th ed. Belmont, CA: Wadsworth.

Wood, J. T., and C. Inman. August, 1993. In a different mode: Masculine styles of communicating closeness. *Journal of Applied Communication Research* 2(3): 279–295.

CHAPTER 3

Gender, Masculinities, Identities, and Interpersonal Relationship Systems

Men in General and Gay Men in Particular

James W. Chesebro

POINTS TO BE ADDRESSED

- Variations in the links among gender, sexual preference, identity, and relationship system
- Various ways of defining *masculinity*
- How *masculinity* functions as a social and symbolic construction
- Factors affecting/determining how masculine a man is
- Viewing relationships in terms of language usage
- Viewing relationships in terms of quasi-marriage and sexual faithfulness
- Viewing relationships in terms of idealized and fantasized relationships

If it weren't for gay men, I'd never talk to men at all.

—Margaret Cho

In the first edition of this book, back in 1993, Arliss and Borisoff posited that gender can directly affect the formation and maintenance of identity, which in turn, can determine the kind or type of interpersonal relationships a person has. This proposition is outstanding in several respects. First and foremost, in this age when everything is assumed to be caused by multiple variables, Arliss and Borisoff dared to posit that a single variable can make a difference. Certainly, a single variable such as gender is not exclusively determining, but they recognized that it possesses a noteworthy influence over who we are and how we function in interpersonal relationships. As Arliss and Borisoff (1993, p. v) articulated the proposition in the first paragraph of the first edition of this book some ten years ago: "Boys and girls, and women and men, learn distinct communication styles. Their attitudes toward relationships, toward the world of work, and toward participating in the family, are distinct. Even the stereotypes and behavioral expectations we have for women and men differ." Arliss and Borisoff explicitly and directly addressed "the effect of gender on our capacity to develop intimate relationships" (v). In this subsequent edition, Arliss and Borisoff continue to explore the social construction of gender and its effect on intimate relationships.

Much has occurred since the first edition was published. We now more fully recognize that gender itself is a complicated construct. Indeed, we do not go amiss by suggesting that gender admits of ambiguity and is now more of an issue than a crisp and precise construct. The ambiguity and issues are particularly vivid when we explore how the notion of gender affects specific minorities. Indeed, in this chapter, we examine some of the ways in which gender affects men in general. But we specifically focus on how gender affects one minority group, gay men, and how gender ultimately influences their identities as well as their interpersonal relationship systems.

Let's begin this exploration by considering explicitly some of the ambiguities that exist when we consider how a construct such as gender works in the lives of different kinds of gay men. Consider the five scenarios that follow, but as you do, I ask you to keep several questions in mind. Even though each scenario is a creation of a man who is homosexual:

1. Doesn't every homosexual man have a very different identity?
2. Doesn't every homosexual man create a different set of experiences, expectations, and standards for what his interpersonal relationships can and should be?
3. Do gender and sexual preferences alone explain the differences among these men?
4. Is there a single generalization that can be made about the identity and interpersonal relationships of these people simply because they are men?

Scenario 1:

Like most gay men I know of my generation, I spent the better part of my late teens and twenties trying to convince myself to go to bed with

> women while my eyes knew they were following the hips and shoulders of men. It wasn't that I wasn't interested in women, didn't find women beautiful, didn't get aroused by the kiss or embrace of a woman. My neurophysiological responses functioned just fine with the opposite sex though perhaps a little less quickly. The great fear, my great fear, was that should the woman at hand catch my errant glance at a man, should she divine my lust for a male breast, I would be undone. I would be revealed as a fraud. I would be other than a man. (Browning, 1998: 4)

Scenario 2:

Bob Paris and Rod Jackson are two well-known men in the world of body building who held a widely publicized wedding ceremony in Los Angeles in the early 1990s. In 86 pages of 11" x 13" black-and-white as well as color pictures, Tom Bianchi photographed Bob Paris and Rod Jackson nude in a series of playful, emotional, sexual, erotic, and affectionate poses and situations. In the final product, a volume entitled *Bob & Rod*, distributed nationally, Bianchi (1994: 7–8) has reported,

> The Jackson–Paris marriage, the publicity which has attended that union, has been important to the imagination of the gay and lesbian community. To the straight world, a message was sent which challenged stereotypes. Never before had men so visible announced so publicly that they were gay, married, and proud. Their honesty lent dignity to gay people as individuals and raised the general awareness of the love shared by homosexuals.

Scenario 3:

Browning (1998) has provided this description of his friend Raimundo, who is a married man, with a daughter, and a "closet case."

> [He has] a voracious appetite for men. . . . He has a profound adoration for his daughter. His wife, he told me, is the other half of his soul. "Why," he asked me quietly, "should I want to be gay?". . . Raimundo, by contrast, appears to be the epitome of all [that the gay-rights movement has] sought to escape. His life, it would seem, represents shame—ours, pride.
>
> Neither emotion, however, seems remotely related to how he experiences his life, homosexually or heterosexually. The most intense pride he feels, he says, is directed at his daughter. The only shame is the occasional twinge at being perennially short of money. Sex is . . . just that: sex is. It exists. It is a pleasure. It is an appetite.
>
> "And what of love?" I remember asking.
>
> "I am already in love," he answered, without elaboration, but of course he meant with his wife. . . . (1998: 12)

Scenario 4:

John and Dan met twenty years ago. John was active in the gay liberation movement at its inception, and later, he was active in gaining recognition for gay men, lesbians, bisexuals, and transgendered people in his professional association. Dan has been known as gay most of his adult life, a self-recognition that was accepted relatively easily by his parents and other brothers. John and Dan began living together permanently three months after they met. All of their straight and gay friends as well as their professional colleagues are aware of the intimate nature of their relationship, although John and Dan seldom mention the relationship explicitly or feel the need to justify and defend their lifestyle. In terms of Kinsey Institute researchers Bell and Weinberg (1978: 23), John and Dan are classified as a "closed couple," for they are in a "quasi-marriage with few sexual problems, with few sexual partners other than their mate during the year, and they engage in little cruising." The Kinsey Institute has reported that some 13.8 percent of all gay men are "closed couples" (Bell and Weinberg, 1978: 23).

Scenario 5:

Charles is an African-American man, with a Ph.D.—a professor who teaches at a major college in the Northeast region of the country. He now identifies himself as "effeminate" and a "black queer." For him "home is a site of both contradiction and contention. As a site of contradiction, home is experienced as a mediated event. As a site of contention within the home, my childhood was a mixed environment of liberation and domination" (Nero, 2000: 55). Among the many events shaping his life, he specifically recalled that it

> was through television that I first imagined the possibility of being gay and living as member of the African-American post–civil rights professional middle class—the group I was being educated to enter. I vividly remember watching Hal Holbrook, Hope Lange, and Scott Jacobi in the 1973 television movie *That Certain Summer*, in which a white man divorced his wife for a male lover. I was a junior in high school and I remember being emotionally moved by poignant scenes such as the one in which Lange, the wife, tells Holbrook, her husband, that she doesn't know how to compete with a man and the anger of young Scott Jacobi, the sensitive son with whom I identified, when he discovered that his father was gay.
>
> Did this film create unrealistic expectations for me? Did they lead to personal frustration because I could not attain the image of home as presented in the media? No, because I also remember several disquieting moments in the movie. Holbrook and his lover, played by Martin Sheen, never displayed affection toward each other. (I had recently viewed Marlowe's *Edward II* on PBS, and it seemed to me that for the entire program the King and Gaveston did nothing but kiss.) It also occurred to me that Holbrook and Sheen, for all intents and purposes, were not the least bit effeminate like me. Yet, *That Certain Summer* allowed me to imagine the possibility of being in love with another man. It also reinforced the idea that personal happiness was a worthy goal, and, on later reflection, that one's quest for personal happiness might be a cause for the unhappiness of others. In other words, I realized that announcing I was gay would require me to weigh my happiness against that of my parents. For me that became an intellectual task beyond homophobia—a critique of heterosexuality itself. (Nero, 2000: 55–56)

Having considered these five scenarios, let me return to and answer the four questions I asked before introducing these five scenarios.

1. Doesn't every homosexual man have a very different identity? *Yes.* Every gay man has a unique identity.
2. Doesn't every homosexual man create a different set of experiences, expectations, and standards for what his interpersonal relationships can and should be? *Yes.* Every gay man has his own set of interpersonal experiences, expectations, and standards.
3. Do gender and sexual preference alone explain the differences among these men? *No.* Gender and sexual preferences alone do not explain the differences among gay men.
4. Is there a single generalization that can be made about the identity and interpersonal relationships of these people simply because they are men? *Yes.* Despite our answers to these first three questions, there is a single generalization that can be made about the identity and interpersonal relationships of these people simply because they are men. Indeed, there are a host of generalizations that can be made about the identity and interpersonal relationships about gay men simply because they are gay men.

In the balance of this chapter, I want to outline a framework that allows us to make generalizations about the identities and interpersonal relationships of gay men even though each gay man has a unique identity, has his own set of interpersonal experiences, and even though we recognize that gender and sexual orientation do not account for the totality of any single personality. I want to end the chapter by proposing a concept that allows us to discuss all men—gay or straight—as equals in terms of their gender orientations, their identities, and their interpersonal relationships. I do not expect universal acceptance of this concept, nor do I expect agreement about its power to create equality among men. But, I do hope it allows us to reconsider all men—gay or straight—as possessing forms of masculinity that can each be assessed for its relative value as a way of dealing with gender, identity, and interpersonal relationships.

Understanding Masculinity: Definitions and a Construct

A tremendous range of diverse, if not contradictory, conceptions of masculinity now exist. As a point of departure, we need to explore what masculinity is, what it is not, and how it functions.

A Definition of Masculinity

I want to suggest that masculinity is profoundly and ultimately a communication concept, a socially and symbolically constructed notion, that every culture and every era revisits and redefines in different ways. In this sense, people decide what masculinity is and what it is not. Therefore, to understand what masculinity is, we need to examine how each specific group of people defines manliness at any given point in time. Accordingly, we begin by considering how this social and symbolic view of masculinity squares up with other views of masculinity. Other views of masculinity have been embedded in religious, psychological, and scientific views of manliness. Because of how powerful each of these views has been in influencing how we think about masculinity, each of these views deserves mention.

For one group, sexuality is linked to and is part of a religious orientation, and all forms of sexuality become God-given. In this view, masculinity is frequently understood as a set of traits that must be "balanced" against feminine qualities. These traits and qualities, as articulated by Payne are "finally rooted in God." In this view, masculine behavior should naturally manifest itself in three roles: "husbands, fathers, and leaders" (1995: 10). In this framework, the current "crisis in masculinity" exists because society has failed to "affirm" these God-given roles. Payne has specifically maintained that, "very few men" are "adequately affirmed as men today, and many are pathologically split off from their masculinity altogether." For Payne, within an ideal society, "The masculine within is called forth and blessed by the masculine without" (11). Within this religious context, Osterhaus has maintained that the "American ideal of the rugged individualist standing invulnerable to the world" must be reconceived so that men form "bonds of iron," creating "lasting male relationships" (1994: 7–8). As Osterhaus has explained, "To be truly human, exhibiting God's image, is to be in relationships with other people" (17). Men must, Osterhaus has maintained, develop a "love of friendship" that "rejoices in the freedom of the friend, and thus lets the friend go continually to grow and become all that the friend was meant to be" (25).

For others, masculinity is an internal or innate quality and trait. Employing a male sex role identity (MSRI) paradigm, Pleck concluded that masculinity is an innate trait of males that "develops from within, rather than being arbitrarily imposed from without: Because of an innate psychological need to develop sex role identity, the individual is preprogrammed to learn a traditional sex role as part of normal psychological development" (1981: 4). In Pleck's view, a "man's efforts to attain a healthy sex role identity" is "thwarted" by paternal absence, maternal overprotectiveness, the feminizing of the schools, and "general blurring" of male and female roles that is "occurring now in society" (2–3).

For another set of people, the explanations offered by science can override all religious and psychological considerations. For these scientifically minded folk, chromosomes can be a relevant framework for defining masculinity. While the XY chromosome formula "sets into motion all the mechanisms of sexual differentiation that cause a man to be a man instead of a woman," Badinter has concluded that "although XY is certainly the primary condition of the male human being, it does not suffice to characterize him" (1992/1995: xiii).

Others suggest that the notions of masculinity and femininity are a product of chemical differences in the bodies of men and women due to testosterone. The greater strength, activity level, and aggressiveness associated with the male's higher level of testosterone are a physical fact. But, even the potential energy associated with testosterone must be channeled and manifested in social and cultural ways. As Sullivan has noted, testosterone-based activities are "refracted through the prism of our own history and culture" (2000: 45).

How, then, might masculinity be formally defined? Ultimately, as I have suggested, masculinity is predominantly a communication issue and masculinity itself is a social and symbolic construction. In this view, masculinity is not divinely inspired, innate, or biological. Masculinity is a product of human interaction; it is social construction. Masculinity is a product of the images and characterizations that humans decide to attribute to men as a group; it is symbolic construction. This view of masculinity, I would hold, allows people to deal with masculinity as a researchable, diverse, ubiquitous, and cross-cultural concept.

Despite the alternative, if not contradictory, approaches used to define the essence and circumscribe the boundaries of masculinity, viewing masculinity as a social and symbolic construction appears to be the most satisfying in a host of ways. At a minimum, masculinity should be defined in a way that allows it to be researchable. Whatever definition of masculinity is used, it should provide—if not encourage—ways of investigating how masculinity has been understood, used, and how it has functioned in a host of diverse cultures in different eras. Viewing masculinity as an innate psychological trait, religious experience, chromosome formula, or chemical reaction in the body fails to reveal and highlight the different forms that masculinity has assumed in different cultures at different times in human history. Accordingly, a reasonable conception of masculinity should allow one to emphasize and highlight the social, cultural, and historical nature of the concept. In this view, ultimately masculinity is a social rather than biological notion.

In this regard, *Webster's Third International Dictionary* provides an apt, if not commonly recognized, orientation for defining masculinity. *Webster's* defines masculinity as a "class of words or grammatical forms characteristically referring to males" (1986: 1387). As a functional concept, masculine terminologies should describe and prescribe; masculine terminologies should provide a convenient model for identifying appropriate and reliable role behaviors for males. Ideally, then, masculinity might function ideologically as but one coherent and systematic set of concepts for characterizing human life and culture, epistemologically as but one way of explaining the human condition, and morally as but one special set of standards for judging and improving human life and culture.

There is little question that masculinity is a ubiquitous cross-cultural concept. Masculinity can and has manifested itself in a tremendous variety of ways. In the medieval period (from approximately A.D. 500 to 1500), a unique set of struggles and crises defined masculinity. Marking a major transformation in what being a man meant, in the medieval period masculinity was undergoing a complicated shift. As Lees (1994) has articulated this shift, masculinity was being transformed from a kind "male humanity" (22) to the "male warrior class" (xxiii). In its wake, this transformation "victimized" women "by their exclusion" and created "male victims," particularly "heretics, homosexuals, Jews, and rebels who didn't fit the mold [who were] turned into women" (22).

In sharp contrast, in England from A.D. 1600 to 1800, the struggles and crises of masculinity focused on defining men in terms of their sexual behaviors. As Hitchcock and Cohen have succinctly put the matter, "before the eighteenth century in England, men did not define themselves in terms of their sexual behavior, whether homosexual or heterosexual" (1999: 3). The struggles and crises of eighteenth-century England were to determine how "masculine" men were to be distinguished from other groups by their sexual behaviors, distinctions that ultimately separated "masculine" men from other groups, particularly women and homosexuals (see, e.g., Hitchcock and Cohen, 1999).

But, the concepts defining medieval men as masculine and eighteenth-century English men as masculine were remarkably different from the defining experiences of men in the United States as they moved from the nineteenth into the twentieth century. In *Manhood in America: A Cultural History*, Kimmel (1994: 78) maintained that between the end of the nineteenth century and the beginning of the twentieth century, men at all levels of the societal system and in all geographic regions of the United States faced a "crisis in masculinity." This crisis was generated by three factors: (1) An unprecedented level of industrialization that challenged the image of the man as self-made; (2) the entry into the labor market of women, newly freed slaves, and immigrants, who demanded rights traditionally reserved for and defining men; and (3) the closing of the frontier, denying the self-made man new options for independence.

More recently, in the United States, during the late twentieth century, some have again underscored the meaning of masculinity as a social and symbolic construction. Defining masculinity as it is socially used and understood, Cicone and Ruble have defined masculinity in terms of "people's beliefs about males" (1978: 5). Based upon a compilation and synthesis of findings from several studies, Cicone and Ruble have specifically suggested that the "typical male" has three distinct traits: (1) *active and achievement-oriented* (including qualities such as adventurous, ambitious, independent, courageous, competitive, leader, and active); (2) *dominant* (including qualities such as aggressiveness, powerful, assertiveness, and boastful); and (3) *level-headed* (including qualities such as logical, realistic, stable, unemotional, and self-control) (11).

Additionally, when masculinity is socially and symbolically defined, its ability to affect and influence people cannot be ignored. It is a persuasive, if not ideological, construct. In this way, the social constructions of masculinity have led to an exploration of its symbolic meaning and uses in a social system. In this sense, in the United States during the end of the twentieth century and the beginning of the twenty-first century, the dominant use of masculinity might reasonably recognize its function as a hegemonic system, creating hierarchies, modes of dominance and subordination, as well as related systems of wealth and power, which serves a relatively few men at the expense of many other groups (see: Carrigan, Connell, and Lee, 1987; Connell, 1987; Hanke, 1992: 190–192). Constructed as a social vision designed to be viewed as common sense and conventional morality, articulated conceptions of masculinity seldom appear destructive. Consider, for example, the qualities of "naturalness," if not inevitability, attributed to the notion of masculinity offered by Oxford University biologist Ben Greenstein (1993/1994: 61) in *The Fragile Male: The Decline of a Redundant Species:*

> Generally speaking, men want to be men. They want to be acknowledged as men, and . . . this need may be programmed into the neural circuitry. . . . In the first place, the appearance of physical proof of manhood is eagerly awaited by every boy. The first signs of pubic and facial hair are celebrated not only by the boy himself, but by a relieved father, and both parents joyfully guide their son to his manhood.
>
> Boys want not only the more private manifestations of manhood. They passionately want those which proclaim their masculine success to the world. They want height, impressive musculature and the strength that goes with it. This desire for the trappings of manhood is so widespread it is tempting to believe that these feelings are instinctive, part of the proto-male that survives to this day.

Or, consider the sense of inevitability as well as the sense of an enduring tradition that anthropologist and sociologist Lionel Tiger (1969: xiv) has associated with masculinity:

> We know from many studies how important male groups are in virtually all known communities; the division of labour along sexual lines is one of the most important recurrent cross-cultural regularities which social scientists have identified. A self-evident concomitant of such division of labour is the existence of all-male groups and all-female ones. I will argue later that the exclusion of females from certain categories of all-male groups reflects not only a formalized hostility to females, but a positive valence, or "attraction," between males.

Of course, we have predominantly emphasized how masculinity is socially understood and functions symbolically in the United States during a very specific period of time. Accordingly, it is useful to understand how masculinity operates within a larger set of cultures in different times and places. We need, then, to conceive of masculinity as a broader construct that explains how men understand themselves and act together in a wider range of cultures and eras.

Masculinity as a Social and Symbolic Construct

When we discuss gender, we traditionally understand that two concepts are cast as opposites, *masculinity* and *femininity.* For example, after considering the addition of *androgynous* (high masculinity and high femininity) and *undifferentiated* (low masculinity and low femininity) to the masculine–feminine continuum, Pearson and Davilla reported that:

> Social scientists are more likely to focus on gender or gender roles because they have traditionally examined our social lives. Nonetheless, a relationship exists between sex and gender. Indeed, women are more likely than men to behave in a feminine way, while men are more likely than women to behave in a masculine manner. (1993: 3)

More useful, however, is the question of what determines masculinity: *What variables influence the construction of masculinity?* But the question becomes more immediate and personal if we ask: *What determines if a particular man is masculine?*

Relying on the work of Freimuth and Hornstein (1982), Franklin (1984) has articulated a framework for exploring some of the factors that affect how masculine a man is:

1. Androgen / Testosterone Level Relative to Estrogen / Progestin Level. The physiology and chemistry of our bodies determines how masculine or feminine each of us is. Certainly, biology is not destiny, but high levels of androgens are correlated with particular characteristics associated with manliness and men, such as higher arousal levels, greater tension levels, and greater aggressiveness during confrontational or sexual situations. Certainly, a higher androgen/testosterone to estrogen/progestin ratio in men does not guarantee them greater psychological dominance, confident physicality, and high self-esteem. As Sullivan aptly noted, "To be sure, because human beings are also deeply socialized, [the] impact [of hormonal differences] is refracted through the prism of our own history and culture" (2000: 46). Indeed, in a host of social and cultural environments, men's disproportional hormonal imbalances work against them in overwhelming ways.

2. Gender-Related Physical Characteristics. Certain physiological characteristics are consistently associated with manliness and men, such as more facial hair, a deeper voice, certain genitals, larger body sizes, a higher ratio of muscle to fat, and a greater upper-body strength.

At the same time, specific correlations between masculinity and specific physical characteristics must be carefully examined. As early as 1936, for example, Terman and Miles found small correlations between scores from a masculine-feminine test and a number of physique measures such as hip width, shoulder width, weight, and sitting height. They concluded that, "one can only say that if there is any correlation between masculine-feminine scores and any of the physical measures we have used it is probably not very large" (1936: 86). Another study (Gilkinson, 1937) also used an early version of the Terman-Miles masculine-feminine test and found that for a group of college men, masculine-feminine scores are negatively correlated with the highness of voice pitch and unrelated to either hip and shoulder size or amount of body hair. Additionally, specific types of physiques have not been correlated with high masculinity scores, although some evidence was found for suggesting that more muscular men have more masculine interests than men with female-like bodies (Child and Sheldon, 1941). In subsequent studies, however, Bayley (1951) and Honzik (1951) found no correlation between more muscular men and more masculine interests, ultimately concluding that the outstanding fact was that type of physique and masculine interests are largely independent of each other.

There is, however, evidence to suggest that those in authority positions early in children's lives begin to assert a correlation between type of physique and behaviors traditionally associated with masculine behavior that more formal measures have failed to establish. For example, Biller (1968) found that teachers evaluated kindergarten boys with greater height and greater chest girth as more active and energetic, more likely to lead other children, and as participating more frequently in sports. Additionally, Biller found that teachers ranked boys who are tall-broad or short-broad as significantly more masculine than boys who are tall-thin or short-thin. Using alternative measurements, similar findings regarding junior high school boys were also reported by Biller and Liebman in 1971. In 1976, LaVoie and Andrews attempted to replicate Biller and Leibman's 1971 study; they found that "physique" (in any height-weight ratio) was not related to sex-role adoption, preference, or orientation for this age group. After reviewing studies of this kind, Doyle and Paludi concluded that:

> The low expectations that parents and teachers have with respect to girls' motor performance, in addition to the lack of rewards given to girls for such activities, apparently combine to produce low motivation and low performance levels for girls in the behaviors that have been socially defined as appropriate for boys. (1985: 81)

In all, then, we must be careful in how we draw conclusions at this point. The evidence suggests that specific types of physical characteristics frequently associated with men do *not* correlate in any significant way with high masculinity scores. Nonetheless, certain physical characteristics and masculinity are socially and symbolically linked or correlated by people. While the link may not exist by any direct observation or independent measure, people fashion a link between certain types of physical characteristics traditionally associated with men with behaviors uniquely associated with masculine behaviors. Within this context, the ways in which a man enacts those physiological features associated with manliness affect, in part, the degree of masculinity associated with a specific man.

3. Gender-Related Sociocultural Roles. In every society, role playing and role taking are universal. Indeed, the ability to adopt roles as others understand them is cross-culturally a measure of reaching adulthood. As social psychologists Lindesmith, Strauss, and Denzin (1999: 267) have argued, "When a child has developed the ability to grasp the role or attitude of one other person at a time, he or she is on the road to becoming a social being. However, before the child can participate in organized adult activity, he or she must be able to conceive his or her own social identity systematically from the standpoint of all other participants." In this regard, Lindesmith, Strauss, and Denzin have reported that, "no society fails to embody in its practices and language the fundamental biological distinction between the sexes. . . . Femininity and masculinity are socially defined terms added to these sex classes" (1999: 267). At the same time, Lindesmith, Strauss, and Denzin were also careful to observe that, "*Gender* (like *sexuality*) is a discursive term; its meanings are established through discourse and performance" (267). Within this sociocultural context, Franklin (1984: 130) has observed that every culture has implicit standards about the appropriate roles that men must enact if they are to be judged masculine: "Judgments regarding the enactment of masculine gender roles are made on the bases of cultural and subcultural definitions of masculine." In other words, a particular male's behavior is subjectively compared by others to some idealized "prototypical male." While it probably goes without saying, men must enact certain roles if they are to be viewed as masculine, but in other sociocultural contexts, they may also initiate actions that challenge and change the discourse, performances, prototypes, and standards a culture employs to define what is masculine.

4. Gender Preference. As Franklin (1984: 130) directly put it, "For many people, the single factor determining a male's masculinity more than any other is his choice of a sexual partner." The sex of a man's sexual partner can be an overwhelming factor. "If a male chooses another male as a sexual partner, many people will automatically question his masculinity" (130). At the same time, Franklin's observation more directly reflects a dominant perspective in the United States rather than a more universal viewpoint. While cross-cultural studies of homosexuality have not been regularly undertaken, referring to the review completed by Hoch and Zubin (1949), Wardell B. Pomeroy (1969: 4), coauthor of the famous Kinsey studies, reported: "A study of 193 world cultures, for example, showed that 28 percent accepted homosexuality while only 14 percent rejected it; in the remaining 58 percent, there was partial acceptance or some equivocation involved." Accordingly, of the United States, Pomeroy has concluded, "Our own culture is plainly in the minority, not only in rejecting homosexuality but also in rejecting male homosexuality more forcibly than female homosexuality. Among the religions of the world, the Judeo-Christian system gives one of the harshest condemnations of homosexuality" (1969: 4).

But, the effect of gender preference on masculinity can operate far more subtly. If a man selected a partner who is opposite in all gender characteristics to his sex, he becomes more masculine than if he selects a partner who shares characteristics of his sex. This principle of gender difference appears to function as strongly for heterosexuals as gay men. As Franklin (1984: 131) has noted, "a male who chooses a masculine female sexual partner may differ only minimally from a male who chooses a masculine male sexual partner."

5. Subjective Gender Identity. Franklin (1984: 131) suggested, "a male's perception of himself is critical in determining his gender. Does he think he is highly masculine, moderately masculine, or minimally masculine?" Franklin has observed, moreover, that "most men tend to rank themselves somewhat below their prototypes of masculinity but with sufficient distance from femininity." At the same time, subjective gender identity functions independently of the other factors determining masculinity, and it is therefore possible that if a male perceives himself as feminine, this may set in motion other behaviors by himself and others that will refute any initial categorization of himself as masculine. Similarly, despite the behaviors of a man that warrant his self-classification as masculine, the perception of and responses by others to him may challenge, if not overwhelm, other defining variables, ultimately leading a man to believe he is somehow less than masculine. In this sense, while subjective gender identification might initially be viewed as a predominately personal self-conception, ultimately the responses of others can dramatically, if not decisively, affect one's subjective gender identity.

6. Gender-Related Age Identity. Because it can be mostly readily observed and measured in young women, puberty itself has often been measured by the age of first menstruation in young women. Konner (1998: A15) has reported that, "in 1840, the average young woman in Europe and the United States menstruated for the first time at the age of 17; her modern counterpart reaches the age of menstruation at about 12." Similarly, Anne Peterson (1979: 45), Director of the Laboratory for the Study of Adolescence at Chicago's Michael Reese Hospital and Medical Center and professor in the Department of Psychiatry at the University of Chicago, has reported, "In the United States, the average age of first menstruation has declined from 14.2 in 1900 to about 12.45 today."

For various reasons, many people prefer not to recognize that puberty has been occurring at an earlier and earlier age for each successive generation and prefer to define younger males as asexual, perhaps to preserve their innocence longer or perhaps because parents are not ready to deal with their children as sexual entities at the age of 11 or 12. (Nonetheless, the failure to recognize—and therefore to not talk about sex with children—results in unfortunate experimentations and misunderstandings about sex and the meanings of sexual activity, especially in an age when AIDS and other sexually transmitted diseases can so dramatically affect the life activities and even the life span of individuals.) Thus, a male's age can affect how masculine he is and how masculine others view him. Two groups of males—the young and the old—are placed at the greatest disadvantage because of how age and masculinity are and are not connected by others.

Indeed, boys normally are not classified as masculine or feminine until they begin to approach puberty. But, even puberty is not an invariant or purely physiological factor. Sociocultural factors such as the nutritional quality of food, sanitation, the quality of medical care, and so forth, can affect the age at which puberty occurs. Likewise, elderly men are seldom viewed as sexual. As Nussbaum and his colleagues have put it, "older people are rarely portrayed as gay men and lesbians; the media, when doing stories on homosexuality, constantly interview and photograph young gay men and lesbians. However, elderly gay men and lesbians do exist and maintain friendships throughout their lives" (2000: 226).

Specifically, older men are frequently presumed, stereotypically, to be the group most susceptible to impotence. As Lindesmith, Strauss, and Denzin (1999: 369), observe, "impotence generally refers to the inability of a man to achieve and maintain an erection sufficient to engage in intercourse." While Lindesmith, Strauss, and Denzin go on to argue that impotence can be the product of either organic (and therefore potentially age-related) or psychological conditions, they maintain that impotency is "more commonly" a psychological condition that affects men "between the ages of 37 and 40" (370). Lindesmith, Strauss, and Denzin specifically conclude that, "Although a decline in sexual interest and activity during old age is related to organic change (de Beauvoir, 1952; Hamilton, 1939; Hite, 1976), the connection is not sufficiently close to be called a causal one" (370). Indeed, Masters and Johnson's (1968, 238–270) intensive study of a sample of aging men and women gives strong evidence that despite organic changes, frequent sexual activity can be enjoyed well into old age.

If a decline in sexual interest and activity are *not*, in fact, causally related to old age, then why are older men stripped of their masculinity? Physical, anatomical, and organic factors are not responsible for the view that older men are less active sexually and therefore less masculine. Older men are viewed as less active sexually and therefore as less masculine, because of the social and symbolic constructions of others. Referring to Masters and Johnson's (1968) work, Lindesmith, Strauss, and Denzin have concluded that "actual declines in sexual interest and gratification" are likely to be "*psycho- and sociophysiological problems*" that directly result from "widespread cultural attitudes toward aging as nonsexual or asexual" (1999: 370).

In this sense, for both younger and older men, masculinity is not physiological. It must ultimately be understood as a social and symbolic construction.

7. Gender-Related Racial and National Identities. Racial and nationality stereotypes are employed to define and characterize what is and is not masculine. Some people believe, for example, that African men are more masculine than white men, because they are assumed to have larger penises and are more potent in terms of procreation. Others believe that Asian men are less masculine than white men, because they are assumed to have smaller penises and are more docile than white men. However, evidence does *not* exist to sustain these beliefs. Ideally, then, it would seem that we should be able to dismiss such beliefs as nothing more than the stereotypes that they are. Nonetheless, when we maintain that masculinity is a social and symbolic construct, we need to consider seriously all of the factors shaping the meaning of masculinity, including ill-formed and misinformed beliefs. At the same time, by seriously considering these stereotypical beliefs, the negative and harmful consequences of using these stereotypes can be explicitly identified. Likewise, when we explicitly deal with the racial and nationality stereotypes linked to masculinity, we also hope to discourage the use of these stereotypes, because of the negative consequences they produce.

While false and misleading racial and nationality stereotypes can exist when people make judgments about masculinity, we also need to admit that the published research in the discipline of communication is not as powerful as we need when it comes to dismissing such stereotypes. Indeed, much of the existing research seems only to have established a preliminary foundation for dismissing racial and nationality stereotypes about masculinity.

The relationships between racism and communication have been recognized for half a century (see, e.g., Baird, 1956: 93–121; Brigance, 1943: 265–293, 329–362, 387–433; Wrage and Baskerville, 1960: 150–212). More recently, the relationships between whiteness and communication have also been explored (see, e.g., Chesebro, 1996; Martin, Krizek, Nakayama, and Bradford, 1996; Mumby, 1996; Oliver, 1996). The interrelationships among whiteness, nonwhiteness, communication, and sexuality, and specifically masculinity and sexual preference, have been recognized and explored in preliminary ways but not investigated in the depth they seem to warrant (see, e.g., Nero, 2000; Ringer, 1994; Stephens, 1999). Likewise, the links between nationality and masculinity have yet to be explored in extended ways (see, e.g., Sandell, 1996). Accordingly, at this juncture, our explorations of the relationships among race, nationality, and masculinity must be viewed as heuristic, but nonetheless they may be extremely informative in terms of understanding how masculinity is socially and symbolically constructed for individual men.

I want to begin this exploration by determining what is meant by ill-formed and mistaken stereotyping. Certainly, in terms of general attraction to others and in terms of explaining their interpersonal decisions involving the choice of a partner, people may prefer a man who is lighter or darker skinned or who has attributes that may be linked to certain racial or nationality categories. Particularly in interracial cultures, skin color and nationality are not easily ignored nor diminished as variables. Skin shade and certain nationality features may determine and explain what is attractive about a specific person or why a particular individual is more appealing as an interpersonal choice.

While we recognize that racial and nationality decisions are made, we also need to ask a critical question: *When is the use of race and nationality a form of stereotyping?* Of course, honest and decent people disagree about when stereotyping occurs and when stereotyping is misinformed and negative. Scollon and Scollon (1995) provide a useful framework when defining inappropriate stereotyping. For Scollon and Scollon, a distinction must be drawn between description of what exists and what they identify as "ideological statements" and "stereotyping." They argue their case in this fashion:

> We have said that a balanced cultural description must take into consideration the full complexity of cultural themes. When one of those themes is singled out for emphasis and given a positive or negative value or is treated as the full description, then we would want to call that ideology rather than cultural description. A much more common term for such cultural ideological statements is "stereotyping."
>
> Ideological statements or stereotyping often arises when someone comes to believe that any two cultures or social groups, or, as we prefer to call them, two discourse systems, can be treated as if they were polar opposites. (1995: 155–156)

In this view, stereotyping occurs under four conditions: (1) when one feature of a group is used as if it is the only characteristic of the group; (2) when one feature of a group is used as if it is a full description of the group; (3) when a universal social characteristic is used as if it is a description of only one group; and (4) when a universal social characteristic is used to distinguish or separate one group from another.

Accordingly, when we consider how race and nationality have been used to define masculinity, we need to recognize the stereotypes involved. No single race or nationality has only large or only small penises. Likewise, every race and nationality have some men who are potent and others who are not. Likewise, every race and nationality have some individuals who are aggressive while others are docile.

At the same time, these stereotypes are used, and they can exert a powerful influence on how men define and understand themselves. These influences frequently displace other characteristics and prevent other influences from emerging. At this juncture, we can appropriately consider the stereotyping effects on African-American and Asian men.

African-American Men. While some may define black masculinity in terms of penis size and sexual potency, the scope, significance, and issues involved in black masculinity, particularly for African-American men, are revealed, in part, by events such as the October 16, 1995, Million Man March in Washington, D.C. Designed to promote personal responsibility and community involvement, the march was also an "emotional celebration for thousands of black men" (Franken, 1995) as well as an effort to devise ways in which individual black men might deal with crime, voting issues, poverty, children, and even genocide within with their communities.

Black masculinity issues are compounded when black men are gay. In 1989, continuing challenges from members of Congress to the National Endowment for the Arts reached a peak with Senator Jesse Helms's attacks on Robert Mapplethorpe's retrospective exhibition, "The Perfect Moment." Harper (1994: 141) has argued that the controversy stemmed "largely from the intensely conflicted issues of race, power, and sexuality raised by the photographer's aestheticized images of black male faces, bodies, and genitalia." Yet, Mapplethorpe's exhibition did not initiate the issues raised by black gay men. As Harper has maintained, "While the black gay man seems to have become a key figure for crises that, at present, threaten the very foundations of institutionalized culture in the United States, this should not be taken to mean that his representations have not functioned to buttress (often specifically by *challenging*) normative conceptions of race, sexuality, and gender identity since at least the Black Power era of the late 1960s" (141–142). Indeed, as Harper articulated the issue, not only is the "absence of a gay subjectivity" an issue, but any particular "representation" of "another" black gay man may be a "distoration" of another's black gay man's "self-representation." Hence, for example, Harper observed that many black gay men believed that Mapplethorpe had "objectified" his black male subjects. Broadly speaking, Harper concluded that, "Print, cinematic, and videographic depictions of the range of sexual activities engaged in by men of African descent, however they identify their sexuality, are essential" to "African American men's expanded sense of self" (147).

In this more extended formulation, in which both straight and gay black men are implicated, Majors and Billson (1992) explored the contradictions in black manhood in their volume *Cool Pose: The Dilemma of Black Manhood in America*. Seeking to find a representative anecdote that captures the social and symbolic reality of black men in America, Majors and Billson describe the "cool pose" as a strategic masculine response that can explain "how a sense of self is created in the face of daily insults and oppression" (xi). While a "powerful cultural statement," Majors and Billson have maintained that the "cool pose" may also hide "deeper vulnerabilities" and "mask" problems such as "dropping out of school, getting into trouble, sliding into drug and alcohol abuse, and being sucked into delinquent or criminal street gangs" (xi). In greater detail they have suggested that the "cool pose" simultaneously reveals and conceals the "dilemmas of black masculinity":

> Striving for masculinity presents dilemmas for the black male because it is so often grounded in masking strategies that rest on denial and suppression of deep feelings. On the other hand, cool pose embodies the kaleidoscopic brilliance of the black male self. People are drawn to the power of the cool black male because he epitomizes control, strength, and pride. He presents a mysterious challenge. He is charismatic, suave, debonair, entertaining.
>
> On the other hand, being cool can become more important than life itself. Unfortunately, it can exact a price that seems destructively high. We believe that cool pose helps to explain the fact that African-American males are more deeply involved in criminal and delinquent activities; that they drop out of school and are suspended more often than white children; and that they have more volatile relationships with women. Cool pose is implicated in the fact that, as Gibbs and others have noted in the

> 1980s, the young black male in America is an endangered species. (Majors and Billson, 1992: 2)

In this sense, the cool pose is a paradoxical strategy for it protects and defends black men against daily insults and oppression, but it simultaneously masks their problems by preventing them from asking for help in dealing with some of the most overwhelming and self-defeating problems any man can face.

While the cool pose is the representative anecdote of black masculinity for Majors and Billson, for Belton the "black male body" is a metaphor for violence in America:

> Historically, the black male body has been scapegoated in the cultural imagination to represent the violence we fear as a nation. The irony in this, of course, is that the black male body has perhaps endured the most sustained and brutal punishment of all in the building of our nation, and all for the existential crime of being black instead of white. During the first quarter of this [twentieth] century, the public hanging, castration, and burning of black men was not only a regular event in the South and the Midwest but a public rite and form of civic government. . . . As this [twentieth] century ends, black men have already been named an "endangered species" in popular and academic discussion. The national discussion about black men's lives is very often one in which the voices of black men are marginalized or silenced—one in which the only authorized voices are those of the "experts" such as journalists, sociologists, undertakers, policemen, and politicians. (1995: 2).

In this context, while some focus on penis size and sexual potency to characterize black masculinity, Belton emphasizes the hangings, castrations, burnings, and demise of the black male body as the dominant metaphor of American violence and black masculinity.

Indeed, in this same volume, Bell suggested that the emphasis on the sexual activity of the black man is a "diversion" or

> tactic in preventing the oppressed from recognizing the true sources of their oppression, [such as the] hundreds of black men [who] were lynched, thousands [who] were victims of racist violence and intimidation, and literally millions [who] were exploited on farms and at mostly menial labor where their pay failed to cover the food and other necessities they were often required to purchase from their employers. (quoted in Belton, 1995: 145–146)

Likewise, in Thelma Golden's 1994 volume *Black Male: Representations of Masculinity in Contemporary American Art*, Gates identified the masculine image of black men that dominated the United States at the onset of the twentieth century: "Indeed, it would have been possible for the average American in 1900 to encounter . . . nothing but images of black people devoid of reason, simian or satanic in appearance, and slothful, lustful, or lascivious in nature. And the bulk of these threatening images are of black men" (quoted in Golden, 1994: 12). Referring to black male imprisonment, college graduation, high school drop out, poverty, and murder rates and numbers, Gates found virtually no change for the black man in America by the end of the twentieth century: "When we consider the plight of black males today in American society, we encounter the most horrible statistics, reflecting a nightmare reality for a large percent of that half of the African-American community" (quoted in Golden, 1994: 13). In all, while predominately communicating visually, Golden herself wrote that:

> One of the greatest inventions of the twentieth century is the African-American male—"invented" because black masculinity represents an amalgam of fears and projections in the American psyche which rarely conveys or contains the trope of truth about the black man's existence. . . . Black masculinity suffers not just from overrepresentation, but oversimplification, demonization, and (at times) utter incomprehension. (1994: 15)

Golden (1994: 200) has aptly concluded her analysis by focusing on "the camp and crazy 'carnivalesque' qualities of Little Richard—the original Queen of Rock and Roll," who has been "in the popular vanguard when it comes to sexual politics." For Golden, "Little Richard's outrageousness" satirizes "the whole masquerade of masculinity itself. By destabilizing signs of race, gender and sexuality these artists draw critical attention to the cultural constructedness, the artifice, of the sexual roles and identities we inhabit."

Asian Men. While derived from alternative historical and cultural origins, the image of Asian males as masculine has also been constructed through a series of contradictory social and symbolic images and experiences. These historical and cultural origins have been derived from a host of different perspectives, several different countries in the Asian area, and different historical eras. For example, while extremely popular and massive in its undertaking, Bornoff's 1991 volume, *Pink Samurai: Love, Marriage & Sex in Contemporary Japan* provides but one of many of the perspectives that might be employed when reconstructing the origins of the contemporary Asian man's sense of his masculinity. An alternative view of Asian masculinity is provided in the early, pre-Hollywood films of John Woo (see, e.g., Sandell, 1996).

One of the most intriguing of these formulating experiences appears in Jackson and Sullivan's 1999 volume *Multicultural Queer: Australian Narratives.* As Jackson and Sullivan have aptly observed, the Australian experience is particularly vivid because the Commonwealth of Australia publicly and formally adopted, in 1901, an Immigration Restriction Act, which came to be known as the "White Australia Policy" and remained the law of the land until 1958. This White Australia Policy was designed to preclude the entry of "unwanted races." Facing severe labor shortages in the 1950s, Australia began to make exceptions to its White Australia Policy. By 1971, Australia had formulated an immigration policy, which would not discriminate on grounds of "race or colour of skin or nationality." Jackson and Sullivan (1999: 10) reported that, "Since the early 1970s successive Australian governments have been committed to a version of cultural pluralism called multiculturalism."

Yet, this historical reality has provided a context for shaping the "politics of identity" that have shaped notions of masculinity for Asian men in Australia. Responding to the context created by these historical experiences, Ayres has provided this personal report:

> Sexuality, as far as I understand it, is fluid. In my case, when I first became conscious of being gay, there was not a particular kind of male body I was attracted to. To be honest, anything with a dick would have done. However, as I became a participant in the gay world, I found myself increasingly influenced by the imagery which determined what was desirable. An "Ideal Body" began to take form in my head. . . . The images of the Ideal Body which saturate mainstream and gay media and cultures gradually insinuated themselves into my fantasies. There was no single Ideal Body. Advertisements are variously filled with blondes, brunettes, latinos, chunky men, lean men. But, the closer you look at what is considered "sexy," "hunky," "desirable," the more you realize that there is a limited range of parts which make up Ideal Bodies. The recurring themes are youth, masculinity, and race. (1999: 91)

As Ayres began to personalize his experiences, he realized that Asian men were never part of the image defining the masculine:

> The act of making the Ideal Body concrete by giving it physical expression—whether through photographs, films or live shows—is a political act. It defines in a social sense what is deemed to be desirable. And it is from this arena that the Asian man has been excluded. Gay magazines rarely use Asian men in their pictorial spreads. Gay-targeted advertising rarely, if ever, uses Asian models. State and territory AIDS Councils in Australia rarely use images of Asian men in safe sex campaigns, except in campaigns targeted specifically at gay Asian men. Gay pornography—American, European or Australian—almost never includes Asian actors, except for porn targeted at the "rice queen" subculture. Each of these sins of omission contributes to the invisibility of the Asian man's body on the scene. (1999: 91)

At a later junction, Ayres also began to realize that the Asian invisibility is a byproduct of stereotyping:

> In gay media photos of Caucasian men the focus of attention is often the man's erect penis, the most aggressive symbol of masculinity. In contrast, the focus in photos of Asian men is the curve of the body, a typically feminine emphasis. This representation shows the Asian male as passive and subservient. Mirroring this feminine image is the stereotypical Asian/Caucasian relationship. In this the western man is older, the Asian man is younger. The western man is wealthy, the Asian man is poor. The western man is sexually active, the Asian man is sexually passive. (1999: 94)}

The consequences of omitting and stereotyping Asian men are multiple and profound. For one, Asian men may begin to devalue themselves. As Ayres (1999) recalled: "Our daydreams are populated by handsome Caucasian men with lean, hard Caucasian bodies. This creates the phenomenon of the Asian man who does not find other Asian men attractive. For most of my adult life, this has certainly been true of me" (91). Another consequence is that Caucasians do not find Asians attractive. As Ayres has put it, "Another consequence of being unseen within the mainstream of gay culture is that we are also invisible in other people's fantasies. This is the phenomenon of the Caucasian man who does not find Asian men (as a category) attractive" (92). Finally, invisibility may be internalized as a personal reproach, and some Asian men may place themselves in sexual positions that compromise their health, if not their survival. Ridge, Hee, and Minichiello (1999: 56–60) noted, when Asian men are not traditionally defined as attractive, some can define their "failure in the sexual currency system" to be a "personal failure" rather than a "gay cultural issue." Accordingly, "competition for a limited number of Caucasian partners" can emerge, which—among other things—can place Asian men at a "distinct power disadvantage." In this context, if an Asian man is "inexperienced" in terms of appropriate cruising norms and behavior, and if an Asian man has "difficulties refusing sexual advances" because of the "non-confrontational manner" of his Southeast Asian background, his apparent "passivity or ambivalence can be interpreted as consent for sex." In all, these circumstances place Asian males at "considerable disadvantage if they cannot avoid or directly say no, even to unprotected anal intercourse. It can take experience of cross-cultural misunderstandings before Asian men become more aware of these kinds of power issues."

In all, then, how masculine a given man is perceived to be is a function of several factors. Certainly, physiological factors—such the ratio of one's androgen/testosterone to estrogen/progestin levels—affect how masculinity is enacted. But, even these physiologically derived factors are mediated and evaluated by the cultural system in which they exist. More profoundly, virtually all of the factors determining one's masculinity are the product of a social and symbolic construction process within one's sociocultural environment, which defines the behaviors associated with manliness as well as the *meanings* of the behaviors associated with manliness. Accordingly, one's masculinity is a function of how others respond to us. One's masculinity is a function of the social perception of and symbolic meanings attributed to factors such as physical characteristics, sociocultural roles, gender preferences, self-conceptions, age, race, and nationality. These recognitions lead us, now, to consider the types of interpersonal relationship systems that reflect and reinforce the forms of masculinity that define men.

Interpersonal Relationship Systems

As we noted at the outset of this chapter, interpersonal relationship systems are ultimately a function of or are derived from the sense of identity men have of themselves. In this chapter, we are particularly concerned with gay men and the ways in which their sense of masculinity affects how they perceive and understand themselves. In this regard, we begin with the premise that the factors determining masculinity are many rather than few. Accordingly, because these factors can interact in any number of ways, they create many rather than one form of masculinity. In this sense, the term *masculinities,* in its plural form, rather than masculinity, in its singular form, more accurately reflects the understandings conveyed in this chapter. And, as you know, men prefer to participate and function in social groupings or interpersonal relationship systems that reflect their own style of masculinity. Our attention thus turns to one central question: *What kinds of interpersonal relationship systems do gay men employ?*

Interpersonal relationship systems continually change and adjust to the changing sociocultural organizations (for details regarding these specific changes that follow here, see: Chesebro, 1981). In the 1950s, homosexual or homophile organizations were private, "closeted," high-risk environments, designed only for gay men who were particularly brave and willing to handle tremendously negative social consequences if they were even identified as gay. After the Stonewall riots of 1969, which created the gay liberation movement, new kinds of social organizations developed and emerged, far more public and political, involving the parents and straight friends of gay men, and ultimately even transformations in the political, social, and cultural systems of the United States. After the outbreak of AIDS in 1982, again the interpersonal relationship systems of gay men necessarily underwent dramatic and profound transformations when young men unexpectedly began to die, affecting the personal lives of virtually all Americans. And, as gay men began to recover from the disastrous and devastating effects of AIDS, insofar as that was possible, new interpersonal relationship systems also emerged (see, e.g., Chesebro, 1994 and 1997).

Accordingly, several kinds of specific interpersonal relationship systems can be identified. Three of these systems are considered here. Each of these systems is intentionally selected, because each reflects a different way of thinking about interpersonal relationships at a different sociocultural historical point in time as well as a different understanding of the lifestyles and social organization of gay men. Of course, given the perspective of this chapter, what is most intriguing about these systems is the assumption each makes about how gender, masculinity, and identity affect how gay men are defined, organized, and understood.

In 1976, Joseph J. Hayes proposed to examine "gayspeak," the "language" of "America's largest subculture, homosexuals" (256). To "account for some specific behavior patterns" and the "contextual framework" of gay men, he identified three different "settings" within the gay community, the "secret," the "social," and the "radical activists" settings. Each deserves special mention for the ways in which Hayes understood the organization system, types of interpersonal relationship styles, and types of masculinity that dominated the gay community in the 1970s.

In the secret setting, gay men are "covert in expressing their gay identity, separatists (from the straight world specifically but often from the gay community as well), apolitical, and conservative. . . . [These men take] great pains to avoid any mannerisms or language which would stereotype them" (Hayes, 1976: 257). In this setting, men not only avoid the use of gay-identifying language, they avoid, according to Hayes, the use of any kind of "specific gender reference" or they become "adept at switching gender references when there is a perceived threat" of "exposure" as a gay man (257–258). For this group, then, being publicly identified as gay is a denial of masculinity, for masculinity is perceived as a product of the sexuality of heterosexual men.

In the social setting, gay men are gathered predominantly in the "gay bar or club" (Hayes, 1976: 258). The men who gather in this setting, according to Hayes, "may be open about their subcultural identity with friends or fellow workers in the straight world" (257). More particularly, Hayes believed that a "vast metaphor of theatre" dominates this setting. The social setting includes:

> role stereotypes, clear notions of approved sexual behavior and the rewards and punishments that are assigned according to one's ability or failure to use the symbols assigned by sex role. . . . Thus, the humor in Gayspeak, especially camp, is often cynical because it is based on a serious relation to the world. In the social setting, Gayspeak suggests that there is always a vast gulf between what people pretend to be and what they are. (1976: 258)

In this social setting, at least two types of masculinity exist, one that is appropriate for heterosexual men and another that is appropriate for gay men. However, the cynicism that dominates camp as well as the "irony" used to deny masculine imagery whenever it emerges (Hayes, 1976: 261) suggest that gay masculinity is, at least, extremely flexible. A harsher judgment of the language choices made in such social settings might suggest that these gay men ultimately deny that they possess any meaningful sense of identity as men and that they predominantly dehumanized themselves with the language choices they make, for they define "gays largely in terms of specific sexual practices" (Hayes, 1976: 259).

In the radical-activists setting, "although they may not have formal ties with the gay liberation movement, they are usually highly political and freely expressive about their identity. . . . Because of their association with the counterculture, [they are] sometimes alienated from people who move only in secret and social settings" (Hayes, 1976: 257). At the same time, in Hayes's view, this group seeks to "stop both the process of alienation and ghettoization and to reject the value system which Gayspeak has incorporated from the mainstream culture" (262). In all, according to Hayes, the language choices of the radical-activist seek to "dramatize and intensify rather than trivialize," for the radical-activist must often verbally and physically confront, challenge, and deny the conceptions offered by gay men in the larger established society. As Hayes himself has concluded, "radical-activist rhetoric or discourse reflects a more traditionally 'masculine' tone" (263).

In sharp contrast to the interpersonal relationship systems described by Hayes, Alan P. Bell and Martin S. Weinberg (1978), two researchers from the

Kinsey Institute, sought to describe the interpersonal relationship systems of gay men in terms of six criteria: (1) the degree to which gay men are involved in a "quasi-marriage"; (2) how much they regret being homosexual; (3) the number of sexual problems they have; (4) how many sexual partners they report having over the past year; (5) the amount of "cruising" they do; and (6) the "level of their sexual activity."

While the criteria used by Bell and Weinberg would clearly seem to reflect an explicit bias against homosexual men, the criteria generated a set of five categories or lifestyles designed to reflect the interpersonal relationship systems of gay men. In this scheme *closed couples* were defined as those in quasi-marriage, with few sexual problems, few partners other than their "mates," and who engage in little cruising. *Open couples* were defined as those in a quasi-marriage who are high on one of the following variables: number of sexual partners, number of sexual problems, or amount of cruising. *Functionals* were defined as those who are not in a quasi-marriage and who also reported a large number of sexual partners, a high level of sexual activity during the year, and little regret over being homosexual. *Dysfunctionals* reported regret over being homosexual although they also reported having a large number of sexual partners and are extremely active sexually. Finally, *asexuals* reported having few sexual partners during the previous year, had a low level of sexual activity, and possessed a great deal of regret over being homosexual. While 29.7 percent of those they interviewed could not be classified into their five-part category system, in terms of specific numbers and the relative significance of each of these categories, Bell and Weinberg (1978) reported the following categories and statistics:

Style	***Gay Men***		***Lesbians***		***Gay Men and Lesbians***	
	N	%	N	%	N	%
Closed Couples	67	13.8	81	38.0	148	21.0
Open Couples	120	24.7	51	24.0	171	24.5
Functional	102	21.0	30	14.0	132	18.9
Dysfunctional	86	17.7	16	7.5	102	14.6
Asexual	110	22.0	33	15.6	143	20.5

Bell and Weinberg (1978: 23) concluded, "Our hope is that, at the very least, it will become increasingly clear to the reader that there is no such thing as the homosexual (or the heterosexual, for that matter) and that statements of any kind which are made about human beings on the basis of their sexual orientation must always be highly qualified."

For many, the category system itself seems unduly restrictive in terms of reflecting "lifestyle" preferences of gay men. For one thing, many gay men believe they have been legally, institutionally, and psychologically restricted or discouraged from participating in a quasi-marriage, which would suggest that participation in a quasi-marriage is an externally derived heterosexual standard for measuring the lifestyles of gay men. Additionally, it is unclear that the number of sexual acts, sexual partners, and sexual problems is an appropriate standard for identifying lifestyles, especially if some 15 to 20 percent of men identifying themselves as homosexual have never had a sexual experience (see, e.g., Task Force on Homosexuality, 1971: 48), some 25 percent of men engaging in sex with other men in quasi-public arenas such as men's rooms espouse some of the most oppressive condemnations of homosexuality (Humphrey, 1970), and "only 1 percent of the behavior of those classified as 'exclusively homosexual' involves any kind of sexual release with another person of the same sex" (Karlen, 1971: 525). In all, then, actual sexual behavior constitutes a relatively small percentage of total human behavior.

Nonetheless, if a quasi-marriage and sexual behavior are used as the constitutional elements and measures of lifestyles, then concomitantly conceptions of masculinity are necessarily derived from these measures. Accordingly, among gay men, one would expect that one of the partners is the "active," "top," "inserter," or "penetrator" and therefore the "male" and "masculine," while the other partner is "passive," the "bottom," the "insertee," or "penetratee" and therefore the "female" and "feminine."

Ultimately, while Bell and Weinberg's system provides one view of how the interpersonal relationship systems of gay men might be viewed if gay men were more like heterosexuals, the scheme appears to have severe limitations. Of the many hesitations one might have about Bell and Weinberg's findings, at a minimum it would seem appropriate to note that sexual activity is now far more varied and diverse in its engagements than the two roles suggested here.

Finally, we might consider an interpersonal relationship system of gay men that is based upon their sexual fantasies. Needless to say, such a scheme does not rely upon what is, but rather it presumes that because of the restrictions of society, gay men have been unable to construct the kind of social system they truly desire. Additionally, fantasy presumes an almost unrestricted set of choices in how life might be organized, when total freedom is seldom an option. Accordingly, we are exploring what a system of relationships might look like if it could be built solely upon one's pleasure principles, a system that emphasizes the "culture of desire" that Browning (1993) has maintained constitutes the core of "gay lives today."

In a series of papers presented in 1999 and 2000, I began to work out a scheme for describing gay men's idealized or fantasized interpersonal relationship systems based upon a textual reading of gay pornography (Chesebro, 1999; 2000a; 2000b; 2000c). Among several other objectives, a content analysis of gay pornography should reveal the idealized relationships as well as the idealized conceptions of manliness of gay men.

As a point of departure for such an analysis, it should be noted that gay pornography plays a central role in organizational, social, and symbolic environments of gay men. As I (Chesebro, 2000c: 38) have previously argued:

> First, these videos create and unify the gay community. . . . Gay pornographic videos provide part of the verbal and nonverbal symbols that constitute and define the gay community . . . for they serve as a unifying set

> of verbal and nonverbal symbols proclaiming homosexuality, confronting those who would silence and shame gay men, and ultimately reconstructing the relationships between public and private spheres. . . .
>
> For gay men, a second function of gay pornographic videos is its ability to more fully and completely represent the nature, emotional meaning, culture, and idealized views of "male homosexual sex." . . .
>
> Third, for gay men, gay pornography videos also serve . . . to "validate and legitimate homosexuality to its viewers."
>
> Fourth, these videos are "educational" in the most basic sense of sex education. . . .
>
> Fifth, gay pornographic videos literally show gay men various styles of masculinity, and they frequently "recommend" one style as more appropriate than another. . . .
>
> Sixth, and perhaps paradoxically, gay men use gay pornographic videos as a way of confronting the reality created by and adjusting to the heterosexual world.

Given the central functions that gay pornographic videos play for gay men, especially because they "show gay men various styles of masculinity and . . . frequently 'recommend' one style as more appropriate than another," I examined 242 summaries of gay pornographic videos provided in the *Adam Gay Video 1999 Directory.* These summaries identify the content themes of these videos in several different ways (see Chesebro, 2000c, p. 42). Ultimately, 640 themes from these videos were extracted and coded into a system emphasizing idealized age, sexual acts, number of partners, personality type and images of sexual partners, race and nationality of partners, and "miscellaneous."

Two major conclusions from this study regarding masculinity are particularly relevant here.

First, traditional concepts of masculinity, as reflected in the images of the "bodybuilder," "jocks and sports," "straight men," and "motorcyclists" constituted . . . "a relatively small percentage of 1999 gay pornographic features videos" (Chesebro, 2000c: 43). Second, as I have previously argued, the

> data derived from this content analysis of 1999 gay pornographic feature videos provides a tentative warrant for the growing importance of the concept of masculinities or multiple standards and lifestyles when defining what masculine is. . . . In this sense, "straight men" are no longer the ideal type. The diversity of occupational differences associated with "personality type and image" suggests men in all social strata from "blue collar" to "bears" are being cast as objects of desire. . . . [Additionally], "Asian, Black, European, and Latin men are cast as desired types or classes of men and perhaps even as cultural alternatives to the culture created by white people." In this regard, interracial interactions and sexual acts constituted 22 percent of the themes in this category.

In all, while we are dealing with fantasies about idealized forms of masculinities, the examination of these gay pornographic videos suggests that "a transformation has been occurring in the self-conception gay males possess. . . . Many, rather than one, forms of masculinity are emerging" (Chesebro, 2000c: 47).

CONCLUSION

When we consider how gender affects gay men, a host of diverse issues emerge regarding the meanings we have of *gender, masculinity, identity,* and *interpersonal relationships.* Indeed, the complexity becomes almost overwhelming. We are tempted simply to claim—as some postmodernist and queer critics and advocates have—that all gender categorization is oppression (Jagose, 1996: 59 and 96–100) and then argue for the elimination of all such gender categorizations. However, gender categorizations continue to be far too pervasive within our language and even in our thought patterns to hope that they will go away if we develop cogent and convincing arguments. Indeed, as I see it, gender and its derived sexuality terminologies—such as masculine, feminine, bisexual, and so forth—are not predominantly personal, private, or interior self-conceptions that somehow "fit" us comfortably as individuals, but rather gender and its derived sexual terminologies are part of the vocabulary or linguistic categories created by and reflecting dominant political and sociocultural systems. We can therefore abandon our interest in gender classifications only if we eschew any commitment to investigate and analyze the vocabulary and linguistic categories created and used by dominant political and sociocultural systems.

In this analysis, we have considered the various ways in which gay men describe themselves as men. The descriptions are extremely diverse, suggesting that little agreement exists about what is and is not masculine. Accordingly, we have reviewed the various approaches used to define masculinity, ultimately arguing that masculinity is a social and symbolic construction, with historical characteristics that can be investigated and traced over time and across cultural systems. Within this framework, I have argued that specific men are viewed as more or less masculine depending upon their adrogen/testosterone–estrogen/progestin ratio, their physical characteristics, how well they enact different sociocultural roles, the gender of their sexual partner, their own subjective gender identification, their age, and their race and nationality. This determination of the degree to which men are or are not masculine provided a foundation for considering several different kinds of interpersonal relationships. Each of these systems offers a different view of the interpersonal relationship systems of gay men.

I suggest that men—straight or gay—are more likely to respond humanely to others and to themselves if the notion of masculinities, in its *plural* form, displaces masculinity, as a *singular* noun. Masculinities, as a concept, is a flagrantly open-ended concept, and this flexibility is exactly why the concept can be so useful and powerful in today's society. For some, masculinities refers to the changing goals and styles of manliness across historical eras (see, e.g., Breitenberg, 1996; Hitchcock and Cohen, 1999; Lees, 1994). For others, masculinities characterizes the different social groupings and regroupings that emerge within contemporary societies (see, e.g., Connell, 1995; Pringle, 1995). For another group, masculinities refers to the different goals, self-conceptions, and styles of men of different races and nationalities (see, e.g., Molloy and Irwin, 1998; Conway-Long, 1994). And, perhaps mostly usefully for researchers, masculinities has been viewed as a concept that crosses all demographic categorizations or can arise from any one demographic category (see, e.g., Hearn and Collinson, 1994). Indeed, Messner (1991) and Brod and Kaufman (1994) have suggested that the notion of masculinities can be employed usefully when linked to demographic categories in a variety of different ways.

From my perspective as a communication critic, masculinities is a way of equalizing or leveling the playing field, of creating a social and symbolic enclave in which men of all types are appreciated as masculine regardless of the specific groups they are part of or the unique form of masculine identity each might formulate and enact as an individual. Certainly, not each form of masculinity promotes civility and solace, nor can each be said to work toward humane ends. But, the notion of masculinities asks us to avoid predeterminations and traditional understandings about what masculinity is and means and to be open to fresh and new interpretations about the meaning of different men's motivations, understandings, and behaviors when they define themselves and act as men.

For Further Discussion

1. What is your personal definition of masculinity? Make a list of ten men you know fairly well and whom you consider to be the most masculine men you know. These men may be members of your everyday life or media personalities. After the list is completed, go through the list and identify the relative body size of each man (e.g. large, medium, or small), muscles to fat ratio, vocal quality (low pitched, moderate pitch, and high pitched), race, nationality, age, occupation, marital status (married, single, divorced, divorced and remarried), and parental status. Then make a judgment about each man's apparent subjective gender identity (confident and highly masculine, moderately confident and moderately masculine, and less confident and less masculine). When you made a judgment about each man's characteristics, go through the list and tabulate the characteristics that appear most often. The most frequent characteristics determine and define your sense of what is masculine. Is your conception of masculine traditional, subculture-specific, or more radical (androgynous or a mix of masculine and feminine characteristics)?
2. How should men communicate with women? Does sexual preference or an alternative conception of masculinity affect how effectively a man can communicate with a woman? Are you using stereotypes to answer these questions? Margaret Cho has suggested that heterosexual women and gay men communicate better than heterosexual

women and men. A similar perspective is reflected on the television series *Will and Grace.* What characteristics do gay men have to possess to be able to communicate with heterosexual women? How would you classify these characteristics: Are these characteristics predominately masculine or feminine? Are there any ways that heterosexual men adopt these characteristics when they communicate while still preserving their preferred mode of masculinity?

3. Who have been your models of masculinity and femininity? Where did you learn about what masculinity and femininity are? Did your models of masculinity and femininity come from your parents and/or your relatives? Who was the first person who told "what a man should be" or "what a woman should be"? Do you think there are implicit standards for determining masculinity and femininity in your church, educational institutions, media, and political institutions? Why? How powerful are these standards? Do you believe that masculinity and femininity can be viewed as physiological and/or innate psychological traits?
4. What is the history of masculinity? How do conceptions of masculinity differ from one culture to another? What criteria were used to construct and determine masculinity in ancient Egypt? In ancient Greece and Rome? Compare and contrast the criteria for constructing and determining masculinity in two contemporary cultures such as Japan and the United States or Iran and the United States. What are the most useful resources to identify the primary characteristics of masculinity in a culture?
5. How are we socialized in terms of masculinity? Which socialization processes and institutions are the most traditional? The traditional concept of masculinity in twentieth-century America holds that "real" men are active and achievement-oriented, dominant, and rational or level-headed. Which social institutions in the United States most take pride in and promote these standards for masculinity? The military? The educational system? Religious institutions such as marriage? The political system? Which social institutions have done the most to undermine traditional conceptions of masculinity?
6. Which industries and corporations promote diversity and multiculturalism? Which do not? Focusing on visual advertisements designed for mass audiences on television, on videotapes, or in magazines, identify the number and percentage of men who are Caucasian, African American, North American Indian, and Asian American in each of these media systems. Do certain industries use minority men in these advertisements more frequently than other industries?

References

Arliss, L. P., and D. Borisoff, eds. 1993. *Women and Men Communicating: Challenges and Changes.* Fort Worth, TX: Harcourt Brace Jovanovich.

Ayres, T. 1999. China doll—The experience of being a gay Chinese Australian. In P. A. Jackson and G. Sullivan, eds., *Multicultural Queer: Australian Narratives.* New York: Harrington Park Press/The Haworth Press, 87–97.

Badinter, E. 1992. *XY: On Masculine Identity.* New York: Columbia University Press.

Baird, A. C. 1956. *American Public Address 1740–1952.* New York: McGraw-Hill.

Bayley, N. 1951. Some psychological correlates of somatic androgyny. *Child Development* 22: 47–60.

Bayley, N., and L. M. Bayer. 1946. The assessment of somatic androgyny. *American Journal of Physical Anthropology* 4: 433–462.

Bell, A. P., and M. S. Weinberg. 1978. *Homosexualities: A Study of Diversity among Men and Women.* New York: Simon and Schuster.

Belton, D., ed. 1995. *Speak My Name: Black Men on Masculinity and the American Dream.* Boston: Beacon Press.

Bianchi, T. 1994. *Bob and Rod.* New York: A Stonewall Inn Studio Book/St. Martin's Press.

Biller, H. B. 1968. A multiaspect investigation of masculine development in kindergarten-age boys. *Genetic Psychology Monographs* 78: 89–139.

Biller, H. B., and D. A. Liebman. 1971. Body build, sex-role preference, and sex-role adoption in junior high school boys. *Journal of Genetic Psychology* 118: 81–86.

Bornoff, N. (1991). *Pink Samurai: Love, Marriage & Sex in Contemporary Japan.* New York: Pocket Books.

Breitenberg, M. 1996. *Anxious Masculinity in Early Modern England.* New York: Cambridge University Press.

Brigance, W. N., ed. 1943. *A History and Criticism of American Public Address* (Vol. I). New York: McGraw-Hill.

Brod, H., and M. Kaufman, eds. 1994. *Theorizing Masculinities.* Thousand Oaks, CA: Sage.

Browning, F. 1998. *A Queer Geography: Journeys toward a Sexual Self* (rev. ed.). New York: Farrar, Straus and Giroux.

Carrigan, T., B. Connell, and J. Lee. 1987. Hard and heavy: Toward a new sociology of masculinity. In M. Kaufman, ed., *Beyond Patriarchy: Essays by Men on Pleasure, Power and Change.* Toronto: Oxford University Press, 139–192.

Chesebro, J. W., ed. 1981. *Gayspeak: Gay Males and Lesbian Communication.* New York: The Pilgrim Press.

———. 1994. Reflections on gay and lesbian rhetoric. In R. J. Ringer, ed., *Queer Words, Queer Images: Communication and the Construction of Homosexuality.* New York: New York University Press, 77–88.

———. 1996, December. Unity in diversity: Multiculturalism, guilt/victimage, and a new scholarly orientation. *Spectra* 32: 10–14.

———. 1997. Ethical communication and sexual orientation. In J. M. Makau and R. C. Arnett, eds., *Communication Ethics in an Age of Diversity.* Urbana and Chicago: University of Illinois Press, 126–151.

———. 1999, December. *Masculinity as a Symbolic and Social Construction in Pornography.* Paper read at the annual meeting of the Speech Communication Association of Puerto Rico, San Juan, PR.

———. 2000a, March 27. *Social and Symbolic Constructions of Masculinity.* Paper read at New York University, New York, NY.
———. 2000b, April 5. *Social and Symbolic Constructions of Masculinity.* Paper read at the University of Minnesota, Minneapolis, MN.
———. 2000c, April 28. *Exploring the Symbolic and Social Constructions of Masculinity and Sexual Preference in Pornography.* Paper read at the annual meeting of the Eastern Communication Association, Pittsburgh, PA.
Child, I. L., and W. H. Sheldon. 1941. The correlation between components of physique and scores on certain psychological tests. *Character and Personality* 10: 23–34.
Cicone, M. V., and D. N. Ruble. 1978, Winter. Beliefs about males. *Journal of Social Issues* 34: 5–16.
Connell, R. W. 1987. *Masculinities.* Berkeley: University of California Press.
Conway-Long, D. 1994. Ethnographies and masculinities. In H. Brod and M. Kaufman, eds., *Theorizing Masculinities.* Thousand Oaks, CA: Sage, 61–81.
de Beauvoir, S. 1952. *The Second Sex.* New York: Alfred A. Knopf.
Doyle, J. A., and M. A. Paludi. 1985. *Sex and Gender: The Human Experience.* Dubuque, IA: Wm. C. Brown.
Franken, B. 16 October 1995. An emotional celebration for thousands of black men. http://www.cnn.com/US/9510/megamarch/10-16/wrap/index.html
Franklin, II, C. W. 1984. *The Changing Definition of Masculinity.* New York: Plenum Press.
Freimuth, M. J., and G. A. Horstein. 1982. A critical examination of the concept of gender. *Sex Roles* 8: 515–532.
Gates, H. L., Jr. 1994. Preface. In T. Golden, ed., *Black Representations of Masculinity in Contemporary American Art.* New York: Whitney Museum of American Art/ Harry N. Abrams, 11–14.
Gilkinson, H. 1937. Masculine temperament and secondary sex characteristic: A study of the relationship between psychological and physical measures of masculinity. *Genetic Psychology Monographs* 19: 105–154.
Golden, T., ed. 1994. *Black Male: Representations of Masculinity in Contemporary American Art.* New York: Whitney Museum of American Art/Harry N. Abrams.
Greenstein, B. 1993/1994. *The Fragile Male: The Decline of a Redundant Species.* New York: A Birch Lane Press Book/Published by Carol Publishing.
Hamilton, G. 1939. Changes in personality and psychosexuality with age. In E. V. Cowdry, ed., *Problems of Aging: Biological and Medical Aspects.* Baltimore, MD: Williams and Wilkens, 459–482.
Hanke, R. 1992. Redesigning men: Hegemonic masculinity in transition. In S. Craig, ed., *Men, Masculinity, and the Media.* Newbury Park, CA: Sage, 185–198.
Harper, P. B. 1994. Walk-on parts and speaking subjects: Screen representations of black gay men. In T. Golden, ed., *Black Men: Representations of Masculinity in Contemporary American Art.* New York: Whitney Museum of American Art/Harry N. Abrams, 141–148.
Hayes, J. J. 1976, October. Gayspeak. *Quarterly Journal of Speech* 62: 256–266.
Hearn, J., and D. L. Collinson. 1994. Theorizing unities and differences between men and between masculinities. In H. Brod and M. Kaufman, eds., *Theorizing Masculinities.* Thousand Oaks, CA: Sage, 97–118.
Hitchcock, T., and M. Cohen, eds. 1999. *English Masculinities, 1660–1800.* New York: Longman.

Hite, S. 1976. *The Hite Report: A Nationwide Survey of Female Sexuality.* New York: Dell.

Hoch, P. H., and J. Zubin. 1949. *Psychosexual Development in Health and Disease.* New York: Grune and Stratton.

Honzik, M. P. 1951. Sex differences in the occurrence of materials in the play construction of preadolescents. *Child Development* 22: 15–35.

Humphrey, L. 1970. *Tearoom Trade: Impersonal Sex in Public Places.* Chicago: Aldine.

Jackson, P. A., and G. Sullivan, eds. 1999. *Multicultural Queer: Australian Narratives.* New York: Harrington Park Press/The Haworth Press.

Jackson, II, R. J. 1999. *The Negotiation of Cultural Identity: Perceptions of European Americans and African Americans.* Westport, CT: Praeger.

Jagose, A. 1996. *Queer Theory: An Introduction.* Washington Square: New York University Press.

Karlen, A. 1971. *Sexuality and Homosexuality: A New View.* New York: Norton.

Kimmel, M. 1996. *Manhood in America: A Cultural History.* New York: The Free Press.

Konner, M. (1998, February 14). Quoted in E. Rothstein, How childhood has changed! (Adults too). *New York Times,* A13 and A15.

LaVoie, J. C., and R. Andrews. 1976. Facial attractiveness, physique, and sex role identity in young children. *Developmental Psychology* 12: 550–551.

Lees, C. A., ed. 1994. *Medieval Masculinities: Regarding Men in the Middle Ages.* Minneapolis: University of Minnesota Press.

Lindesmith, A. R., A. L. Strauss, and N. K. Denzin. 1999. *Social Psychology* (8th ed.). Thousand Oaks, CA: Sage.

Majors, R., and J. M. Billson. 1992. *Cool Pose: The Dilemmas of Black Manhood in America.* New York: A Touchstone Book/Simon and Schuster.

Martin, J. N., R. Krizek, T. K. Nakayama, and L. Bradford. 1996, Spring. Exploring whiteness: A study of self labels for white Americans. *Communication Quarterly* 44: 125–144.

Masters, W., and E. Johnson. 1968. *Human Sexual Inadequacy.* Boston: Little, Brown.

Messner, M. A. 1991. Masculinities and athletic careers. In J. Lorber and S. A. Farrell, eds., *The Social Construction of Gender.* Newbury Park, CA: Sage, 60–75.

Molloy, S., and R. M. Irwin, eds. 1998. *Hispanisms and Homosexualities.* Durham, NC: Duke University Press.

Mumby, D. K. 1996, February. Feminism, postmodernism, and organizational communication studies: A critical reading. *Management Communication Quarterly* 9: 259–295.

Nakayama, T. K., and J. N. Martin, eds. 1999. *Whiteness: The Communication of Social Identity.* Thousand Oaks, CA: Sage.

Nero, C. I. 2000. Black queer identity, imaginative rationality, and the language of home. In A. Gonzalez, M. Houston, and V. Chan, eds., *Our voices: Essays in Culture, Ethnicity, and Communication.* Los Angeles, CA: Roxbury, 54–59.

Nussbaum, J. F., L. L. Pecchioni, J. D. Robinson, and T. L. Thompson. 2000. *Communication and Aging* (2nd ed.). Mahwah, NJ: Lawrence Erlbaum.

Oliver, M. B. 1996, Summer. Influences of authoritarianism and portrays of race on Caucasian viewers' responses to reality-based crime dramas. *Communication Reports* 9: 141–150.

Osterhaus, J. 1994. *Bonds of Iron: Forging Lasting Male Relationships.* Chicago: Moody Press.

Payne, L. 1995. *Crisis in Masculinity.* Grand Rapids, MI: A Hamewith Book/Baker Books.

Pearson, J., and R. Davilla. 1993. The gender construct: Understanding why men and women communicate differently. In L. P. Arliss and D. J. Borisoff, eds., *Women and Men Communicating: Challenges and Changes.* Fort Worth, TX: Harcourt Brace Jovanovich, 1–13.

Petersen, A. C. 1979, February. Can puberty come any earlier? *Psychology Today, 12:* 45–46.

Pleck, J. H. 1981. *The Myth of Masculinity.* Cambridge, MA: The MIT Press.

Pomeroy, W. B. 1969. Homosexuality. In R. W. Weltge, ed., *The Same Sex: An Appraisal of Homosexuality.* Philadelphia: Pilgrim Press, 3–13.

Pringle, K. 1995. *Men, Masculinities, and Social Welfare.* London: UCL Press.

Ridge, D., A. Hee, and V. Minichiello. 1999. "Asian" men on the scene: Challenges to "gay communities." In P. A. Jackson and G. Sullivan, eds., *Multicultural Queer: Australian Narratives.* New York: Harrington Park Press/The Haworth Press, 43–68.

Ringer, R. J. 1994. *Queer Words, Queer Images: Communication and the Construction of Homosexuality.* New York: New York University Press.

Sandell, J. 1996, Summer. Reinventing masculinity: The spectacle of male intimacy in the films of John Woo. *Film Quarterly* 49: 23–34.

Scollon, R., and S. W. Scollon. 1995. *Intercultural Communication: A Discourse Approach.* Cambridge, MA: Basil Blackwell.

Stephens, G. 1999. *On Racial Frontiers: The New Culture of Frederick Douglass, Ralph Ellison, and Bob Marley.* Cambridge, UK: Cambridge University Press.

Sullivan, A. 2000, April 2. The he hormone. *The New York Times Magazine,* Section 6, pp. 46–51.

Task Force on Homosexuality of the Human Rights Commission. 1971. *The Isolation, Sex Life, Discrimination, and Liberation of the Homosexual.* St. Paul: Human Rights Commission of the State of Minnesota.

Terman, L. M., and C. C. Miles. 1936. *Sex and Personality.* New York: Russell and Russell.

Tiger, L. 1969. *Men in Groups.* New York: Random House.

Webster's Third New International Dictionary Unabridged with Seven Languages Dictionary. 1986. Chicago: Encyclopaedia Britannica.

Wrage, E. J., and B. Baskerville, eds. 1960. *American Forum: Speeches on Historic Issues, 1788–1900.* New York: Harper and Brothers.

CHAPTER 4

A Cross-Cultural Perspective on Gender

David A. Victor

POINTS TO BE ADDRESSED

- Defining culture
- Understanding the connection between gender and culture
- Arguments explaining male domination
- Cultural approaches toward gender differences
- Interaction attempting to ignore gender differences
- Interaction attempting to reinforce gender differences
- Managing cultural differences

CULTURE AND COMMUNICATION

This chapter discusses cross-cultural differences in gender and communication. Behavioral and communication differences exist between the sexes in every society. The way in which these differences are manifested, however, changes radically from one culture to another. To the extent that culture affects virtually every aspect of life, culture shapes the nature of gender differences in any given society. The concern of communication in all cultures is the transference of one participant's message to another. Culture and communication, however, interact in ways that can impede the transference of that message. As Lillian Chaney and Jeannette Martin (1995) write:

> Whereas communication is a process, culture is the structure through which the communication is formulated and interpreted. Culture deals with the way people live. When cultures interact, adaptation has to take place in order for the culture to communicate effectively. (5)

Additionally, the cultural norms of one's society—including gender norms—tend to act as predictors for what one can reasonably expect to experience in the future. As William Chapel (2000) explains,

> While culture is universal to all persons, the way individuals view the world differs depending upon one's native society and culture. Learning influences, such as family, teachers, media, street knowledge, and so forth, provide the basis for the assumption that what happened before will, under similar circumstances, occur again. This ability to recognize patterns within classifications has social, and even survival significance, yet socialization within one's own native group can become a stumbling block when attempting to communicate with others who have different worldviews. (419)

Finally, the way in which people communicate is inextricably intertwined with the culture in which they were raised. Indeed, as John Condon and Fathi Yousef (1985) have indicated, "we cannot separate culture from communication" (34–35).

Consequently, the premise of this chapter is that the culture in which one is raised directly influences both the way one communicates and the way in which one perceives gender roles.

CULTURE DEFINED

Before proceeding, it is necessary at this point to define the rather protean term culture. Alfred Kroeber and Clyde Kluckhohn (1954) discovered more than 300 definitions of the term in use. The number of definitions has since increased, and these definitions have themselves grown even more unclear because of the fact that living—to use the words of ethnologist James Clifford (1988)—in an "ambiguous, multivocal world makes it increasingly hard to conceive of human diversity as inscribed in bounded independent cultures" (23).

Still, for our purposes we can define culture as what Glen Fisher (1988) calls the programming of a mindset. Culture, in Fisher's definition, begins at birth: "the infant mind is somewhat like a blank tape, waiting to be filled, and culture plays a large part in the recording process" (45). Culture is the part of behavior that is at once learned and collective. In other words, culture is taught rather than instinctive or innate. No particular culture is therefore natural while others are unnatural. And culture is collectively reinforced and handed down, so that culturally determined behavior can function only within the larger context of a group (the members of the culture itself).

Still, culture becomes deeply imbedded in general behavior. In most cases, culture is learned at an early age. Then, as Geert Hofstede (1997) explains, "As soon as certain patterns of thinking, feeling and acting have established themselves within a person's mind, (s)he must unlearn these before being able to learn something different, and unlearning is more difficult than learning the first time" (4). Hofstede goes on to make his now-famous analogy of culture to computer programming, calling the mental programming of culture a type of "software of the mind" (4), the subtitle of his book *Cultures and Organizations: Software of the Mind.*

CULTURE'S INFLUENCES ON COMMUNICATION

Culture affects virtually every aspect of life, from economics to religion, from language to kinship structures. Culture shapes social organization, of which formal and informal views of proper and improper sex roles form an important subset. In almost every culture, people learn to communicate differently with those of the same sex than they do with those of the opposite sex. Indeed, in many languages, the actual formation of the words one uses changes according to whether the speaker is a man or a woman. Additionally, the vast majority of the world's languages strengthen gender distinctions by using gender-linked word construction. In English, gender distinctions exist in the third person singular (that is, whether one uses "he" or "she") and the use of the word "man" to stand for "humankind"—as in the opening lines of the U.S. Declaration of Independence, in which "all men are created equal" (which at least partially formed the defense against woman's suffrage in the United States for well over a century). Culture, however, affects gender roles in many ways beyond linguistic distinctions. Culture, by shaping the way in which its members think and view the world around them, lays the underlying foundation on which are built all gender relations within that particular society—including communication.

In all cultures, men and women are raised differently. Cultural values regarding the roles of men and women are taught, modeled, and learned at an early age. For example, in the United States, girls may be encouraged to play with dolls as pretend babies (a nurturing activity) while boys are likely to be discouraged from such play. This difference in play activity, in turn, begins to reinforce certain cultural expectations of girls and boys. No innate nurturing predisposition necessarily moves girls to play with dolls; the activity is culturally learned. In turn, one can argue that gender role differences in large measure result from the combined activities of such culturally reinforced learned behavior. Deborah Borisoff and Lisa Merrill (1998) explain that these "presumed gender-stereotyped attributes can become the articulated norms of culture and lead to polarization" (71).

Lillian Breslow Rubin (1976) has written that men and women "are products of a process that trains them to relate to only one side of themselves—she, to the passive, tender, intuitive, verbal, emotional side; he, to the active, tough, logical, nonverbal, unemotional one" (116). Rubin's remark is itself admittedly culturally biased; she erroneously describes gender roles in her own country (the United States) as if they were universal. Still, the position Rubin holds remains valid: men and women are taught at an early age to communicate differently.

Other Influences on Gender Roles

It would be incorrect to claim universal agreement that gender role differences derive from cultural factors. While this view is suggested here, it is important to discuss at this point the century-long debate that has raged over the causes of the inequality of the sexes.

The chief argument against culture as the sole determinant of gender differences rests in the high degree of similarity of several factors in gender inequality, regardless of culture. With only a few exceptions among cultures in some parts of Melanesia and among some early Native American societies, male dominance is traditional in virtually all cultures. Additionally, studies of the perception of certain male and female traits have shown considerable universality, regardless of cultural differences. For example, John Williams and Deborah Best (1982) found in a study of gender traits in 29 nations that people associated men with such traits as "dominant," "forceful," and "strong-willed," and associated women with such traits as "emotional" and "submissive" (16). Over a decade and a half later in 1996, a Gallup Poll taken among 1,000 individuals in 22 countries found that respondents characterized women as "emotional" and "affectionate" while finding men to be "courageous" and "ambitious" (Lewin, 1996). In short, these stereotypic divisions persist as numerous researchers have shown (Arliss, 1991; Bem, 1993; Borisoff and Merrill, 1998; Borisoff and Victor, 1998; Powell, 1993; and Wood, 1994).

The preponderance of male dominance has been attributed largely to two causes outside of culture: sociobiology and psychology. The one undebatable conclusion among proponents of all three sources (sociobiological, psychological, and cultural), however, is that with few exceptions most societies traditionally have placed men in a dominant position relative to women. The near universality of traditional male dominance in most societies, regardless of culture, tends to support the view that either sociobiology or psychology is the source of gender inequality.

The Sociobiological Argument

Briefly, sociobiology extremists such as Edward O. Wilson (1975) assert that all behavior is rooted in biology. While such so-called biological determinists represent a minority position among sociobiologists, considerable attention has been given to supposedly innate biological causes of male dominance. These include arguments rooted in the concepts of male bonding genetically reinforced through natural selection to favor male group hunting needs over millennia (Tiger, 1969); in male biologically-caused aggressive behavior leading to male dominance over aggressive females (Goldberg, 1974; Wilson, 1975); in male biological superiority in physical strength and consequently in primitive warfare (Harris, 1974); and in the biological female impediments of childbearing, either through direct removal from the nondomestic area at the time of childbirth (Scheinfeld, 1947) or through greater female vulnerability during pregnancy and the early stages of childrearing (Collins, 1972). It also should be pointed out that while most of the proponents of sociobiological causes of female inequality are themselves men, this is not entirely the case. Notably, such prominent female feminist theorists as Ann Oakley (1972), Alice Rossi (1977) and Janet Sayers (1982) are critical of those who overlook entirely the role of biology in creating gender disparity. While biology is not the central factor, or even a major factor, the presumption of what Sandra Bem (1993) among others has called biological essentialism is used to reinforce the pre-existing stereotypes.

The Psychology Argument

Whether innate and universal psychological differences in male and female behavior lead to male dominance is among the most widely argued of all questions in research on gender differences. In *The Psychology of Sex Differences* (1974), Eleanor Emmons Maccoby and Carol Nagy Jacklin cite over 1,200 articles and books published by the mid-1970s on this subject. The number has since continued to grow. The argument supporting psychological causes of gender inequality has its source in the theories of female castration complex, tentatively set forth by Sigmund Freud in an essay entitled "Some Psychical Consequences of the Anatomical Distinction Between the Sexes" (1925). Although Freud himself questioned the completeness of his observations, his theories on the subject led to arguments among his followers and opponents regarding psychological causes of sex inequality. These debates have manifested themselves in a host of subjects ranging from differences in perception, cognitive styles, learning ability, and achievement motivation to self-concept and self-respect, power relationships, approach-avoidance conflicts, memorization ability, and general temperament. Most feminist theorists have outrightly rejected Freud's theories as inadequately developed, perverted by the pervasive Victorian sexual repressiveness of his own era or (in the case of Jeffrey Masson's scathing 1984 criticism) on the grounds that Freud falsified his observations for personal reasons. Still, several major feminist theorists (Chodorow, 1978; Mitchell, 1974) have suggested that innate psychological differences may exist and that psychological theories—if not necessarily Freud's works—remain applicable to an understanding of the sources of gender differences.

Cultural Approaches toward the Role of Gender Differences

The role of culture in socializing male and female behavioral traits, including communication, was pioneered by Margaret Mead (1963; 1973), who was among the first theorists to recognize that those traits we think of as masculine or feminine are actually culturally taught and learned, not inherent qualities. While Derek Freeman (1983) and others have attempted to raise some doubts regarding Mead's methodology, her central views regarding the way in which cultural factors shape views of gender remain intact and continue to be seen as valid. Still, it would be somewhat too facile to discount all other influences. To some extent, biological or psychological factors may—along with cultural influences—affect gender differences.

What should concern us most here, however, is not the theories behind these differences but the reality of their existence. The fact that sex roles differ is universal but the ways in which those differences manifest themselves are culturally specific. A German sees behavioral differences between the sexes as readily as a Saudi, but the nature of those differences vary markedly precisely because those differences manifest themselves differently in German culture and in Saudi culture. Because of this, communication between and among the sexes in Germany differs, for cultural reasons, from that in Saudi Arabia. Essentially, cultural approaches to gender differences manifest themselves in three broad categories: (1) interaction attempting to ignore gender differences; (2) interaction attempting to reinforce gender differences; and (3) segregation between the sexes with limited interaction.

At this point it is important to note that within-culture differences can occur in the actual way these tendencies are manifested. That is, individual differences or resistance to such categories may represent important exceptions or subcultures varying markedly from the culture as a whole.

Interaction Attempting to Ignore Gender Differences

In the cultures of several nations, including the United States, people have attempted consciously to redefine sex-trait stereotyping. Efforts have been made to ignore gender differences in communication (and actions). Particularly in the realm of politics and the workplace, steps have been taken to eradicate gender stereotyping through legal or face-losing penalties.

For the most part, these attitudes represent a revamping of society—a change from a tradition of male dominance toward an egalitarian ideal. Thus in the United States, a societal ideal—the equality of men and women—has been encouraged and reinforced by antidiscrimination legislation. This has led many contemporary Americans to consider nonsexist language and to ignore perceived gender differences in communication practices (particularly in the workplace or political forum). Moreover, the attempt to eradicate sex-trait stereotyping has led to efforts to disprove assumptions about sex characteristics. Thus, the Russell Reynolds Associates' study entitled *Men, Women, and Leadership in the American Corporation* (1990) was undertaken specifically to determine empirically the validity of commonly held U.S. stereotypes about nurturing (managing style) versus aggressive (leadership style) approaches to work in executive positions. The test, in short, was designed "to test several hypotheses related to the 'glass ceiling' that prevents women from reaching the top-most executive positions in corporations" (3). It is significant that the survey designers expected to find clear sex differences in management approaches, but that "contrary to expectations, the study found that a majority of women in both line and staff positions were leader-style executives. In contrast, male executives tested as expected: leader-style in line positions, manager-style in staff positions" (ii). Moreover, "80 percent of executives in every category (97 percent of male leader-style executives) reported that the gender of people working under them 'didn't matter'" (ii). In short, the Russell Reynolds study indicates a movement toward perceived sexual equality among business leaders.

Perceptions of sexual equality are important because they affect the direction that the business community is likely to follow. Perhaps more important, the move toward sexual equality in the United States signifies a cultural manifestation of U.S. values. The ideal of gender nondifferentiation is no more natural or unnatural than any other culturally derived ideal. Instead, the tendency to strive toward a gender equality in which sex-trait differences are ignored has its roots in culture. U.S. culture (in part, as an outgrowth of its political system) attempts to teach and reinforce an ideal of innate equality among people that is often counteracted by the status and the value of work. The status and the value of work in the United States, in turn, is usually linked directly to the price paid for the labor. Gender equality as an ideal has roots in the U.S. political system of equality for all; the means of its attainment is culturally tied to the economic equality of the sexes.

To some extent, change along these lines is already evident in the United States. The increasing number of women working in a paid occupation and the entry of women into traditionally male occupations has been pervasive in the United States over the last thirty years. As of 1990, two-thirds of all U.S. married mothers with a husband present worked outside the home (Green, 1991). This is significant because women working in traditionally unpaid jobs (for example, childrearing, housework) have no direct economic self-definition. While such work remains work, it nonetheless is judged as unpaid or free labor and therefore is denigrated by U.S. cultural norms. Moreover, the percentage of U.S. women in such traditionally male occupations as engineer, physician, and lawyer has grown from 1.2 percent, 4.1 percent, and 6.5 percent, respectively, in 1950 (Bates et al., 1983) to 6 percent, 17 percent, and 18 percent, respectively, in 1990 (Green, 1991). The result is an increasing trend toward gender integration in business communication and, increasingly, society as a whole.

Still, despite the positive, culturally conveyed messages regarding work for wages and increase of jobs for women in traditionally male occupations, U.S. women remain far from being the economic equals of U.S. men. Women who do work for wages still predominate in the lower paid, so-called "pink collar" jobs. As a result, women make up the vast majority of clerical positions (secretaries, typists, bank tellers), which pay less money for the associated labor than the managerial, technical, or professional occupations in which women, despite increasing numbers, still represent a marked minority.

Interaction Attempting to Reinforce Gender Differences

A second culturally determined view of women is particularly common in the countries of northern Europe and many other highly industrialized nations. This is an economic equality in which sex-trait stereotypes are reinforced or even exaggerated. These cultures reinforce sex-trait stereotypes as a way to bring different human qualities into daily life and, especially, into the workplace. Consequently, more women than men may be called on to use those interpersonal skills that are perceived through culturally learned sex stereotyping as feminine. Conversely, in these cultures, men are seen as naturally better able to carry out tasks requiring those analytic skills that are culturally perceived as being more masculine. The key point here, however, is that both sets of sex-trait stereotypes are viewed as positive by the culture as a whole and in the workplace in particular. As a result, women are not encouraged to behave more like men to succeed, but are encouraged by workplace advancement to cultivate the sex-traits stereotypes attributed to them by the society as a whole.

The most comprehensive analysis of this view toward economic equality retaining sex-trait reinforcement is the Dutch management researcher Geert Hofstede's (1984; 1997) studies on cultural differences in the perception of gender-linked traits in the workplace. Hofstede did not assign given behaviors to either gender, but merely examined—using what he termed a masculinity–femininity index—how often such behavior occurred in the workplace in 40 countries in the early study and 53 countries and cultural regions in the latter study.

Hofstede correlated as feminine those answers that showed people orientation, interdependence, fluid views of sex roles, leveling (rather than excelling), quality of life, sympathy for the unfortunate, intuition, emphasis on serving (rather than achievement), a "work to live" philosophy, and a belief that differences in sex roles should not mean differences in power. He correlated as masculine those responses that indicated a materialistic orientation, emphasis on performance and growth (over quality of life), clearly differentiated sex roles, excelling (versus leveling), decisiveness, sympathy for the achiever, a "live to work" philosophy, and a belief that men should dominate in all settings.

His categories themselves reflect common Dutch stereotypes, a function of Hofstede's own culturally acquired stereotyping of the sexes. None of these traits are themselves biologically feminine or masculine. Still, Hofstede did not link either gender to either category. Men in some cultures could predominantly have feminine behavior; women in some cultures could predominantly have masculine behavior. He found whole societies masculine or feminine. Nevertheless, Hofstede did establish precise correlations between the amount of masculinity or femininity in a culture to the degree of differences between men and women in specific areas. Thus, he found that "in more feminine countries more working women are in the qualified jobs, and in higher education the same courses tend to be taken by women and men" (1984: 203–4). He also indicated that he found "some evidence that in more masculine countries fewer men are positive toward the idea of seeing women in leading positions" (1984: 204). The degree of masculinity or femininity as a work-related value, Hofstede observes, actually affects the types of jobs dominant in different cultures:

> Based on their cultural characteristics, masculine versus feminine countries excel in different types of industries. . . . Industrially developed masculine countries have a competitive advantage in manufacturing, especially in large volume: doing things efficiently, well and fast. [By contrast,] feminine cultures have a relative advantage in service industries like consulting and transport, in manufacturing according to customer specification, and in handling live matter such as high-yield agriculture and biochemistry. (1997: 95)

It is interesting to note that in both the 1984 and 1997 surveys, Hofstede's most feminine countries—notably the four Nordic states—are among those countries most strongly emphasizing economic parity through sex-stereotype reinforcement and are also those having the most parity between the sexes in professional and administrative occupations. Thus, for example in Sweden, 15 percent of the men and 15 percent of the women hold such jobs; and in Norway, 13 percent of the men and 10 percent of the women hold these positions (Taylor, 1985: 361).

Segregation between the Sexes with Limited Interaction

The last category of cross-cultural differences in the perception of gender is one in which gender differences are reinforced and in which men and women are limited or excluded from full interaction. Men are encouraged to interact only with other men and those women who are members of the immediate family. Even then, the subjects and degree of interaction may be limited. Women, in turn, are either expected primarily to interact only with other women and male family members or even to interact with no other person, male or female, outside the family. Thus, women are expected to act within the private sphere while men are expected to act within the public sphere. Women acting in the public sphere are rare and are given a pseudo-male status for the purpose of their actions.

Various arguments exist to explain gender segregation, ranging from the role of religion to theories of labor distribution in agricultural or hunter-gatherer societies. Women are culturally taught to be submissive to men in the public sphere (although they may dominate in the private sphere of the home). The women in these societies may view themselves as oppressed or view themselves as self-fulfilled, depending on the cultural value placed on their role in society.

Managing Cultural Differences in the Perception of Appropriate Communication among and between the Genders

A tendency exists within every individual to view his or her own culture as intrinsically better than other cultures. This is called ethnocentrism. To some extent, ethnocentrism is impossible to overcome entirely, because culture is modeled and learned so early in life that cultural norms appear to be universal norms against which differences are judged. To the extent that an individual will never leave the confines of his or her own culture, an ethnocentric hold poses no problem. The world, however, is growing increasingly multicultural. International information systems, mass media reports, international trade, and other factors make ethnocentrism a weakness.

To the extent that one's own view of gender roles is culturally determined, ethnocentrism plays a part in how one will view gender differences. Because of ethnocentric influences, a tendency exists to see one's own cultural attitudes toward gender roles as right and others' views as wrong. This is even true when a culture is attempting to redefine gender roles and gender roles are therefore in a state of flux. For example, a tendency exists in the United States to denigrate societies in which the sexes are segregated. Discussion of the marked differentiation of the sexes into private-female and public-male life is likely to provoke a negative reaction among North Americans, who are likely to see such divisions as somehow wrong rather than merely different. It is important to note that the sources of such condemnation are themselves culturally rooted and may in themselves have a sexist source. This is precisely because, as mentioned above, the private sphere has no direct economic measurability and is thus devalued according to U.S. cultural norms. The reasons for the U.S. cultural attribute of devaluing the private sphere, however, may have been culturally derived by devaluing the traditional role of women's work.

The key to effective cross-cultural communication is in the suspension of ethnocentric biases as much as possible. Ethnocentrism, in turn, is diminished through increased cross-cultural awareness. As a result, the more one recognizes cross-cultural differences in gender perception as not intrinsically wrong but simply different, the more likely gender-linked differences in culture will no longer impede communication.

Cultural relativity and communicative flexibility are at the heart of cross-cultural communication. Concepts of right and wrong are themselves derived from such culturally linked factors as religion and political organization. In a broader sense, one can believe that one's religion or political system is superior to that of all others, but in an immediate sense it is unlikely that one will convert an individual to one's religion or political persuasion as a prerequisite to communication. Cross-cultural communication, therefore, presupposes, to some extent, the suspension of values of right and wrong.

Differences in what are perceived as proper gender roles across cultures, however, are often so mutually offensive to both parties that communication can not proceed. To illustrate with a simple nonverbal communication example, dress attributions across cultures may prove so marked that communication stops. Thus, Saudis may be so offended by a bare-armed woman that they can not continue to talk. Conversely, North Americans may be so outraged to see a woman in a chador that they feel compelled to end all channels of communication.

The intercultural communicator, then, is faced with an issue that communicators in a single culture do not face. To overcome cultural differences in gender role perception it is necessary to be flexible about what is and is not acceptable behavior for each gender. This chapter has attempted to describe the three broad categories of gender-role perception into which most of the world's cultures fall. No attempt has been made to discuss the individual cultures; such a discussion in a broad overview would be impractical here. It would, however, be highly advisable for the intercultural communicator to prepare in advance for communication with someone from another culture by studying in detail the specifies of gender-role attributions in that culture.

While the intercultural communicator need not in every instance accommodate other cultures' differences in the perception of the proper relationship of the sexes, it is nonetheless a prerequisite to effective communication. If the communicator cannot accommodate such differences, he or she can choose to cut off communication altogether. But once the commitment is made to carry on a dialogue outside of one's own culture, it is necessary to remain as flexible to differences as possible. To the extent that this chapter has provided some direction toward that end, it will have served its function.

For Further Discussion

1. In *The Hidden Dimension,* Edward T. Hall compares culture to a prison insofar as it may constrain individuals and restrict/limit their behavior; their experiences. Do you believe that gender, too, may be compared to a prison? Justify your response in light of this chapter and/or additional readings. (*The Hidden Dimension*, New York: Doubleday, 1966).
2. This chapter addresses the construction of gender with a particular focus on U.S. culture. For discussion, research, compare, and contrast sex-trait stereotypes of either men or women in the U.S. with sex-trait stereotypes of either men or women in another culture. Identify both commonalities and differences.
3. The exercise above asked for a cross-cultural comparison of sex-trait stereotypes. Following the same guidelines, investigate sex-role stereotypes.
4. Identify one tradition from another culture that is associated with gender. Select a tradition that goes counter to what is regarded as norma-

tive and/or acceptable in U.S. culture. Pretend that you are an emissary trying to persuade a group of U.S. residents/citizens why this tradition is both necessary and important. How would you go about preparing and defending your argument?

5. To what extent do you believe that cultural differences between women and men is a matter of power? Justify your position vis-à-vis the larger culture (for example, through laws, economic policy, social institutions, etc.).

REFERENCES

Arliss, L. P. 1991. *Gender Communication.* Englewood Cliffs, NJ: Prentice Hall.

Bates, U., et al. 1983. *Women's Realities, Women's Choices: An Introduction to Women's Studies.* Oxford: Oxford University Press

Bem, S. 1993. *The Lenses of Gender: Transforming the Debate on Sexual Inequality.* New Haven, CT: Yale University Press.

Borisoff, D., and L. Merrill. 1998. *The Power to Communicate,* 3rd ed. Prospect Heights, IL: Waveland Press.

Borisoff, D., and D. A. Victor. 1998. *Conflict Management: A Communication Skills Approach,* 2nd ed. Boston: Allyn and Bacon.

Chaney, L. H., and J. S. Martin. 1995. *Intercultural Business Communication.* Englewood Cliffs, NJ: Prentice Hall.

Chapel, W. B. 2000 International management communication. In Marilyn M. Helms, ed., *Encyclopedia of Management,* 4th ed. Detroit: Gale Group, 419–423.

Chodorow, N. 1978. *The Reproduction of Mothering: Psychoanalysis and the Sociology of Gender.* Berkeley: University of California Press.

Clifford, J. 1988. *The Predicament of Culture.* Cambridge, MA: Harvard University Press.

Collins, R. 1972. Conflict theory of sexual stratification. In H. Dreitzel, ed., *Family, Marriage and the Struggle of the Sexes.* New York: Macmillan.

Condon, J., and F. Yousef. 1985. *An Introduction to Intercultural Communication.* New York: Macmillan.

Fisher, G. 1988. *Mindsets: The Role of Culture and Perception in International Relations.* Yarmouth, ME: Intercultural Press.

Freeman, D. 1983. *Margaret Mead and Samoa: The Making and Unmaking of an Anthropological Myth.* Cambridge, MA: Harvard University Press.

Freud, S. 1925. Some psychical consequences of the anatomical distinction between the sexes. In J. Strouse, ed., *Women and Analysis.* New York: Grossman, 108–141.

Goldberg, S. 1974. *The Inevitability of Patriarchy.* New York: William Morrow.

Green, S. D. 1991. American women and change. *The World and I* 6(4): 469–481.

Harris, M. 1974. *Cows, Pigs, Wars and Witches.* New York: Vintage.

Hofstede, G. 1984. *Culture's Consequences: International Differences in Work-Related Values.* Beverly Hills, CA: Sage.

———. 1997. *Cultures and Organizations: Software of the Mind.* New York: McGraw Hill.

Kroeber, A. L., and C. Kluckhohn. 1954. *Culture. A Critical Review of Concepts and Definitions.* New York: Random House.

Lewin, T. 2 March 1996. Child care in conflict with job. *The New York Times,* 8.
Maccoby, E. E., and C. N. Jacklin. 1974. *The Psychology of Sex Differences.* Stanford, CA: Stanford University Press.
Masson, J. 1984. *The Assault on Truth: Freud's Suppression of the Seduction Theory.* New York: Farrar, Straus and Giroux.
Mead, M. 1963. *Sex and Temperament.* New York: Dell.
———. 1973. *Coming of Age in Samoa.* New York: William Morrow.
Men, Women, and Leadership in the American Corporation. 1990, November. New York: Russell Reynolds Associates, Inc.
Mitchell, J. 1974. *Psychoanalysis and Feminism.* New York: Random House.
Oakley, A. 1972. *Sex, Gender and Society.* New York: Harper Colophon Books.
Powell, G. N. 1993. *Women and Men in Management,* 2nd ed. Newbury Park, CA: Sage.
Rossi, A. 1977. A biosocial perspective on parenting. *Daedalus* 106(2): 1–22.
Rubin, L. B. 1976. *Worlds of Pain: Life in the Working-Class Family.* New York: Basic Books.
Sayers, J. 1982. *Biological Politics: Feminist and Anti-Feminist Perspectives.* New York: Methuen.
Scheinfield, A. 1947. *Women and Men.* London: Chatto & Windus.
Taylor, D. et al. 1985. *Women: A World Report.* Oxford: Oxford University Press.
Tiger, L. 1969. *Men in Groups.* New York: Random House.
Williams, J. E., and D. L. Best. 1982. *Measuring Sex Stereotypes: A Thirty Nation Study.* Beverly Hills, CA: Sage.
Wilson, E. O. 1975. *Sociobiology: The New Synthesis.* Cambridge, MA: Harvard University Press.
Wood, J. T. 1994. *Gendered Lives.* Belmont, CA: Wadsworth.

CHAPTER 5

The Impact of Gender on the Self and Self-Talk

Linda Costigan Lederman

POINTS TO BE ADDRESSED

- The development of the self-concept and gender
- The self as a composite of multiple selves
- Communication within the self: intrapersonal communication
- Relationships within the self: intrapersonal relationships
- Gender differences in intrapersonal and interpersonal communication
- A transactional model of intrapersonal and interpersonal communication

Differences in the ways men and women talk, behave nonverbally, and develop and/or maintain relationships are the subject of much written discussion and analysis. We know, for example, that men and women in our culture are socialized into different ways of handling interactions. In this regard, women learn to emphasize relational dimensions while men generally learn to be more message-attentive. A good deal has been said about the implications of such contrasts for personal and professional interaction. Many related gender issues are raised and discussed in later chapters of this book. This chapter, however, is devoted to an area that is less often written about: gender and the self.

One's sense of self is a critical component of any communication interaction (Cushman, Valentinsen, and Dietrich, 1982; Kuipner and Rogers, 1979; Markus, 1983). This chapter describes the communication that takes place within the self, also known as *intrapersonal communication.* It is argued here that an awareness of intrapersonal communication is critical to individual well-being, particularly because it results in intrapersonal relationships (Lederman, 1988), which, in turn, affect *interpersonal communication.*

In keeping with the theme of this volume, special attention is paid to gender differences in intrapersonal communication. An important question arises as we examine gender issues in relation to the self. If women and men form distinct self-images, what are the implications for male–female communication? Because so many of the significant interpersonal relationships in our culture are cross-sex, this question deserves serious consideration.

Many of the concepts presented in this chapter are illustrated by excerpts from interviews the author has conducted with college students. Although the examples here are quite specific to the lives of the interviewees, they help to demonstrate how a sense of self emerges, how various facets of the self become distinct and subsequently communicate with one another, and how the resultant intrapersonal communication affects relationships with others.

DEFINING THE SELF

Each of us has a sense of self, or self-concept. From the moment of birth, we are in the process of what Carl Rogers (1961) refers to as "becoming." We are in the process of gathering information about ourselves and developing a concept about that self. Our daily experiences continuously shape our understanding of who we are, including a sense of ourselves as male or female. But we do not develop a self-concept in isolation. In fact, most theorists emphasize the profound influence of social interaction on the formation of the self-concept (Gergen, 1982; Goffman, 1972). It is in social interaction that the self is born and developed. We come to think of ourselves as humorous by the laughter of others, as socially attractive by the attention others pay to us, and so on. We also evaluate the quality of our interpersonal relationships by the ways in which others treat us. We come to regard ourselves as good brothers/sisters, wives/husbands, friends, or coworkers based on interaction with others.

Thus, the self is a product of interpersonal communication. At the same time, however, we know quite well that an individual's self-image has a profound effect on his or her communication with others. We make communicative choices based on our current understanding of who we are, assuming that others see us as we see ourselves. An individual who believes he or she is amusing to others will risk offering witticism. An individual who sees him- or herself as a leader will risk offering direction. In truth, the relationship between intrapersonal communication and interpersonal communication is highly complex. The two levels of communication are mutually influential, nearly inseparable. It is very difficult to segment the process of self-concept formation, but, for the purposes of understanding the importance of gender on the emerging sense of self, it may be useful to begin at the beginning—birth.

When a new baby is born, one of the first questions asked is about the child's biological sex. Once others know "what the baby is," they can talk about the baby as "he" or "she" and address it appropriately (Stewart, Stewart, Friedly, and Cooper, 1990). Of course, they know which pronouns to use and whether to suggest a masculine or feminine nickname. But research indicates that adults even use different adjectives to describe male and female infants, focusing on the size, strength, and bodily activity of baby boys and the beauty, sweetness, and facial responsiveness of baby girls. In truth, males and females begin to develop gendered self-images very early in life, first in interaction with parental figures, later with other adults, all of whom are well-schooled in gender-appropriateness and provide distinct messages to boys and girls about "who they are."

As a child grows, the self-concept continues to be influenced by what others say. Through face-to-face interaction, parents, teachers, and peers all provide children with vital information necessary for self-concept formation (Blumer, 1975; Cooley, 1967). For instance, teachers tell children how smart they are through grades and verbal comments. Even young children become remarkably adept at interpreting the meaning of the various symbols used to evaluate their ability. Although teachers are the primary source of information about academic ability, parents and friends often offer verbal comparisons ("You're the smartest girl in your class" or "Your brother is the smart one in the family"). In similar exchanges, we teach children how athletic, attractive, humorous, considerate, and generally desirable they are, which assists them in forming self-images.

Thought of in this way, it is clear that the self arises from social experience. This is why gender-related differences in our culture are part and parcel of how we come to see ourselves. In one of the interviews conducted by the author,[1] a young woman told of a vivid memory from kindergarten. When asked to list the things she had learned about how to treat others, she responded "Be nice, be kind, and hold hands when we cross the street." She went on to explain the source of these lessons: "I think that the voice that I am always criticizing myself with is like an internalized parent figure. Sometimes that voice sounds almost like a mother—like my mother." This explanation demonstrates the close relationship between intrapersonal messages and interpersonal messages. Also, because the "rules" named by the kindergartner were characteristically female, it suggests that her sense of gender-appropriateness was learned in communication with an adult, in this case her mother.

The same interview demonstrates that the messages learned early in life can be quite powerful. Even as an adult, the subject was influenced by her mother's messages: "Like when I will have an argument with her, I will be totally against what she is saying. But then I will start telling myself things that I know are clearly her speaking. Yet I am talking for her and I'm talking to me." Later in the chapter, specific characteristics of "self-talk" and other examples of intrapersonal conflict will be examined in more detail. For now, let's return to the nursery to consider another source of information about the self, a source that is arguably even more powerful than direct messages about gender-appropriateness.

Research has revealed that adults actually behave differently toward boys and girls, just as they behave differently toward mature men and women (Stewart, Stewart, Friedly, and Cooper, 1990). Often behavioral choices contain implicit messages about the significance of being male or female in the culture. Because much of what we know of ourselves is learned in social interaction, examining gender-specific communication is critical to understanding the process of self-concept formation. Through observation and interaction, children learn that females and males behave differently and have different speaking "rights" (Treichler and Kramarae, 1983). Of course, both sexes of parents have a wider range of rights than children, but, in all likelihood, children will notice that fathers typically interrupt more than mothers and engage in more simultaneous speech with their daughters than with their sons.

Such observations are significant, because the sense of self begins in interactions characterized by these and other gender-related inequities in conversational patterns. It is in these interactions that our images of who we are and the behaviors we can expect from others are born and nurtured. No one may have ever explicitly taught us as children that little boys would be interrupted less than their sisters, but such lessons are all too often the outcome of early patterns of interaction between children and adults. When an adult listens to or interrupts a child, the youngster observes the adult's actions and attributes meaning to them. The meanings attached to communicative behaviors become incorporated into the child's sense of self. It is not that anyone necessarily tells girls that they are inherently less worth listening to than boys are. It is that little girls are ostensibly listened to less than the boys with whom they talk. And boys and girls learn from their experience in these interactions that there is something inherently more worth listening to when boys speak (Treichler and Kramarae, 1983). This may explain why so many studies, conducted in diverse settings, indicate that men take far more turns at talk, and considerably longer turns, than their female counterparts.

Of course, adult males and females can challenge such gender-related inequities and work for change in their private and public lives, but it is important to keep in mind that the roots of gender bias are firmly embedded in the self-concepts of many adults.

Recognizing Multiple Selves

Based on the discussion thus far, it may seem that the self is a single entity. In actuality, the self is comprised of multiple parts that evolve and function separately. The notion of multiple selves is critical to understanding intrapersonal communication. The concept was first articulated at the end of the nineteenth century by William James. James (1890) identified three distinct selves: the material self, the social self, and the spiritual self. These categories still apply today. The material self is defined in relation to the physical aspects of the individual and his or her world. It concerns itself with material objects: the individual's body and the various artifacts amassed and used by the individual, such as clothing, jewelry, cars, houses. The social self is concerned with the self in relation to others, with the self as brother/sister, friend, coworker, and so on. The spiritual self cares for the individual's essence, his or her very spirit.

The complex nature of the self was further developed by George Herbert Mead (1934), who differentiated between the "I" and the "me." The "I" is the impulsive, unorganized, unpredictable self. Mead used the term "me" to identify the generalized other, who monitors the "I" and provides direction and guidance. One college student demonstrates how the distinction helped generate the structure for a writing project: "I remember my sophomore year of college, I was taking a short-story class and I was going through a real traumatic time in my life. I wrote a short story about it and what it ended up being was the conversation that was going on in my head. I put it in the form of two different characters."

Our understanding of multiple selves was added to by the transactional psychologists, who identified three ego states: the child, the parent, and the adult (Barnlund, 1970; Berne, 1962; Jung, 1956). The child is the spontaneous self, the parent the ethical self and the adult the rational self. Each of us has all three ego states firmly in place by the time we reach maturity. One ego state may be more powerful in controlling behavior, but, according to the transactional psychologists, intrapersonal conversations between the three ego states are normal and desirable.

The existence of multiple selves creates the capacity for "self-reflection" (Thayer, 1968). That is, because the separate selves exist within one person, they can view one another as "objects" and evaluate one another, variously commending and criticizing. For example, the spiritual and social selves may find fault with the material self, which wants to have all the worldly trappings indicative of success. The spiritual self may disdain the goal, while the social self may object to valuing work over relationships. In recent research conducted on college students' reflection on their own drinking-related behavior, many students indicated that they found that they would evaluate themselves and others the day after drinking too much by talking to themselves about their own behaviors. Said one student, "I told myself, I'm never going to do that again, but then I heard this little voice in my head say, 'yeah, but that's what you said last Friday'" (Lederman, 1998).

In terms of gender differences it is interesting to speculate about whether the various selves develop differently in men and women. In terms of James's triumvirate, for example, it may be that men invest more in their material selves, because of their historical domination of public sphere. Traditionally, men have assumed the burden as "breadwinner," so they may attend more to this aspect of self. Conversely, women have been traditionally the "kin keepers" in our culture, responsible for nurturing family and friendship relationships. Consequently, they may invest more in the social self. Though the lines that divide male and female experiences are becoming less rigid in contemporary times, the majority of early child care is still performed by women, which, in turn, limits their participation in the material world. Their male partners are less likely to be afforded "leaves" to nurture family relationships full-time. It remains to be seen if this contrast is related to decision making among the various selves or is simply the outcome of a sociopolitical environment that does not offer equal freedom for men and women.

Similarly, stereotypes indicate that women are perceived as more emotional than men and men as more rational than women. If so, this distinction may indicate the prominence of the child ego state in females and the adult in males. Women also appear to be more concerned with politeness and etiquette than men, indicating that they may have a more dominant parent ego state. Again, it is unclear whether the various selves gain strength because the social world requires gender-appropriateness or vice versa. One fact remains clear, however. In many cases, life's important decisions are made in tandem with a member of the "opposite sex." As a result, men and women often find themselves engaged in interpersonal, as well as intrapersonal, dialogue as the multiple selves attempt to reconcile competing alternatives and make acceptable choices.

In the next section, the interdependence of intrapersonal relationships and interpersonal relationships is further developed.

Characteristics of Intrapersonal Relationships

As a multifaceted system, the self inevitably develops relationships between its parts. These are called intrapersonal relationships (Lederman, 1988; 1996). Intrapersonal relationships provide important connections among the multiple selves. The resultant relationships affect and are affected by our relationships with others. Attitudes, feelings, and thoughts about the self influence communication just as strongly as attitudes, feelings, and thoughts about the other. Prior to examining the complex interplay between intrapersonal and interpersonal relationships, it is necessary to discuss in more detail the vehicle that makes intrapersonal relationships possible: self-talk.

Just as we learn how to talk to one another, we also learn how to talk to ourselves, offering commentary, reactions, suggestions, and advice. Such utterances may be listened to or ignored, but typically, patterns of self-talk emerge and intrapersonal relationships are formed. Unlike interpersonal exchanges, self-talk is often ongoing and continuous. One woman describes her intrapersonal communication: "It's like an internal Muzak. It just goes on and on and I don't even know it's there until I stop and listen to what it is that I am saying to myself about me" (Lederman, 1996). In comparing her self-talk to the background music played in elevators and restaurants, this interviewee attests to its continuous nature. In addition, her description indicates that she does not always listen. Just as it is possible to sit in a lecture hall and drift away mentally, so too is it possible to drift away while engaging in self-talk.

Indeed, the inner world of self-talk may compete with the external world for the individual's attention. As one college man reports,

> I remember I was sitting there watching TV, but my mind was going off on a tangent. It was telling me, "I should not have done that; I should not have gotten that nasty." I would have to tell myself to come back and watch TV and not worry about it. "You did the right thing." But then I would find myself drifting back off again and I would have to come back again and say "Watch TV. Don't feel bad. You did the right thing."

This description, like the one above, indicates that individuals variously attend to or dismiss messages offered by the self. Self-talk is continuous, but it can be tuned in and out.

All of the interview excerpts provided here demonstrate that individuals can describe self-talk in remarkably vivid and specific terms. In fact, most people can recreate the content and the emotion of the internal dialogues contained in self-talk. Often, such dialogues reveal the quality of an individual's intrapersonal relationships. It should hardly surprise us that intrapersonal relationships can be good or bad, happy or troubled, close or distant (Lederman, 1996). In this regard, they are like any relationship with another person.

Intrapersonal relationships are highly significant because they can enhance or impair self-esteem. Self-talk can potentially provide a constant and rich source of esteem, but this is not always the case. If we continually put ourselves down, we feel differently about ourselves than if we continually praise ourselves. Just as one person who holds another in low esteem can provide disconfirming, destructive messages, so can the self communicate contempt and disapproval. In most instances, self-esteem is not a single, fixed commodity but a dynamic set of entities that is highly variable. Self-esteem can be compartmentalized or distributed unequally among the various selves. One individual may admire the adult part of himself or herself but disapprove of the child. Another may enjoy the child and disapprove of the parent for trying to squelch his or her spontaneity. Similarly, the material, spiritual, and social selves need not be held in equal esteem. Because there are multiple selves, and multiple relationships among the selves, there are multiple levels of self-esteem.

Like all long-term, continuous relationships, intrapersonal relationships are subject to change and modification over time as one party (the self) gets to know the other (itself) more fully. Thus, an intrapersonal relationship, like an interpersonal relationship, has a history (Lederman, 1988, 1996). The nature and valence of the relationships develop and stabilize over a wide range of experiences. We may not even be aware of how we think about and behave toward ourselves because the process becomes so familiar that it is no longer noticeable. Still, most individuals learn to value their intrapersonal voices. As one college man stated, "It is a conscious process when I am trying to work through a problem or when I am trying to decide something. I try to talk to myself as a way to get two different opinions even if they are both my opinion."

An important facet of any intrapersonal relationship is the amount of knowledge we have about our different selves. We may, for example, know more about ourselves as students than we do about ourselves as employees. Similarly, most young adults know more about themselves as children than as parents. According to some researchers, men and women differ greatly in terms of self-knowledge. Women have been reported to pay more attention to themselves as relationship partners. They monitor their own relational behavior and assess their supportiveness, understanding, and so on, in interpersonal terms. Men, in contrast, reportedly possess more self-knowledge about task-related abilities, such as career and athletic talents. They monitor their individual behavior, too, but tend to see it in isolation from or in direct competition to the behaviors of others.

As you might expect, problems sometimes arise in intrapersonal relationships. Often, problems are associated with stressful situations. If we are experiencing difficulties in our personal relationships, we may find ourselves riddled with self-doubt and inner conflict, which, in turn, may further complicate our communication with others. Similarly, when we feel that we have done a poor job on some task and are not happy with ourselves about it, interpersonal problems often emerge. The close relationship between interpersonal conflict and intrapersonal conflict suggested by these two examples is of great significance in male–female communication. Keep in mind that men and women may be troubled by different kinds of stress, but typically call on one another to understand and even empathize.

In sum, many dimensions exist in intrapersonal communication. This means that intrapersonal communication can be affected by gender-related issues, just as interpersonal and mediated communication can. In the next section, a model of interpersonal communication is expanded to include intrapersonal relationships. By taking a more comprehensive view of an interpersonal exchange, we can better clarify the impact of gender.

Modeling Intrapersonal Communication

Because of its complexity and importance, communication within the self must be viewed as an integral part of any dyadic exchange. To illustrate, let's create a simple model of communication between two individuals (A and B). The object of their exchange is labeled X. Figure 5.1 below is a model of that communication.

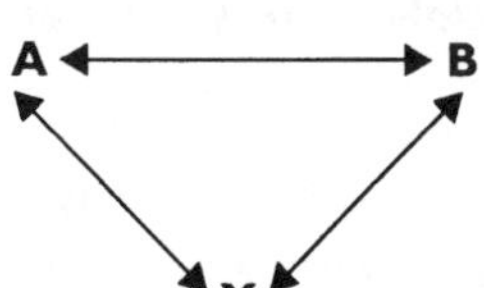

Figure 5.1 Lederman's Transactional Model of Communication

If we view this communication as transactional, we assume that it consists of two parts, the relationships between A and B and the exchange of messages about X. That is, though the talk itself may seem to be about the subject X, the participants also share valuable information about their relationship. In this way, they are attempting to achieve "co-orientation," not only toward X, but also toward one another (Baudhuin, 1974; Newcomb, 1953).

Obviously, the relationship between A and B affects their communication. If, for example, A and B view themselves as friends, and the subject of the conversation is A's brother (X), B will be more apt to speak well of X. If A and B are adversaries, the communication about X might be quite different. Indeed, one of the most significant reasons for using a transactional model to discuss communication is that it points out the impact of relationships on communication. The transactional model makes explicit that messages exchanged between two people do not exist apart from their relationship with one another. As Wilmot (1980) explains, communication between people begins with them taking another into account, a relational dimension.

Of course, it is very difficult to "take another into account" without attending to his or her biological sex. As mentioned, even infants are viewed as distinct based on this information. The gender composition of a dyad, then, can have a profound influence in terms of who says what to whom and in what ways. Two women would logically talk quite differently than two men, even if they were discussing the same event. Presumably, though, the similarity between the partners would facilitate the exchange. Cross-sex exchanges, in contrast, would be more problematic. Studies verify that men and women tend to use different language, different vocal patterns, different turn-taking behaviors, and even different nonverbal behaviors (Stewart, Stewart, Friedly, and Cooper, 1990).

But a simple transactional model does not go far enough in depicting the full impact of gender differences on male–female communication. An expansion is needed that includes potential gender differences in intrapersonal communication. An expanded transactional model is presented in figure 5.2 below.

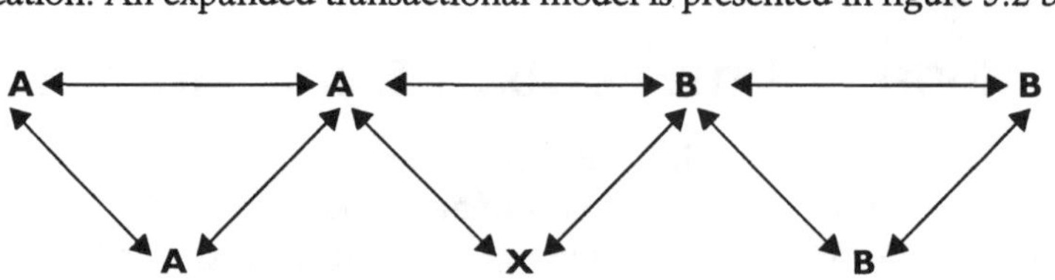

Figure 5.2 Lederman's Expanded Transactional Model of Communication

By adding two sets of intrapersonal relationships (A–A and B–B) to the model, we can more fully realize the complexity of the exchange. Note that in the A–A relationship, the X is replaced by an A and in the B–B relationship, the X is replaced by a B. This is to indicate that A talks to A about self (A) and that B does the same: talks to B about self (B). Thus in an interpersonal interaction, the talk between A and B is X to indicate any subject at all, while in the talk one has with oneself about oneself, all talk is about self. In a recent interview with a student about her self-talk and her partying behavior, a student said, "Bob was telling me how cool I was at the frat party but I just kept saying to myself, 'hey girl, you just can't drink like that and keep the calories down.'" This is an example of the complex role of self-talk in interpersonal interaction. Just as the relationship between A and B affects and is affected by the discussion of X, so too are the intrapersonal relationships of both A and B, which, in turn, act back upon the A–B relationship and the discussion of X. The expanded model accurately reflects the reality of communication. Most important, it indicates that intrapersonal and interpersonal communication occur simultaneously and are mutually influential. This is why all of the arrows in the model go both ways: to signify the potential for reciprocal effects.

The Impact of Gender on Communication

The expanded transaction model provides a useful framework for understanding the profound effect that gender has on communication. As discussed earlier, the self is developed in early communicative exchanges, which tend to be gender-specific. Girls and boys learn who they are through direct messages about themselves and indirect messages contained in gendered communicative choices. By the time they can challenge such inequities, they have already developed a solid self-image, which makes change stressful.

Meanwhile, male–female relationships take on added significance as a child passes through adolescence and into adulthood. Comfortable same-sex friendships among age mates gradually yield to more heterogeneous relationships developed in educational, professional, and social settings. Many important pairings will be cross-sex, so understanding sex differences in intrapersonal communication is critical to effective interpersonal communication.

Many studies indicate that women are more supportive interpersonally than men. Others suggest that men are more honest and critical than women (Treichler and Kramarae, 1983). Similarly, studies verify that women are more accommodating than men (Wheeless and Berryman-Fink, 1985). These and other findings are easier to understand if we attend to the intrapersonal process that accompanies communicative choices. It is not that women do not know how to be more direct and critical. It is not that men do not know how to be more accommodating. Rather, individuals of both sexes have learned to view and evaluate their own behavior in light of the prevailing images of maleness and femaleness in the culture. Indeed, there is no reason to believe that individuals are less critical in self-evaluation than in other types of evaluation, so their intrapersonal messages may be especially harsh in this regard. It is essential that we realize the origin and function of self-talk if we hope to achieve mutually acceptable cross-sex relationships, whether at work or at home.

Communication is a complex and lifelong process. Much of what we become and how we think about ourselves is formed while we talk with one another. Our sense of ourselves and our sense of value to others, indeed our relationships with others, are formed as we talk with others. Men and women in this culture form much of their sense of manliness or womanliness in the same communication process in which we develop our other facets of self-concept. This chapter has provided a review of some of the most important dynamics at work in the process in which that sense of self is formed. Because we are continually shaping and reshaping, defining and redefining that sense of self, knowing about these processes is important. The more we know about how we have come to see ourselves and think of ourselves, the more we know about the power we have to reexamine our self-concepts and to develop the people we are in the process of becoming.

For Further Discussion

1. What, if any, evidence do you have about your own relationship with yourself?
2. How, if at all, does your "internal Muzak" set the tone for your interpersonal interactions on a particular day?
3. What are the most important findings from interpersonal communication that apply to the intrapersonal aspects of communication?
4. In what ways does one's gender influence one's interpersonal interactions?
5. What kind of research needs to be done to understand more about the role of gender in intrapersonal communication and intrapersonal relationships?

Endnote

[1] Seven college women were interviewed about the ways in which they talk to themselves about themselves for a major research project on which the author is working. In addition, three college men were interviewed. These interviews will be referred to throughout the chapter and direct quotes will be taken from them and used as illustrations of some of the concepts discussed in the chapter. Additionally, students interviewed for a recent major research project on the role of communication in college drinking are cited as well.

References

Barnlund, D. C. 1970. A transactional model of communication. In K. K. Sereno and C. D. Mortensen, eds., *Foundations of Communication Theory.* New York: Harper and Row, 83–102.

Baudhuin, E. S. 1974. A general semantics systems model of communication. *Etc.: A Review of General Semantics* 31: 415–424.

Berne, E. 1962. *Transactional Analysis in Psychotherapy. A Systematic Individual and Social Psychiatry.* New York: Grove Press.

Blumer, H. 1975. Symbolic interactionism. In R. W. Budd and B. D. Ruben, eds., *Approaches to Human Communication.* Rochelle Park, NJ: Hayden.

Cooley, C. H. 1967. *Human Nature and the Social Order.* New York: Schocken Books.

Cushman, D. P., B. V. Valentinsen, and D. Dietrich. 1982. A rules theory of interpersonal relationships. In F. E. X Dance, ed., *Human Communication Theory: Comparative Essays.* New York: Harper and Row, 90–119.

Gergen, K. J. 1982. From self to science: What is there to know? In J. Suls, ed., *Psychological Perspectives on the Self,* Vol. 1. Hillsdale, NJ: Erlbaum, 129–149.

Goffman, E. 1972. The presentation of self to others. In J. G. Manis and B. N. Meltzer, eds., *Symbolic Interaction. A Reader in Social Psychology,* 2nd ed. Boston: Allyn and Bacon, 234–244.

James, W. 1890. *The Principles of Psychology.* New York: Holt.

Jung, C. G. 1956. *Psyche and Symbol: A Selection from the Writings of C. G. Jung.* New York: Doubleday and Company.

Kelley, H. H. 1983. *Close Relationships.* New York: W. H. Freeman.

Kuipner, N. A., and T. B. Rogers. 1979. Encoding of personal information: Self-other differences. *Journal of Personality and Social Psychology* 35: 633–678.

Lederman, L. C. 1988, April. Intrapersonal relationships: A new construct. Paper presented to the Eastern Communication Association, Baltimore, MD.

———. 1996. Internal Muzak: An exploration of intrapersonal communication. *Information and Behavior.* Guest Editor, H. Mokros.

———. 1998. Friends don't let friends beer goggle: A case study in the use and abuse of alcohol and communication among college students. *Communication Theory: A Reader,* by L. C. Lederman, ed. Dubuque, Iowa: Kendall Hunt, (Reprinted from E. B. Ray, ed., *Case Studies In Health Communication*). Hillsdale, NJ: Lawrence Erlbaum, 110–119.

Markus, H. 1983. Self-knowledge: An expanded view. *Journal of Personality* 51: 543–565.

Mead, G. H. 1934. *Mind, Self and Society from the Standpoint of a Social Behaviorist.* Chicago: University of Chicago Press.

Newcomb, T. 1953. An approach to the study of communication acts. *Psychological Review* 60: 367–386.

Rogers, C. 1961. *On Becoming a Person.* Boston: Houghton-Mifflin.

Stewart, L. P., A. Stewart, S. Friedly, and P. Cooper. 1990. *Communication Between the Sexes,* 2nd ed. Scottsdale, AZ: Gorsuch Scarisbrick.

Thayer, L. 1968. *Communication and Communication Systems.* Homewood, IL: Richard Irwin.

Treichler, P. A., and C. Kramarae. 1983. Women's talk in the ivory tower. *Communication Quarterly* 31: 118–132.

Wheeless, V. E., and C. Berryman-Fink. 1985. Perceptions of women managers and their communicator competencies. *Communication Quarterly* 33: 137–147.

Wilmot, W. W. 1980. *Dyadic Communication,* 2nd ed. Reading, MA: Addison-Wesley.

PART II

Communicating in Personal Relationships

CHAPTER 6

Times, Places, and Social Spaces for Cross-Sex Friendship

William K. Rawlins

POINTS TO BE ADDRESSED

- Comparison of friendship and romantic love
- Gender differences in same-sex friendship
- Cross-sex friendship as borderwork
- Cross-sex friendship as a rhetorical challenge
- Advantages of cross-sex friendships
- Discovering a broader perspective

Friendship between a woman and a man? For many people the idea is charming, but improbable. Either it leads to "something else"—that is, romantic involvement—or comments by significant others in their immediate social network or by third parties who make the friends feel too uncomfortable to continue their close affiliation. *Whether* and *how* you think such relationships can endure as mutually fulfilling ends-in-themselves indicates your thoughts about several key social issues, including how women and men should behave and feel in personal relationships and what boundaries exist between friendship and love.

This chapter presents some of my thinking on cross-sex friendships, documented here (somewhat artificially) as two points in time, that is, as two different attempts to write the chapter you are reading. The initial attempt was an essay entitled, "Communication in Cross-Sex Friendships," published in 1993 as a chapter in the first edition of this book. That essay reappears virtually unchanged here as the bulk of the present chapter with more-recent citations added. These sections examine research concerning this surprisingly uncommon and often vexing interpersonal relationship in order to identify the communicative challenges facing such friends. I begin by comparing friendship and romantic love to display their similarities and differences. Next, I outline gender patterns in same-sex female and male friendships and the related issue of women's versus men's perceptions of cross-sex bonds. I argue that how women and men view their relationships in general has implications for the possibilities that exist in female–male relationships. I then critically examine the gender disparities in expectations of friendships and suggest certain ideal-typical scenarios of conducting cross-sex friendships. Added to this discussion is society's perception of cross-sex friendships. The chapter closes with a consideration of central concerns in the rhetorical management of cross-sex friendships and a description of their advantages.

But time has passed since this chapter was first written. And I want to raise some questions about social patterns described in the sections I just previewed for you. I am especially interested in how much you, the reader, can relate to or identify with what is said throughout this chapter. Do the findings and issues discussed here speak to your experiences of interpersonal relationships? I would like you to think about this as you read this chapter because I will be asking you this question again, as well as others, toward the end of this essay in a final section entitled, "Epilogue/Dialogue."

Comparing Friendship and Romantic Love

Friendship and romantic love are similar and different in important ways. First, both are personal relationships privately negotiated between particular individuals. People choose friends and romantic partners based on their distinctive qualities as persons. Nobody can compel someone to love or befriend another. However, two individuals can develop a mutual attachment of friendship or romance in unlikely arrangements (like the friendship portrayed in the movie *Driving Miss Daisy*) and even in forbidden circumstances (as when prison guards and their prisoners fall in love). Potentially then, because of private negotiation, both friendships and romances can transcend social dictates and sanctions.

Next, friendships and romantic bonds require a considerable investment of emotional energy (Rawlins, 1982). Close friends as well as lovers feel substantial affection for one another and care deeply about what happens to their partners. Finally, friendship and love both demand loyalty and fidelity. In developing a private relationship characterized by mutual trust, affection, and commitment, lovers as well as close friends depend on the other to be there when needed and to be loyal in times of trouble (Rawlins, 1992).

But there are also significant contrasts between friendship and romance. While romantic love usually involves a strong sexual component, friendship manifests a strong spiritual attraction. Consequently, love relationships are potentially more volatile and characterized by perceived urgency (Rawlins, 1982). Further, love does not imply equality while friendship emphasizes it (Brain, 1976; Horton, 1973; Rangell, 1963). Sometimes in the struggle for "the upper hand" in love relationships, persons withhold commitment from each other, playing games of "brinkmanship" to keep the other off balance or trying to make the other jealous even at the risk of losing the relationship (Sprey, 1969). In contrast, the more "serene" caring of friendship (Lepp, 1966), coupled with its emphasis on equality and mutual benefit, usually results in comparatively fewer passionate struggles (except, of course, for competitions fueled by similarities between friends).

Moreover, Lepp (1966) maintains that romantic love is exclusive because "it can only exist as reciprocity between two people" (53). Roberts (1982) also cites "exclusivity" as a definitive attribute of romantic love in contrast to friendship. The exclusive claims of romantic partners make them possessive about each other. For this reason many societies institutionalize love relationships, thereby socially sanctioning the restricted attachment of two persons (Brain, 1976; Lepp, 1966). By contrast, friendship is typically not as jealous and can be shared; friends are enriched by experiencing the friendship of other people. Rangell remarks, "Friendship stands in fact between genital love, with its exclusivity to one or a few chosen objects, and the 'all-embracing love of others' seen in religious ascetics . . ." (49). Lepp (1966) argues that those who maintain that a person can only have one true friend conceive of friendship as similar to love. However, the fact that some friends do become possessive and jealous suggests that any distinctions between the exclusivity of friendship and romantic love are a matter of degree (Rawlins, 1982).

Lastly, romantic involvement between a man and a woman is much more celebrated than cross-sex friendship in American culture. Brain (1976) argues that romantic love receives "insane intensification" in our culture, both in its own right and as a prelude to marriage. But we need not look any farther than common parlance to hear people regretfully or defensively describing a cross-sex affiliation as "just friends." Meanwhile, other persons report aspiring to "more than friendship" in their cross-sex attachments. In contrast to the countless love stories we hear told in songs and see enacted on screen, cross-sex friendship is rarely acclaimed or depicted as an ongoing, freestanding bond (Werking, 1997). This relational category lacks its own master narrative in our culture. How many stories can you think of that richly portray or endorse the lasting, devoted friendship of a man and a woman as an end in itself? Even the film *When Harry Met Sally,* which attracted so much attention to the question of enduring cross-sex friendship, ultimately proves to be another tale of romantic love. The characters' cross-sex friendship is only a stage in the development of the latter, more celebrated attachment.

GENDER PATTERNS IN SAME-SEX FRIENDSHIPS

Traditional sex roles continue to influence significantly the character of friendships in America. Scholars repeatedly observe differences between males' and females' same-sex friendships across the life course (Monsour, 1996; Rawlins, 1992). Gottman (1986) concludes that "Gender is the most potent psychological determinant of friendship choice in middle childhood" (140). In trying to explain the prevalence of same-sex friendships among children, Rubenstein and Rubin (1984) allude to the well-known preference for similar others in children's friendships, adult encouragement of these choices, and sex-role stereotypes within the peer group that reinforces them.

In comparing the friendships of girls with those of boys, fairly consistent tendencies have been described. Beginning around age seven, boys tend to play in groups, and girls prefer to play with one other girl (Berndt, 1982; Foot, Chapman, and Smith, 1977; Lever, 1976). While fifth and sixth grade boys' friendships are expansive, allowing other boys to join them, Eder and Hallinan (1978) found those of girls to be more exclusive, making it rather difficult for other girls to become friends.

Girls' friendships are also more intimate than those of boys. For example, fourth grade females shared more secrets than males in Rotenberg's (1986) research. And in their study of fifth and sixth graders, Furman and Buhrmester (1985) report that the girls indicated significantly more intimacy, affection, and enhancement of worth than the boys did. Though there were no initial gender differences in the ratings of same-sex friendships across a sample of second, fifth, and eighth graders, the girls exhibited a steady increase in intimate disclosure and a "striking increase during preadolescence in the significance of same-sex friends as intimacy providers" (Buhrmester and Furman, 1987: 1111). In contrast, the boys' levels remained fairly constant. By and large, girls are more apt to have a same-sex "chum" and share greater intimacy as opposed to mere sociability (Seiden and Bart, 1975).

Continuing these trends, adolescent female friendships are characterized as "involved" (Fischer, 1981), more exclusive and intimate than males' (Hunter and Youniss, 1982), closer emotionally (Douvan and Adelson, 1966; Youniss and Smollar, 1985), and more inclined to disclose and discuss personally involving topics (Johnson and Aries, 1983; Youniss and Smollar, 1985). Adolescent girls prize their close friends for evaluating experiences and aiding in their personal development (Richey and Richey, 1980). However, the characteristic emphasis placed on loyalty, confidence, and commitment in these bonds often fosters intense jealousy between friends and rejection of others desiring to join their conversations (Bigelow and La Gaipa, 1980; Douvan and Adelson, 1966; Feshback and Sones, 1971; Karweit and Hansell, 1983; La Gaipa, 1979).

In contrast, adolescent male friendships are described as "uninvolved" (Fischer, 1981), more inclusive and group-related than females' (Kon and Losenkov, 1978), less disclosive, and concerned mostly with activity-oriented issues (Johnson and Aries, 1983; Youniss and Smollar, 1985). Although they do begin to air mutual concerns by mid to late adolescence, males tend mostly to value their friends' companionship and the enjoyment of doing activities together (Richey and Richey, 1980; Smollar and Youniss, 1982). However, since males' friendships typically emphasize activity, achievement, and leadership, closeness can be inhibited or problems can arise due to feelings of competition between friends (Douvan and Adelson, 1966; Karweit and Hansell, 1983; Richey and Richey, 1980).

Throughout their adult lives, modal male patterns of friendship emphasizes each individual's rights and personal autonomy (Gilligan, 1982). While assuming this basic stance toward relationships, they do things together, share activities and fun, and provide instrumental help on a reciprocal basis. But men also typically limit their vulnerability by revealing little about themselves to their friends, largely avoiding the discussion of feelings or personal issues and focusing more on activities and objective issues, such as sports or politics (Rawlins, 1992). Overall, their relationships exhibit restrained emotional involvement (Fox, Gibbs, and Auerbach, 1985).

In contrast, female friends typically enact a moral vision of mutual obligations and responsibilities, wherein relationships are primary and individuals are viewed as essentially connected with one another (Gilligan, 1982). For women, the satisfactions of friendship are usually associated with extensive interdependence. Their pattern of activities interconnects their lives, encourages emotional sharing and intimacy, and incites ongoing tensions between caring versus utility and judgment versus acceptance (Rawlins, 1992). Sharing both mundane and fundamental concerns, disclosing personal feelings and values, and supporting each other by talking things through cultivates close involvement between women friends.

Females' greater intimacy competence in friendships across the life course partially derives from the fact that more females embrace the challenge and consequently learn how to communicate with close friends sooner. Such interaction remains an important part of their everyday lives (Rawlins, 1992). In contrast, a considerable number of males practice the "hail-fellow-well-met" and activity-oriented carriage appropriate for routine male role requirements and ultimately useful for the world of work but not for facilitating intimacy.

Gender Differences in Perceptions of Cross-Sex Friendships

The contrasts evident in male and female same-sex friendships extend to their orientations to cross-sex relationships. Consequently, males and females tend to derive unmatched benefits from their cross-sex friendships. Researchers have found that males confide more in their best female than their best male friends (Hacker, 1981; Komarovsky, 1974; Olstad, 1975). And though undergraduate males mentioned more male "best friends" than female ones in Olstad's (1975) study, they reported spending more time with their best female friends and consulting them more about significant decisions. Finally, young men describe giving less, knowing the other person and being known better, feeling closer (Buhrke and Fuqua, 1987), and obtaining greater acceptance and intimacy in their cross-sex versus same-sex supportive relationships and friendships (Rose, 1985).

In contrast, women receive more acceptance and intimacy from their female than from their male friends; only companionship, an activity-oriented pursuit, increases with males (Rose, 1985). Females declare knowing the other and being known better by same-sex others (Buhrke and Fuqua, 1987). They indicate feeling happy more frequently in close same-sex bonds, as opposed to males' prevailing happiness in cross-sex intimacy (Helgeson, Shaver, and Dyer, 1987: 227). And both men and women are more apt to search for females than males in times of stress (Buhrke and Fuqua, 1987). Finally, though men reported feeling that their same- and cross-sex friendships served similar functions. Rose (1985) observes, "Women's expectations for friendship do not seem to be fulfilled to the same extent by men friends as by women friends" (72). Taken together, the research findings comparing males' and females' same- and cross sex friendships support Komarovsky 's (1976) contention that men have greater emotional dependence than women on their cross-sex relationships. Chodorow (1976), in turn, argues that exclusive relationships with men are insufficient for women, who also need bonds with women.

Males' undifferentiated view of women may overly constrict their behavior options and undermine their emotionally rewarding cross-sex friendships. The stereotypical male outlook includes several tendencies that potentially subvert cross-sex friendship (Rawlins, 1992). First, males are more apt than females to view both men's and women's behaviors in a more sexualized manner (Abbey, 1982). Abbey remarks, "Males do seem to perceive friendliness from females as seduction, but this appears to be merely one manifestation of a broader male sexual orientation" (1982: 830). Second, many males acknowledge their sexual motivations for forming cross-sex friendships, which women recognize, rendering them suspicious and reluctant to form friendships with males (Rose, 1985). On their part, most females describe platonic motives (Rose, 1985). Third, males often perceive a responsibility to take initiative and assert masculine sexuality (Pleck, 1975).

However, it should be noted that attracting a romantic partner is a crucial pursuit during young adulthood for both genders. One study reports that both genders view males more positively than females as "first-initiators" of heterosexual relationships, and that both sexes prefer indirect initiations; in addition, males indicate more willingness to take the lead (Green and Sandos, 1983). Further, being friends prior to romantic involvement: (1) avoids much of the "brinkmanship" of sexual game playing and strategically withheld commitments; (2) presents less risk to either party's self-esteem; and (3) better facilitates a more positively toned and gradual break-up, as well as a return to friendship in the event that the love relationship does not work out (Metts, Cupach, and Bejlovec, 1989; Rawlins, 1982). Viewed in this way, cross-sex friendship makes considerable sense as a precursor to romance.

It is primarily men who find it difficult to develop cross-sex relationships free of romantic involvement. Rubin, Peplau, and Hill (1980) assert that men believe more in a "romantic ideology" and therefore "may be more ready to fall in love quickly with a wider range of partners while women tend to be more deliberate and discriminating about entering into a romantic relationship" (824). Research indicates that males feel they are supposed to take the initiative in cross-sex bonds and try to transform "just friendships" into romantic or sexual relationships (Bell, 1981). Women seem better able to manage their feelings cognitively and are "less likely to be swept off their feet into a deep love relationship" (Rubin, Peplau, and Hill, 1980: 832). Yet, when women do develop romantic attachments to men, they are more liable than men are to withdraw from their same-sex friendships to facilitate exclusive commitment (Rose and Serafica, 1986). Distinctive relational aptitudes and inclinations persist.

Critically Examining Gender Disparities in Friendships

It should be noted, however, that the incongruities typically associated with men's and women's friendships are much less evident in their closer and more enduring bonds (Wright, 1982). While women frequently disclose more to their friends than men do, McAdams (1985) found no significant differences when intimacy motivation was examined. In other words, males who were highly motivated to be close with their friends revealed as much to them as similarly inclined females. Likewise, Ginsberg and Gottman (1986) did not observe gaps in disclosure between comparably close male and female pairs of friends. Finally, in a study of same-sex best friendships, Ashton (1980) reported no difference in the males' and females' self-disclosure, emphasis on communicative ability, or intimacy.

Thus, some quandaries emerge in attempting to appraise and compare the closeness and overall worth of the typically reported same-sex friendships of men and women. For example, Caldwell and Peplau (1982) noted a provocative "discrepancy between subjective reports of intimacy in friendship and objective measures of intimate interactions" (731). Though both men and women were describing best friends, defined abstractly by them in terms of heightened communication, disclosure, and confidence, in actuality, the women emphasized "emotional sharing and talking" privately with a single best friend, while the men stressed "activities and doing things together" with a group of friends (Caldwell and Peplau, 1982). Consequently, the authors suggest that males and females may employ separate standards for evaluating the intimacy of their friendships, and what constitutes closeness for men may not suffice for women (Caldwell and Peplau, 1982).

Apparently, males and females characteristically use different evaluative standards to appraise the disclosure, shared activities, and affection occurring in their friendships (Rawlins, 1992). Women rate communicative exchanges with men lower than their interactions with female friends because they are accustomed to more intimate and personal discussions than men typically pursue, and therefore experience unmet expectations. On their part, men may actually perceive themselves as spontaneous and trusting conversants though they seldom share issues that offer emotional insight or render them vulnerable (Davidson and Duberman, 1982). Further, many men think their feelings are best revealed through their actions and that too much revelation is "unmanly" (Williams, 1985). For these reasons men often must learn from women what it means to talk about their feelings in a manner that women perceive as "opening up" and facilitating closeness. Women, in turn, accommodate male friends in realizing that doing things together comprises a cardinal expression of friendship for them (Helgeson, Shaver, and Dyer, 1987).

Thus, shared activities are coded distinctly by males and females. For men, joint endeavors exhibit mutual liking, though they often include individualized displays of competence, competition, and the accomplishment of instrumental goals, all of which men highly value. For women, common activities are not enough to secure relational involvement; they appreciate indications of mutual and intrinsic concern, even while getting something done. Sustained surface engagements, though entertaining, are unfulfilling.

Finally, females and males view affection in friendship differently. Women appear to use similar criteria for evaluating the closeness of their relationships with both genders, and male friends are often not rated as caring or as close as female ones. Moreover, the sexual potential of relationships does not significantly confound females' views of friendship. In comparison, men seem to employ separate standards in assessing the emotional closeness of their friendships with men and women (Buhrke and Fuqua, 1987; Bukowski, Nappi, and Hoza, 1987). Basically, they seem to play down the caring exhibited in their male friendships while strongly emphasizing the affection displayed by their female friends (Bukowski, Nappi, and Hoza, 1987).

There are a few possible reasons for these inconsistent assessments. First, as female appraisals of male disclosure above imply, because men usually do not communicate affection as directly or sensitively as women, females' baseline expressions receive higher marks from men (Buhrke and Fuqua, 1987). Second, males confuse female friendliness with sexual attraction, view it differently, and rate it more positively than "mere" friendship with other males (Abbey, 1982). Third—and relatedly—males are more homophobic than females; they are more likely to fear being or being labeled homosexual (Lewis, 1978; Morin and Garfinkle, 1978). Such apprehension may lead to repressing feelings of affection for other men and emphasizing the sexual nature of the caring experienced with women (Rangell, 1963). Taken together, these double standards seem to reflect and reproduce traditional sex-role expectations within friendships (Rawlins, 1982).

Cross-Sex Friendship as "Borderwork"

In her discussion of gender arrangements in elementary schools, Thorne (1986) uses the term "borderwork" to describe "interaction across, yet based upon and even strengthening gender boundaries" (172). Interestingly, she derives the idea from Fredrik Barth's "analysis of social relations which are maintained across ethnic boundaries without diminishing dichotomized ethnic status" (Thorne, 1986: 172). I argue that in pursuing cross-sex friendship, participants simultaneously engage in two forms of borderwork: (1) addressing the boundaries between sex-typed male and female behavior, and (2) addressing the distinctions between friendship and romantic love.

Traditional sex roles appear to influence significantly the possible trajectories of cross-sex relationships. As Hess (1972) observes, "The fusion of friendship with the sex role is so nearly complete through most of the life course that 'friend' in popular usage . . . generally refers to another of the same sex" (364). Cross-sex friendships often face the added exigencies of being perceived within and outside of the dyad as unconsciously or deceptively rehearsing, enacting, or obstructing romantic involvement and the normative adult path to selecting a spouse (Rawlins, 1982). As a result, the partners must rhetorically manage internal and external perceptions of the dyad as comprising "more than friendship" (Brain, 1976; Rawlins, 1982). These bonds also violate the "homosocial norm," which describes a tendency in our culture "for the seeking, enjoyment, and/or preference for the company of the same sex" (Rose, 1985: 63). Of course, sex-role expectations vary in precision and scope, and individuals differ in their degrees of internalizing or enacting stereotypical sex-role behaviors (Chafetz, 1974). Accordingly, the analysis in the following section will link females and males with several ideal-typical trajectories for conducting cross-sex relationships. These gender alignments are based on modal patterns identified in the research literature. But all of these patterns must be relationally constituted in actual dyads, and any of the approaches described below could characterize either males or females in given cases.

Three other factors should also be considered. First, certain patterns may be more indicative of the specific individuals' adherence to overarching cultural visions of romantic love or ideals of friendship than to specific gender-linked behaviors. Next, misunderstandings arising from expressing or repressing erotically charged feelings may develop within same-sex dyads as well (Rangell, 1963; Werebe, 1987). Finally, notions of romantic love or friendship may be subsumed by a utilitarian or instrumental conception of relationships whereby others in general are typically viewed as means to ends rather than as ends in themselves. This outlook may influence how a person conducts all of his or her relationships, and cross-sex relationships simply comprise one example.

Scenarios of Cross-Sex Borderwork

As we have already discussed, males and females exhibit distinctive orientations to both same-sex and cross-sex relationships. Typically, males sharply distinguish between same-sex and opposite-sex relationships but view their associations with women rather uniformly. Same-sex bonds are sources of friendship, though many of these relationships are not particularly close or involving. Cross-sex bonds offer more disclosure, intimacy, and emotional involvement, which many males have difficulty interpreting as something other than precursors to romance. Males, experiencing competition and limited intimacy with other males, may therefore look to females as potentially loyal, caring, and supportive partners. But, informed by the socially conditioned alternatives of either friendship or romance, they often enact their cross-sex friendships as "not friendship," that is, as possible romances.

By contrast, females differentiate less markedly between same-sex and opposite-sex relationships, but make distinctions among their male partners. They are able to form close relationships with females and males. And they clearly distinguish between the males they consider friends and those they regard romantically. Even so, because their close same-sex friendships often involve jealousy and possessiveness, they view males as potentially easygoing and fun to be with as friends. Accordingly, their cross-sex friendships are typically enacted as "not romance," that is, as possible friendships.

In the ongoing management of cross-sex friendships, these outlooks counteract and complement each other in various ways that can reshape or reinforce stereotypical notions of appropriate male and female relational participation and their associated conceptions of friendship and romantic love. Let us consider five ideal-typical trajectories in negotiating cross-sex friendship.

1. When an individual's cross-sex "friendship as not friendship" approach meets with a similar cross-sex "friendship as not friendship" reaction from a potential "friend," the persons may play out a positive definition of the relationship as romance, *not* friendship, and begin to behave according to the ideology of heterosexual romantic involvement. This trajectory affirms traditional sex-typed distinctions between the genders (especially when initiated by the male), and asserts that cross-sex friendships and romantic love occupy a teleological continuum, with the former relationship comprising an understudy or prelude to, and/or fallback for, the latter. In this scenario, cross-sex friendships merely constitute what Freud called, "aim-inhibited sexuality or aim-inhibited love" (quoted in Rangell, 1963).

2. When a person's cross-sex "friendship as not romance" agenda receives cross-sex "friendship as not romance" responses from a desired opposite-sex partner, the individuals may negotiate a positive definition of the relationship as friendship, not romance, and begin to behave according to the ideals of friendship. This trajectory asserts

more commonalities between the genders, even though role-typical behaviors may also persist, and emphasizes the distinctions between cross-sex friendship and cross-sex romantic love as options for continuing involvement between males and females.

3. When a male enacts a cross-sex "friendship as not friendship" approach and encounters a female's cross-sex "friendship as not romance" orientation, he may simply perceive rejection and decide not to be friends at all. Frequently, males are irritated at having to abandon an asymmetrical, future-oriented, means-to-an-end viewpoint of relationships. Romantic ideology calls for heightened experience of self's potentials and exclusive possession and use of another person for one's own desires, including enhanced public status and sexual gratification (Brain, 1976; Roberts, 1982; Rubin, Peplau, and Hill, 1980). Ironically and regrettably, they return to only moderately supportive relationships with other males (unless they have a particularly close same-sex or cross-sex friend), and may try again for cross-sex "friendship as not friendship," or dating. This trajectory also reinforces gender distinctions and conceptions of cross-sex friendship as neither friendship nor romantic love, but a stepping stone to the latter.
4. When a female enacts a cross-sex "friendship as not romance" approach and encounters a male's cross-sex "friendship as not friendship" orientation, she may simply perceive rejection and attempted exploitation and wonder if they were ever friends at all. Often, females are resentful or hurt by having to relinquish a symmetrical, present-oriented, end-in-itself conception of the relationship. This stance is consistent with the ideals of friendship as mutually expressive and beneficial. Still, they return to emotionally supportive relationships with females and consider other involvements with males on a case-by-case basis. This trajectory also sustains gender disparities and definitions of cross-sex friendship as neither friendship nor romantic love, but an ulterior version of the former and one-sided instance of the latter.
5. When one person's cross-sex "friendship as not friendship" or "friendship as not romance" outlook meets with mostly contrasting responses from an appealing other, neither party may experience their differences as either simple negations or simple affirmations of sex-typed behaviors, or of friendship or romance. Put simply, they may continue spending time together because they like and enjoy each other, yet without explicitly defining the nature of their relationship. However, there are few cultural guidelines or positive sanctions for conducting such a relationship.

Consequently, these relationships involve potentially unstable interplay between platonic and romantic communicative practices and activities (Block, 1980; Rangell, 1963). Rangell notes that the exchange of tenderness in "friendship-love" is mutable, "conflict-laden, and vulnerable" (41).

According to personal feelings, perceived injunctions to act out genderized scenarios and cultural visions of relational alternatives, and interpersonal events, the relationship may become friendship, romantic love, or neither. Or the bond may persist as a mutually and dynamically contingent arrangement, which continually challenges while sometimes reflecting the pieties of sex-roles and the socially expected behavior between the genders.

Cross-Sex Friendship as a Rhetorical Challenge

Persons participate in the greatest number of freestanding cross-sex friendships during young adulthood; these dwindle when people get married and continue to decrease across the rest of the life course (Adams, 1985; Booth and Hess, 1974; Rawlins, 1992). By and large, cross-sex friendships reflect the traditional social order and sex roles. They tend to develop: (1) between males and females who work together; (2) between nonmarried men and women, since "friendship" can be viewed as a euphemism for dating and hence, a stage in the "natural" progression to publicly acknowledged romance and possibly marriage; and (3) between married (not to each other) people if sanctioned by one or both friends' spouse(s) or romantic partner(s), thereby reinforcing the primacy of marriage and/or romance in heterosexual relations.

No neat conceptual category for cross-sex friendship exists because of its unusual and uncertain alignment with and threat to sex-type conceptions of opposite-sex bonds. Thus, such friendships potentially undermine the pieties of sex roles and the normatively constrained thoughts and behaviors socially constructing and perpetuating gender differences. Accordingly, such friendships are extremely vulnerable to labels of deviance. Further, because friendship can connote both attraction and love, a nuance of expression by a third party may suggest that two individuals are "really" lovers. Brain (1976) observes:

> We have been brought up as "dirty old men," assuming the worst when two men are constantly and devotedly together or when a boy and girl travel together as friends—if they share the same bedroom or tent, they must be lovers. We have imbued friendly relations with a smear of sexuality, so that frank enjoyment of a friend for his or her sake is becoming well-nigh impossible. (46)

Because of their unusual nature and subversive potential, many cross-sex friends experience ongoing judgments, insinuating remarks, and pressures from third parties.

In a frustrating cultural setting, cross-sex friends must orchestrate social perceptions of their relationship as well as develop a shared private definition (Rawlins, 1982). Thus, maintaining cross-sex friendship constitutes a rhetorical challenge, an ongoing array of predicaments requiring strategic management through communication with each other and with third parties. A rhetorical view of these relationships proposes a conscious supervision of interpersonal communication to achieve predetermined as well as emergent goals. Situational constraints include the degree to which sex-role expectations restrict individuals' behavioral options and the extent of social pressure experienced by the partners (Rawlins, 1982).

Often the rhetorical issues remain implicit in ongoing relationships for various reasons. First, unselfconscious cross-sex friends may be unconcerned with third party innuendoes because they are innocent of, or less preoccupied with, the bases for them. Next, the "mystery" of unactivated or undiscussed sexuality may innervate a relationship without ever being overtly expressed. Finally, one or both members may want to preserve the possibility of a sexual relationship.

I hold that as long as sex-typed behaviors remain tacit concerns, cross-sex friends are especially vulnerable to similarly unspoken or subtle cultural injunctions. The friends may be following stereotypical relational paths without full awareness. As Laing (1972) notes in the family context, "Unless we can 'see through' the rules, we only see through them" (105). He argues further that commenting upon the unstated rules governing a given relationship reduces their power, thus the importance of explicit negotiation. Wood (1982) also advocates openly discussing relational definitions.

Because the development of friendship into romantic love or vice versa occupies an experiential continuum, there must be an expressive continuum for communicating or masking such transitions. I suggest a compendium of rhetorical issues and negotiated views of the other and of the relationship that avoids constraining, sex-typed choices and facilitates the maintenance of cross-sex friendship. The following discussion assumes that the friends' definition of their relationship will eventually affect how it is perceived by the social world at large.

Cross-Sex Friends' Definition of Their Relationship

Several authors indicate that a mutual definition of a relationship is essential and unavoidable (Haley, 1963; Wood, 1982). In any friendship, and especially in cross-sex ones, a shared definition is necessary because there are few institutional guidelines for establishing such private cultures (Brain, 1976; Suttles, 1970; Wood, 1982). In defining their relationship, cross-sex friends must emphasize males' and females' commonalities more than their differences, and the friendship should be stressed as an end in itself. Regarding crucial definitional concerns, such as the role of sexuality and equality, partners should clarify and demystify their positions. Verbal statements are congruently qualified by gestures, tone of voice, and the context in which they occur (Haley, 1963). If sexually suggestive vocal tones or actions accompany discussions of the platonic nature of the bond, for example, then an incongruent definition of the relationship is being proposed (Haley, 1963). A pattern of such incongruent behavior may cause tension, promote second-guessing of the other's actions, and/or weaken confidence in the person's friendly overtures.

In general, romance is avoided. All friends communicate affection, but cross-sex friends monitor the behaviors that qualify such expressions because they can alter the interpretation of the message to include romantic intent. Basically, either friend might ask himself or herself, "How would I make this statement to a friend of my own sex?" or "Am I smuggling romance into this conversation?"

The activation or deactivation of sexuality is pivotal in most cross-sex friendships. Overt sexual behavior is liable to alter the definition of a relationship to something besides friendship (Block, 1980; Booth and Hess, 1974) or convert it to the unstable friendship-love. Brain (1976) remarks:

> The fact is that sex can be switched on or off as a situation demands—between brother and sister for example—and frequently this favors a more lasting friendship. We all know that sexual appetites once aroused are destructive of friendship, but they can and often do remain dormant. (46)

Thus, in friendship sexuality is deemphasized in favor of companionship (Bell, 1981). Of course, "sexual activity" can encompass a wide spectrum of behaviors with varying degrees of associated intimacy. And I do not deny that unexpected, romantically charged circumstances sometimes result in overt sexuality between male and female friends. Nevertheless, I argue that such actions usually reflect a change in the permissible behaviors of the friends that is negotiated by a series of rhetorical clues and cues subject to conscious management.

Cross-sex friends manage not only the presence or absence of sex in their relationship but the meaning that sexuality holds for them. The sex act can symbolize various things—from a relatively casual expression of affection or sharing of pleasure to the profound consummation of a love relationship. Developing a mutual view of sex that either upholds or opposes broader social conventions necessitates discussion. Talking about the significance of sexual involvement or noninvolvement in the friendship may help relieve any residual feelings of guilt or inadequacy that might accompany a rejection of deeply internalized sex-typed injunctions.

Further, a spirit of equality pervades cross-sex friendship. Inequality and power plays suggest a different type of relationship—for example, a patron–client (Paine, 1969) or superior–subordinate one—and recall traditional social mores. Of course, there are friendships between individuals of different status, ability, attractiveness, or age, but often some facet in the friendship functions as a leveler (Brain, 1976). Stressing equality minimizes the risk of exploitation (Fiebert and Fiebert, 1969; Kurth, 1970). Though self-interest is part of any realistic bond, exploitation is not. Thus, considerations of equity as well as equality may mediate what is given and expected in the relational exchange (Hatfield and Traupmann, 1981; Walster, Walster, and Berscheid, 1978). Females and males must not extend the double standard into their friendships with each other, though research data indicate this practice frequently occurs (Booth and Hess, 1974; Rawlins, 1992).

Finally, cross-sex friends relinquish exclusive claims to their friends; restricting freedom is antithetical to friendship (Rawlins, 1983). As von Hildebrand affirms, the special affection of friendship accentuates an intention of good over union (cited in Owens, 1970). Lovers, not friends, tend to be possessive.

In summary, cross-sex friends manage several rhetorical issues within their relationship: (1) A mutual definition of the relationship as a friendship is sustained by consistently congruent messages. (2) Romance is avoided. (3) Overall, sexuality is deemphasized. (4) However, the meaning and possibility of overt sexuality, with its potential for altering the definition of the relationship, may require discussion. (5) Equality is fostered. (6) Personal freedom is permitted.

Social Definitions of Cross-Sex Friendships

I have suggested that cross-sex friends embrace certain recurring rhetorical challenges in defining their relationship. Here I maintain that they may also need to adopt a strategic posture vis-à-vis those who would threaten the relationship with rumors and attributions. The friends' goal is to convince third parties that the friendship is authentic. This task is difficult because the defining features of cross-sex friendships are different from other opposite-sex bonds but are not always observable. What publicly distinguishes spiritual from sexual relationships if, in both cases, their most intimate moments are confidential? In short, the friends must manage the privacy and publicity of their actions.

Privacy is an important prerogative in all personal relationships. However, it poses an inherent threat to others' perceptions of a cross-sex friendship as legitimate. While both friends and lovers value privacy for sharing the unique features of their bond, with cross-sex friends privacy is seen to reflect the exclusiveness associated with love. Bell (1981) reports, "Frequently, a sexual relationship is assumed to exist between friends who keep their friendship private, whether or not it is actually the case" (105).

Thus, the visibility of the relationship comprises an ironic predicament: the more hidden and private the friends' actions, the more suspect; the more open and public, the more idiosyncratic behaviors may be compromised or restricted (Paine, 1969). Self-consciousness about "public performance" (Paine, 1969) may undermine the friends' natural inclinations for enjoyment of each other. Clearly, the rhetorical challenge implied here is discovering modes of interaction to interconnect the friendship's private and public spheres (Rawlins, 1989a; 1989b).

Unfortunately, it is difficult to recommend specific strategies for loosening the Gordian knot of societal reactions and attributions. Some friendships may become more public to preserve themselves while sacrificing much of their private moralities and proprietary norms. Others may adopt a rather defiant and self-righteous attitude and continue their relationship unchanged until others get their message, "This friendship is fundamentally not different from others though it is special to us. We will not compromise its essence." Such a policy stares "the smear of sexuality" square in the face by announcing that there is no sexual agenda and exploitation, simply an equitable and spiritual relationship. Given the intense socialization to experience cross-sex intimacy differently, it is interesting to consider how dyadic cultures can undermine the program by adopting a private morality.

Summary and Conclusion

Presently, stereotyped sex-role expectations appear to prevail in American cross-sex friendships (Rawlins, 1982; 1992). Ironically, friendships in general and cross-sex friendships in particular constitute privately negotiated contexts where sex-typed behavior may be ruled out. Yet such relationships are highly susceptible to scrutiny and attributions by third parties, especially if the friendship is perceived to threaten culturally sanctioned bonds like romantic or steady dating relationships, marriage, or kinship.

Cross-sex friendships are inherently ambiguous. Societal expectations, personal values, sexual orientations or motivations, third party pressures, and coordinated or clashing assumptions and perceptions all combine in shaping the dynamics of given relationships. Whatever occasions the shift, romantic involvement apparently alters cross-sex friendships. And the somewhat apologetic or defensive description of those dyads remaining "just friends" reflects the tendency throughout life to marginalize these bonds and to view them as precursors, threats, or understudies to more institutionalized or socially endorsed romantic relationships (Rawlins, 1992).

Ultimately, the woman and man in a cross-sex friendship must negotiate its morality. This rhetorical challenge is twofold. On the one hand, the friends *demonstrate to each other a commitment* to maintain the relationship as a friendship free of over sexuality or exploitation. The friends must also convince third parties of the viability and authenticity of their bond. In doing so, they create a *social context for the friendship that allows* it to flourish.

Acknowledging cross-sex friendship as a viable interpersonal option yields several advantages. For one thing it makes friendship possible with the other half of the persons comprising society (Bell, 1981; Chafetz, 1974). Next, cross-sex friendship allows individuals to see the world from the perspective of someone of the opposite gender (Sapadin, 1988). Participants may also expand their repertoires of friendship styles (Rawlins, 1992). Females may learn about and enjoy the prevailing agentic friendship style of men with its emphasis on activities and individual freedom. Males, in turn, may discover and practice the communal style of female friendships, emphasizing involved conversation, caring, and interdependence.

Moreover, persons learn about the pitfalls and vagaries of traditional sex roles as they attempt to transcend them in cross-sex friendships and treat each other more compassionately as particular individuals. Learning to value someone outside of materialist and sexist expectations is worthwhile in itself. It also enhances conceptions of personal worth by reducing objectification in viewing oneself and one's relations with others (Rawlins, 1991). Neither self nor other is reduced to merely a role occupant or an object of self-gratification. Further, while kinship relations tend to perpetuate established patterns of interaction and keep an individual at a status quo, cross-sex friendship promotes personal experience in new modes (Douvan and Adelson, 1966). Thus, there is liberation from the constraints and expectations of ascribed relationships, an opportunity for independence and spontaneous actions (Dubois, 1974). Finally, cross-sex friendship breaches the image of love or affection as a "zerosum game" (Chafetz, 1974). Chafetz advises: "Indeed, it is unlikely that any one individual can ever fill all of another person's emotional needs. To gain a full life and have a variety of their needs met, humans must develop deep emotional commitments to more than one individual in more than one way." (163).

Epilogue/Dialogue

Now that you have read this essay, how much of this discussion of cross-sex friendship rings true for you? To what extent do you identify with the patterns, issues, and challenges described in this chapter? Can you think of specific incidents or relationships in your own life that seem to uphold what is said here? Or in your opinion, have times, social practices, and cultural and media representations changed enough since this essay was first written to find you questioning its assertions (Adams and Allan, 1998)? Are there generational differences in the possibilities or exigencies of cross-sex friendship that are not addressed here? Can you recall examples of events or relationships that challenge the validity of these general conclusions about males' and females' actions and options for behaving and feeling?

If you do not identify with any or several of the modal patterns reviewed in this chapter, there may be other reasons why. First of all, despite my attempts to qualify encompassing statements made about males and females, making generalized comparisons of males' and females' social lives and relationships may exaggerate the differences between them. To what degree do these types of categorical statements function to reinforce stereotypes instead of clarifying what may be occurring in given cases? On the other hand, to what extent do they help us to recognize and question our own and others' stereotypical thoughts and actions? Moreover, there may be significant commonalities in males' and females' experiences and perceptions of their cross-sex friendships that are obscured by contrasting the genders. Meanwhile, there is extensive and meaningful variety within each gender's interpersonal relationships due to the participants' race, ethnicity, sexual orientation, and socioeconomic class that goes understated.

How, for example, do issues of sexual orientation and gender role orientation influence our descriptions of and participation in cross-sex friendships? And how are cross-sex as well as same-sex friendships developed among gays, lesbians, and heterosexual or bisexual men and women further enabled or constrained by ideologies and enactments of masculinity and femininity (Nardi, 1992)? What assumptions are enacted about gender, that is, what it means to be a feminine or masculine woman, or a masculine or feminine man, in our discussions and experiences of friendship? Does being masculine (in gay, lesbian, and heterosexual relationships) mean being assertive and initiating sexual activity, and does being feminine mean wanting to get to know a person for who he/she is before or perhaps instead of pursuing sexual relations (Nardi, 1992)? How are females and males "supposed" to act and feel in ongoing relationships lived and breathed in highly scripted cultural contexts? How sex-typed are our judgments and attributions about self and others in the contexts of caring relationships? To what extent do relational participants define themselves (and other people define them) as women or men according to sexual (or other activities and practices), participation in procreation and/or raising children, etc.?

Viewed in this way, I wonder to what degree the dominant heterosexist ideology is reproduced in our talk about cross-sex friendship. Don't persistent concerns about whether cross-sex friends will become lovers merely inscribe a heterosexual/ist drama? We sometimes talk about cross-sex friendships as if the identical problems do not occur in same-sex ones (e.g., jealousy, possessiveness, sexual attraction, and hetero- and homosexist attributions and injunctions by third parties). Individuals do enact differing and similar sexual orientations, gender role orientations, notions of friendship, romance, and sexual involvement. And friendships vary in their practices for reconciling troublesome divergences in outlook and actions. But don't all friends face these challenges to greater or lesser degrees?

For Further Discussion

1. In looking at your own friendships, do you have more same-sex or cross-sex friendships? With whom are you more comfortable communicating—same- or cross-sex friends?
2. Do you agree with the statements made in this chapter about the patterns of same-sex male friendships? Same-sex female friendships? Explain your answer.
3. Describe a cross-sex friendship that you have. How do you think others perceive this relationship?
4. How should an individual handle a situation in which he/she wants to become romantically involved with a cross-sex friend? A same-sex friend?

5. Name the advantages you gain from your cross-sex friendships. Are there any disadvantages?
6. How do factors such as race, ethnicity, sexual orientation, and socioeconomic class affect your friendships?
7. Do your parents, or others of their generation, have cross-sex friendships?

References

Abbey, A. 1982. Sex differences in attributions for friendly behavior: Do males misperceive females' friendliness? *Journal of Personality and Social Psychology* 42: 830–838.

Adams, R. G. 1985. People would talk: Normative barriers to cross-sex friendships for elderly women. *The Gerontologist* 25: 605–610.

Adams, R. G., and G. Allan. 1998. *Placing Friendship in Context.* Cambridge: Cambridge University Press.

Ashton, N. L. 1980. Exploratory investigation of perceptions of influences on best-friend relationships. *Perceptual and Motor Skills* 50: 379–386.

Bell, R. R. 1981. *Worlds of Friendship.* Beverly Hills, CA: Sage.

Berndt, T. J. 1982. The features and effects of friendship in early adolescence. *Child Development* 53: 1447–1460.

Bigelow, B. J., and J. J. La Gaipa. 1980. The development of friendship values and choice. In H. C. Foot, A. J. Chapman, and J. R. Smith, eds., *Friendship and Social Relations in Children.* New York: John Wiley, 15–44.

Block, J. D. 1980. *Friendship.* New York: Macmillan.

Booth, A., and E. Hess. 1974. Cross-sex friendship. *Journal of Marriage and the Fam*ily 36: 38–47.

Brain, R. 1976. *Friends and Lovers.* New York: Basic Books.

Buhrke, R. A., and D. R. Fuqua. 1987. Sex differences in same- and cross-sex supportive relationships. *Sex Roles* 17: 339–352.

Buhrmester, D., and W. Furman. 1987. The development of companionship and intimacy. *Child Development* 58: 1101–1113.

Bukowski, W. M., B. J. Nappi, and B. Hoza. 1987. A test of Aristotle's model of friendship for young adults' same-sex and opposite-sex relationships. *The Journal of Social Psychology* 127: 595–603.

Caldwell, M. A., and L. A. Peplau. 1982. Sex differences in same-sex friendship. *Sex Roles* 8: 721–732.

Chafetz, J. S. 1974. *Masculine/Feminine or Human?* Itasca, IL: Peacock.

Chodorow, N. 1976. Oedipal asymmetries and heterosexual knots. *Social Problems* 23: 454–468.

Davidson, L. R., and L. Duberman. 1982. Friendship: Communication and interactional patterns in same-sex dyads. *Sex Roles* 8: 809–826.

Douvan, E., and J. Adelson. 1966. *The Adolescent Experience.* New York: John Wiley.

Dubois, C. 1974. The gratuitous act: An introduction to the comparative study of friendship patterns. In E. Leyton, ed., *The Compact: Selected Dimensions of Friendship.* St. Johns, Newfoundland: Institute of Social and Economic Research, 15–32.

Eder, D., and M. T. Hallinan. 1978. Sex differences in children's friendships. *American Sociological Review* 43: 237–250.

Feshback, N., and G. Sones. 1971. Sex differences in adolescent reactions toward newcomers. *Developmental Psychology* 4: 381–386.

Fiebert, M. S., and P. B. Fiebert. 1969. A conceptual guide to friendship formation. *Perceptual and Motor Skills* 28: 383–390.

Fischer, J. L. 1981. Transitions in relationship style from adolescence to young adulthood. *Journal of Youth and Adolescence* 10: 11–23.

Foot, H. C., A. J. Chapman, and J. R. Smith. 1977. Friendship and social responsiveness in boys and girls. *Journal of Personality and Social Psychology* 35: 401–411.

Fox, M., M. Gibbs, and D. Auerbach. 1985. Age and gender dimensions of friendship. *Psychology of Women Quarterly* 9: 489–502.

Furman, W., and D. Buhrmester. 1985. Children's perceptions of their personal relationships in their social networks. *Developmental Psychology* 21: 1016–1024.

Gilligan, C. 1982. *In a Different Voice.* Cambridge, MA: Harvard University Press.

Ginsberg, D., and J. Gottman. 1986. Conversations of college roommates: Similarities and differences in male and female friendship. In J. M. Gottman and J. G. Parker, eds., *Conversations of Friends: Speculations on Affective Development.* Cambridge: Cambridge Univ. Press, 241–291.

Gottman, J. M. 1986. The world of coordinated play: Same- and cross-sex friendship in young children. In J. M. Gottman and J. G. Parker, eds., *Conversations of Friends: Speculations on Affective Development.* Cambridge: Cambridge University Press, 139–191.

Green, S. K., and P. Sandos. 1983. Perceptions of male and female initiators of relationships. *Sex Roles* 9: 849–852.

Hacker, H. M. 1981. Blabbermouths and clams: Sex differences in self-disclosure in same-sex and cross-sex friendship dyads. *Psychology of Women Quarterly* 5: 385–401.

Haley, J. 1963. *Strategies of Psychotherapy.* New York: Grune and Stratton.

Hatfield, E., and J. Traupmann. 1981. Intimate relationships: A perspective from equity theory. In S. Duck and R. Gilmour, eds., *Personal Relationships 1: Studying Personal Relationships.* London: Academic Press, 165–178.

Helgeson, V. S., P. Shaver, and M. Dyer. 1987. Prototypes of intimacy and distance in same-sex and opposite-sex relationships. *Journal of Social and Personal Relationships* 4: 195–233.

Hess, B. 1972. Friendship. In M. W. Riley, M. Johnson, and A. Foner, eds., *Aging and Society: A Sociology of Age Stratification,* Vol. 3. New York: Russell Sage Foundation, 357–393.

Horton, M. 1973. Alternatives to romantic love. In M. E. Curtin, ed., *Symposium on Love.* New York: Behavioral Publications, 107–121.

Hunter, F. T., and J. Youniss. 1982. Changes in functions of three relations during adolescence. *Developmental Psychology* 18: 806–811.

Johnson, F. L., and E. J. Aries. 1983. Conversational patterns among same-sex pairs of late-adolescent close friends. The *Journal of Genetic Psychology* 142: 225–238.

Karweit, N., and S. Hansell. 1983. Sex differences in adolescent relationships: Friendship and status. In J. L. Epstein and N. Karweit, eds., *Friends in School.* New York: Academic Press, 116–130.

Komarovsky, M. 1974. Patterns of self-disclosure of male undergraduates. *Journal of Marriage and the Family* 36: 677–686.

———. 1976. *Dilemmas of Masculinity: A Study of College Youth.* New York: Norton.

Kon, I. S., and V. A. Losenkov. 1978. Friendship in adolescence: Values and behavior. *Journal of Marriage and the Family* 40: 143–155.

Kurth, S. B. 1970. Friendships and friendly relations. In G. J. McCall, M. M. McCall, N. K. Denzin, G. D. Suttles, and S. Kurth, eds., *Social Relationships.* Chicago: Aldine, 136–170.

La Gaipa, J. J. 1979. A developmental study of the meaning of friendship in adolescence. *Journal of Adolescence* 2: 201–213.

Laing, R. D. 1972. *The Politics of the Family.* New York: Vintage.

Lepp, L. 1966. *The Ways of Friendship.* New York: Macmillan.

Lever, J. 1976. Sex differences in the games children play. *Social Problems* 23: 478–487.

Lewis, R. A. 1978. Emotional intimacy among men. *Journal of Social Issues* 34: 108–121.

McAdams, D. P. 1985. Motivation and friendship. In S. Duck and D. Perlman, eds., *Understanding Personal Relationships: An Interdisciplinary Program.* London: Sage, 85–105.

Metts, S., W. R. Cupach, and R. A. Bejlovec. 1989. I love you too much to ever start liking you: Redefining romantic relationships. *Journal of Social and Personal Relationships* 6: 259–274.

Monsour, M. 1996. Communication and cross-sex friendships across the life cycle: A review of the literature. In B. Burleson, ed., *Communication Yearbook, 20.* Newbury, CA: Sage, 375–414.

Morin, S., and E. M. Garfinkle. 1978. Male homophobia. *Journal of Social Issues* 34: 29–47.

Olstad, K. 1975. Brave new man: A basis for discussion. In J. Petras, ed., *Sex: Male/Gender: Masculine.* Port Washington, NY: Alfred.

Owens, T. J. 1970. *Phenomenology and Intersubjectivity: Contemporary Interpretations of the Interpersonal Situation.* The Hague: Nijhoff.

Paine, R. 1969. In search of friendship: An exploratory analysis in "middle-class" culture. *Man* 4: 505–524.

Pleck, J. H. 1975. Man to man: Is brotherhood possible? In N. Glazer-Malbin, ed., *Old Family/New Family.* New York: D. Van Nostrand Co, 229–244.

Rangell, L. 1963. On friendship. *Journal of the American Psychoanalytic Association* 11: 3–54.

Rawlins, W. K. 1982. Cross-sex friendship and the communicative management of sex-role expectations. *Communication Quarterly* 30. 343–352.

———. 1983. Negotiating close friendships: The dialectic of conjunctive freedoms. *Human Communication Research* 9: 255–266.

———. 1989a. A dialectical analysis of the tensions, functions and strategic challenges of communication in young adult friendships. In J. A. Anderson, ed., *Communication Yearbook* 12. Newbury, CA: Sage, 157–189.

———. 1989b. Cultural double agency and the pursuit of friendship. *Cultural Dynamics* 2: 28–40.

———. 1991. On enacting friendship and interrogating discourse. In K. Tracy, ed., *Understanding Face-to-Face Interaction: Issues Linking Goals and Discourse.* New York: Lawrence Erlbaum, 101–115.

———. 1992. *Friendship Matters: Communication, Dialectics, and the Life Course.* Hawthorne, NY: Aldine de Gruyter.

Richey, M. H., and H. W. Richey. 1980. The significance of best-friend relationships in adolescence. *Psychology in the Schools* 17: 536–540.

Roberts, M. K. 1982. Men and women: Partners, lovers, friends. In K. E. Davis and T. Mitchell, eds., *Advances in Descriptive Psychology,* Vol. 2. Greenwich, CT: AI Press, 57–78.

Rose, S. M. 1985. Same- and cross-sex friendships and the psychology of homosociality. *Sex Roles* 12: 63–74.
Rose, S., and F. C. Serafica. 1986. Keeping and ending casual, close and best friendships. *Journal of Social and Personal Relationships* 3: 275–288.
Rotenberg, K. J. 1986. Same-sex patterns and sex differences in the trust-value basis of children's friendship. *Sex Roles* 16: 613–626.
Rubenstein, C., and C. Rubin. 1984. Children's fantasies of interaction with same and opposite sex peers. In T. Field, J. L. Roopnarine, and M. Segal, eds., *Friendships in Normal and Handicapped Children.* Norwood, NJ: Ablex, 99–124.
Rubin, Z., L. A. Peplau, and C. T. Hill. 1980. Loving and leaving: Sex differences in romantic attachments. *Sex Roles* 6: 821–835.
Sapadin, L. A. 1988. Friendship and gender: Perspectives of professional men and women. *Journal of Social and Personal Relationships* 5: 387–403.
Seiden, A. M., and P. B. Bart. 1975. Woman to woman: Is sisterhood powerful? In N. Galzer-Malbin, ed., *Old Family/New Family.* New York: D. Van Nostrand, 189–228.
Smollar, J., and J. Youniss. 1982. Social development through friendship. In K. H. Rubin and H. S. Ross, eds., *Peer Relationships and Social Skills in Childhood.* New York: Springer-Verlag, 279–298.
Sprey, J. 1969. On the institutionalization of sexuality. *Journal of Marriage and the Family* 31: 432–440.
Suttles, G. D. 1970. Friendship as a social institution. In G. J. McCall, M. McCall, N. K. Denzin, G. D. Suttles, and S. Kurth, eds., *Social Relationships.* Chicago: Aldine, 95–135.
Thorne, B. 1986. Girls and boys together . . . but mostly apart: Gender arrangements in elementary schools. In W. W. Hartup and Z. Rubin, eds., *Relationships and Development.* Hillsdale, NJ: Lawrence Erlbaum, 167–184.
Walster, E., G. W. Walster, and E. Berscheid. 1978. *Equity Theory and Research.* Boston: Allyn and Bacon.
Werebe, M. J. G. 1987. Friendship and dating relationships among French adolescents. *Journal of Adolescence* 10: 269–289.
Werking, K. J. 1997. *We're Just Good Friends: Women and Men in Nonromantic Relationships.* New York: The Guilford Press.
Williams, D. G. 1985. Gender, masculinity-femininity, and emotional intimacy in same-sex friendship. *Sex Roles* 12: 587–600.
Wood, J. T. 1982. Communication and relational culture: Bases for the study of human relationships. *Communication Quarterly* 30: 75–83.
Wright, P. H. 1982. Men's friendships, women's friendships, and the alleged inferiority of the latter. *Sex Roles* 8: 1–20.
Youniss, J., and J. Smollar. 1985. *Adolescent Relations with Mothers, Fathers, and Friends.* Chicago: University of Chicago Press.

CHAPTER 7

When Myths Endure and Realities Change

Communication in Romantic Relationships

Laurie P. Arliss

POINTS TO BE ADDRESSED

- Cultural messages about romantic interaction
- Unique aspects of romantic communication
- Linguistic forms used to refer to romantic partners
- Impact of gender equality on romantic interaction
- Causes and effects of ambiguity in romantic interaction
- Conflict in romantic relationships

How we struggle to label comfortably that special someone who is neither a platonic friend nor a family member. The formal marriage ceremony is accompanied by widely used role labels (husband, wife, spouse) and, just before the marriage, the future partners easily identify themselves as "engaged to be married" and comfortably pronounce the label "fiancé." Yet we have not coined an appropriate label for the relationship partner with whom future marriage is in doubt.

Many simply refer to the person-in-question as a boyfriend or girlfriend. But these are the same labels used by naive young children. They are also the labels used, at least by females, to refer to same-sex associates. Possessive pronouns, used in conjunction with more adult words, emphasize the exclusive ownership of the individual (this is "*my* guy" or "*my* woman"). Forward thinkers of the 1970s coined the term "significant other," a gender-neutral label that seems less possessive, but it is difficult to imagine two individuals gazing at one another as they declare that they are now significant others. More realistically, they will probably declare (or discover) that they are lovers. Assertive types at this stage frequently begin to refer to one another as such, knowing full well that the label implies a sexual relationship. But, for many, privacy issues make the term inappropriate for use in social introductions.

Scholars have had slightly less trouble identifying and naming these elusive pairs. They are typically called "romantic pairs," "intimates" or simply "dating couples." The broad term "romantic relationships" is used to title this chapter, but there are frequent references to the social practice called "dating." The emotional state experienced by participants in romantic relationships is often called "romantic love." This term may seem redundant, since romance is believed to be synonymous with love despite the fact that many loving relationships are clearly not romantic. *The American Heritage Dictionary* equates the terms in one section and uses the more provocative term "love affair" in another. But the primary listing that follows the word "romance" is as follows: "1. a. A medieval narrative telling of the adventures of chivalric heroes. b. A long, fictitious tale of heroes and extraordinary or mysterious events. c. A quality suggestive of the adventure and idealized exploits found in such tales." This definition reveals the powerful, mystical, extraordinary adventure associated with the pursuit of a "significant other" in our culture.

Romantic Myths: Communication about Romantic Relationships

In our society, still dominated by the nuclear family, individuals are expected to select a singular suitable mate, and dating is understood to be part of the process used to locate the right person and negotiate intimacy.[1] But the practical aspects of the mate selection process are downplayed in discussions of dating; discussion of this highly significant male–female experience is dominated by the glorified language of romantic love. The mythology of romantic interaction has survived generations of retelling. Even in modern times, we continue to envision a sublime (albeit difficult to obtain) state of euphoria (Mehta and Clark, 1994). Indeed, the content of our love stories has changed very little over time, despite the development of new technologies for marketing them. By the time we reach adulthood, images of true love are closely linked to culturally created images of masculinity and femininity.

Childhood Narratives

Most children become familiar with magical fantasies of daring heroes who rescue beautiful maidens. Cinderella, Sleeping Beauty, Snow White are all sweet, pure, young maidens in the midst of terrible predicaments. Fortunately, they are rescued by strong, handsome, capable princes. Each helpless maiden is saved in a magic moment by a kiss from her man or by a shoe that fits just right. Notice how the childhood characters that have survived intergenerational storytelling are aligned with the prevailing gender stereotypes: gentle, sweet, pure, young women and strong, powerful, resourceful, young men. The plot is equally traditional: the woman waits passively (often, she's asleep) for the man to make the move that will ensure that they both live happily ever after. (Note: the gender dynamics of children's literature are far more complicated than this discussion suggests. Consider, for example, that it is usually an ugly, evil, powerful woman who causes the maiden's troubles in the first place.)

Smith and Midlarsky (1985) have argued that gender stereotypes are both embodied and perpetuated in fairy tale images and plots. These stories are commonly told to children who, according to experts, are just learning their own gender identity and seeking information about how to behave appropriately (Intons-Peterson, 1988). Children seek positive evaluations of their own gender (Cross and Markus, 1994), so it is not surprising that most young girls idealize the heroines. After all, these fictive maidens are beautiful and kind (although helpless and unbelievably gullible). It seems easy for little boys to emulate the heroes; they are capable, righteous, handsome, and usually of royal blood. Of course, children of both sexes appreciate the goodness of the opposite sex characters. But, Bem (1987: 265) explains that children are likely to "reject any way of behaving that does not match their sex." In the case of fairy tale images, this choice would have serious implications for young girls seeking to solve their own problems.

As children mature, so does their knowledge of romantic relationships. Children complement an increasing collection of romantic fictions with a number of firsthand observations. Most prominently in our culture, they learn about the institution of marriage, which may or may not explain the family relationships in their own lives but is an important cultural institution nonetheless. Even before children have a clear understanding of reproduction, many associate having a baby with being married and being married with positive feelings for a member of the opposite sex. Hence, it is not uncommon for some children to declare that they intend to marry their opposite sex parent, which demonstrates both children's naiveté about the conventions that make certain partners taboo and their wisdom that the marriage partner should be a special loved one of the opposite sex.

Adolescent Fantasies

When children become adolescents, the element of sexuality is inevitably added to the romantic fantasy. At the onset of puberty, young people are physically capable of reproduction and, simultaneously, become interested in "the opposite sex," although they are commonly not well-versed in what is necessary to make the liaison. Therefore, despite the physical readiness, most cross-sex adolescent interaction is little more than a rough imitation of adult romance (Hill, 1982; Wright, 1999). Picture teenage boys and girls strategically planning social pairings, sharing secrets about the desirable aspects of the opposite sex, and reflecting on the exhilarating emotions associated with young love. As you might image (or perhaps remember), "the romantic adventures of adolescents seldom feature the sort of extended, social interaction which might let (them) explore mutual interests and lay the foundation for a friendship" (Rubin, 1980: 105). In fact, Rubin (1980) speculates that romantic interest during this period does more to facilitate same-sex relating than cross-sex relating. Both boys and girls tend to converse more with same-sex peers about girlfriends or boyfriends than with the particular admired other. More often than not, they send messages and notes through same-sex confederates and arrange meetings in groups. Thus, the mystical nature of romance is largely created and preserved in the midst of the adolescent's developing sense of himself or herself as male or female.

Given the adolescent's tendency to reflect on the success of various cross-sex experiences with members of the same sex, it might be argued that boys and girls develop values pertaining to all-important *heterosexual* interaction at a time when life is decidedly *homosocial* (Eggert and Parks, 1987; Wright, 1999). So, it is neither surprising nor comforting to realize that men and women leave adolescence with different expectations and impressions of romantic interaction. Girls tend to emphasize getting noticed by boys, often by one special boy. They may even begin to fantasize about true, lasting love. A good deal of time in female groups is devoted to the refinement of appearance through clothes, hairstyles, make-up, and the like (Rubin, 1986). Girls also devote time to various activities in which they provide support for male activity (Wilks, 1986). Being a cheerleader is often accorded a higher status than being a star athlete. Indeed, *who* you date may be the most important determinant of status. In line with stereotypic myths, athletes, social leaders, and those with material possessions are believed to be good catches.

Like their female counterparts, adolescent boys also attribute great status to sexual maturity, and they too are concerned with appearances, though they typically do not primp publicly. They tend to emphasize overt signs of maturity, strength, and athleticism as evaluated by male peers (Hill, 1982). Talk of athletic achievements dominates their conversations, but adolescent boys, like adolescent girls, also confide in friends about the opposite sex (Rubin, 1986). Seldom is true, lasting love a theme in their conversations. Rather, adolescent boys tend to emphasize sexual activity in their discussions (Youniss and Smollar, 1985). Thus, who you date may be significant for boys as well as girls, but how you did on the date is a special preoccupation in all-male discussions. According to Johnson (1997: 54), the impact of sex differences such as these are especially important because "Although [early experiences] powerfully shape what we experience as reality, we're rarely aware of this, especially while it's happening."

The fact that sex differences continue in adolescence to characterize perceptions of romantic interaction may disturb us, but should not surprise us. One study revealed that adolescents, particularly boys, hold very rigid traditional images of men and women (Lewin and Tragos, 1987). Their experience with members of the opposite sex is not likely to be sufficient to challenge the traditional, stereotypic notions they adopted in childhood. Moreover, it appears that the nature of their same-sex interaction during adolescence does little to broaden their minds.

Myths for Adults

The continued dominance of traditional gender images among today's children and adolescents may indicate that the heralded "age of gender equality" has not yet arrived (Johnson, 1997). An alternative explanation might be that young people understandably experience the world using simple categories consistent with early stages of cognitive development (Cross and Markus, 1994). If the latter explanation is correct, we would expect to see adult men and women, rich in experience and knowledge, portray more flexible images of gender in their communication about romance. We might expect college students to report a gender-neutral understanding of romantic interaction. But despite liberal attitudes about professional and legal issues, today's young adults continue to express conservative views of male–female interaction in personal relationships. Research reveals that both sexes still endorse traditional values concerning dating relationships, especially about who should pay for the expenses, initiate sexual intimacy, and propose marriage (McKinney, 1987; Wood, 1994; Wright, 1999).

Granted, the expressed values of research subjects represent talk about romantic interaction. McKinney (1987) acknowledges that those surveyed may or may not display more gender-neutral standards in their lived experience. But, if men and women are more traditional in their private cross-sex relationships than in their public cross-sex relationships, it might very well be because contemporary visions of love are simply not peopled with aggressive women and dependent men. That is not to say that nontraditional women and men are not gaining prominence, particularly in the media. But seldom do nontraditional couples appear to "live happily ever after." Indeed the "emasculating female" has become nearly as prominent on daytime dramas (i.e., soap operas) as the "trusting, innocent maiden." Both characters are likely to be seen engaging in romantic interaction, but the virtuous, gentle female is more likely to find true love, despite interference from the jealous, aggressive female (Cassata, Skill, and Boadu, 1983; Bate and Bowker, 1997). It seems the portrayals of romance enjoyed by adult consumers are not substantially different from those available in fairy tales.

Snapshots of contemporary male–female entanglements are also readily available on daytime talk shows (Livingstone, 1994; Nelson and Robinson,

1994). Experts concur that these programs offer portrayals of men and women and interpersonal problems that are not statistically typical, but analysts disagree about whether the individuals featured are viewed as realistic. If the audience considers the guests as credible, the tendency to incorporate professionals to provide "counsel" may reinforce the perception that nontraditional ways of acting result in relationship "illness."

Popular magazines also offer images of men, women, and romance. In 1981, a review by Jean Umiker-Sebeok revealed that print images emphasize men engaged in activity and women just "looking pretty." Portrayals of women typically included children in their care and/or men with whom they appeared to be romantic. During the same period, articles in magazines marketed to women focused almost exclusively on being attractive and developing personal relationships. A 1994 content analysis of women's magazines reported a number of articles dealing with politics and social issues (Demarst and Garner), but they did not outnumber articles dedicated to appearance and guile as the means to "catching and pleasing a man." Magazines marketed primarily to men during the same time period also included articles about significant contemporary issues, as well as discussions of "fashion" and "getting in shape." Indeed, one popular men's magazine emphasizes fashion and appearance (*Gentleman's Quarterly*). However, most top-selling men's magazines highlight pictorals of women, not men. Even magazines organized around traditional male topics, such as automobiles and hunting, commonly include photographs of attractive women. Magazines and television, of course, must be consumed to endure, and experts who control media content are keenly aware of what the buying public appreciates. It is unclear whether popular media reflect or create the prevailing mythology about men, women, and romance, but what is clear is that adults continue to consume media images that reinforce early lessons learned about female passivity and male resourcefulness.

Ultimately, as adults, we realize that neither media images nor fairy tales hold the truth about developing a steady and exclusive partnership. Nevertheless, individuals in our culture are pressured to find and win a desirable mate. Courtship in other cultures may amount to the negotiation of goods or the introduction of pre-assigned partners, but in our culture it involves identifiable *communication* events—attempts to appear attractive to members of the opposite sex, strategies to win the affections of desired individuals, and ultimately the negotiation of a single, highly personal connection with a *significant other*, all events that are both a product of and an influence on each individual's self-image. To the extent that one's self-image is gender-specific, romantic interaction will be understandably traditional. A dominant theme in this book is that future generations of men and women may consider themselves (and others) to be more gender-neutral than they do today. If so, traditions about romantic interaction may be challenged, but, according to DiIorio (1989), personal relationships between men and women have always been, and will continue to be, highly resistant to change.

Not-so-Romantic Realities: Communication in Romantic Relationships

Perhaps it is because we hold the mythology of love so dear that the realities of romantic interaction are so difficult to accept. The challenge of attracting a desirable person (preferably selected from a host of desirable alternatives) is one for which childhood lessons and adolescent rehearsal do not adequately prepare most of us. Even those who are considered successful at the sort of casual, short-lived entanglements typical among teenagers may find themselves ill-equipped to negotiate and sustain the singular intimate relationship revered in our culture.

Ironically, the aspects of romantic interaction that make it special are often the very causes of difficulty. To begin with, romantic relationships are voluntarily entered into in our culture. Each individual is expected to find a suitable life partner, one who is sufficiently similar to facilitate mutual decision making, yet also sufficiently dissimilar. If the relationship takes its full course, cultural norms predict that it will become legal and binding through the institution of marriage. According to most present legal systems, the chosen marriage partner cannot be a family member and must be of the opposite sex, so the relationships that dominate youthful interaction are not likely to provide ready partners. In reality, finding a romantic partner amounts to negotiating a close relationship with a stranger.

Add to the mystical, adventurous nature of romance the expectation that romantic bonds are expected to become gradually more intense and more significant in our lives. Unlike the family relationships we experienced as children, which must become less intense in order to set us free to become adults, and friendships, which vary greatly in intensity, adult romantic pairings must either progress or be dissolved. It is difficult to state with certainty when rehearsals begun in adolescence become serious, but Duck (1988) suggests that "Typically, people seek a marriage partner most actively between the ages of about 16 and 26." This is probably a good estimate, since the median age of (first) marriage in the United States is approximately 27 years for men and 25 years for women.

Interaction between prospective partners used to be called "courtship" and, in past decades, was governed by established, gender-specific rules. There were proper and improper behaviors for males and females, communicated as "rules" by parental figures. During the 1950s, young adults rebelled against both the label "courtship" and the imposition of parental control. The term "dating" was coined, which, according to Pearson (1989), is now "dated." Dating was presumably different from courtship because it focused on aspects of the present social arrangement between two people, with no inference about the future.

But new traditions emerged during the 1950s and 1960s to mark the development of romantic relationships. Communication events involving the exchange of promises and usually a symbolic gift for the female signified relationship states. Couples agreed to "go steady" or "get pinned." Female partners displayed their steadies' class ring or fraternity pin or school jacket to signify their status—*taken*. (Notably, the male partners seldom displayed any complementary token.) The obvious communicative markers that depicted relationship development helped the partners to clarify their increasing degree of intimacy. In turn, the relationship became progressively more exclusive, a characteristic of romantic pairings that is often a source of conflict.

According to one survey, young people today are questioning the utility of all these "new" traditions. Seventy-eight percent of the college-aged respondents prefer "informal meetings in social settings" to "formal dates." Dates are limited to formal occasions like proms, which are still in vogue and still very traditional. The "semantics of dating" have also changed. The most common way to refer to a nonplatonic male–female relationship is to note that the two individuals are "seeing each other" (Sacks, 1990). Although researchers have found it useful to distinguish "casual dating" from "serious dating" (Tolhuizen, 1989), many college students simply remark that they are "not seeing others." The new phrases are noticeably ambiguous. There are no clear-cut labels for relationship stages. This may be related to Baxter and Wilmot's (1985) finding that discussing the state of a close relationship is a taboo topic. Tolhuizen (1989) found that only about 29 percent of his respondents used "relationship negotiation" to intensify a dating relationship and even less (14 percent) offered verbal declarations of affection such as "I love you." Owens's (1987) data indicate that, in some cases, individuals use verbal declarations unilaterally and strategically to intensify a relationship, while in others, dating couples report simultaneously discovering that a relationship has grown closer. In a related study by Marston, Hecht, and Roberts (1989), many subjects who identified themselves as involved in a heterosexual "love relationship . . . used no relational constructs in their definition of love" (390).

Along with relationship labels and other verbal constructs, nonverbal relationship markers are also becoming less common. Only a small percentage of subjects in Tolhuizen's study (1989) reported giving tokens of affection, inviting partners to meet family or friends, or staging events to make partners jealous. Also, despite the fact that self-report data indicate the prevalence of premarital sexual involvement (Sprecher and McKinney, 1994; Woodward, 1990), physical intimacy is not necessarily viewed as a relationship intensifier. Christopher and Cate (1985) found that dating couples vary greatly as to the connection between sexual involvement and relationship intensification. However, the majority (61 percent) believed that sex should follow, not cause, recognition by both partners that they are a "couple" (200).

It is interesting to speculate about the current state of the romantic world. For some, sex and love continue to be closely connected. For others, sex is separate from and desirable without love. Critics of contemporary values argue that the separation of sex, love, and marriage leads to serious social problems (Footlick, 1990). According to Johnson (1997), men have always been willing to separate sex from commitment, but women have not. He contends that, as part of a growing desire for autonomy, some women are now separating sexual involvement from commitment.

The ambiguity that now characterizes romantic interaction is undoubtedly due to social changes young people regard as positive—the movement away from strict parental control of "courtship" and the questioning of traditional gender divisions. However, as the title of this book suggests, with these changes come inherent challenges. Ambiguity is not necessarily comfortable. The prospect of negotiating male–female relationships in the absence of cultural traditions and rules is at once exhilarating and frightening. It is a challenge that, like so many others, calls for effective communication. In the remaining sections of this chapter, several of the specific challenges inherent in romantic interaction are discussed.

Initiation

As the discussion above suggests, if relationships are to progress, it is necessary for one or the other member to initiate that progress. Traditionally, when it came to romance, male partners were expected, even pressured, to do the asking, the proposing, and the like. Similarly, traditional images of physical interaction suggested that the man, not the woman, should "make the moves" that we know as precursors to sexual intimacy. Females who asked men on dates or who were too forward physically earned a "bad reputation." Of course, as gender restrictions become less rigid, partners should be expected to share the freedom and responsibility to initiate social and sexual activity.

However, some studies suggest that young people are not altogether willing to abandon traditions when it comes to initiation in romantic pairs. Men are still far more likely to ask for a woman's company on a date than vice versa (Green and Sandos, 1983). Women continue to occupy a relatively passive position when it comes to "seeing someone" they are interested in. They wait and react, or perhaps take indirect or subtle action. Since the same young women report that they are willing to suggest social liaisons in platonic relationships (Buhrke and Fuqua, 1987), it seems that potentially romantic relationships inspire otherwise assertive females to behave in traditionally "feminine" ways.

The gender stereotypes "aggressive" and "passive" also continue to influence the initiation of sexual intimacy. As Grauerholz and Serpe (1985) report, men continue to be "sexually proactive," while women continue to be "reactive." This boils down to greater freedom for men to *initiate sex* and greater freedom for women to *refuse* sex—both prerogatives that ideally should be available to either a male or a female in a free society. The researchers conclude that the proposed "single sexual standard does not yet exist" (Grauerholz and Serpe, 1985: 1049).

Men also continue to be more proactive than women in the symbolic aspects of relationship development. The practice of gift-giving as a symbol in male–female interaction continues to be dominated by male giving and female receiving. Florists still deliver most of their valentine flowers to females, and no widely accepted male counterpart of the engagement ring has emerged. The language of our wedding ceremonies has been revised so that the woman no longer has to "love, honor and obey," but a tender moment continues to be shared between father and daughter as he symbolically "gives her away" to the new husband. No such giving away is necessary for the groom.

All the aforementioned sex-specific behaviors are being challenged in some dating relationships, according to DeLucia (1987). She points out that psychological gender orientation, a term coined by Bem to identify an individual's self-perception that he or she is "masculine" or "feminine" or some combination thereof, is important in determining behavior in romantic interaction. Specifically, men who see themselves as "very masculine" and women who see themselves as "very feminine" are likely to conform to traditional standards. But those who see themselves as androgynous (possessing both male and female qualities) may cross the lines somewhat (DeLucia, 1987). Still, it is important to note that behaving "unfeminine" or "unmasculine" in romantic situations may be more costly than in professional or social situations.

Feminists have argued that women should take more initiative in our society, and many men and women have agreed, at least when it comes to legal and social reforms. However, according to feminist critiques, "efforts to equalize women's status through legal reforms guaranteeing equal rights and formal equality may be insufficient for creating true sex equality since in the private and intimate spheres of life . . . women still find themselves subordinate to their boyfriends, lovers and husbands" (DiIorio, 1989: 94).

The issue of subordination is not settled by simply citing that men tend to be proactive and women tend to be reactive. Young men might argue that it is the woman who holds the power in romantic relationships, because she can either accept or reject the advances of the man. Also, the receiving of gifts may constitute a superior position in some people's eyes. Both these arguments hinge on the proposed control of resources that are valuable in romantic relationships. In the next section, the control of such resources is examined.

Control of Resources

Traditionally, researchers have defined power in male–female interaction as a function of controlled resources (McDonald, 1980). Thus, if the male partner initiates social action, provides necessary transportation, accepts responsibility for expenses, and so on, he may be assumed to be more powerful than the female. But, from another perspective, because the male partner is actually providing resources, giving of his own wealth and services to the female, he maybe interpreted as subordinate to her. In fact, Sprecher (1985) found the latter interpretation to be more popular among both males and females currently involved in dating relationships. However, her interviews also suggested an interesting caveat. To the extent that the male dating partner perceived that he had "other options" (i.e., other females willing to date him), the freedom to initiate encounters and control the resources was seen as empowering. Conversely, women without "other options," who must "wait passively for someone else to show an interest," perceived themselves as less powerful than their male partners (Sprecher, 1985: 458). Apparently, perceptions of power in dating relationships may be based on the relative social dependency of the partners on one another, not on the actual size of the resource contribution.

The above discussion defines resources in traditionally male terms. But the dreaded "turndown" has been identified as one of several "feminine resources." Some analysts argue that women also control certain "services" that men want but cannot, or would rather not, buy (Carroll, Volk, and Hyde, 1985). It is interesting to note that nearly any service traditionally provided by women, even bearing and mothering children, can now be purchased for the right price. Obviously, the resources labeled as "feminine" are valuable commodities that might be used for bargaining with the romantic partner. But it is not difficult to imagine how, once contributed, these resources reduce the power of the giver. Research reveals that women who "give" a great deal in relationships tend to surrender power. They tend to become highly dependent on their male partners for the very same resources they formerly controlled, namely love and sex (Sprecher, 1985).

It seems that inequities continue to characterize male–female interaction when it comes to premarital romantic interaction. Unless men and women redistribute the resources so that both are free to initiate and pay for social encounters, and both are free to initiate and reject sexual advances, romantic relationships will continue to be dominated by traditional gender-specific guidelines

EXCLUSIVITY AND POSSESSIVENESS

Questions about initiation and resources are most pressing in the early stages of romantic relationships. Other challenges emerge in later stages, as couples attempt to negotiate progress toward exclusivity. The marriage commitment in our culture mandates exclusivity, so it is not surprising that romantic couples move toward exclusivity. But, short of becoming engaged, there is no recognized public ritual designating a pairing as exclusive, so the partners must negotiate their status privately and decide how to communicate to others that they are "taken."

Perhaps the most pressing issue is sexual exclusivity. As mentioned earlier, traditionally there have been different cultural standards for men and women when it comes to sexual exclusivity. The so-called "double standard" allows greater sexual freedom for men than for women, and may even regard many sexual partners for a man as a mark of social success. The negative image of women who engage in sex with many partners is evidenced in the words by which we refer to them, words that typically have no male counterpart. Our tendency to speak of women as "easy" or "loose" or worse, but not to refer to men in this way, demonstrates our understanding that women, at least stereotypically, are supposed to attach sex to emotional commitment, while men are understood to equate sex with pleasure, which can be separated from commitment.

In fact, surveys reveal that college women typically cite "emotional reasons" for engaging in sex, while college men more often cite "pleasure" as the reason for sex (Sprecher and McKinney, 1994; Whitely, 1988). In one study, this trend was correlated with biological sex—not psychological gender orientation—which means that even men and women who perceived themselves as "androgynous" conformed to gender-specific standards in explaining the reasons for sexual activity (DeLucia, 1987).

Regardless of the reason for engaging in sex, sexual exclusivity continues to be a defining characteristic of commitment. Both men and women expect their partners to be "faithful," and feel that "cheating" would constitute a major threat to the romance (Hansen, 1985). But the issue of exclusivity in romantic relationships often extends beyond the bounds of sexual loyalty. Partners may struggle with the degree to which they are allowed other freedoms, such as time to spend with same-sex friends, family, and so on. Self-report data suggest that both men and women expect that certain outside relationships, particularly cross-sex friendships, will be subordinate to coupledom, even during the early stages of romantic bonding (Hansen, 1982). However, females tend to believe that dating relationships mandate more devotion to one's partner, and women tend to be more disturbed when their partners spend time with friends or family (Hansen, 1985).

Being a couple seems to create a situation in which time management can be a difficult issue. Couples have to negotiate about how to allocate social and work time, keeping in mind "each individual's need for privacy and intimacy" (Duck, 1988: 103). As if the internal pressures are not difficult enough, couples may be treated as a single unit by outsiders and pressured to decide together which social invitations to accept and which to decline (Cate and Lloyd, 1988). Attending separate social events may be evidence that the couple is either very secure about the relationship or not totally devoted, but such decisions are sure to be noticed in a couple-oriented social world.

VOLATILITY

One of the truly unique aspects of romantic relationships is their degree of volatility. Individuals who "fall in love" often experience intensely joyful moments, but they also experience moments of intense depression or anxiety. In some cases, the joy of finding one another and/or the threat of losing one another can be so emotional that individuals behave totally out of character.

Consider the metaphors we use to describe this highly emotional condition: "crazy in love," "head over heels in love," "love-struck."

Researchers have verified that, just as the metaphoric language of love suggests, individuals may be literally overcome with the intense emotions they feel. So it is not surprising that, as the degree of intimacy in a male–female relationship increases, so does the threat of violence. According to Gamache (1998) one out of ten high school students and one out of five college students have experienced physical violence in a dating relationship. Both men and women revealed having made or received threats of physical abuse, witnessed violent destruction of inanimate objects, and/or experienced "real violence" (Deal and Wampler, 1986). Although young people of both sexes report having inflicted or received physical abuse from a romantic partner, it is important to note that abuse of females by males tends to be more severe in terms of both physical and psychological consequences (Gamache, 1998).

Although physical abuse is clearly the most disturbing form of dating violence, it is important to note that psychological abuse also increases as couples become "closer" (Pipes and LeBov-Keeler, 1997). Psychological abuse, in fact, may seem all too familiar when defined by example: hostile verbal communication such as insults or swearing or constant criticism; the issuing of orders and ultimatums; instances of social humiliation or public degradation; and constant surveillance or accusations of infidelity (Pipes and LeBov-Keeler, 1997: 592.) The line that distinguishes acceptable levels of negative interaction from psychological abuse may be a fine one, but Hoffman (1984) distinguishes psychological abuse based on the perception of the abused partner that the ability to work, interact in the family and society, and enjoy good health is threatened.

Ironically, those who report high instances of psychological abuse are more likely to be in "serious" relationships, considered by both partners to be "committed" and objectively categorized as "long standing" in duration (Kasian and Painter, 1992). While abuse does not appear to be limited to heterosexual romance, research of its prevalence in committed male–female dyads is disturbing. Felmlee (1994) cites the power differentials between men and women as a contributing factor. To complicate matters, cross-sex pairings are logically ill-equipped for interaction involving extreme negative emotions, because men and women deal quite differently with negative feelings. Men tend to "mask" sadness and fear with expressions commonly associated with anger, while women tend to "mask" anger with tears (Crester et al., 1983; Ross and Mirowsky, 1984). Thus, confusion and frustration can result when invisible emotions are misconstrued based on visible behaviors.

Ultimately, words may fail to resolve love-sparked violence, and negative feelings may be expressed through physical separation or violence. Although separation seems preferable to violence, it can feel just as threatening. "Breaking up" often embodies the ultimate threat because the romance itself is valued so highly. The thought that the relationship will be dissolved, and replaced by another, may be more than some can bear.

Yet, the statistical reality of contemporary romance is that few who promise total, enduring devotion are able to fulfill their promises. A good deal is at stake in making these relationships last, but they are so fragile and so volatile that most do not succeed.

In closing, it is worth noting that today's young men and women seem to be deliberately postponing marriage—indirectly creating an extended period of the life span characterized by movement in and out of romantic entanglements. Thus, the topics discussed in this chapter are likely to increase in prominence. Males and females who seek the mythological happiness associated with romance will need to develop their communication skills in order to initiate these highly significant relationships, intensify them as appropriate, and control the intense emotions associated with romantic love.

For Further Discussion

1. Collect and discuss a set of contemporary images of romance. You may look at television or film images, greeting cards, magazine contents, contemporary song lyrics, or any other source that offers romantic images. If you were a stranger to our culture, what would you learn about romance through examining these images?
2. What changes, if any, can you find in the portrayal of male and female heroes in the stories consumed by children over the past few decades? To answer this question, examine best selling children's books, top box office movies, and popular television programs created for children.
3. Discuss the similarities and differences between romantic relationships and platonic relationships. Which type of cross-sex pair seems to contribute most to personal well-being? Personal problems? Does the answer differ for the male vs. the female partner?
4. How many romantic relationships do you consider an ideal number? How many sexual/romantic partners should an individual know prior to marriage?

Endnote

[1] Consistent with the focus of this volume, this chapter emphasizes communication in cross-sex dyads, but the reader is encouraged to consult the growing body of research that explores relationship negotiation between same-sex romantic partners.

References

Bate, B., and J. Bowker. 1997. *Communication and the Sexes.* 2nd ed. Prospect Heights, IL: Waveland.

Baxter, L. A., and W. W. Wilmot. 1985. "Taboo topics" in close relationships. *Journal of Social and Personal Relationships* 1: 253–269.

Bem, S. L. 1987. Gender schema theory and the romantic tradition. In P. Shaver and C. Hendrick, eds., *Sex and Gender.* Newbury Park, CA: Sage, 251–271.

Buhrke, R. A., and D. R. Fuqua. 1987. Sex differences in same- and cross-sex supportive relationships. *Sex Roles* 17: 339–1.

Carroll, J. C., K. A. Volk, and J. S. Hyde. 1985. Differences between males and females in motives for engaging in sex. *Archives of Sexual Behavior* 15: 131–139.

Cassata, M., T. Skill, and S. Osel Boadu. 1983. Life and death in the daytime television serial: A content analysis. In M. Cassata and T. Skill, eds., *Life on Daytime Television. Tuning-in American Serial Drama.* Norwood, NJ: Ablex, 47–70.

Cate, R. M., and S. A. Lloyd. 1988. Courtship. In S. W. Duck, D. F. Haley, S. E. Hobfoll, W. Ickes, and B. Montgomery, eds., *Handbook of Personal Relationships.* Chichester, UK: Wiley.

Christopher, F. S., and R. M. Cate. 1985. Premarital sexual pathways and relationship development. *Journal of Social and Personal Relationships* 2: 271–288.

Crester, G. A., W. K. Lombardo, B. Lombardo, and S. C. Mathis. 1983. Fer cryin' out loud—there is a sex difference. *Sex Roles* 9: 987–996.

Cross, S. E. and H. R. Markus. 1994. Gender in thought, belief, and action: A cognitive approach. In A. L. Weber and J. H. Harvey, eds., *Perspectives on Close Relationships.* Boston: Allyn and Bacon, 55–98.

Deal, J. E., and K. S. Wampler. 1986. Dating violence: The primacy of previous experience. *Journal of Social and Personal Relationships* 3: 457–471.

DeLucia, J. L. 1987. Gender role identity and dating behavior. *Sex Roles* 17: 153–161.

DiIorio, J. A. 1989. Being and becoming coupled: The emergence of female subordination in heterosexual relationships. In B. Risman and P. Schwartz, eds., *Gender in Intimate Relationships.* Belmont, CA: Wadsworth, 94–107.

Duck, S. 1988. *Relating to Others.* Chicago: Dorsey Press.

Eggert, L. L., and M. R. Parks. 1987. Communication network involvement in adolescents' friendships and romantic relationships. In *Communication Yearbook 10.* Newbury Park, CA: Sage, 283–322.

Felmlee, D. H. 1994. Who's on top? Power in romantic relationships. *Sex Roles* 31: 275–295.

Footlick, J. K. 1990. What happened to the family? *Newsweek Special Issue,* Vol. CXIV, No. 27: 14–20.

Gamache, D. 1998. Domination and control: The social context of dating violence. In B. Levy, ed., *Dating Violence: Young Women in Danger.* Seattle: Seal Press, 69–83.

Grauerholz, E., and R. T. Serpe. 1985. Initiation and response: The dynamics of sexual interaction. *Sex Roles* 12: 1041–1059.

Green, S. K., and P. Sandos. 1983. Perceptions of male and female initiators of relationships. *Sex Roles* 9: 849–852.

Hansen, G. L. 1982. Reactions to hypothetical jealousy producing events. *Family Relations* 31: 513–518.

———. 1985. Dating jealousy among college students. *Sex Roles* 12: 713–721.

Hill, J., ed. 1982. Early adolescence. *Child Development* 53.

Hoffman, P. 1984. Psychological abuse of women by spouses and live-in lovers. *Women and Therapy* 3: 37–47.

Intons-Peterson, M. J. 1988. *Children's Concepts of Gender.* Norwood, NJ: Ablex.

Johnson, A. G. 1997. *The Gender Knot: Unraveling Our Patriarchal Legacy.* Philadelphia: Temple University Press.

Kasian, M., and S. L. Painter. 1992. Frequency and severity of psychological abuse in a dating population. *Journal of Interpersonal Violence* 7: 350–364.

Lewin, M., and L. M. Tragos. 1987. Has the feminist movement influenced adolescent sex role attitudes? A reassessment after a quarter century. *Sex Roles* 16: 125–135.

Livingstone, S. 1994. Watching talk: Gender and engagement in the viewing of audience discussion programmes. *Meida, Culture & Society* 16: 429–447.

Marston, P. J., M. L. Hecht, and T. Roberts. 1989. "True love ways": The subjective experience and communication of romantic love. *Journal of Personal and Social Relationships* 4: 387–408.

McDonald, G. W. 1980. Family power: The assessment of a decade of theory and research, 1970–1979. *Journal of Marriage and the Family* 42: 841–854.

McKinney, K. 1987. Age and gender differences in college students' attitudes toward women: A replication and extension. *Sex Roles* 17: 353–358.

Mehta, P., and M. S. Clark. 1994. Toward understanding emotions in intimate relationships. In A. L. Weber and J. H. Harvey, eds., *Perspectives on Close Relationships.* Boston: Allyn and Bacon, 88–109.

Nelson, E. D., and B. W. Robinson. 1994. "Reality talk" or "telling tales"? The social construction of sexual and gender deviance on a television talk show. *Journal of Contemporary Ethnography* 23: 51–78.

Owens, W. F. 1987. The verbal expression of love by women and men as a critical communication event in personal relationships. *Women's Studies in Communication* 10: 15–24.

Pearson, J. 1989. *Communication in the Family. Seeking Satisfaction in Changing Times.* New York: Harper & Row.

Pipes, R. B., and K. LeBov-Keeler. 1997. Psychological abuse among college women in exclusive heterosexual dating relationships. *Sex Roles* 36: 585–602.

Ross, C., and J. Mirowsky. 1984. Men who cry. *Social Psychology Journal* 47: 138–146.

Rubin, L. 1986. *Just Friends.* New York: Harper & Row.

Rubin, Z. 1980. *Children's Friendships.* Cambridge, MA: Harvard University Press.

Sacks, R. 1990. The Dating Game: An update on the rituals of courtship. *In View* 23: 16.

Smith, P., and E. Midlarsky. 1985. Empirically derived conceptions of femaleness and maleness: A current view. *Sex Roles* 12: 313–327.

Sprecher, S. 1985. Sex differences in bases of power in dating relationships. *Sex Roles* 12: 449–461.

Sprecher, S., and K. McKinney. 1994. Sexuality in close relationships. In A. L. Weber and J. H. Harvey, eds., *Close Relationships.* Boston: Allyn and Bacon, 193–216.

Tolhuizen, J. H. 1989. Communication strategies for intensifying dating relationships: Identification, use and structure. *Journal of Personal and Social Relationships* 64: 413–434.

Umiker-Sebeok, J. 1981. The seven ages of women: A view from American magazine advertisements. In C. Mayo and N. Henley, eds., *Gender and Nonverbal Communication.* New York: Springer-Verlag, 209–252.

Whitely, B. E. 1988. The relation of gender-role orientation to sexual experience among college students. *Sex Roles* 9: 849–852.

Wilks, J. 1986. The relative importance of parents and friends in adolescent decision making. *Journal of Youth and Adolescence* 15: 323–334.

Wood, J. T. 1994. *Gendered Lives: Communication, Gender and Culture.* Belmont, CA.: Wadsworth.

Woodward, K. 1990. Young beyond their years. *Newsweek Special Issue,* Vol. CXIV, No. 27: 54–60.

Wright, D. E. 1999. *Personal Relationships: An Interdisciplinary Approach.* Mountain View, CA: Mayfield.

Youniss, J., and J. Smollar. 1985. *Adolescent Relations with Mothers, Fathers and Friends.* Chicago: University of Chicago Press.

CHAPTER 8

First Marriage Families
Gender and Communication

Kathleen Galvin
Carma Bylund

POINTS TO BE ADDRESSED

- The definition and status of first marriage families
- The influence of cultural norms and of family-of-origin experiences on gender and communication in first marriage families
- The gender-based patterns of marital and family interaction
- The changes in gender related communication patterns across family developmental stages

Near the close of many weddings, the new husband and wife approach the altar. Each picks up one of two lighted candles, they jointly light a third central candle and then, the bride and groom each blow out the two original candles—symbolically blowing themselves away. In this romantic and ritualistic way, the couple portrays to assembled family and friends that two persons have now become one. Much of the mythology surrounding marriage supports the coming together of two halves to make a whole, the merging of oneself with another. Yet the lived marriage reflects a different reality, and for many persons, male and female, the candle ritual portrays neither reality nor a desirable dream.

The marriage vows incorporate phrases that contain the cultural expectations for adult life as a partner in marriage and family life. "With this ring, I thee wed." With these six words a man and woman embark on a quest for a shared lifetime, that routinely concludes the fairy tales' "happily ever after." Some expect to reach fulfillment simply through the marital declaration of commitment and legalization of the union, believing marriage itself is the desired end. Others may be less certain about the promise of predictable and lasting contentment. Yet each couple enters the ceremony hoping or praying that their marriage will be different from others they have witnessed, that their marriage will continue "as long as we both shall live." In a recent poll 86 percent of Americans answered "yes" when asked "If you were to marry today would you expect the marriage to last a lifetime?" (*The New York Times*, 2000). For most persons, this dream also includes forming a perfect family that matches an internal, and often ideal image. For most young people, the first marriage family is seen as the realization of that dream. The term "first marriage family" suggests a system created through the unbroken union of a man and woman and including their biological and adopted children.

At a time when marital and family commitment are in a state of uncertainty, choosing to create a first marriage family may be viewed as a courageous act on the part of a young man and woman. Although there are many perspectives one could use to examine the development of such a relationship, the twin lenses of gender and communication serve to shed light on the experiences of a committed, long-term familial relationship. Gender and communication may be viewed as organizing principles of family life that influence structures, beliefs, meaning, relationships, and change (Galvin and Brommel, 1999; Goldner, 1989; Orbuch, Veroff, and Holmberg, 1993). They undergird the development, maintenance, and struggles of marital and family relationships, but may be taken for granted or ignored as crucial issues by persons in such relationships.

Although each couple intuitively understands that their marriage will be different from any other, what the bride and groom may not understand is, just as there are two variations of human development, male and female, there are two marriages for each couple, "his marriage" and "her marriage." Their realities may be quite different (Bernard, 1972; Gottman, 1994). Today's young people, those who form the greatest percentage of first marriages, come to this union with more possibilities, options, and questions than their grandparents, yet once married, their familial and cultural patterns emerge as powerful forces driving them toward the traditional and familiar.

First marriages usually take place during early adulthood. A sharp increase in age at first marriage has occurred over the last three decades from 20 for women and 23 for men in 1965 to 24 for women and 26 for men in 1988. In 1998, the median age for first marriages in the United States was 26.7 years for men and 25 years for women (Spraggins, 2000). For many young couples, the transition to a family comes quickly; approximately one-fifth of all children are conceived before marriage and many others are conceived within the first two years. Yet some couples, particularly dual-career couples, may marry later or postpone childbearing until their early to middle thirties. Although the average length of a first marriage ending in divorce is eight years, these first marriages have the potential to last a half a century or more. In contrast, a century ago a typical couple lived together for an average of thirty-one years before losing a spouse to death.

Even "first marriage" is a difficult term because what may be the first for one partner may not be for the other. In 1990, approximately 65 percent of marriages were the first, 26 percent were the second and 9 percent were the third for either the bride or the groom (Rosewicz, 1996).

Although divorce rates dropped slightly after a significant rise from 1960 to 1990, the words of the marriage ceremony "as long as we both shall live" apply only to the relatively small proportion of first marriage couples who will celebrate a fortieth or fiftieth anniversary. The family type known variously as the "nuclear," "intact," "first," or "traditional" family serves as a life stage for many couples and as a lifetime experience for a smaller number. Many individuals will create partnerships or families outside of the marital pattern; cohabitating pairs are increasing, having reached four million at the turn of the century; one child in four is born to an unmarried mother (Marano, 1997) who may or may not ever marry.

With marriage also comes "normative assumptions and legal expectations . . . unlike those in any other type of relationship" (Nock, 1998: 228). Because of these legal expectations, the role of the government in marriage has received increased attention recently. "Covenant marriage," a legally binding type of marriage that makes it more difficult to get married and to get divorced, is seen by some as a way to prepare couples for marriage and to help them keep their promises. Currently, couples in Louisiana and Arizona, when purchasing a marriage license, may select a covenant marriage. In Louisiana, a divorce may be granted to couples married under the "covenant marriage" only in cases involving adultery, abandonment, abuse, spouse imprisonment, or marital separation (Anderson, 1998), and the Arizona law is similar. Other states now offer discounts on marriage licenses for engaged couples who take marital education classes or have premarital counseling.

The concepts of gender and communication in first marriage families are important because: (1) the marriage incorporates the gender beliefs and communication patterns of each spouse's sociocultural traditions and family-of-origin, (2) the spouse's interaction patterns reflect significant male–female differences that affect both the marital and the parent–child relationships, and (3) the marital experience of gender and communication patterns will vary across family developmental stages, impacted by culture and peer groups.

Marital Culture

"I take you to be my lawfully wedded wife/husband." Throughout the ages the wedding ceremony has served to initiate a man or woman into a new self-identification, husband or wife. Yet over the past decades, family life experience for males and females has been transformed. Even within the flux of shifting gender roles and expectations, the weight of social and individual history presents itself in conscious and unconscious ways. Couples in every culture make some sort of metaphysical bargain at the onset of their relationship, determining not only whether they will marry, but also setting the rules for the relationship (Walsh, 1989). These rules are constructed within an overall cultural frame that reflects tradition and at the same time reflects the specific life experiences or particular family-of-origin experiences of the individuals involved.

Gender roles reflect centuries of consistent and predictable distinctions between, and expectations for, men and women. These traditional distinctions are captured in the prescriptive characteristics contained in Figure 8.1 (Feldman, 1982: 355).

The Female Role	The Male Role
Women are expected to be (or allowed to be) the following:	*Men are expected to be (or allowed to be) the following:*
1. Home oriented, child(ren) oriented.	1. Ambitious, competitive, enterprising, worldly.
2. Warm, affectionate, gentle, tender.	2. Calm, stable, unemotional, realistic, logical.
3. Aware of feelings to others, considerate, tactful, compassionate.	3. Strong, tough, powerful.
4. Moody, high-strung, temperamental, excitable, emotional, subjective, illogical.	4. Aggressive, forceful, decisive, dominant.
5. Complaining, nagging.	5. Independent, self-reliant.
6. Weak, helpless, fragile, easily emotionally hurt.	6. Harsh, severe, stern, cruel.
7. Submissive, yielding, dependent.	7. Autocratic, rigid, arrogant.

Figure 8.1 Psychological Dimensions of the Female and Male Roles: Traditional Distinctions

Traditional gender roles prepared husbands to distance themselves in the world of work and to function in a rational, judgmental manner; to suppress feelings; convey a sense of control; and maintain close ties in the outside world. They prepared wives to take care of the home, children, and emotional concerns; to function in a dependent and sensitive manner; to suppress independence and to maintain close ties to family and community. These patterns were tied to common assumptions, such as the male being the "head" of the family household, the female being the one to maintain the household, and the family being more important to the woman while work is more important to the man. The roles of husband and wife carried specified utilitarian functions; neither expected the other to meet extensive emotional needs or to serve as a best friend. Historically, male and female marital communication occurred within strongly segregated and highly predictable patterns. However, with today's expectation of companionate marriages much is expected of the other. Today careful distinctions are made between gender expectations assigned to masculinity and femininity. The reality is that gender role socialization pertains to the process by which women and men learn what roles are appropriate to their sex. Although the gender role of a feminine person has been identified as nurturing, flexible, and child loving and that of a masculine person includes independence, aggressiveness, and mechanical skill, not all masculine individuals are male and not all feminine individuals are female (Pearson, West, and Turner, 1995).

Unique multigenerational family patterns combine with the sociocultural forces to influence new families. Multigenerational systems contain patterns that are shared and eventually recreated in younger members; they affect new families because the husband's and wife's heritages reflect those family-of-origin influences (Hoopes, 1987). Families of origin provide blueprints for the communication of future generations as attitudes and rule-bound behaviors are transmitted to a newly forming system. Each spouse arrives with beliefs about what it means to be female or male and what it means to be a wife/mother or husband/father. Issues of dominance, decision making, intimacy, emotional responsiveness, and conflict styles are bound to historical family gender patterns. A woman who comes from a family line of strong females, with a family theme "A woman must be able to support herself," will move to create a different marriage than a woman who witnessed generations of dependent females. These familial patterns also reflect ethnic heritages that may embody strong gender beliefs (McGoldrick, Giordano, and Pearce, 1996).

These historical patterns counterbalance current forces seeking to release males and females from highly gender-bound structures. Contemporary young couples are attempting to work out nontraditional gender arrangements, but find themselves struggling to create relationships for which there may be few lifetime models. "Even as women are rebelling against having responsibility for making family relationships, holidays and celebrations, they typically feel guilty for not continuing to do what they are expected to do" (McGoldrick, 1989b: 200). These nontraditional marital relationships tend to be less prescriptive, less role bound, less predictable, and characterized by high levels of problem solving and negotiation. Males and females are attempting to create emotional and functional partnerships quite different from those their parents or grandparents experienced.

Dual-career families represent attempts to create a gender-flexible lifestyle. These collaborative marriages move beyond traditional gender expectations but still struggle with the issues of dominance and dialectical issues of autonomy and connection, especially when parenting is involved. Such marriages have to be renegotiated every time there is a move or major change; even daily crises require discussion and negotiation. Traditional gender patterns seldom serve as predictable guides for behavior.

MARITAL/FAMILY INTERACTION PATTERNS

". . . in good times and in bad . . . to have and to hold." Promises of presence and support undergird most marriage vows, although their actual meaning is determined by each couple. Contemporary couples expect to create a companionate marriage, a union with emotional connectedness at its core. Spouses are expected to be best friends or emotional partners as well as to serve instrumental or pragmatic roles. Expectations for a companionate marriage place extensive focus on communication, particularly nurturing or interaction. This emphasis on emotional substance in marriage appears to be related to enhanced well-being for both women and men but is especially important for women (Williams, 1988). Yet this expectation can place high pressure on men because their friendship history may not include this dimension. Women are more likely to have a greater history of emotionally based same-sex friendships, and may have different definitions for "best friend." The communication and gender related assumptions underlying such first marriages are (1) the couple serves as the architect of the system, (2) marital communication, the core of the family system, incorporates gender-based interaction patterns.

It appears there is a gendered approach to maintenance communication behaviors in marriages. Women talk more about and focus on relationship issues more often than men (Acitelli, 1992) and they are more aware of such issues (Ragsdale, 1996). In their study of couples Weigel and Ballard-Reisch (1999: 267) found "Wives appear to be more positive, to remain open, to reaffirm the importance of the relationship, to do things together and to perform agreed upon tasks when they and their husbands feel more positively about their marriages." In contrast husbands' use of maintenance behaviors do not appear to be influenced by these feelings or perceptions of marital quality.

Researchers have found the pattern of female demand/husband withdraw to happen more frequently than husband demand/wife withdraw. Some have attributed this difference to women desiring more change in their husbands than husbands desiring change in their wives. However, Caughlin and Vangelisti (1999) found that husbands and wives did not differ on their desire for change in the other, even though female demand/husband withdraw was more frequent.

Wives are more likely to use a range of affective responses than are husbands. Studies of marital interaction during the discussion of relationship problems tend to underscore sex differences, with wives being more likely to express their negative feelings directly and to be more emotional. In general, wives appear to show a great range of affection while males demonstrate a lack of behavioral responses and expressivity (Noller and Fitzpatrick, 1990). Women tend to express a broader range of emotion in marriage with more tenderness, fear, and sadness. Many men tend to limit themselves to control anger, a reflection of sociocultural and family-of-origin patterns that discourage softer emotions. Overall, women tend to be more expressive and affectionate than men in marriages (Thompson and Walker, 1989). Gender differences in conflict style may have roots in socialization patterns and physiological responses to stress (Gottman, 1994).

Males and females may differ in the ways they use or value relational currencies, in their ways of sharing affection. For example, although during courtship men are willing to spend intimate time with women, after marriage they tend to spend less and less time talking to their wives, often considering doing chores around the house to be an adequate demonstration of caring and intimacy. Husbands feel mystified about what women want when they seek more contact in the marital relationship (McGoldrick, 1989b).

Many modern couples engage in debriefing conversations defined by Vangelisti and Banski as "the conversations that couples engage in to inform one another about the events, thoughts, and emotions they experienced during the day when they were separated" (1993: 149). These researchers found women felt their husbands spent significantly more time talking about their day than men thought women did. Women reported they talk more than men did, but each thought the other talked for longer periods of time.

Self-disclosure is a primary communication relational currency used to deepen and strengthen interpersonal relationships. Historically, spouses disclose more to each other than to anyone else, yet wives tend to disclose more than husbands. Earlier studies suggested younger, more educated couples may be moving toward a pattern of more equal and intimate disclosure by both sexes as disclosure is higher among men and women with egalitarian sex role attitudes (Peplau and Gordon, 1985).

The nature of the message affects marital self-disclosure. For example, face honoring, face compensating, and face neutral emotions are disclosed more frequently and preferred more than face threatening disclosure. In other words, messages that are positive, supportive, or neutral are seen as more desirable than messages that threaten the other's identity. Overall, husbands and wives do not differ in their actual disclosure of emotions, but wives reported that they disclosed more emotions and that they value the disclosure of emotions more than husbands (Shimanoff, 1985). Recent reviews of the self-disclosure literature suggest that verbal emotional disclosure is a more feminine style of relating, whereas a more masculine style may value joint activities (Wood and Inman, 1993), and there is an inherent bias that self-disclosure is good (Dindia, 2000).

The conflict styles men and women bring into marriage frequently differ. Gottman (1994) reports common patterns in how the sexes interact in marriage. He suggests women are generally more comfortable in intimate relationships and "in marital relationships, women tend to be the emotional managers" (138) whereas men are more reluctant to delve into emotional issues. He attributes this in part to socialization as well as to physiological differences in managing emotional conflict.

The quality of marital communication affects marital satisfaction. Williams (1988) suggests the beneficial effects of marriage are tied to the quality of dyadic communication between spouses: "It appears that it is the affective quality of the marital relationship rather than the marriage per se that is more important for the well-being of individuals" (465). More recent work reports that husbands' tendency to disclose and express themselves affects both husbands and wives relational satisfaction more than wives' ability to be open (Vangelisti and Banski, 1993). About one-third of wives find it easy to raise issues of change with their husbands. These wives and their husbands report higher levels of marital satisfaction (McQuillan and Ferree, 1998). In addition, there appears to be a relationship between marital satisfaction and the husband's ability to read nonverbal messages. In a study of married couples reading nonverbal clues, results indicated a positive relationship between marital satisfaction and nonverbal competence but only for husbands reading their wives' nonverbal cues. In comparison to male strangers, the husbands of satisfied wives were more able to read their wives' nonverbal cues, while the husbands of dissatisfied wives were less able to read them (Gottman and Porterfield, 1981). Fitzpatrick and Badzinski (1985) suggest a strong correlation between marital satisfaction and self-reports of communication in marriage; that is, the happily married believe they have good communication with their spouses. Finally Vangelisti and Banski's study of couples' debriefing conversation led them to conclude: "the amount of time that individuals reported talking with their spouses about the events in their day was positively and significantly associated with relational satisfaction" (1993: 153).

Marital satisfaction is also related to the types of attributions husbands and wives make about each other's behavior. When compared to couples with higher marital satisfaction, couples who report lower marital satisfaction tend to make attributions about the other's behavior that decrease the impact of positive events (i.e., "He only brought me flowers because he feels guilty about something.") and increase the impact of negative events (i.e., "She was late getting home because she knows that makes me mad.") (Bradbury and Fincham, 1990). These authors also report that there is evidence to suggest that there is not only a correlation between types of attributions and marital satisfaction, but that types of attributions have a causal effect on judgments of marital satisfaction.

Yet generalizations can be misleading, because each marriage is different. Work on marital typologies reveals similarities among groups or types of marriages and families. For example, Fitzpatrick's work (1988, 1997) on classifying couple types identifies three major types—independents, separates, and traditionals—plus mixed types. Independents accept uncertainty and change, do considerable sharing, and negotiate autonomy. They do not avoid conflict, they value independence, and they are more likely to support androgynous and flexible sex roles. Separates differ from independents in greater conflict avoidance, more differentiated space needs, fairly regular schedules, and less sharing. In relationships, they experience little sense of togetherness or autonomy. Separates usually oppose an androgynous sexual orientation. Traditionals uphold a fairly conventional belief system and resist change or uncertainty because it threatens their routines. Their high level of sharing leads to a high degree of interdependence and low autonomy. Traditionals will engage in conflict but would rather avoid it. Uncertainty and change in values upset them. Traditionals demonstrate strong sex-typed roles.

Though this chapter is primarily centered on functional marriages, it is important to recognize that there are highly dysfunctional marriages, some of which are violent in nature. Some research suggests that men and women participate equally in marital violence (Barnett, Miller-Perrin, and Perrin, 1997). Difficulties in accurately measuring marital violence contribute to this confusion. Although causes for domestic violence are considered to be somewhat elusive, certain risk factors for domestic abuse have been established (Miller and Knudsen, 1999). An extensive study of aggression in early marriage suggests that for men, violence in the family-of-origin, and that for women, violent actions against others, serve as predictors of later marital aggression (O'Leary, Malone, and Tyree, 1994).

Developmental Stages

"From this day forward as long as we both shall live . . ." This short phrase may describe a marriage of six months or sixty years. A developmental approach recognizes that marriage and family life are not static realities; each life stage may appear different. In arguing for a life course perspective for understanding marriage, Cooney and Hogan (1991) suggest the patterning of the individual's life course is influenced largely by the interplay of changing historical conditions, social structures, and individual biological and psychological development. Therefore the marital experience must be understood within this context as the experience of a marriage changes across time.

The developmental perspective is particularly effective for recognizing cultural shifts of the past two or three decades. Most persons who married twenty or thirty years ago set out to create a marriage and family that reflected strong gender role differences; contemporary young couples enter marriage with multiple options and different expectations.

Most models of family stages apply to the middle-class, intact American family life cycle. Historically, experiences such as untimely death or divorce placed those families outside the normal developmental patterns. Contemporary family theorists are beginning to call these "temporary interruptions," thus considering divorce as one normal stage for some persons and suggesting a "Y," or "fork in the road" model of development (Ahrons and Rodgers, 1987; Aldous, 1990).

Traditionally, the first or intact family developmental model includes the following life cycle stages: forming the couple, birth of the first child, family with young children, family with adolescents, launching children, couple in later life, and death of one spouse. This model presumes the couple will become parents. Although some couples will not parent, this group remains a small minority. Communication within intact family systems changes across the individual life span and family life cycle. Researchers hypothesize that explicit verbal communication decreases, and implicit forms of communication increase over the marital life span (Sillars and Wilmot, 1989). In general, marital satisfaction appears to decline with the birth of the first child and increase after children leave home (Orbuch et al., 1996). The following overview of stages highlights some of the gender and communication issues.

Forming the Couple

This is a time of romance that eventually moves into reality. In the previous chapter, Arliss described many of the romantic "happily-ever-after," notions likely to characterize views of first marriages. These views may be fed or fostered by media portrayals or fairy tale promises, yet they are characterized by male–female inequities even in terms of premarital interaction. In many marriage ceremonies the woman is "given away" by her father to another man; she wears a ring to symbolize the new affiliation, he may not. She may have attended showers while he attended stag parties, both of which reinforce traditional gender roles (Imber-Black, 1989). Newlywed couples frequently make allowances for behavior that isn't quite acceptable because spouses focus on what they are getting, and differences seem enhancing. Later, differences become annoying and call out for resolution (Lederer and Lewis, 1991).

These early stages of courtship and marriage involve the couple's attempt to create a relational culture, establish rules for communication, and find ways to deepen communication. The initial stage of first marriage is characterized by close monitoring of the relationship and more frequent and intense communication about the relationship than at any other stage (Sillars and Wilmot, 1989). Couples may negotiate such issues as the place of old friends, attachment to families-of-origin, time spent together or apart, closeness, and conflict. Couples may manage the autonomy/connection tensions by relying on tradeoffs (Hause and Pearson, 1994). This is a time for investing in a relationship, engaging in high self-disclosure, communicating about sexual life, developing negotiation and conflict styles, and planning for future years. Young couples must resolve such issues as the initial integration of separate personalities and subsequent transformation from couple to family particularly dealing with gender role expectations and reality.

Families with Young Children

The arrival of the first child irrevocably changes the couple's life. The pair becomes a threesome, with all the change in communication patterns such a shift implies. Pregnancy occurs relatively close to the wedding for most couples; although some couples, particularly dual-career couples, may marry later or postpone childbearing and have a baby in their early to middle thirties. No matter what the age, taking on a role of "father" or "mother" is a major life transition, with strong gender and communication implications (Stamp, 1994). Three factors influence couples during the transition to parenthood: their views on parental responsibilities and restrictions, the gratification childrearing holds for them as a couple, and their own marital intimacy and stability. Views on parenthood reflect sociocultural backgrounds. For example, middle-class mothers differ from lower-class mothers in their response to the stress of motherhood both during pregnancy and in the years following.

Once men and women become parents they tend to do different things with and for their children, with mothers becoming more involved because "our culture still leaves women with primary responsibility for childrearing and blames them when something goes wrong" (McGoldrick, 1989b: 200). Mothers appear to give more care, attention, response, and nonverbal comfort than fathers. They are more likely to spend long periods of time alone with a child. Yet fathers who are actively engaged in child care may be as competent as mothers in providing attention, stimulation, and care. Contributions of fathers to their children's lives are multiple. Amato (1998) reports fathers' education and income to be positively associated with children's well-being. The quality of the father–child relationship has also been shown to be positively associated with children's well-being. Couples who share traditional gender role attitudes find the transition to parenthood less stressful (Huston and Vangelisti, 1995).

In studying couples from marriage through the birth of their first child, Gottman found that some couples are able to make the transition to parenthood easily and not suffer the decline of marital satisfaction that is widely reported. Such couples have the following characteristics: (1) the husband spontaneously cxpresses fondness and admiration of his wife; (2) the husband's use of language indicates solidarity and inclusiveness, such as "we" and "us"; and (3) they establish "cognitive room"—both husbands and wives allow for time to talk about details of the history of their relationship and each other's "everyday" world (Gottman, 1998).

The birth of a first child appears to have a traditionalizing effect on the marriage. "There is likely to be some movement away from the degree of explicit communication and negotiation required by role sharing and greater implicit adjustment based on role delegation" (Sillars and Wilmot, 1989: 234). The major research on the transition to parenthood indicates that it is accompanied by a general decrease in marital satisfaction and a reversion to more traditional sex roles, even by dual-career couples. Very few couples share household and children responsibilities equally (White, 1999). Dual-career or dual-job couples face the greatest challenge, because they have few predictable roles and rules to guide them; constant renegotiation becomes a challenge.

Within this stage, the couple must deal with the following communication related issues: (1) renegotiating the roles of husband and wife and assuming roles of mother and father, (2) transmitting culture and establishing a community of experiences, and (3) developing the child's communication competence. Such tasks are inevitably bound up with gender socialization of children.

The growth of the first child and births of subsequent children add complexity, if not chaos, to the couple's interactions. Time together seems to disappear, and talk tends to focus on pragmatic child-centered concerns, including the gender socialization of the children. Given the increasing practical demands it is no wonder marital satisfaction has declined. These couples tend to manage their dialectical stresses through topic selection and tradeoffs (Hause and Pearson, 1994).

Adolescents frequently add stress to the family system. Historically, this is a period when many young women struggle with self-identity and choose intimacy with a male as a way to find self-definition. Conventional gender values appear to be at an all-time high during adolescence (McGoldrick, 1989b). The predictable teenage struggles with individuation, particularly in areas of sexuality, identity, and autonomy, may coincide with parental mid-life issues. Opposite sex parents and children may find a gulf between them as a response to the power of the "incest taboo." Parental conflict with teenagers may provoke husband–wife conflicts, although the adolescent's daily schedule may provide more time for spouse interaction. Depending on the parental generation, the life choices that are identified by their children may appear rewarding or may be viewed as a rejection of traditional gender values.

Midlife Couples

Smaller families and greater life expectancy have given couples a more extensive midlife period. During this stable period, implicit role expectations should increasingly substitute for explicit communication, and couples may experience a blurring of personalities due to long-term interdependence (Sillars and Wilmot, 1989). There is a tendency for men and women to go in opposite directions psychologically as their children move out into their own lives. Men may seek the closeness they missed during the career-building years, and women, usually done with childrearing by their early 50s, may feel more energized about developing their own lives (McGoldrick, 1989b). They may become more assertive and focused on career development or individual fulfillment. Different generations may experience this quite differently; for example, women who are younger when their children move out of the house may not have been gone from the workforce for long. Thus, the transition from childrearing to rejoining the ranks of employment may not be as difficult for them as it would for older women who have been away from the workforce for a long time. Equity in the tasks of cooking, homemaking, and providing economic support increases across the stages, with the greatest growth in the launching stage and middle years after the children leave home. The children, while requiring minimal attention, are still a source of conflict. Levenson, Cartsenson, and Gottman (1995) found that conflict topic rankings, in order of importance, are: children, money, communication, recreation, and sex.

This period often involves grandparenthood, a role less complicated if the parenting couple has stayed together. In her review of related research, Downs (1989) reports women indicated higher satisfaction with the grandparent role and were better socialized for the role than men. Both males and females report similar perceptions about their responsibilities for discipline or helping out with grandchildren. Some gender-related communication patterns develop at this stage. Whereas grandmothers tend to discuss subjects of emotional or relational content with their grandchildren, grandfathers often communicate in terms of practical aspects and relate more to grandsons (Hagestad, 1988).

By this point the couple that has remained together expects contact with children and grandchildren, but usually not primary responsibility for their lives. Older couples with no children in the home are happier than those with children (Pittman and Lloyd, 1988). Living independently from children and grandchildren allows time and energy for redefinition and reinvigoration of the original couple relationship. Sometimes this is publicly celebrated in a renewal of vows. A study of persons married an average of 29 years suggests married couples appear to "use the renewal event to weave together their past, their present, and their future commitments to one another" (Braithwaite and Baxter, 1995: 193).

Older Couples

Couples who remain together and enter into the later life stages typically exhibit a commitment to the relationship, interdependence, and reasonably high marital satisfaction. Their self-disclosure tends to decline, or such communication becomes more implicit. This period often coincides with retirement, historically of the male, but increasingly of both partners. These couples may face issues of transition adjustment but most manage well. According to Zietlow and Sillars (1988), retired couples appear less analytic and more noncommittal and they exhibit a remarkable passive and congenial style. A comparison of later life and middle-aged couples found the former revealed less potential for conflict and greater potential for pleasure (Levenson, Cartsenson, and Gottman, 1993). A few exceptions of conflict-habituated retired couples do exist, and this pattern appears to continue. Sources and topics of conflict tend to be different at this point than they were during earlier stages of marriage, with salient topics, in order of importance, being communication, recreation, money, children, and sex. Communication issues may reflect a more intense togetherness (Dickson, 1997).

Retirement appears to be a period of more flexible male and female roles. Men appear to become more reflective, dependent, and affiliative, and females become more assertive. Retired men and women see themselves as having less normative pressures to fit either masculine or feminine molds subsequent to parenting and retirement, so the sexes may become more similar and androgynous (Sillars and Wilmot, 1989).

These changes tend to bring about increased sharing and companionship. Satisfaction with an intimate relationship is related to life satisfaction and psychological well-being, especially for elderly women (Thompson and Nussbaum, 1988). At 35–44 years of marriage, levels of marital satisfaction are higher than they were even in the first four years of marriage (Orbuch et al., 1996). Decline in work and parental responsibilities explain a large portion of the increase in marital satisfaction in this period (Orbuch et al., 1996). For couples in good health, this stage may truly be the "golden years of communication."

Death of One Spouse

At some point the couple faces the reality of the words "as long as we both shall live." Women are more likely to outlive their husbands. In cases where a woman dies first, the widower is at especially high risk of death and suicide for a year because of the loss, loneliness, and lack of caretaking (McGoldrick, 1991). Widowers and widows are faced with acknowledging the loss and openly grieving, learning to function physically and emotionally alone, and creating connections of interest and to a larger social network. The need for supportive communication especially from children and extended family is critical.

Conclusion

Life in first marriage families represents a long-term commitment to a life that involves the negotiation of gender issues and the development of communication patterns that create meaning in members' lives. The first marriage trajectory includes tough times and greater thoughts of divorce in the 15–19 years, but after 20–24 years such thoughts decrease and marital satisfaction increases (Orbuch et al., 1996). When considering the candle-lighting ceremony of the marital ritual, the lasting importance of the two original candles should be clear. According to Carter and McGoldrick (1988), "Marriage tends to be misunderstood as a joining of two individuals. What it really represents is the changing of two entire systems and an overlapping to develop a third subsystem" (15). Perhaps the candle lighting ceremony, described in the beginning of this chapter, would come closer to the truth if three lighted candles were left on the altar, one for the man, one for the woman, and one for the marriage and family created by their union.

For Further Discussion

1. Analyze a fictional or actual marriage in order to identify the marital culture, or what makes this couple a "country of two." Talk in terms of verbal and nonverbal patterns unique to this relationship and the way they play out gender roles.
2. Describe the messages you received from your family-of-origin about the ways males and females should relate to each other in a romantic partnership and explain to what extent these messages are congruent with your current beliefs or practices. If you have been in a serious romantic relationship or marriage, identify two or three gender patterns that evolved within that relationship.
3. Respond to the statement: "Though traditionally described as less assertive in the world at large, in marital relationships women tend to be the emotional managers. They are usually better attuned than men

to the changing emotional climate in their relationship and more willing to confront problems" (Gottman, 1994: 138). In the response state and defend your points of agreement or disagreement with Gottman.

REFERENCES

Acitelli, L. K. 1992. Gender differences in relationship awareness and marital satisfaction among young married couples. *Personality and Social Psychology* 18: 102–110.

Ahrons, O., and R. Rodgers. 1987. *Divorced Families.* New York: Norton.

Aldous, J. 1990. Family development and the life course: Two perspectives on family change. *Journal of Marriage and the Family* 52: 571–583.

Amato, P. R. 1998. More than money? Men's contributions to their children's lives. In A. Booth and A. C. Crouter, eds., *Men in Families: When Do They Get Involved? What Difference Does It Make?* Mahwah, NJ: Lawrence Erlbaum, 241–278.

Anderson, E. 17 August 1998. Covenant marriage: Some do, more don't; It'll catch on, big backer says. *The Times Picayune,* A1.

Barnett, O. W., C. L Miller-Perrin, and R. D. Perrin. 1997. *Family Violence across the Lifespan.* Thousand Oaks, CA: Sage.

Bernard, J. 1972. *The Future of Marriage.* New York: Guilford Press.

Bradbury, T. N., and F. D. Fincham. 1990. Attributions in marriage: Review and Critique. *Psychological Bulletin* 107(1): 3–33.

Braithwaite, D. O., and L. A. Baxter. 1995. "I do" again: The relational dialectics of renewing marriage vows. *Journal of Social and Personal Relationships* 12: 177–198.

Carter, B., and M. McGoldrick. 1988. Overview: The changing family life cycle—A framework for family therapy. In B. Carter and M. McGoldrick, eds., *The Changing Family Life Cycle,* 2nd ed. Boston: Allyn and Bacon, 3–30.

Caughlin, J. P., and A. L. Vangelisti. 1999. Desire for change in one's partner as a predictor of the demand/withdraw pattern of marital communication. *Communication Monographs* 66(1): 66–89.

Cooney, T., and D. Hogan. 1991. Marriage in an institutionalized life course: First marriage among American men in the twentieth century. *Journal of Marriage and the Family* 53: 178–190.

Dickson, F. C. 1997. Aging and marriage: Understanding the long-term, later-life marriage. In W. K. Halford and H. J. Markman, eds., *Clinical Handbook of Marriage and Couples Intervention.* New York: John Wiley and Sons, 255–266.

Dindia, K. 2000. Sex differences in self-disclosure, reciprocity in self-disclosure, and self-disclosure and liking: Three meta-analyses reviewed. In S. Petronio, ed., *Balancing the Secrets of Private Disclosures.* Mahwah, NJ: Lawrence Erlbaum.

Downs, V. C. 1989. The grandparent-grandchild relationship. In J. Nussbaum, ed., *Life-span Communication: Normative Processes.* Hillsdale, NJ: Laurence Erlbaum, 257–281.

Feldman, L. 1982. Sex roles and family dynamics. In F. Walsh, ed., *Normal Family Processes.* New York: Guilford Press, 345–382.

Fitzpatrick, M. A. 1988. *Between Husbands and Wives.* Beverly Hills, CA: Sage.

———. 1997. Interview in Family Communication Teleclass Available from PBS Adult Learning Satellite Service, 1320 Braddock Place, Alexandria, VA.

Fitzpatrick, M. A., and D. M. Badzinski. 1985. All in the family: Interpersonal communication in kin relationships. In M. L. Knapp and G. R. Miller, eds., *Handbook of Interpersonal Communication*. Beverly Hills, CA: Sage, 687–736.

Galvin, K., and B. Brommel. 1999. *Family Communication: Cohesion and Change*, 5th ed. New York: HarperCollins.

Goldner, V. 1989. Generation and gender: Normative and covert hierarchies. In M. McGoldrick, C. Anderson, and F. Walsh, eds., *Women in Families*. New York: W. W. Norton, 42–60.

Gottman, J. 1994. *Why Marriages Succeed or Fail*. New York: Simon and Schuster.

———. 1998. Toward a process model of men in marriages and families. In A. Booth and A. C. Crouter, eds., *Men in Families: When Do They Get Involved? What Difference Does It Make?* Mahwah, NJ: Lawrence Erlbaum, 149–192.

Gottman, J., and A. Porterfield. 1981. Communicative competence in the nonverbal behavior of married couples. *Journal of Marriage and the Family* 43: 817–824.

Hagestad, G. O. 1988. Demographic change and the life course: Some emerging trends in the family realm. *Family Relations* 37, 405–410.

Hause, K., and J. Pearson. 1994, November. The ebb and flow of marriage: Relational dialectics over the family life cycle. Paper presented at the meeting of the Speech Communication Association, New Orleans, LA.

Hoopes, M. 1987. Multigenerational systems: Basic assumptions. *American Journal of Family Therapy* 15: 195–205.

Huston, T., and A. Vangelisti. 1995. How parenthood affects marriage. In M. A. Fitzpatrick and A. L. Vangelisti, eds., *Explaining Family Interactions*. Thousand Oaks, CA: Sage, 147–176.

Imber-Black, E. 1989. Rituals of stabilization and change in women's lives. In M. McGoldrick, C. Anderson, and F. Walsh, eds., *Women in Families*. New York: W. W. Norton, 451–470.

Lederer, G., and T. Lewis. 1991. The transition to couplehood. In F. H. Brown, ed., *Reweaving the Family Tapestry*. New York: W. W. Norton, 94–113.

Levenson, R., L. Cartsenson, and J. Gottman. 1993. Long marriages: Age, gender, and satisfaction. *Psychology and Aging* 8: 301–313.

Marano, H. E. 1997, September/October. Another round, honey? *Psychology Today* 20.

McGoldrick, M. 1989. Women through family life cycle. In M. McGoldrick, C. Anderson, and F. Walsh, eds., *Women in Families*. New York: Norton, 200–226.

———. 1991. A time to mourn: Death and the family life cycle. In F. Walsh and M. McGoldrick, eds., *Living Beyond Loss*. New York: W. W. Norton.

McGoldrick, M., J. Giordano, and J. Pearce. 1996. *Ethnicity and Family Therapy*. New York: Guilford Press.

McQuillan, J., and M. M. Ferree. 1998. The importance of variation among men and the benefits of feminism for families. In A. Booth and A. C. Crouter, eds., *Men in Families: When Do They Get Involved? What Difference Does It Make?* Mahwah, NJ: Lawrence Erlbaum, 213–225.

Miller, J. L., and D. D. Knudsen. 1999. Family abuse and violence. In M. Sussman, S. K. Steinmetz, and G. W. Peterson, eds., *Handbook of Marriage and the Family*, 2nd ed. New York: Plenum Press, 705–741.

The New York Times. 7 May 2000. The way we live now poll. *New York Times Magazine*.

Nock, S. L. 1998. Marriages in men's lives. In A. Booth and A. C. Crouter, eds., *Men in Families: When Do They Get Involved? What Difference Does It Make?* Mahwah, NJ: Lawrence Erlbaum, 227–237.

Noller, P., and M. A. Fitzpatrick. 1990. Marital communication in the eighties. *Journal of Marriage and the Family* 52: 822–843.

O'Leary, K. D., J. Malone, and A. Tyree. 1994. Physical aggression in early marriage: Prerelationship and relationship effects. *Journal of Consulting and Clinical Psychology* 62: 594–602.

Orbuch, T., J. House, R. Mero, and P. Webster. 1996. Marital quality over the life course. *Social Psychology Quarterly* 59: 162–171.

Orbuch, T., J. Veroff, and D. Holmberg. 1993. Becoming a married couple: The emergence of meaning in the first year of marriage. *Journal of Marriage and the Family* 55: 815–826

Pearson, J. 1989. *Communication in the Family.* New York: HarperCollins.

Pearson, J., R. West, and L. Turner. 1995. *Gender and Communication*. Madison, WI: Brown and Benchmark.

Peplau, L., and S. Gordon. 1985. Men and women in love: Gender differences in close heterosexual relationships. In R. O'Leary, R. Unger, and B. Washington, eds., *Women, Gender and Social Psychology.* Hillsdale, NJ: Lawrence Erlbaum, 257–291.

Pittman, J., and S. Lloyd. 1988. Quality of family life, social support, and stress. *Journal of Marriage and the Family* 50: 53–67.

Ragsdale, J. D. 1996. Gender, satisfaction level, and the use of maintenance strategies in marriage. *Communication Monographs* 6: 354–369.

Rosewicz, B. 1 September 1996. Here comes the bride . . . and for the umpteenth time. *Wall Street Journal*, B1, B10.

Shimanoff, S. 1985. Rules governing the verbal expression of emotions between married couples. *The Western Journal of Speech Communication* 49: 147–165.

Sillars, A., and W. Wilmot. 1989. Marital communication across the life span. In J. Nussbaum, ed., *Life-span Communication*. Hillsdale, NJ: Lawrence Erlbaum, 119–135.

Spraggins, R. E. 2000. U.S. Census Bureau census brief: Women in the United States: A profile. *Current Population Reports.* Washington, DC: Department of Commerce.

Stamp, G. 1994. The appropriation of the parent role through communication during the transition to parenthood. *Communication Monographs* 61: 2, 80–112.

Thompson, L., and H. Walker. 1989. Gender in families: Women and men in marriage, work, and parenthood. *Journal of Marriage and the Family* 51: 845–871.

Thompson, T., and J. Nussbaum. 1988. Interpersonal communications: Intimate relationships and aging. In C. W. Carmichael, C. H. Botan, and R. Hawkins, eds., *Human Communication and the Aging Process.* Prospect Heights, IL: Waveland Press, 95–110.

Vangelisti, A. L., and M. A. Banski. 1993. Couples debriefing conversation: The impact of gender, occupation, and demographic characteristics. *Family Relations* 42: 149–157.

Walsh, F. 1989. Reconsidering gender in the marital quid pro quo. In M. McGoldrick, C. Anderson, and F. Walsh, eds., *Women in Families.* New York: Norton, 267–285.

Weigel, D. J., and D. S. Ballard-Reisch. 1999. How couples maintain marriage: A closer look at self and spouse influences upon the use of maintenance behaviors in marriages. *Family Relations* 48: 263–270.

White, J. M. 1999. Work-family stage and satisfaction with work-family balance. *Journal of Comparative Studies* 30: 163.

Williams, D. G. 1988. Gender, marriage, and psychosocial well-being. *Journal of Family Issues* 9: 452–468.

Wood, J. T., and C. C. Inman. 1993. In a different mode: Masculine styles of communicating closeness. *Journal of Applied Communication Research* 21: 279–295.

Zietlow, P. H., and A. L. Sillars. 1988. Lifestage differences in communication during marital conflicts. *Journal of Social and Personal Relationships* 5: 233–245.

CHAPTER 9

Communication in the Stepfamily
Transitions Bring Challenges

Joyce Hauser

POINTS TO BE ADDRESSED

- Ending the traditional nuclear family: The divorce
- Reorganizing after divorce
- The remarried dyad
- Children in the new blended family
- Gender issues and stepparents

Noah's Ark has definitely sprung a leak! We are no longer a "two-by-two" society which is clearly reflected by the statistics on divorce over the past ten years (Hauser, 1988). In the United States today there is an emerging American family, interwoven and complicated—two families, usually created by divorce, mingled and connected with new stepsisters or stepbrothers, grandparents, aunts, uncles, and either one or two new stepparents (Glick, 1989, cited in Galvin and Cooper, 1990). This so-called "blended family" is no longer an anomaly in American society: It's a norm.

The family as a significant, evolving, and complex institutional structure has been studied extensively by many in a wide range of disciplines; however, the remarried family as a specific variant of the nuclear family has until recently received only occasional and limited investigation. One reason is the complexity and the uniqueness of the stepfamily. Questions about issues such as blending different lifestyles, defining the steprole, forming new attachments while maintaining ties with the old, and achieving a new remarried family identity, must be addressed to gain understanding of the stepfamily.

The End of One Stage: The Divorce

Weiss (1975) believes that a person goes through two distinct phases during divorce: transition and recovery. The transition period begins with separation and is characterized by separation distress and then loneliness. In its later stages, most people begin functioning in an orderly way again, although they still may experience periods of upset and turmoil. The transition period generally ends within the first year of a divorce. At this time, individuals have already begun making decisions that provide the framework for new selves. They have entered the role of single parent or absent parent, have found a new place to live, have made important career and financial decisions, and often have begun to date. Their lives are taking shape.

Contrary to most beliefs, divorce does not end the relationship between spouses, especially if there are children involved. It transforms it into a new, complex and often ambiguous relationship. As part of the Divorce Mediation Research Project (1984), Pearson and Thoennes interviewed divorcing and/or divorced parents. They found that most families were facing an array of problems, including physical relocation of one or both parents, financial stresses, and uncertainties about the future.

Even with the changing roles of men and women, with more women in the workplace, life still remains difficult for women after divorce. Professor Weitzman (1985) of Harvard University found that, on average, women with minor children experience a 73 percent decline in the standard of living during the first year after divorce whereas their husbands experience a 42 percent increase in their standard of living. Weitzman (cited in Wallerstein and Blakeslee, 1990) predicted a two-tier society with women and children as an underclass.

The record for men paying court-mandated child support is dismal, regardless of socioeconomic class. Wallerstein and Blakeslee (1990) reported that some men arbitrarily cut or reduced child support when they remarried, especially if they had acquired stepchildren or had more children with the second wife. Building a new life for the divorced woman, even if she had a job before marriage, is a matter of survival. Being the sole reliable provider for herself and her children, she carries the burden of feeding them, clothing them, and caring for them, while keeping her own self-confidence and not allowing resentment to set in. Granted, the courts are willing to go after men who do not make child support payments, but the divorced mother must file delinquent charges and wait for the system to assist her.

A related issue stems from the exchange of money between an ex-husband and an ex-wife via child support. The child support money can become a metaphor for control and other unresolved emotional issues. By regulating the flow of resources, he is still in charge (Crosbie-Burnett and Ahrons, 1985; Walsh, 1992).

In another study, Wallerstein and Blakeslee (1990) found that a third of the divorced women and a quarter of the men, mostly the older ones, felt that life was unfair, disappointing, and lonely. The researchers further reported that

> Men who divorce undergo less psychological change than women in the wake of divorce. The male social roles tend to be defined by employment, whereas women tend to separate work and family roles. After divorce, a man's job, status, and contacts of work are relatively unchanged, so a major part of his life remains stable. Many women are completely different people ten years after divorce. Not so the men. (42)

The Child's View after Divorce

According to Pearson and Thoennes (1984), many divorced parents feel so overwhelmed they find it difficult to assess what their children are experiencing. In the words of one mother: "I didn't notice any immediate changes (in the children) but I might have been too busy trying to be competent and not fall apart myself, so I might not have noticed" (114). Around 20 percent of the parents in the Pearson and Thoennes study (1984) reported that their child seemed angry with at least one of the parents because of the divorce. Interviews with the children confirmed their anger with parents. The anger grew directly out of the divorce experience.

Loyalty conflicts are a key concern of children. A number of children indicated that they worried about having to take sides with one parent, putting them directly in the middle of the divorce. About 30 percent of the parents indicated the child's unwillingness to discuss the divorce. Interviews with children confirmed that for many the primary coping mechanism was avoidance. In the words of several children: "I don't think about it. That's how I handle problems"; "I don't think about them and they go away."

Most children have reconciliation fantasies, and many blame the divorce on their own failures or limitations. Divorce changes how children think about and relate to parents. Children have difficulty deciding where they belong and articulating what their problems are and what can be done to alleviate them. Most professionals believe that parents must communicate the reasons for divorce and stress that the divorce is not the child's fault.

On a positive note, divorce does not necessarily have to have a deleterious effect on a child's growth and development. Although idyllic images of a warm, loving, intact nuclear family continue to dominate cultural expectations, it is possible to appropriately manage divorce situations.

The Effect of Age in Children and Divorce

In California, Wallerstein and Blakeslee's (1990) team of researchers reported preliminary findings on a 10-year follow-up study of children from divorced families. The study was intended to determine which emotional issue was heightened at each development stage. This study looked at the effects of divorce on preschool, school-age, and adolescent children.

In most studies, boys seem to be harder hit than girls. Preschool boys of divorced parents tend to be unpopular with male peers, to have difficulty gaining access to play groups, to spend more time with younger compatriots and females, and to engage in more activities traditionally considered feminine. Young boys tend to be more vehemently opposed to the divorce, to long more for their father, to feel rejected by him, and to feel uncertain about their masculinity. They are more likely than girls to become depressed and angry. Many have problems developing intimacy throughout their life, and build lifestyles of solitary interest and habits (Wallerstein 1984). Keep in mind that men are still more likely to play the role of "noncustodial" parent, even though joint custody arrangements are common.

In contrast, Mavis Hetherinton of the University of Virginia (1987) found that teenage girls have special problems following divorce. Specifically, she discovered a pattern of low self-respect and sexual precocity among teenage girls living with a divorced mother who has remarried. This pattern did not hold true among girls living with a solo mother due to the death of the father. Thus, it is possible that active hostility from a father who is present in the home, not his absence, causes a disturbance among teenage girls. Wallerstein concurs that teenage girls are quite confused about the separation of their father from the family and treat it sometimes with glorification and other times with suspicion.

Preschoolers. The youngest children at the time of the divorce regress at home and in nursery school during the first 18 months after the divorce. They display a range of emotional disorders and serious learning problems, with boys being more severely affected than girls. These problems can be attributed to the child's sensitivity to change in the parents. Mother becomes more anxious and less available. Because the mother usually has custody, the child senses the loss of the father and panics at the idea that a parent is gone. This leads to the fear that the mother might leave as well, heightening the child's separation anxieties.

School-Age Children. Children ages 6–11 seem to cope the best. Their heightened sense of loss and sadness is significant but less extensive than that of the other age groups. Psychiatrist J. Visher (1990), who works with many stepfamilies, questions the concept that a child's values are firmly established by age five or six. By showing the school-age child what may be gained by change, rather than having a totally negative view of divorce, parents can increase the likelihood for change to be less debilitating.

Adolescents. According to McLoughlin and Whitfield (1984), family life before separation seems to have an impact on how adolescents respond to their parents' divorce. In their study, 76 percent of the adolescents reported that there had been conflict in the marriage before separation. Sixty percent of the conflict was verbal, but 38 percent was both verbal and physical. In spite of the reported conflict, almost half of this group were surprised that their parents split up. They had come to view conflict as a normal part of marital life.

According to Strong and DeVault (1979), adolescents usually experience immense turmoil after their parents divorce but will protect themselves by separating themselves from the emotional conflict. They may appear outwardly cool and detached. Unlike younger children, they rarely blame themselves, and are more likely to be angry with both parents, who they feel have upset their lives.

Also, adolescents often react dramatically to divorce because this is the period in their lives that is usually the most difficult in terms of change for them. The adolescent is groping, questioning, and evaluating the values that will guide him or her in life, and the problems of divorce only add to the confusion of the adolescent (Ackerman, 1958). Adolescence is the beginning of the struggle to resolve identification with two parents and to build from this identification a personal identity (Ackerman, 1958). If parents are unable to provide stability in the adolescent child's environment then the adolescent's own instability is augmented (Curran, 1985).

One significant gender difference, according to Visher (1990), is in girls' heightened need for the father. Daughters from divorced homes often feel compelled to contact their fathers and share their closest feelings with them. This is especially the case when the child and the parent have had little contact over the years. The child's attempts at intimacy can be quite anxiety-provoking for the father, who may wonder why the child is only now willing to open up.

Older Children. Long-range coping is often harder for children who are older at the time of divorce because they retain so many memories of their parents' struggles. Also, because they have lived for a longer period in an intact family, their sense of loss may be more profound. These children poignantly describe their sadness at recalling the fights and recriminations. For this group, as well as for adolescents, the divorce remains a central aspect of their lives and continues to evoke strong feelings.

Wallerstein and Blakeslee (1990) note that there is a "sleeper effect" that affects girls more than boys because it appears that, at first, girls are more psychologically at ease with divorce than boys. However, a girl's problems usually surface when she becomes a woman, and they often affect her romantic attachments. At this point, men do better. A young woman's fears of abandonment and betrayal are often overwhelming at this stage of her life. One of the ways the young woman copes with the emotional complications is that she will date and marry an older man. The relationship apparently seems less precarious to her.

A New Life after Divorce

Although divorce is an "event," it is clear that many view it as an ongoing stage. Others have been more interested in the communicative challenges inherent in "moving on," particularly the special challenges of creating a viable stepfamily. Social researchers explain that the remarriage family lacks the shared family experience, the symbols, and the rituals characteristic of the first marriage family. Interpersonal communication in the remarriage family, therefore, poses adaptation problems. Lacking symbols or models, the new family must devise new rules in its relationships. And remarried couples are especially aware that, if they do not rethink past behavior, they are destined to make the same mistakes in the new family (Ackerman, 1958; Einstein, 1982).

Preparing children for a new marriage more often than not isn't handled well. Before the marriage perhaps the stepmother/father often didn't consider the child an integral part of future life or vice versa. A marriage, however, may involve substantial changes, such as a physical move or the introduction of new family members and events. Of course, if a parent or stepparent did not pay too much attention to the child before the remarriage the tendency is to follow the same pattern or even resent the child. Marriage, however, often heightens the child's expectations. The painful fact is that stepfamily life is fragile (Jewett, 1982).

Children, according to Visher and Visher (1979), often have difficulty figuring out where they belong. If parents acknowledge children's fears regarding family reorganization, then they can be better prepared to attend to their needs. Concerns need to be expressed and feelings accepted, so that a clearer delineation of new roles can be successfully negotiated. According to Bohannan and Erickson (1978), roles and boundaries in the new family have to be clearly spelled out as earlier roles from the former family are relinquished and/or redefined. Uncertainty breeds power struggles and manipulations. If there is to be a change of caretaker, for example, the child who is appropriately prepared for the change is given a chance to anticipate where she or he will live and who will keep her or him safe. Any of these experiences of sharing can help children complete their understanding of the changes occurring in their lives so that they can move on to new relationships with their self-esteem intact while continuing to care deeply about the lost family member.

Healthy mourning, according to Freud (1946), is achieved when people accept the changes in their external life, make corresponding changes in their internal life, and finally make the reorientation necessary to be able to feel attachment again. In the mourning process, after an acute period of denial, there usually comes guilt and anger, followed by despair or depression (Visher and Visher, 1979). It is important that parents anticipate this process in their children and that they allow grieving to occur in an environment that is supportive.

Remarriage, ironically, may be appropriately thought of as both the last phase of a divorce and the first phase of a brand new, and highly complex, family.

The Formation of a Remarriage Family

Romantics say love is better the second time around. When applied to remarriage, this idyllic notion of songs and movies fails to mention the "leftovers" from former family relationships: children, former spouses, child support and alimony, anger, guilt, jealousy, and fear (Bray, 1995; Einstein, 1982). One of the consistent findings in research is that "step-parenthood does not recreate the nuclear family" reports Furstenberg and Nord (1985: 895), "It does not put the family back in Humpty Dumpty fashion."

Effective communication skills are especially important to the success of the remarried couple. Not only is it important for the new couple to be aware of communication problems between the two of them but, as mentioned earlier, if there are children from the first marriage, they need to be considered. The ideal situation would be if stepparents could perfect their interpersonal skills with the children before the new marriage. Sometimes a long courtship is advocated before the remarriage as it allows children to move into the relationship at a slow and stable pace. This time also allows the stepparent to get to know the children and create a history from singlehood to remarriage with adequate time for everyone to adjust to the new situation.

A tension may exist because of differences between the individual's need for maintaining a sense of personal identity and the need for the couple to maintain stability (Askham, 1976). Conflict is natural in intimate relationships. That is the paradox of love: the more intimate a couple becomes, the more likely they are to have differences. If this is understood, then the meaning of conflict can be mediated. Conflict will not necessarily represent a crisis in the relationship.

How a couple addresses the differences between them will affect relationship satisfaction. As suggested, the period between dating and remarriage is the time to sort out feelings and weigh reactions under a variety of circumstances. A couple should determine when they will be stepping on each other's toes in questions of discipline, authority, money, relations with the other natural parent, modesty within the home, and social habits. It takes time to work through these issues, and it's best done before the final commitment. This period allows the couple to learn about the issues that are likely sources of conflict (Hunt, 1977).

Visher and Visher (1979) identify the following five characteristics that distinguish the blended from the intact family:

1. In blended families almost all members have lost an important primary relationship. The children may mourn the loss of their parent or parents, and the spouses the loss of their former mates. Because of this perceived loss, anger and hostility may be displaced onto the new stepparent.
2. One biological parent lives outside the current family. He or she may either support or interfere with the new family. Power struggles often occur between the absent parent and the stepmother/father.
3. The relationship between a parent and his or her children predates the relationship between the new partners. Children have often spent con-

siderable time and have grown accustomed to living in a single-family structure. A new husband or wife may be regarded as an intruder in the children's special relationship with their parent. A new stepparent may, in turn, find that he or she must compete with the children for a spouse's attention.

4. Stepparent roles are ill-defined. No one quite knows what he or she is supposed to do as a stepparent. Most stepparents try role after role until they find one that fits.
5. Many children in blended families are also members of the noncustodial parent's household, living in one household and visiting the other. Each home may have differing rules and expectations. When conflict arises, children may try to play one household against the other.

Researchers say it often takes from four to seven years for a new stepfamily to become stable, to work out a sense of "we." It starts with the fantasy "Oh, it's going to be better the second time around. I'm going to be a better spouse and parent." But, for many, early stages of remarriage actually bring chaos, confusion, and craziness. That's when many people give up, and, sadly, a disproportionately high number of second marriages collapse. If a new family can survive early disappointments, however, they can begin to resolve problems and understand what to expect (Bernard, 1956; Hunt, 1966; Jones, 1977; Visher and Visher, 1979). Mutual acceptance, tolerance, and developing new family traditions are important strategies for bringing family members closer together.

Mutual acceptance requires getting to know and appreciate new family members as they are, not as they would like each other to be. This is important in all stages of family development, but appears to be especially challenging during separation, divorce, and remarriage. Marrying for the first time or remarrying with the idyllic notion that an insensitive partner will somehow magically become sensitive, for example, is an invitation to disappointment and divorce (Strong and DeVault, 1979).

There are, as mentioned, also conflicts with stepchildren who have experienced parental loss through divorce. They are frequently hesitant to invest their feelings in a new person for fear of reexperiencing the pain. The parent who can be tolerant of the child's feelings and not insist on his or her liking the stepparent is off to a good beginning. The parent who can convey the attitude, "I know it takes time and you don't like your stepparent yet" is giving the child room to develop positive feelings. The parent who verbalizes that this new spouse does not have to displace the absent parent is recognizing the child's concern for preexisting family ties (Cantor and Drake, 1983).

Jewett (1982) devised a way to help the child understand that he or she can have a parent–child relationship with more than one parent or set of parents. One helpful technique is what she calls the "candle ritual." As the child lights a new candle for each caretaker in his or her life, he or she can see vividly that the love and warmth once felt with earlier caretakers does not have to be "blown out" as new bonds are established, and as new candles are lit. The ceremony helps even the youngest children understand that new family constellations do not demand the death of old relationships.

Gender Issues in the Nontraditional Family

The formal and legal structure of traditional marriage is linked to male dominance, but the reality of marriage varies widely in this regard. Sociologist Bernard (1972) makes an important distinction between authority and power in marriage. Authority is based in law but power is based in personality. A strong, dominant woman is likely to exercise power over a weak, passive man simply by force of her personality. Accordingly, Bernard feels both men and women can exercise power in marital dyads.

Despite Bernard's assertion, gender stereotypes regarding power persist and they affect expectations in the nontraditional family. Other gendered expectations carry implications about nurturance and emotional expression and, these too, contribute to the complexity of communication in the remarriage family.

The Stepmother Role

It is difficult to accept that the stereotypical "wicked stepmother" image in *Cinderella, Hansel and Gretel*, and *Snow White* could actually perpetuate negative connotations about female stepparents, but there is evidence that the stereotype influences both perceptions and subsequent behaviors of women who become parents through marriage. Stepmothers, for example, often are afraid to discipline stepchildren or to engage in any meaningful interactions that might provoke conflict for fear of confirming their wickedness. When a stereotype is strongly negative, it seems that the stereotyped individual may become the object of prejudice or work unnaturally hard to avoid fulfilling stereotypic expectations (Ehrlich, 1973; Schneider, Hastorg, and Ellsworth, 1979).

The latest research on the "wicked stepmother," though, suggests that some social scientists are wondering whether this stereotype is justified. Scientists researching modern stepfamilies generally agree that families with a full-time stepmother do fare worse than families with a stepfather. According to Daly and Wilson (1999) this is not so much because of the sterotypical "wicked stepmother" syndrome, but because the stepmother's role is simply more difficult, given the children's strong bond with the biological mother. Even if no such maternal bond is competing, it is difficult for the stepmother to match the idealistic expectations of the mother role. As White and Booth (1985) note, "a man can be a decent stepfather simply by being a provider and a nice guy, but a stepmother is often called upon to establish 'gut-level' empathy and attachment—traits that are difficult."

A woman growing up never dreams that one day she will become a stepmom. In most instances, she is stepping into a role for which she is almost never prepared. In this paradoxical environment where she is not trained or ready, she is expected to take on the responsibility of bringing strength, safety, and happiness to others. She has been taught that, as a parent, she has a right to be respected, and, as a new spouse, she should expect to be happy, yet she is struggling to nurture his kids and possibly her own, as well as their mutual children—and her marriage (Norwood, 1989). Many women are understandably overwhelmed.

Female contributors to Neufeld's study (1988) describe the trauma caused by trying to make the stepfamily an instant, traditional family. Women speak in voices laced with anger, bitterness, and unacknowledged hurt. A few women depict men as explicitly rejecting involvement because their notions of masculinity encourage authoritarian roles or distancing behaviors.

Even for women with the desire, opportunity, and skills to step out of their situation to reflect on it, the emotional urgency of negotiating the complexities of lives in stepfamilies can supersede intellectual understanding and feminine consciousness (Maglin and Schniedewind, 1988). What she knows and what she feels are at odds. Thus, insight—or any kind of reflective stance—while meaningful and clarifying, still may not match the power of the emotional experience.

The stepmother's relationship with her stepchildren is another puzzle. How does she maintain a relationship with the stepchild and with her own biological children without worrying about favoritism? The stepmother, in many cases, is haunted simultaneously by the images of the imperfect stepmother and the perfect (biological) mother. We have learned that a woman is the nurturer, the emotional linchpin for family members, and that subsequently she has the primary responsibility for meeting others' needs. While some women have found this effort workable, most have found it painful or self-defeating.

Aside from stereotypic expectations, adapting to the role of stepmother is inherently difficult because women make judgments based on prior knowledge of their own children's reactions, with little knowledge about probable reactions from their stepchildren. For children who live with their biological parent, the arrival of a stepparent (and perhaps stepsiblings) may be regarded as an intrusion. Frequent complaints from stepmothers concern, among other things, how nasty children can be, indifferent husbands, and their own feelings of inadequacy. They want emotional support to help assuage these feelings of anger and self-doubt.

Being a stepmother is sometimes having all the responsibilities and none of the privileges of motherhood. The stepmother is faced with many troubling times especially at holidays. "On Mother's Day I made dinner for my stepchildren and then their natural mother picked them up to go for dessert," notes one stepmother. A stepmother raising someone else's child may get more than she bargained for. Being a stepmother to a child who doesn't accept you, or whose natural mother hates you, can be emotionally destructive. A stepmother can become very insecure with feelings that everyone is against her (Neufeld, 1988). But, according to Peterson (1999), this must change. She has the right to both respect and happiness as she struggles to nurture his kids, as well as their mutual children—and her marriage.

Deutsch (1973) explains the difficulties in the steprelationship in the following manner. When the father remarries, the child loses an exclusive relationship with him that is often established after the break-up of the family. After the remarriage, the child must share the father with the stepmother. Although the father was originally shared with the natural mother, the prior positive nurturing of the mother toward the child and child's wish to maintain this relationship led to a positive identification with the mother, thus facilitating sharing the father. Because this "store" of love and nurturing is absent when the stepmother comes on the scene, the child has greater difficulty sharing the parent with the stepparent.

Moreover, the sexual nature of the relationship between the father and the new wife stirs up "hate impulses" of children of both sexes against the stepmother. The child in the stepsituation has greater difficulty resolving the Oedipal conflict than when the natural mother is present. The natural mother continues to be "good" and is idealized, while the stepmother is cast in the role of the "bad" mother and is vilified. These unconscious phenomena feed the negative symbols and images of the "bad stepmother" even when the behavior of the stepmother is not consistent with that image. Both the concepts of unresolved Oedipal conflicts and splitting of good and bad images have been useful to therapists in work with children in the remarried family.

In their work with stepmothers Visher and Visher (1979) found nine common problem areas most stepmothers must face in relation to their role:

1. Expectation of instant love for and from stepchildren
2. Tendency to rush in and come on too strong
3. Difficulty in handling rejection from stepchildren
4. Difficulties with the wicked stepmother myth
5. Unsuccessful attempts to keep everybody happy
6. Inability to achieve close family unity
7. Anger, jealousy, and competition for love and affection from spouse
8. Anger at ex-spouses
9. Guilt generated by all of the above

What can be done? For the wife, the issues in stepparenting are complex. To begin to make a success of this new role, women need to acknowledge the fact that stepparenting is a difficult task. Patience and sanity will be tested repeatedly. Overnight successes are rarely found. A stepmother should not demand instant love from stepchildren. She must recognize that love takes time to develop.

Many experts see the father as a key player in successful stepmother–stepchild communication. At the onset, an appropriate helping message is simply: "This is my wife. You will be courteous to her or you will answer to me." This establishes a simple foundational expectation for communication in the new dyad, drawing on an authority dynamic between the father and child which is long standing. If the father's message is acted upon, time will allow the family to move on to stage two. It is during stage two that a relationship can be developed between the stepmother and the stepchildren. However, if the stepmother is made the heavy in stage one, the family may get caught up in stage one, never moving on to stage two: the new role of adult-friend.

The Stepfather Role

The predivorce relationship between father and children is not necessarily a predictor of the postdivorce relationship. Attentive fathers before divorce can become distant, or, fortunately, closer. Fathers who have left the development of their children to the mother often become interested and involved, taking great pride in the newly active parental role. The noncustodial father remains a significant psychological presence regardless of his level of participation in the child's lives. Children *need* to have a positive image of their parent in order to develop a strong self-esteem and will protect the image of the natural father even if he has been abusive or negligent. Thus, it is rare for a stepfather to become a substitute for a father, although this sometimes happens when the child is young at the time of the divorce. (Ricci, 1980; Jewett, 1982; Wallerstein and Blakeslee, 1990).

Despite loyalties to the biological father, there is some strong evidence that stepfathers have an easier task than do stepmothers. Duberman (1973) studied 88 stepfamilies in which each adult in the family was interviewed and given an opportunity to rate familial relationships and to evaluate the closeness of the family. Neither sex nor age of stepchildren influenced stepfather relationships, but stepmothers had better relationships with stepchildren under the age of 13 than with teenage stepchildren.

Bohannan and Erickson (1978) reported research that found that children in stepfather households got along as well with their stepfathers as children in natural households got along with their natural fathers. However, natural fathers rated their children as significantly happier than the stepfathers rated their stepchildren, and natural fathers rated themselves as significantly better fathers than the stepfathers rated themselves. Thus, stepfathers viewed themselves and their stepchildren as less successful and happy than did natural fathers, even though the stepchildren and their mothers did not feel that way.

One of the major differences between the stepmother's role and the stepfather's role is that, while the stepmother tends to fight actively for her place in the family, the stepfather tends to withdraw (Schulman, 1981). As a result, the relationship between a stepfather and his stepchildren tends to remain underdeveloped rather than negative. The stepfather's role in the family is poorly articulated—particularly in relation to discipline. In fact, discipline seems to create a great deal of difficulty for a stepfather, especially when each stepparent has unique methods of disciplining children. One stepfather was very frustrated about his new stepdaughter, who was brought up in a household where there were very few rules and regulations about eating on time, staying out late, and so on. Major conflicts were created because his children had many restrictions, which created problems not only for the parents but for the stepsiblings.

Visher and Visher (1979) in their work with stepfathers indicate that there are seven general psychological tasks that stepfathers are faced with in relation to their role:

1. Joining a functioning group and establishing a place for himself (This is the reverse of the situation faced by the woman who marries a man whose wife has custody of his children.)
2. Working out rules regarding family behavior
3. Handling unrealistic expectations both on his part and on the part of the new family
4. Dealing with feelings of guilt about his previous family
5. Money
6. Adoption, naming, and inheritance questions with reference to his stepchildren
7. Sexuality in the stepfamily

The new stepfather may find family issues frustrating, especially when he has not had much prior experience raising a biological child. For example, take the businessman who exclaimed, "I run a department of sixty people, worth upwards of 60 million dollars, and everything is pretty orderly. Then I go home and have to face this awful child who looks at me with such disdain that I wonder if this marriage wasn't a mistake."

Roberts and Price's (1987) study included both remarriage mothers and first-married fathers (i.e., stepfathers). The results indicated that the wives perceived their husbands as more concerned with the external consequences of the stepchildren's behavior than with the inner development of character and moral values in the children. Apparently, the new male parent may be perceived by his wife as seeking to create order and structure in her previously single-parent family. According to Keshet (1988), males may feel a greater need than females for order and hierarchy in a home with children, or they may simply perceive their new wives as too lenient. Fine, Ganong, and Coleman (1997) also found that stepfathers were more satisfied with their marital and family lives when they reported frequent engagement in authoritative parenting behaviors.

Gender and the Stepchild Experience

In a study of remarried couples, White and Booth (1985) specifically identified the presence of stepchildren in the home as a principal source of strain in second unions. Of course, stepparents may overestimate the difficulties, but there is substantial detail in the research about the negative aspects of becoming a stepchild. As might be expected, gender, along with age, figures prominently in explaining those difficulties.

For the majority of children their world has been turned upside down. The familiar "givens" are no longer present. An oldest child may no longer be the oldest child or youngest child the youngest. An only child may suddenly have two or three siblings; the mother or father now needs to give time and attention to three or four children rather than to one child.

For older children the displacement and confusion can be even greater. Imagine a teenage boy who has been the "man of the house" for several years suddenly being asked to relinquish this status to a newcomer to the family. No longer does the adolescent have the responsibility for cleaning the car, washing the windows, or carrying the heavy loads for his mother. Perhaps he complained bitterly about the tasks at the time, but he did have a recognized status in the home, which is now eliminated.

Or take the situation of a 16-year-old girl who did the housework and cooking for her father and younger brother for several years. Her father is planning to remarry a woman with strong motivation to be a superwife and mother, and is preparing for her new stepfamily. The stepmother-to-be is full of the very best of intentions, but the daughter who has been running the household feels upstaged, replaced, and crowded into a very small corner (Wallerstein and Blakeslee, 1990).

The diversity provided by having a membership in two households can eventually give children in remarried families additional role models and a wider variety of experiences from which to learn and grow. Many children, however, do not perceive the back-and-forth trek from one household to another in a positive light. They feel helpless and out of control. They seem to be faced with constant change that feels like complete "culture shock." The sets of rules in the two homes may be quite different. Unless the children have some help in recognizing that there are many different acceptable patterns of living rather than a "right" and a "wrong" way, they may constantly battle at least one pattern. Without this mindset they can cut themselves off from one parent as well as from a richness of experience that is available to them (Ricci, 1980).

Some of the studies that have investigated the effects of remarriage on children have suggested that remarriage inflicts some degree of trauma on all children, regardless of gender. There are some differences, though. Stepsisters generally have a more difficult time with stepbrothers than stepbrothers do with stepsisters, and girls whose divorced mothers remarry may be particularly at risk. Boys benefit from having a stepfather more than girls; young boys positively reacted to the entry of stepfather into the home, rapidly attaching themselves to him (Bitterman, 1968; Bowerman and Irish, 1962; Wallerstein and Kelly, 1980). Similarly, Clingempeel, Brand, and Ievoli (1984) found that girls in stepmother families did better the longer they lived in the remarried home. Heatherington, Cox, and Cox (1985) compared divorced families where the mothers had remarried with those where she had not, and with families that were not divorced. They found that boys showed more long-term problems when their mothers divorced and did not remarry, whereas girls showed more problems when their mothers remarried. However, improvement was found for the girls in later stages of remarriage over girls in the early stage, though stepdaughters continued to see themselves, and be seen by their stepfathers, as having more problems than girls in nondivorced families.

Most of the studies point out the life stresses in stepfamilies. Girls in stepfamilies reported more negative stress than either girls in nuclear families or boys in stepfamilies. While girls in stepfamilies report more stress in their lives, their own self-concept and intellectual functioning do not seem to suffer. However, both mothers and stepfathers report that these girls exhibit more behavioral problems than do girls in nuclear families. It seems that girls in stepfamilies respond to the added stress by acting out and misbehaving, rather than feeling bad about themselves. The same is true for boys who seem to experience less negative stress than girls, but also act out and misbehave.

For the most part, the stepmother–stepdaughter relationship seems to be the most difficult of all steprelationships. This is particularly true when the daughter is an adolescent. Usually this is true because a girl's emotional development is more complicated than a boy's. The main problem seems to be that little girls want to be "Daddy's girl." Little boys outgrow the stage of wanting to be "Mama's boy" and begin to emulate their fathers very early in development. The "Daddy's girl" syndrome lasts well into adolescence (Thompson, 1966). Wallerstein and Kelly's (1989) team reported on gender differences in their 10-year follow-up study of children from divorced families.

1. Boys from divorced families experience an intense, rising need for their fathers during adolescence—even if the divorce occurred ten years earlier. Before that time fathers were less important in their sons' lives.
2. Many of the girls in the study had problems with identification at adolescence. They were afraid to identify with a rejected mother, but they still wanted to be like her. They loved their mother but were afraid they too would be rejected. If she loved and admired her mother would she be cast away also?
3. In some cases a young woman may be fearful of surpassing her mother, of doing better in the world of love and marriage. She might have taken on many of the decisions and responsibilities for her mother after the divorce, and it is difficult to leave that role and find her own identity. The fear of success had its roots in this young woman's identification with her mother, she did not want to leave her mother behind by being better than her.
4. There was no conclusive evidence that one sex feels more or less pain, but girls were more inclined to readily express their feelings. The girls who denied their loss and pain experienced the "sleeper effect" in later years. Those repressed feelings were only placed on hold.

5. Boys were more apt to "shut out" their feelings to avoid the hurt and pain. These feelings create so much psychic energy that they had no energy to deal successfully with future relationships.

Wallerstein and Kelly's (1980) intent "was not to argue against divorce but rather to raise the consciousness of the community about the long-term effects of divorce on children. The first step in solving a problem is to acknowledge it. Only then can the transition get at the complex tasks that lie ahead."

Of utmost importance is that the stepchild must realize that while certain behaviors might be unacceptable, the child is important. This can be accomplished by explaining "I like you, but not some of the things you do." Deciding what is intolerable and what can be acceptable is important because in the long run, the more acceptance there is in the stepfamily, the more successful it can be (Visher and Visher, 1979).

CONCLUSION

The traditional law defined the basic rights and obligations of spouses based on gender, creating a sex-based division of family roles and responsibilities. The woman was to devote herself to being a wife, homemaker, and mother in return for her husband's promise of lifelong support. As Clark wrote in 1968:

> The courts say that the husband has a duty to support his wife, that she has a duty to render services in the home, and that these duties are reciprocal. . . . A reading of contemporary judicial opinions leaves the impression that these roles have not changed over the last two hundred years. (281)

At the time of Clark's observation, the state placed the burden for economic support of the family squarely on the husband and the responsibility for care of the home and children on the wife. He was required to provide "necessities," while she was required to provide domestic service, companionship, and child care. The postdivorce family reflected these expectations.

More recently, there have been several changes in the patterns of alimony, or "spousal support" awards, as they are now called, which suggest that attitudes about men's and women's roles are shifting. First, in an effort to create "self-sufficient" ex-partners, permanent awards that suggest continued dependence have been replaced with time-limited transitional awards. Since most in need of "transitional" assistance are females, the standards of the new law seemingly dictate that the ex-wife must become able to "support" herself. If she had even a marginal employment history prior to the divorce, she may not receive spousal support as she is presumed capable of supporting herself (Hauser, 1987).

The reality of women's lives after divorce, however, suggests that in many cases a female, often with children to support, is not able to go it alone. Women often seek assistance through remarriage, creating a brand new challenge—the stepfamily. Despite her hope to the contrary, this new family may be just as challenging as the single-parent family of her initial postdivorce life.

Although many argue that families have changed too much over recent decades, it may be equally true that other institutions have changed too little. American's work policies are antiquated, designed for a time when most moms weren't in the workforce and most dads didn't understand the joys of being involved in child care. Our school schedules are out-of-date, designed for a time when kids were needed to assist at home with milking and haying. Political debates now focus on whether to help parents stay home or invest in better daycare, preschool, and afterschool programs, when most industrialized nations have long since learned it's possible to do both (Coontz and Song, 1999).

It is time to redefine the family and the designated roles for men and women not only in their professional lives, but also in marriage and, yes, remarriage. The storybook nuclear family—breadwinning husband, homemaker wife, and 2.4 problem-free children—is a relic. The logical first step in strengthening the stepfamily is to redefine it in terms that more accurately reflect its special composition and dynamics. It is important to stop feeling that any alternative to the traditional arrangement is something less than a family.

References

Ackerman, N. 1958. *The Psychodynamics of Family Life.* New York: Basic Books.

Askham, J. 1976. Identity and stability within the marriage relationship. *Journal of Marriage and Family* 38: 535–547.

Bernard, J. 1956. *Remarriage.* New York: Dryden Press.

Bitterman, C. 1968. The multimarriage family. *Social Casework* 49: 218–221.

Bohannan, P., and R. Erickson. 1978, January. Stepping in. *Psychology Today,* 46–53.

Bowerman, C., and D. Irish. 1962. Some relationships of stepchildren and their parents. *Marriage and Family Living* 24: 113–121.

Bray, J. H., (1995) Role integration and marital adjustment in stepfather families. In K. Pasley and M. Ihinger-Tallman, eds., *Stepparenting: Issues in Theory, Research and Practice.* Westport, CT: Praeger, 69–86.

Cantor, D., and E. A. Drake. 1983. *Divorced Parents and Their Children.* New York: Springer.

Clark, H. 1968. *The Law of Domestic Relations in the United States.* St. Paul, MN: West Publishing Co.

Clingempeel, W., E. Brand, and R. Ievoli. 1986. Stepparent-stepchild relationships in stepmother and stepfather families: A multimethod study. *Family Relations* 33: 465–473.

Coontz, S., and S. Song. 1999, November. The American family. *Life* 22(12).

Crosbie-Burnett, M., and C. R. Ahrons. 1985. From divorce to remarriage: Implications for therapy with families in transition. *Journal of Psychotherapy and the Family* 1: 121–137.

Curran, D. 1985. *Stress and the Healthy Family.* Minneapolis, MN: Wilson Press.

Daly, M., and M. Wilson. 1999. The truth about Cinderella. *U.S. News & World Report* 127(21).

Deutsch, H. 1973. *The Psychology of Women: Women, Motherhood; A Psychoanalytic Interpretation*. New York: Bantam.
Duberman, L. 1973. Step-kin relationship. *Journal of Marriage and the Family* 35: 283–292.
Ehrlich, N. J. 1973. *The Social Psychology of Prejudice.* New York: Wiley.
Einstein, E. 1982. *The Stepfamily.* Boston: Shambhala.
Fine, M., L. Ganong, and M. Coleman. 1997, September. The relation between role construction and adjustment among stepfathers. *Journal of Family Issues* 7: 222–232.
Freud, A. 1946. *The Ego and the Mechanisms of Defense.* New York: International Universities Press.
Furstenberg, F. Jr., and C. Nord. 1985. *Recycling the Family: Remarriage after Divorce.* Beverly Hills, CA: Sage.
Galvin, K., and P. Cooper. 1990. *Development of Involuntary Relationships, the Stepparent-Stepchild Relationship.* Paper presented at the International Communication Association Convention, Dublin, Ireland.
Glick, P. C. 1989. Remarried families, stepfamilies, and stepchildren: A brief demographic profile. *Family Relations* 38: 24–27.
Hauser, J. 1987. *An Analysis of Divorce Mediation.* Unpublished doctoral dissertion, at Union Graduate School, Cincinnati, OH.
———. 1988. Divorce mediation: A growing field? *The Arbitration Journal* 43: 15–22.
Heatherington, E. 1987. Family relations six years after the divorce. In K. Parsley, M. Ihinger, and B. Tallman, eds., *Remarriage and Stepfamilies: Current Research and Theory.* New York: Guilford, 185–205.
Heatherington, E., M. Cox, and R. Cox. 1985. Effects of divorce on parents and children. *Journal of Family Psychology* 7: 39–56.
Hunt, Morton. 1966. *The World of the Formerly Married.* New York: McGraw-Hill.
———. 1977. *The Divorce Experience.* New York: McGraw-Hill.
Jewett, C. 1982. *Helping Children Cope with Separation and Loss.* Harvard, MA: The Harvard Common Press.
Jones, N. 1977. The impact of divorce on children. *Consultations Courts Review* 15 (2).
Keshet, J. K. 1988. The remarried couple: Stresses and successes. In W. R. Beer, ed., *Relative Strangers.* Totowa, NJ: Rowan & Littlefield, 132–146.
Maglin A., and N. Schniedewind. 1988. There for each other: A stepmothers' support group. In M. Bauer and N. Schniedewind, eds., *Women and Stepfamilies.* Philadelphia: Temple University Press, 321–332.
McLoughlin, D., and R. Whitfield. 1984. Adolescents and their experience of parental divorce. *Journal of Adolescence* 7: 155–170.
Neufeld, A. 1988. One step away from mother: A stepmother's story. In M. Bauer and N. Schniedewind, eds., *Women and Stepfamilies.* Philadelphia: Temple University Press, 77–91.
Norwood, P. 1989. *Enlightened Stepmother: Revolutionizing the Role.* New York: Avon Press.
Pearson, J., and N. Thoennes. 1984. *Divorce Mediation Project.* Denver, CO: Research Unit, Association of Family and Conciliation Courts.
Peterson, K. 1999. A stepmother movement: New research, new concerns for this often difficult role. *USA Today.*
Ricci, I. 1980. *Mom's House, Dad's House.* New York: Macmillan.
Roberts, T. W., and S. J. Price. 1987. Instant families: Divorced mothers marry never-married men. *Journal of Divorce* 11(1): 71–92.
Schneider D., A. Hastorg, and P. Ellsworth. 1979. *Person Perception.* Reading, MA: Addison-Wesley.

Schulman, G. 1981. Divorce, single parenthood and stepfamilies: Structural implications of these transitions. *International Journal of Family Therapy* 9: 87–112.

Snyder, M., and W. Swann. 1978. Behavioral confirmation in social interaction: From social perception to social reality. *Journal of Experimental and Social Psychology*: 148–168.

Strong,. B., and C. DeVault. 1979. Inside America's new families. *Family Life Educator* 1(3): 9–11.

Thompson, H. 1966. *The Successful Stepparent*. New York: Harper & Row.

Visher, J. 1990, October. *Clinical Intervention with Stepfamilies.* Paper presented at the Annual Meeting of the American Association for Marriage and Family Therapy, Washington, DC.

Visher, E. B., and J. Visher. 1979. *Stepfamilies: A Guide to Working with Stepparents and Stepchildren.* New York: Brunner/Mazel.

Wallerstein, J. 1984. Children of divorce: Preliminary report of a ten year follow-up of young children. *American Journal of Orthopsychiatry* 54: 444–58.

Wallerstein, J., and S. Blakeslee. 1990. *Second Chances: Men, Women and Children a Decade After Divorce.* New York: Ticknor & Fields.

Wallerstein, J., and J. Kelly. 1980. *Surviving the Breakup. How Children and Parents Cope with Divorce.* New York: Basic Books.

Walsh, W. 1992. Twenty major issues in remarriage and families. *Journal of Counseling and Development* 70: 709–715.

Weiss, R. 1975. *Going It Alone.* New York: Basic Books.

Weitzman, L. 1985. *The Divorce Revolution. The Unexpected Social and Economic Consequences for Women and Children in America.* New York: Free Press.

White, L. K., and A. Booth. 1985. The quality and stability of remarriages: The role of stepchildren. *American Sociological Review* 60: 689–698.

PART III

Communicating in Professional Environments

CHAPTER 10

Gender Issues in Corporate Communication

Lea P. Stewart

POINTS TO BE ADDRESSED:

- Changing nature of the workplace
- Legal issues and gender in corporations
- Changing nature of work-related communication
- Managerial communication styles
- Challenges and issues for the future

As the twenty-first century begins, our attention is drawn to the dramatic changes that the U.S. workplace has undergone in the last several decades; it is poised for even more changes in the future. As Helgesen (1990) notes: "Pressed by global competition and a fast-changing technology characterized by flexibility and innovation, companies are casting aside old-culture values, trimming the pyramid, and rooting out cumbersome and bureaucratic structures" (xviii–xix). Imagine working for a large corporation today. What is your job like? What does your workplace look like? Who are your coworkers? How do you handle conflicts between family responsibilities and the demands of your job? Does your company offer flexible work schedules so that you can choose your working hours, depending on other obligations in your life? Does your company have a good history of promoting women into

The author would like to acknowledge Dianne Clarke-Kudless for her extensive knowledge of the workplace and for her contributions to the first edition of this chapter.

higher levels of management? Are there opportunities for alternative career paths within the company? If your company makes a product, does it strive to maintain gender-neutral product packaging and promotion? All of these questions are relevant to gender issues in corporate communication and have been addressed by researchers in this area.

One of the most dramatic changes in the contemporary workplace is the increasing diversity of the workforce. And the workplace of the future will be even more diverse than the workplace as we know it today. A landmark study from the 1990s, the Hudson Institute's Workforce 2000 report, predicted that the workforce of the future would be dramatically more diverse in terms of both gender and ethnic background (Duke, 1991). At the same time, the U.S. Bureau of Labor Statistics predicted that by the year 2000 only 30 percent of new entrants into the workforce would be white males.

The increased diversity of the workforce is both a challenge and an opportunity. Although this chapter primarily focuses on gender issues in the workplace, it is important to be aware of issues raised by multiculturalism and other factors such as the aging of the workforce and the increased openness about sexual orientation. Many of the issues of gender bias discussed in this chapter also are applicable to people from diverse ethnic groups, to older workers, and to gay males and lesbians. Noting parallels with these groups can expand one's perspective on the effects of the changing workforce and the communication issues that are raised by these changes.

How are today's corporations responding to these issues? Public opinion concerning gender bias in the workplace has resulted in legislation, landmark court cases, and citizens' efforts to counter bias. Progress has been made in the internal workings of corporate practices such as employment interviews and corporate-sponsored social activities. For example, job applicants are rarely asked questions about marriage plans, desire for children, or child care arrangements. Major corporations are even opening their own on-site day-care centers to accommodate working parents (Northcraft and Gutek, 1993). In terms of corporate social activities, few companies pay membership fees for corporate officers who belong to male-only or racially segregated clubs.

Nevertheless, as Lee (1993) notes:

> Although sex discrimination in employment has been illegal since 1964 under federal law, and for even longer under some state civil rights laws, it persists in many employment settings. Furthermore, systematic discrimination against women, such as occupational segregation and depressed wages for employees in female-dominated occupations, remains a serious social problem that is seemingly impervious to legislative or judicial solutions. (246)

Today's workplace still contains inequalities based on sex segregation and sex differences in earnings. Sex segregation is the "concentration of men and women in different occupations, jobs, and places of work" (Reskin and Padavic, 1994: 45). This means that men and women may do different tasks at the same work site (female nurses work in hospitals with male surgeons) or the same tasks at different times or in different places (a convenience store may have a female manager during the day and a male manager at night). Sex segregation may inhibit a woman's opportunity for advancement or an increase in salary. The higher the proportion of women in an occupation, for example, the less that *both* men and women employees earn (Reskin and Padavic, 1994). Although some progress has been made in equalizing women's and men's salaries, parity is still not the norm. In 1997, U.S. Department of Labor statistics indicated that women were paid approximately 25 percent less than men across all job categories (Equal pay, 1999). White women earned an average of $462 per week compared with $631 for white men, and minority women earned an average of $369 per week compared with $415 earned by minority men. The Institute for Women's Policy Research estimated that "if women were to receive wages equal to those of comparable men, working families across the United States would gain a staggering $200 billion in family income annually, with each working woman's family gaining more that $4,000 per year" (1).

Women have made progress in the managerial ranks. The percentage of women in managerial and executive positions has been steadily increasing from 18 percent in 1970, to 40 percent in 1990, to 48 percent in 1997 (Reskin and Padavic, 1994; Women in American boardrooms, 1997). Nevertheless, African-American women have fared particularly badly in terms of gaining access to managerial jobs. In 1988, only 2 percent of managers in the U.S. were African-American women. A report by the Women's Research and Education Institute predicts that it may take 75 to 100 years to overcome inequities in hiring, promotion, and other aspects of employment (Rich, 1990).

This discussion has been a brief overview of some of the issues faced by corporations as the twenty-first century begins. Obviously, corporate communication will be affected by these changes. The next part of this chapter contains a review of some of the legal issues in corporations that relate to gender. The rest of the chapter addresses the impact of gender issues on managerial communication, how corporations have been communicating their commitment to equality, and challenges for the future. More extensive discussions of other communication issues affecting men and women in organizations can be found in Fairhurst (1986), Powell (1999), and Stewart, Cooper, Stewart, and Friedley (2001).

GENDERED LEGAL ISSUES

Two of the most important legal issues in the workplace that have a gendered component are (1) affirmative action and equal opportunity legislation, and (2) sexual harassment.

Since 1964, most companies have been required by the federal government to follow *affirmative action and equal opportunity* guidelines that prohibit discrimination on the basis of race, color, religion, sex, and national origin. More recent additions to this legislation include age, physical disability, pregnancy, and childbirth or related medical conditions. Some local communities have also included sexual orientation in their antidiscrimination laws. These laws are designed to give all members of the workforce equal access to opportunities for jobs and to prevent employees from unnecessary harassment. It is evident from the previous discussions, however, these laws do not guarantee that all people progress through the organizational hierarchy at an equal rate. Although affirmative action (recruiting and hiring people who have been underrepresented in specific job categories) has become a controversial topic and one that may be prohibited by the courts (Lee, 1993), workplaces should be committed to avoiding discrimination and to providing equal employment opportunities for all employees.

A second area of legal policy that has received a great deal of attention and communication-based research is *sexual harassment.* Sexual harassment continues to be a problem in the workplace for women and even for some men (Lee, 1993). Sexual harassment has been defined by the Equal Employment Opportunity Commission as

> unwelcome sexual advances, request for sexual favors, and other verbal and physical conduct of a sexual nature . . . when (1) submission to such conduct is made either explicitly or implicitly a term or condition of an individual's employment, (2) submission to or rejection of such conduct by an individual is used as the basis for employment decisions affecting such individuals, (3) or such conduct has the purpose or effect of unreasonably interfering with an individual's work performance or creating an intimidating, hostile, or offensive work environment. (Mastalli, 1981: 94)

Thus, sexual harassment appears in two primary forms: hostile work environment and quid pro quo. Hostile work environment includes unwanted sexually oriented behaviors such as inappropriate email of a sexual nature, verbal harassment, and unwanted touching. Quid pro quo harassment is the demand for sexual favors in order to retain a job or gain a promotion.

From a communication perspective, sexual harassment is an exchange between two people in which one exhibits sexual approach behaviors, the other counters with sexual avoidance behaviors, and the first subsequently exhibits additional sexual approach behavior (Simon and Montgomery, 1987). Such sexual approach behaviors often appear in ascending stages. In other words, the harasser may begin with more subtle behavior such as joking that escalates to a more extreme behavior such as physical touching (Booth-Butterfield, 1986). One survey (Loy and Stewart, 1984) found that approximately half the reported incidents of sexual harassment were verbal commentary (sexual messages delivered through innuendo or off-color jokes). Thirty-six percent of the incidents reported in this survey involved physical contact such as unwanted touching or groping. Verbal negotiation (explicit requests to exchange sex for economic or career benefits) occurred 10 percent of the time. Three percent of the reported incidents involved actual physical assault. Sexual harassment is an important workplace issue not only because it has negative effects on employees' health and well-being, but because companies are responsible for their employees' behavior and can be held legally liable for the negative consequences suffered as a result of this behavior (Sandroff, 1988).

Women in nontraditional jobs are often the targets of sexual harassment. A report issued by the National Council for Research on Women (*Sexual Harassment*, 1995) points out that many occupations, ranging from construction worker to neurosurgeon, have been historically dominated by men with 25 percent or less of the job holders being women. Women working in these professions are often the targets of harassment both from coworkers and supervisors.

Women of color may suffer a particularly negative impact of sexual harassment. As Crenshaw (1991) notes: "Pervasive stereotypes about black women not only shape the kinds of harassment that black women experience but they also influence whether black women's stories are likely to be believed, and even when they are believed, whether their insult or violation matters" (cited in *Sexual Harassment*, 1995: 30). African-American women may be harassed due to both race and sex (*Sexual Harassment*, 1995).

Communicating Equality

Corporations are responding to the changing workforce, including gender issues, in a variety of ways. Many *job qualifications* have been altered to accommodate women applicants. For example, in many communities, the physical test required to become eligible to be a firefighter has been modified to identify qualified applicants without discriminating against women due to their smaller size and weight. *Training programs* reflect the diverse composition of the workforce and have eliminated bias in the content and presentation of programs. For example, it is not acceptable to use sexist language or all-male terminology in case study materials (such as referring to "salesmen" or assuming that all machine operators are male or that all secretaries are female) or to use visual media that portray women and minorities only in support roles and men only in decision-making roles. In addition, on-the-job training programs have been designed to prepare both men and women for jobs that have traditionally been held by men. A woman doing telephone repair work may be a result of this type of program.

Some companies have expanded their *employee services* by adding child care support, flexible work schedules, and programs where special interest groups address the needs of a more diverse employee population. For example, one survey found that 56 percent of 259 major employers offer some type of child care aid, 56 percent allow flexible scheduling, and 42 percent grant unpaid parental leave (Fierman, 1990). The Family and Medical Leave Act was passed in 1993 and entitles employees to unpaid leave to care for newborn or adopted children or family members who are ill. This legislation is an important step in recognizing the complicated relationship between work and personal life. Nevertheless, some experts worry that since more women than men take advantage of this benefit, employers may be increasingly reluctant to hire or promote women (Lee, 1993).

Employment interviewing is another area that is receiving increased attention in terms of preventing gender bias in organizations. Changes in interviewing practices include advertising, recruitment, interview structure, decision-making, and record-keeping requirements. Job advertisements may contain a statement encouraging women and minority applicants. Many companies conduct outreach recruitment efforts designed to attract a more diverse applicant pool. The structure of an employment interview is often carefully planned to include the job description, hiring criteria, and assessment of the applicant's qualifications. Decision making is based on multiple contacts and clear documentation. In addition, companies must keep accurate records that contain nondiscriminatory applicant profiles and clearly specify the results of the interviews.

Graves (1999) provides a comprehensive assessment of the research literature on employment interviewing and gender issues (see also chapter 10 of this text). She concludes that both the observational and experimental studies of gender bias in employment interviews yield mixed results. She notes: "The prevalence of complex interactions between applicant gender and other factors suggests that the critical issue is not whether gender bias occurs, but under what conditions it occurs" (153). For example, women who are perceived as unattractive or obese are more likely to be victims of discrimination than men with the same characteristics.

Chapter 10 examines fully issues related to gender and the employment interview. However, applicants in employment interviews can ask themselves the following questions to identify signs of gender bias:

1. Did I feel comfortable? Was I treated with courtesy and respect?
2. Did I experience any direct examples of discrimination (questions, jokes, social references)?
3. Does the company have a public image of fair action? (Look for a corporate mission statement or code of ethics.)
4. What opportunities for training and advancement are available? How does my performance affect consideration for promotion?
5. Are there special group activities, benefits, and projects that are of interest to me?
6. Check references and referrals. Some companies are recognized particularly for their progress on gender issues. Review the annual report and product literature and talk to customers.

The more applicants know about a company, the better they can evaluate their opportunities for career advancement.

Once an applicant is hired, the commitment to eliminating gender bias should continue. *Performance appraisals* have been revised in many companies to avoid gender bias. Modifications have occurred in the structure and scheduling of performance appraisals, in the training and decision making of the appraiser, and in improvement programs used as follow-ups to the appraisal. Appraisals should be performance-based and results-oriented. They should be evenly distributed throughout the work year and routinely administered. Appraisers should be trained to eliminate bias in delivering feedback to employees, and their decisions may be subjected to third-party review in order to ensure consistency in appraisals. While males traditionally have used informal communication networks to their advantage in organizations, females may have been excluded. Thus, companies may assign mentors to female employees to facilitate their success in meeting the goals identified in a performance appraisal.

A great deal of research has been conducted that identifies various factors that could lead to bias in performance appraisals. Bartol (1999) has written a comprehensive review of this research and concludes that "studies to date suggest that neither males nor females give higher ratings to same gender ratees, nor do they consistently give higher or lower ratings to opposite-gender ratees" (169).

Managerial Communication Styles in Organizations

In the past, organizations emphasized productivity, competition, and independence (Grant, 1988). In this way, much of the formal communication in organizations is based on a traditionally masculine model of interaction. According to Devine and Markiewicz (1990), "organizations pride themselves on their creation of rational structures based primarily on a male perspective of interaction. Workers are expected to set aside interpersonal behaviors that do not directly contribute to task performance" (333). Workers have been expected to focus on competition, strategy, and "bottom-line results." This type of thinking has occurred because "organizations have traditionally been established and managed by men. Rational structures were consciously created where decision-making processes, communication patterns and norms of interaction were based on normative male experiences of relationships and approaches to work" (Devine and Markiewicz, 1990: 333).

Yet, according to Devine and Markiewicz (1990):

> as more women enter organizations at managerial levels, they bring with them their own norms of relationship, friendship and interaction. . . . The importance of relationships for women is reflected in such tendencies as (1) women's emphasis on assisting others to achieve the others' goals; (2) the emphasis on establishing the security of intimate relationships prior to consideration of personal achievement; (3) women's tendency to define themselves in relation to others; (4) women's inclination towards self-disclosure and the development of close relationships with others. (333)

Related themes in men's lives include:

> (1) relationships (e.g., mentor, spouse, friends) as instrumental to attaining one's career goals or "dream"; (2) the emphasis on succeeding in one's career during early adulthood; (3) the importance of work and

> achievements in defining male identity; (4) men's tendency to avoid self-disclosure and to develop few, if any, close relationships with coworkers. (Devine and Markiewicz, 1990: 333)

Grant (1988) believes that "women's greater ease with the relational world could help make organizations places in which affiliation, friendship, connection, and personhood could also be valued in a more integrated manner" (60). She criticizes organizations in the past for creating "she-males"—women who have moved up the organizational hierarchy of success and who strongly identify with the male model of managerial success. Of course, the "she-male" is often negatively perceived by her male peers. For example, one consultant notes, "the most common lament of top management men is 'She's too shrill. She's too aggressive. She's too hard-edged'" (Fierman, 1990: 46). Women often feel trapped by these attitudes. If their communication style is "too feminine," they are perceived as too soft; if they adopt a more traditionally masculine style they are seen as abrasive (Fierman, 1990).

Although we have come a long way from the "power pumps era" of the 1970s and 1980s in which many women believed that to win the corporate game required a poker-faced mentality and an imitation of men's behavior (Oldenburg, 1990), working closely with women continues to make some male executives uncomfortable (Fierman, 1990). Ellie Raynolds, a partner at Ward Howell International, notes that:

> Corporate males still don't know how to deal with women. They are afraid to yell at them or to give them negative feedback. It's as though they think they are yelling at their mothers or their wives. Men often worry women will run from the room in tears, or worse yet, yell back. They're not really sure the women will come through for them. They don't trust them as much as the guys with whom they talk football. (Fierman, 1990: 42)

To find out how men and women in organizations actually communicate with each other, Statham (1987) surveyed a matched sample of women and men in management jobs and interviewed their secretaries. The managers worked for three diverse organizations—a financial institution, a manufacturing firm, and a technical institute. The female managers described themselves as both "people oriented" and "task oriented." The male managers focused more on the importance of their jobs (called "image engrossment" by Statham). Statham concluded that the women used their people orientation to accomplish tasks while the men valued autonomy in their jobs. This difference in managerial style was most clear in the area of delegation. Women felt a need to be involved with their subordinates while men believed that good management entailed *not* being involved in what their subordinates were doing. These styles were often resented by employees of the other sex. For example, women perceived male managers' autonomy as neglect, and men felt that women managers' need to be involved was an indication that women managers were not confident in their male subordinates' abilities to carry out a task. Statham differentiates between the male ethos of "give everybody space to do their jobs" and the female desire to "look over their shoulders" (422). Although Statham acknowledges several exceptions in which women were concerned about autonomy and men were more involved, she concludes:

> Men managers leave women subordinates to struggle on their own because they believe this is the "best way to manage." Men subordinates resent women managers who "stand over their shoulders" because this signals to them a lack of confidence, while the woman believes she is demonstrating her "concern for the employee." And women resent men who "dump the work" onto others or who in other ways are perceived as not contributing as much as women. (425)

Thus, men and women in organizations may see the same behavior and attach different meanings to it.

Helgesen (1990) examines "women's ways of leadership" and finds that women are more likely than men to view unscheduled tasks and encounters not as interruptions but as a natural part of the workday. Thus, informal communication (such as dropping by to ask a coworker about a sick child) is seen as an important way to let employees know that a manager cares about them. Helgesen uses words such as "caring, being involved, helping, and being responsible" (21) to describe the female managers she studied. Helgesen also points out that women managers preferred face-to-face communication to conversations over the telephone, but that the mail was seen as a valuable way to maintain relationships with peers in the workforce.

In general, women have a more positive attitude than men toward women as managers, but people who have worked with a woman manager have a less traditional view of women as managers than those who have not had this type of work experience (Wheeless and Berryman-Fink, 1985). Thus, as more women become corporate executives and more people have experience working with women executives, attitudes toward them are changing.

Although perceptions of women in leadership positions are changing, there is still a relative absence of women in the very top managerial levels of corporations—the so-called "glass ceiling effect." Researchers at the University of California at Los Angeles Graduate School of Management and Korn/Ferry (a corporate recruiter) surveyed approximately 700 top executives and found that between 1979 and 1990 neither women nor minorities increased their ranks at the level of senior vice president or above by more than 2 percentage points (Silver, 1990). The U.S. government's Glass Ceiling Commission estimated that women held only 5 percent of senior executive positions in 1996 (Women in American boardrooms, 1997). All of the respondents in one study (male and female managers as well as their secretaries) mentioned a "point beyond which women could not go" (Statham, 1987). Thus, it appears that there has been little progress after almost 20 years of growing awareness of the importance of promoting women and minorities.

According to a report by the Women's Research and Education Institute, the lack of women at the top of corporate hierarchies cannot be explained solely by their recent entry into those professions. Women have not reached the top of the corporate hierarchy in part because of the gender stereotype held by many corporate decision makers that women do not have the personality characteristics necessary for top leadership roles (Rich, 1990). *Fortune* magazine polled 1,000 CEOs to determine why women are not progressing into the highest levels of corporate management. Of the 241 respondents to the survey, 81 percent attributed the problem to stereotyping and preconceptions (Fierman, 1990). As one authority notes, "it's a little bit surprising that there hasn't been more breakthrough [for women and minorities]. There're barriers imposed if you don't share the same interests or follow the same football teams" (quoted in Silver, 1990).

The type of organization may influence attitudes toward women in leadership positions. Companies that deal with high technology products and small start-up companies are often more accommodating to women executives. Since new industries are less likely to be run by the old boys' network (Fierman, 1990), they allow women to maximize the benefits of their own communication style.

CHALLENGES FOR THE FUTURE

As you can see from the discussion presented above, many challenges face workers as we move into the twenty-first century. According to Colwill and Erhart (1985), "education, attitude change, the establishment of women's networks, and improved communication between men and women [are] catalysts for sex-role change" in organizations (30).

Thus, one of the best communication strategies for women to use to overcome barriers in the workplace is *networking*. As noted previously in this chapter, although women are entering organizations in increasing numbers, their progress to the highest level of the corporate ladder is often blocked by barriers, such as gender bias that limits the advancement and compensation of female executives. Colwill and Erhart (1985) found that women who used networks such as membership in private clubs or on corporate boards were more successful than women who did not have these contacts. Networking can be through formal information channels such as head-hunting firms or informal channels such as family and friends (Bartlett and Miller, 1985). These networks are often successful because over 40 percent of managerial jobs are discovered by word of mouth (Corcoran, Datcher, and Duncan, 1980). Helgesen (1990) found that the successful women managers she studied maintained a complex network of relationships with people outside the office as did their male counterparts. Although women's networking may include contacts with groups that include men, the number of business networks solely for women is increasing (Northcraft and Gutek, 1993).

In addition to networking, women are also seeking *mentors*. Some companies have formed mentoring programs for their women employees, and the Small Business Administration has established a Women's Network for

Entrepreneurial Training that pairs successful women business owners with new business owners (Northcraft and Gutek, 1993).

Telecommuting is an organizational phenomenon that is increasingly available to workers today. Experts expect that this work option will help women in particular by allowing them to work from home while caring for small children. Companies are beginning to offer employees training in telecommuting including advice on setting up appropriately designed home offices as well as assistance in coping with the isolation from coworkers (Johnson, 1997). Some theorists even speculate that the availability of telecommuting will encourage men to become more involved in their family's day-to-day activities. Northcraft and Gutek (1993) note that "flextime scheduling and telecommuting provide ways for men to retain career involvement while becoming primary caregivers for their children" (223).

Prospects for better pay for women are also increasing. According to one authority, "a shrinking labor force is expected to force employers to compete for workers and that is expected to mean better pay for women" (Mann, 1990). Hopefully, this change in the workforce will also help to eliminate the glass ceiling. As one researcher notes, "our best hope for the future are women who don't see the ceiling but the sky" (quoted in Fierman, 1990: 62).

Many corporations have introduced programs to help their employees deal with and manage the increasing diversity of the workforce. *Managing diversity* means that managers' performance is judged on their ability to manage a diverse workforce (Duke, 1991). Also, as managing cultural diversity programs become more popular, all employees are being challenged to confront their own negative stereotypes about people who are different from themselves (Duke, 1991). These changes should also contribute to the increased understanding between men and women and to the increased success of women in organizations.

In addition to increased diversity within a corporation, to be successful in today's competitive business environment, organizations must meet the needs of a more diverse customer base. For example, cosmetics manufacturers need to acknowledge the needs and preferences of women of color as well as Caucasian women. A contemporary corporation cannot be successful without responding to the diversity of the marketplace. Thus, issues of gender have a particular importance for corporations attempting to meet the needs of the future both in terms of encouraging creativity and adaptability in the workforce and rejecting traditional managerial stereotypes that limit hiring and responsiveness to customers (Northcraft and Gutek, 1993).

For Further Discussion

1. Collect the annual reports of at least twenty major corporations. Read them carefully and analyze them for signs of gender bias. How many women are on the boards of directors? How many women are corpo-

rate officers? How are women portrayed in pictures? Are any special programs for increasing diversity mentioned? What can you conclude about the organizations' commitment to workplace diversity and to the advancement of women, in particular?

2. Identify specific women's networks in your area. Interview several people active in each one. Answer the following questions about each network: (1) Is this a formal, national network or an informal group of people trying to help each other?; (2) Are men encouraged to become part of the network or excluded from it? Why or why not?; (3) What is the network designed to accomplish? How successful is it?; (4) What communication strategies are used by network members to achieve success in their careers?
3. Collect examples of at least ten training programs designed to help employees. Analyze each one for signs of gender bias. How are the programs designed to overcome gender bias? How are they indicative of gender bias? Did you find any signs of "hidden bias"—for example, all-male referents, lack of female examples, or male-oriented content?
4. Make a list of potential conflicts between the workplace and family responsibilities. How can organizations best deal with these conflicts? What types of arrangements can be implemented to help employees cope with these conflicting demands?
5. Have two people role-play a stereotypical feminine managerial communication style and a stereotypical masculine managerial style. Which style do you feel is most successful? Now have the male and female switch roles (that is, the male acts like a "feminine" manager and the female acts like a "masculine" manager). What differences do you observe? How do you evaluate these styles now?

References

Bartlett, R. L., and T. I. Miller. 1985. Executive compensation: Female executives and networking. *AEA Papers and Proceedings* 75: 267–270.

Bartol, K. M. 1999. Gender influences on performance evaluations. In G. N. Powell, ed., *Handbook of Gender and Work.* Thousand Oaks, CA: Sage, 165–178.

Booth-Butterfield, M. 1986. Recognizing and communicating in harassment-prone organizational climates. *Communication Quarterly* 9: 42–51.

Colwill, N. L., and M. Erhart. 1985. Have women changed the workplace? *Business Quarterly* Spring: 27–31.

Corcoran, M., L. Datcher, and G. J. Duncan. 1980. Most workers find jobs through word of mouth. *Monthly Labor Review* 103: 33–35.

Crenshaw, K. 1991, November. Presentation at the Center for the American Woman in Politics Forum for Women State Legislators, San Diego, CA.

Devine, I., and D. Markiewicz. 1990. Cross-sex relationships at work and the impact of gender stereotypes. *Journal of Business Ethics* 9: 333–338.

Duke, L. 1 January 1991. Cultural shifts bring anxiety for white men. *Washington Post*, A1, A14.

Equal pay for working families: A national overview. 1999. *Institute for Women's Policy Research Research-in-Brief.* Washington, DC: Institute for Women's Policy Research, 1–4.

Fairhurst, G. T. 1986. Male-female communication on the job: Literature review and commentary. In M. McLaughlin, ed., *Communication Yearbook* 10. Newbury Park, CA: Sage, 83–116.

Fierman, J. 30 July 1990. Why women still don't hit the top. *Fortune*, 40–62.

Grant, J. 1988. Women as managers: What they can offer to organizations. *Organizational Dynamics* 16(3): 56–63.

Graves, L. M. 1999. Gender bias in interviewers' evaluations of applicants: When and how does it occur? In G. N. Powell, ed., *Handbook of Gender and Work.* Thousand Oaks, CA: Sage, 145–164.

Helgesen, S. 1990. *The Female Advantage: Women's Ways of Leadership.* New York: Doubleday.

Johnson, K. 17 December 1997. Limits on the work-at-home life. *The New York Times*, B1, B4.

Lee, B. A. 1993. The legal and political realities for women managers: The barriers, the opportunities, and the horizon ahead. In E. A. Fagenson, ed., *Women in Management: Trends, Issues and Challenges in Managerial Diversity.* Newbury Park, CA: Sage, 246–269.

Loy, P. H., and L. P. Stewart. 1984. The extent and effects of the sexual harassment of working women. *Sociological Focus* 17: 31–43.

Mann, J. 17 August 1990. The shatterproof ceiling. *Washington Post*, D3.

Mastalli, G. L. 1981. Appendix: The legal context. *Harvard Business Review* 59(2): 94–95.

Northcraft, G. B., and B. A. Gutek. 1993. Point-counterpoint: Discrimination against women in management—Going, going, gone or going but never gone? In E. A. Fagenson, ed., *Women in Management: Trends, Issues and Challenges in Managerial Diversity.* Newbury Park, CA: Sage, 219–245.

Oldenburg, D. 29 October 1990. Cracking the ceiling with a smile. *Washington Post*, B5.

Powell, G. N., ed. 1999. *Handbook of Gender and Work.* Thousand Oaks, CA: Sage.

Reskin, B., and I. Padavic. 1994. *Women and Men at Work.* Thousand Oaks, CA: Pine Forge Press.

Rich, S. 26 April 1990. Women's pay still far behind men's, group reports. *Washington Post*, A9.

Sandroff, R. 1988, December. Sexual harassment in the Fortune 500. *Working Women*, 69–73.

Sexual Harassment: Research and Resources. 1995. New York: National Council for Research on Women.

Silver, L. 14 August 1990. Few women, minorities at the top. *Washington Post*, A1, A5.

Simon, S., and B. M. Montgomery. 1987, May. *Sexual Harassment: Applying a Communication Perspective.* Paper presented at the meeting of the Eastern Communication Association, Syracuse, NY.

Statham, A. 1987. The gender model revisited: Differences in the management styles of men and women. *Sex Roles* 16: 409–429.

Stewart, L. P., P. J. Cooper, A. D. Stewart, and S. A. Friedley. 2001. *Communication and Gender,* 4th ed. Boston, MA: Allyn and Bacon.

U.S. Department of Labor. 1989, December. *Facts on Working Women, Women's Bureau No. 89-4.* Washington, DC: U.S. Government Printing Office.

Wheeless, V. E., and C. Berryman-Fink. 1985. Perceptions of women managers and their communicator competencies. *Communication Quarterly* 33: 137–148.

Women in American boardrooms: Through a glass, darkly. 1997, March/April. *Women in Management* 7(3): 3.

CHAPTER 11

Intersections of Gender and Employment Interviewing

Steven M. Ralston
Amber E. Kinser

POINTS TO BE ADDRESSED

- Federal employment practice (FEP) laws
- Summary of the research literature
- Explanations for inconsistent findings
- Verbal and nonverbal grammars of the ideal candidate profile
- Gender and the grammar of the ideal candidate profile

Recently, one of the authors was told the following story by a woman who had applied for a position in the insurance industry. After following the usual protocol of submitting a letter of interest and resume, the woman received notice that she had been selected to participate in a phone interview. She was excited about the opportunity and prepared for what she hoped would be a chance to demonstrate her knowledge and interest. Unfortunately, the interview was anything but what she had expected. Shortly into the conversation, the male interviewer (who was also the office manager) began asking questions about the woman's marital status, child care plans, and the like. Flustered at first, the woman recovered and asked why the interviewer wanted to know about such personal, job-irrelevant information. The interviewer responded that he didn't believe that a woman with a husband and children would have the time and energy to do the job well. Disgusted, the woman ended the interview. Eventually, the woman found a rewarding job, and to end one of those "there is justice in the world" stories, the insurance organization to which the woman originally applied for a job went out of business shortly after the interview.

Unfortunately, what happened to the woman in the story might not be an isolated case. Clearly, women have made significant inroads toward workplace equality. However, it is unwise to confuse *movement toward* a destination with *arrival* at that destination. Because women began their movement toward equality from what Felice Schwartz (1992) calls a "zero point" (as cited in Murphy and Zorn, 1996: 214), they are farther behind than where men currently stand. Recent evidence suggests that women continue to report bias in the workplace. For instance, Lord (1999) indicates that discrimination complaints among pregnant women were up 48 percent in 1994 from what was reported in 1990. Others (Rheem, 1999; Stuart, 1992) suggest that despite their increased presence in the workforce, women remain disadvantaged in obtaining middle- and upper-management positions. Similarly, Eagly, Makhijani and Klonsky's (1992) meta-analysis of published research showed that women remain disadvantaged in assuming leadership positions, albeit the effect size is smaller than in the past. Echoing this sentiment, Hite and McDonald (1995) found that although women hold 42 percent of management positions, only 5 percent are in top-level positions. One only has to read these and other recent accounts of apparent gender inequity to conclude that what goes on in contemporary organizations may not always be fair and just.

The employment interview plays an important role in establishing and maintaining workplace equality. Kirkwood and Ralston (1999) posit, "the employment interview is more than just a gateway to the organization. Whatever transpires between parties during interviews is part of their long-term relationship" (56). In addition, it is through the interview that employers mold political and cultural organizational force by recruiting and selecting new employees (Ralston and Kirkwood, 1995). Given its centrality to establishing women's roles in the workplace, the intersection of gender and employment interviewing is explored in this chapter. First, we briefly examine federal employment practice (FEP) law that has relevance to employment interviewing discrimination. The second section considers the research literature on gender and employment interviewing. In the third section, we explore gendered behavior and relevant cultural assumptions in an effort to sharpen the seemingly blurry picture of gender bias in employment interviewing painted by the research literature.

Federal Employment Practice Law

Title VII of the 1964 Civil Rights Act, the Age Discrimination in Employment Act (ADEA) of 1967, and the Americans with Disabilities Act (ADA) of 1990 conjointly specify that employers with 15 (Title VII and the

ADA) or 20 (ADEA) employees cannot discriminate on the basis of race, color, religion, national origin, age (if 40 or older), disability or gender. These federal laws are most clearly manifest in the concepts of "disparate (different) impact" and "disparate treatment."[1] Disparate impact refers to policies and practices that may seem evenhanded but in fact have a discriminatory impact on applicants. For instance, imagine that hiring criteria for a particular position mandated that qualified candidates must meet certain height and weight requirements, and yet such demographics are neither a business necessity nor job-relevant. Imagine, too, that most women cannot meet these criteria. In such instances, the hiring benchmark could be said to have a disparate impact on women applicants. Disparate impact is a matter of procedural justice because it involves the perceived fairness of a particular hiring procedure. As Bible (1998) puts it, "a shorthand way of explaining 'disparate impact' is that it involves policies which are fair in form but [are] discriminatory in fact" (9).

Disparate treatment occurs when an employer discriminates against an otherwise qualified candidate on the basis of race, age, gender, and so forth. For example, disparate treatment would cover instances wherein a fully qualified woman is denied employment because of her marital status. The unfortunate woman in our opening story who was questioned about her marital status and child care arrangements experienced a form of disparate treatment. Presumably, the employer did not ask similar questions of male applicants, and men were not held to the same hiring standards. In other words, disparate treatment falls under the category of distributive justice, which is the similar treatment of all job candidates participating in the interview process.[2]

The importance of disparate impact and treatment for the intersection of gender and employment interviewing is most evident in employers' questioning protocols. Roehling, Campion, and Arvey (1999) posit four ways in which FEP law impacts employers' questioning of applicants. First, the ADA and some states strictly prohibit questioning about some topics (albeit the list is relatively small). For example, the ADA prohibits questions about the existence of applicants' disabilities or the severity of a given disability. Second, Roehling et al. further indicate that disparate questioning across groups of candidates violates FEP. Generally speaking, all candidates should be asked the same questions. The third way FEP affects questioning is that although few topics are outright denied to the employer (see point 1), the EEOC (Equal Employment Opportunity Commission, 1981) makes it clear that questions regarding the candidate's race, ethnicity, gender, and so forth, are looked upon with disfavor. Roehling et al. point out that "unless such questions are otherwise explained, courts have frequently viewed them as evidence of discriminatory intent" (56). Barring questions that apparently seem neutral, but that actually involve selection criteria that result in adverse impact, is the fourth way FEP influences interview questioning.

The proliferation of advice to female job candidates about responding to illegal questions effectively suggests that women face unique challenges in employment interviewing, despite efforts to legislate away the problem. For instance, in an effort to help women respond to such questions effectively, Wilson (1991) offered eight response categories: termination of the interview, direct refusal, direct refusal with reason, asking how information relates to job qualification, indicating that the requested information is personal, acknowledging employer concern about what the question addresses, answering employer's perceived concern, and answering the question and the employer's perceived concern (48). It seems clear that gender-related issues remain important in the study and practice of employment interviewing. We now summarize the research literature on gender and employment interviewing, where we will find that the literature presents a rather muddy picture.

SUMMARY OF THE RESEARCH LITERATURE

What can the research literature tell us about gender bias in employment interviewing? This section summarizes the current research literature in an effort to better understand women's experiences in the employment interview. The importance of gender-based interview discrimination is evidenced by the numerous reviews of the literature (e.g., Arvey, 1979; Arvey and Campion, 1982; Campion and Arvey, 1989; Graves, 1999; Harris, 1989; Roehling, Campion, and Arvey, 1999). We first consider the extent to which research demonstrates that gender bias occurs as a result of employment interviews. We then examine variables associated with possible gender bias in interviews. We conclude this section of the chapter by positing three possible explanations for the discordant research findings.

The Occurrence of Gender Bias in Employment Interviewing

The research about gender bias in job recommendations based on employment interviewing provides few definitive answers. On the one hand, some studies have found evidence of sex discrimination in employment interviewing. For example, Kinicki and Lockwood (1985) sought to uncover factors used in making hiring recommendations by observing recruiters interviewing students. The researchers discovered that recruiters employed many job-irrelevant, subjective factors, including gender similarity (the likeness of sex between the interviewer and interviewee), in making hiring decisions. Similarly, Hitt and Barr's (1989) investigation of policy-capturing (the variables and processes involved in making personnel decisions) and interviewer decisions examined the relative influence of job-relevant information (e.g., experience) and job-irrelevant demographic information (e.g., gender) on employment decisions. Sixty-eight managers used videotaped oral resumes to rate 16 applicants and to make salary recommendations. The results showed that managers in the study used job-irrelevant information when rating applicants and when making salary recommendations. In particular, female applicants were rated lower and received lower salary than males. Similarly, Marlowe, Schneider, and Nelson's (1996) investigation found clear evidence of gender bias. Specifically, their data indicated that men were judged more suitable for an executive position than were women.

Some research found no bias against women, while some studies showed bias in favor of women. For instance, a series of investigations (e.g., Cable and Judge, 1997; Graves and Powell, 1996) discovered that female applicants were more favorably evaluated than men. To make the issue even more confounding, some research (e.g., Graves and Powell, 1995) has found favoritism toward men by female interviewers, whereas other investigations (e.g., Kacmar and Hochwarter, 1995) reported no evidence of favoritism toward either female or male applicants. For example, unlike similar investigations (e.g., Hitt and Barr, 1989; Kinicki and Lockwood, 1985), Raza and Carpenter (1987) discovered that interviewers consistently used job-relevant information over job-irrelevant information, including gender, when making hiring decisions.

Russo and Ommeren's (1998) investigation found no evidence of gender-based hiring discrimination. These researchers subjected data gleaned from surveys from over 20,000 job vacancies to a sophisticated statistical modeling procedure. The results indicated that male and female applicants have the same statistical chances of being hired. The data did reveal, however, that the gender composition of the applicant pool is significantly related to hiring decisions. In other words, if significantly more males make up an applicant pool for a given position, then it is likely that a man will be hired.

Variables Associated with Gender Bias

Our review of the research provides no conclusive evidence of meaningful gender bias in the employment interview. Yet, since the early 1970s, research has identified many variables relevant to gender that are believed to play an important role in the interview processes and associated outcomes. How sex role stereotypes and applicant and interviewer characteristics interact with gender to influence the employment interview are examined next.

Sex Role Stereotype. Among the most interesting research areas regarding gender and employment interviewing are studies examining the extent to which gender-based job stereotypes influence employers' perceptions of candidates and hiring recommendations. Simply put: Does the perception of jobs as having a male or female orientation affect employers' judgments and decisions? In one of the earliest investigations on the matter, Cohen and Bunker (1975) asked recruiters to assess the employment materials (i.e., resume, application, test scores, references) of a hypothetical applicant (male or female) for either a male-oriented position (technician) or female-oriented position (editorial assistant). The results indicated that males were significantly more often recommended for the male-oriented position than were women; women were recommended significantly more often than were males for the female-oriented job. A decade later, Arvey, Miller, Gould, and Burch's (1987) study also found evidence of sex role stereotyping. When applicants' sex and age were compared with interview judgments, the data showed that female candidates were given significantly higher evaluations for a retail clerk position (female orientation) than were men.

Futoran and Wyler (1986) also investigated the sex role stereotype phenomenon. Subjects in their investigation read packets of information about one of two job candidates (male or female) and were asked to form an impression of the candidate. Afterward, subjects were asked to rate the candidate's suitability from a list of nine occupations, which had been previously rated as having either a masculine or feminine orientation. The results confirmed that candidates' gender functioned as an independent, job-relevant variable in the matching of candidates and positions. Commenting on their results, the researchers noted, "candidates were considered more suitable for occupations with which their gender was stereotypically consistent than for those with which their gender was inconsistent" (489). Futoran and Wyler's (1986) findings are similar to those of Davis and Penner (1986), who confirmed the presence of sex matching when men evaluated women for male- and female-oriented positions. No such pattern was found for women evaluating men.

More recent investigations (Zebrowitz, Tenenbaum, and Goldstein, 1991) further establish the link between applicant sex and position stereotype. Similar to past studies, Heilman (1984) and Heilman, Martell, and Simon (1988) found evidence of sex role stereotyping in employment decisions. Zebrowitz, Tenenbaum, and Goldstein (1991) conducted two studies investigating job applicants' facial maturity, gender, and level of achievement on hiring decisions. Their data showed that women were preferred for jobs perceived to require warmth and submission, whereas males were preferred for jobs perceived to require shrewdness and leadership. The researchers concluded by suggesting that female and babyfaced applicants are most likely to be discriminated against when applying for higher status positions. Concluding their own investigation on the issue, Van Vianen and Willemsen (1992) posited that "women are less likely to be selected for jobs which are sex typed as masculine" (487). More recently, Perry (1994) found less support for sex stereotyping, noting however that the matching of positions with sex may be in greater evidence when employers' decisions are less easily censored and when applicant gender is considered along with other job-irrelevant variables, such as age.

Overall, the research tends to support evidence of sex stereotyping in employment interviewing. As women make significant strides into positions that were once mostly occupied by men (and as men assume jobs once thought to have feminine orientation), we would expect less evidence of sex role stereotyping. Nonetheless, given that women appear to experience some difficulty ascending to upper management positions (see Hite and McDonald, 1995), it would appear that sex role stereotyping remains a problem. We now consider how gender interacts with characteristics of applicants and interviewers to influence employment interview processes and outcomes.

Applicant and Recruiter Characteristics. In addition to examining how sex role stereotyping influences women's employment opportunities, research has also considered how characteristics of both applicants and interviewers interact with gender to influence the interview. One recent avenue of research has investigated the similarity-attraction hypothesis. The similarity-attraction hypothesis predicts that when interviewers perceive applicants as similar to themselves, applicants will be rated more favorably and will receive stronger employment recommendations. Gallois, Callan, and Palmer's (1992) study indicated that female interviewers judged women applicants similar to themselves and judged men less like themselves. Male interviewers did not make similar distinctions between men and women applicants. Overall, however, the data showed that women were generally rated more favorably than men. Following up on Gallois et al.'s findings about differences between male and female recruiters, Graves and Powell (1995) found that female recruiters rated male applicants as more qualified than female candidates, whereas in 1996 Graves and Powell (1996) found just the opposite: Female recruiters rated female applicants over males. Graves and Powell commented that perhaps organizational imperatives, such as an emphasis on diversity, might explain the discordant findings.

Other investigations have addressed the effect of interviewer sex on applicant reactions and likelihood of accepting a job offer. Liden and Parsons (1986) studied the impact of recruiter sex on entry-level job applicants. Their data showed that while female recruiters were viewed as more personable and informative than their male counterparts, applicants who were interviewed by females had less positive reactions to the job than when they were interviewed by men. However, recruiter sex was not significantly related to applicant intentions to accept job offers. Similarly, Taylor and Bergmann's (1987) investigation explored the impact of recruiter age, gender, race, experience, job tenure, education, training, and job type on applicants' perceptions of company attractiveness and likelihood of accepting job offers. Among the many interesting findings, Taylor and Bergmann discovered that female applicants were more likely to accept job offers when interviewed by men. Male applicants showed no preference for either male or female recruiters. Likewise, Maurer, Howe, and Lee (1992) showed that women reacted more favorably when interviewed by men than when interviewed by women. Turban and Dougherty (1992) also examined the effect of recruiter–applicant similarity on employment interviewing. Contrary to the other studies cited here, these researchers discovered that males were more attracted to jobs when interviewed by male recruiters and less attracted when interviewed by women. Female applicants reported no preferences.

A series of investigations also explored how gender interacts with oral communication style and tactics to influence employment interviewing. In addition to examining potential effects for recruiter sex, Gallois, Callan, and Palmer (1992) also studied the interaction of communicator style and gender on hiring recommendations. The results were mixed. Generally, recruiters preferred an assertive communication style, irrespective of applicant sex. Yet, nonassertive women were viewed somewhat more favorably by some recruiters than were assertive women. Gallois et al. tentatively concluded, "These results are encouraging for assertive women who are concerned that a 'masculine' communication style may be inappropriate in an employment interview" (1055). In studies conducted in the mid-1970s, Dipboye and Wiley (1977; 1978) also found that recruiters preferred moderately aggressive males and females to passive applicants. More recently, Buttner and McEnally (1996) discovered that males using assertive styles (i.e., pressure) were more likely to receive hiring recommendations than when they used rational tactics (i.e., logic). However, women whose style emphasized rational tactics were more favored than when they behaved assertively.

Also addressing communication style and gender, Cianni-Surridge and Horan (1983) investigated the relationship among assertive job-seeking behavior, applicant sex, and industry size. Sixteen assertive behaviors were examined including applicant calling to arrange an interview appointment, applicant calling to arrange a second interview after the initial meeting went poorly, and applicant rescheduling an interview after the interviewer scheduled the initial meeting. Although the interaction among the variables produced some rather complex results, it was clear that applicant sex was not relevant to hiring decisions in the study. Similarly, Williams, Radefeld, Binning, and Sudak (1993) examined the impact of applicant and recruiter gender, applicant playing "hard-to-get," and objective information (e.g., GPA) on interviewers' evaluations of candidates. For the purposes of the study, "hard-to-get" involved applicants indicating if they were considering or not considering other job opportunities. Williams et al. did not find any significant differences in the way female and male applicants were evaluated. However, the results did show that male recruiters were more lenient in their judgments of application materials than their female counterparts.

Another fascinating area of research involving gender and interviewee characteristics centers on nonverbal attributes. In particular, studies have addressed facial maturity, physical attractiveness, and attire. Zebrowitz, Tenenbaum, and Goldstein's (1991) study on applicants' facial maturity, gender, and achievement found evidence of the interplay between applicant nonverbal characteristics and employment interviewing. The results of two investigations showed that raters favored job candidates who were either "babyfaced" or female for positions that involved displays of warmth and submission. On the other hand, either "maturefaced" or male candidates were preferred for positions in which shrewdness and leadership were a job requirement. Zebrowitz et al. concluded that "the jobs for which male and maturefaced applicants were favored were those for which high-achieving applicants were favored, which suggests that female and babyfaced applicants are most apt to be discriminated against when applying for higher status job" (525).

Marlowe, Schneider, and Nelson (1996) explored how applicant gender, attractiveness, and managerial work experience influenced employment suitability ratings. The results showed that in general, men are more likely to receive high ratings than women. Specifically, attractive men were more likely to receive higher employment suitability ratings for executive positions than attractive or unattractive women. However, attractive women were more likely to be rated higher than unattractive women. In effect, for executive positions, gender played the most important role. However, among women, attractiveness played an interactive role. To put it another way, women rated as unattractive were significantly less likely to receive positive recommendations for executive positions. Similarly, Pingitore, Dugoni, Tindale, and Spring (1994) found that overweight women were less likely to be hired than were overweight men. Yet, in an earlier investigation, women rated as unattractive were favored over attractive women for male-oriented management positions (Heilman and Saruwatari, 1979). Summarizing the research on physical attractiveness, gender, and employment interviewing, Morrow (1990) concluded:

> PA [physical attractiveness] is generally an asset for men. For women, the findings vary with the type of job. For managerial (masculine) jobs, PA is probably a handicap for women. Unattractive women, who might be regarded as less feminine and therefore more appropriate for the job, are preferred. However, if the managerial job is defined such that interpersonal skills are stressed, attractive females may not be penalized compared to unattractive females. For nonmanagerial jobs, PA is desirable; attractive women are rewarded more than unattractive females. However, attractive males will still be rewarded more highly than attractive females in these positions. (49)

Forsythe, Drake, and Cox (1985) and Forsythe (1990) examined the effect of female applicants' attire on male and female interviewers' selection decision for management positions. Costumes representing four levels of masculinity were used. Masculine attire was operationalized as vertical lines, straight silhouettes, strong angular lines, large-scale details, heavy textures, strong color contrasts, and dark or dull colors. Feminine costume was achieved though horizontal lines, rounded silhouettes, curved lines, small-scale details, soft, delicate textures, and light colors. The most masculine costume consisted of a dark navy, tailored suit and embodied the design elements identified above; the least masculine attire was a soft beige dress with the design characteristics associated with feminine dress. The two other costumes were intermediate designs along this masculine–feminine continuum. Prior to the study, all costumes were rated as appropriate for women in management positions.

After viewing videotaped interviews of one of four applicants who were dressed in one of the four costume conditions, interviewers made hiring recommendations. The results from both investigations indicated that clothing type affected interviewer judgments. Forsythe (1990) also found that masculinity of dress was associated with perceptions of interviewees' self-reliance, aggressiveness, dynamism, decisiveness, and forcefulness. Commenting on the results, Forsythe (1990) suggested, "the data show that increased costume masculinity resulted in more favorable hiring recommendations, regardless of the respondents' occupation or gender" (1588). Forsythe also indicated that contrary to the popular myth that masculine clothing is important only in conservative occupations, research suggests that masculine clothing is preferred across position types. Forsythe's two studies are consistent with previous research regarding attire. For instance, Harp, Stretch, and Harp (1985) showed that women newscasters were judged as more credible when wearing a more masculine business suit than when wearing less masculine attire. Damhorst and Reed (1986) found that women who wore dark colors were judged more favorably than women who wore light colors in an employment interview.

In an effort to synthesize the research and explain gender-based selection decisions, Perry, Davis-Blake, and Kulik (1994) proposed a comprehensive model in which cognitive and contextual explanations are melded together. Cognitive explanations include interviewers' use of personal schemas, such as an ideal applicant prototype, for the selection of men and women into different jobs. Contextual explanations refer to factors, such as the gender composition of the workforce and organizational structure, that predict gender segregation. Regrettably, space here does not permit a lengthy discussion of Perry et al.'s work. Essentially, the model indicates that contextual factors tend to affect cognition, which, in turn, prompts gender-based or gender-neutral selection decisions. However, Perry et al. propose a highly complex interaction of factors contributing to employment process and decisions. For instance, one of the model's twelve propositions suggests that decision makers are less likely to use existing gender-associated jobholder schemas when selection decisions are scrutinized by powerful external constituents. Another proposition notes that gender is more likely to be associated with decision makers' jobholder schemas when the applicant pool is occupied primarily by persons of one gender. Perry et al. offer a sophisticated and rich model for testing the myriad factors associated with gender and employment interviewing.

Explanations for the Research Findings

Perry, Davis-Blake, and Kulik's (1994) model notwithstanding, the research on gender and applicant/recruiter characteristics presents a puzzling and sometimes contradictory picture of gender and interviewing. Why did we not find more compelling evidence of gender bias in the employment interview? Given the convincing data already presented, suggesting the occurrence of gender bias in the workplace, and given the symbiotic relationship between interviewing and organizational culture (Kirkwood and Ralston, 1999; Ralston and Kirkwood, 1995), one would expect to find more evidence of gender bias in the employment interviewing research. We offer three possible explanations for this inconsistency: (1) past research methods failed to capture what actually goes on in the employment interview, (2) capturing the complexity of gender and employment interviewing is difficult, and (3) gendered assumptions about female and male behavior powerfully direct employment interview processes, yet they are so deeply embedded and firmly planted that they are difficult to uproot and examine.

Unreliable Research Methods. Constructing an investigation addressing a topic as sensitive as gender in a manner whereby participants provide reliable answers, rather than socially acceptable responses, is difficult. In their review of the gender and race research literature, Rosenstein and Hitt (1986) admonished researchers, stating, "Future research with more imaginative and complex designs and larger sample sizes are needed" (215). Ralston (1988) made the same point when he posited that research demands characteristics, such as experimental instruments, procedures, and task requirements, which often intrude upon normal responses to yield unreliable data. Ralston noted that "the researcher is charged with the difficult task of studying discrimination without giving the appearance of doing so" (222).

Simply put: The extant research might be unreliable because study participants may have behaved in a manner inconsistent with what they might have done in more normal circumstances. In statistical terms, the research findings could represent a Type I error, that is, not finding significance when, in fact, significance exists. To the extent that past research methods are unreliable, we must be very cautious in making generalizations about what actually occurs in the employment interview.

Complex Research Variables. Closely related to the first explanation, the second account for variance between the research literature and reports of gender discrimination concentrates on the complex nature of the phenomenon. Two principal arguments can be advanced here. First, since significant efforts have been made by federal and state governments to raise awareness of and to combat discrimination, it is entirely possible that many study participants were careful not to use gender in their hiring decisions. Yet, we see from studies that participants frequently reacted differently to members of the opposite sex than they did to members of their own sex (e.g., similarity-attraction), but apparently these varied reactions had no bearing on their hiring recommendations. To put it another way, gender-related differences might affect the interview process yet sometimes fail to influence hiring recommendations (i.e. outcomes). This explanation differs from the "socially acceptable" explanation in which study participants provide "acceptable"' responses during the interview process, rather than what they actually might do in circumstances that are not under scrutiny. The second argument that can be made about research complexity centers on the number of factors that contribute to personnel selection and employment interviewing. Graves (1999) posits that the "complex interactions between gender and a variety of other variables [makes] it difficult to assess the extent of gender discrimination" (160). Campion and Arvey (1989) reached the same conclusion, observing, "When more contextually rich and sophisticated research methods are used, puzzling differences occur across studies" (69). That is, the numerous and complex variables associated with gender and employment interviewing interact in such a way that rarely produce simple conclusions. Given the difficulty of constructing and carrying out studies on gender and employment interviewing, made all the more formidable by the sheer complexity of the phenomenon, we should not be surprised by the mixed results.

Cultural Assumptions. The third explanation for coming to terms with the discordant research literature and reports of continued gender bias suggests that cultural assumptions about gender and work make it difficult to investigate the matter and interpret the findings with clarity. There are probably very few of us who realize the extent to which our everyday behavior and our expectations for the behaviors of others are directed by gender stereotypes. As we have already discussed, legislation has been passed to guard against gender bias at work, and employers' sensitivities to gender bias have indeed increased. Yet, as we have also argued, such moves seem to have met with only relative success. Clearly, research is influenced by gender bias and stereotypes that likely undergird the types of questions asked, how studies are conducted, and how results are interpreted. Moreover, research participants are nonetheless guided by perceptions of gender and work, which, in turn, affect their behavior and responses to research manipulations. Until we take a more discerning look at our own gendered assumptions and those that thrive and proliferate, we will never be able to interpret the effect of gender bias in employment interviewing or elsewhere. Toward gaining a better understanding of the issue, the next section of the chapter explores in greater detail some cultural "taken for granted" assumptions about gender. We will find that these assumptions are embedded so deeply and planted so firmly as to make the study of gender and employment interviewing difficult.

Deeply Embedded Assumptions about Gender

The prevailing communication standards and tendencies for male and female interviewees are examined in this section of the chapter. Our goal is to illustrate that, while gender bias may not always be manifest in observable interviewing practices, it is alive and well beneath the surface. In an effort to identify and challenge the norms and practices that feed such bias, we foreground what Frey, Pearce, Pollock, Artz, and Murphy (1996) call "the grammars that oppress or underwrite relationships of domination" in employment interviews. Typically, the term "grammar" refers to those known or knowable elements and sequences of language that instantiate particular meanings and generate particular responses in interactions. Extending Wittgenstein's concept of grammar, as illuminated in Baker and Hacker (1985) and Frey et al. (1996), we apply the term here to gendered interactions. Having foregrounded these grammars, we can then reconstruct them in a way that promotes equality in the employment interview. First, we consider verbal and nonverbal languages of the ideal job-candidate profile. Second, we translate these languages to reveal how they can create and sustain gender bias in employment interviewing.

The Ideal Candidate Profile

An examination of almost any literature on employment interviewing reveals easily identifiable and cross-organizational norms for interviewer and interviewee communication. Whether one examines popular literature (Drake, 1997; Green, 1996; Yeager and Hough, 1998), professional literature (Ballard, 1999; Hagevik, 1998; Koonce, 1997; Meyer, 1999; Society for the Advancement of Education, 2000), academic literature (Cable and Judge, 1997; Graves and Powell, 1996; Jenkins and Atkins, 1990; Rynes and Gerhart, 1990), or job search sites on the Internet (www.collegegrad.com; www.jobsontheweb.com), a fairly consistent profile emerges of the effective interviewee. The most competitive job candidates communicate their fit with the job and the organization through specific verbal and nonverbal tactics.

In general, the employment interview literature (e.g., Kirkwood and Ralston, 1996; Ralston and Kirkwood, 1995; 1999) suggests that effective job candidates recognize and embrace the competitive nature of job interviewing; they believe interviewing in many respects is a contest and they are there to compete and "win." Effective candidates cultivate their interview communication skills beforehand, anticipating questions that interviewers are likely to ask. They formulate and practice the answers interviewers want to hear most. Successful candidates accept their lower status in the interview and the responsibility to mold their behavior according to expectations held by higher status interviewers. For instance, one tactic used by effective candidates during interviews is modeling their own behavior after interviewers' communicative styles (Ralston and Kirkwood, 1999). Perhaps most importantly, successful job applicants are fluent in the verbal and nonverbal languages of the "ideal candidate profile" (Buzzanell, 1999). The grammars of these verbal and nonverbal languages and implications for female and male interviewees are explored next.

Verbal Languages

The ideal candidate profile prescribes specific communication rules to which interviewees should adhere. Verbal standards for interviews require candidates to be orally fluent in particular kinds of corporate languages. One such language is that of assertiveness and competitiveness.

The Language of Assertiveness and Competitiveness. Interviewees should demonstrate confidence and self-assurance, and be unafraid to reveal their genuine nature (albeit merely a performance) for interviewers to see.[3] When asserting themselves, however, interviewees must be careful not to come across as aggressive, since this oversteps their lower status. Candidates should also be able to "talk the talk" of the interviewer's organization—whether they are interviewing to sell mutual funds or operate heavy machinery. Communicating confidence, assertiveness, and demonstrating connectedness with the host organization while avoiding messages of aggressiveness are integral to interviewing success. Effective applicants tend to speak this language fluently.

The Language of Task/Results Orientation. According to the ideal candidate profile, the second verbal language in which applicants should be proficient is that of a task/results orientation. Interviewees can demonstrate fluency in this language three ways. First, how well candidates answer Patterned Behavior Description Interview (PBDI) questions, such as, "Tell me about a time when you demonstrated effective leadership in your last job," and Situational Interview (SI) questions, like, "What would you do if any angry customer began yelling in your office" provides information that interviewers use to determine the extent to which applicants are focused on meeting specific job-relevant goals. As such, these are conversational opportunities for interviewees to show their attention to ends rather than means, and results and achievement before relationships (Buzzanell, 1999). Second, interviewees might also demonstrate fluency in this language by guarding against answers that reveal fears, personal issues, or affiliative coworker relationships. Instead, interviewees should communicate that they are able to zero-in on solving problems, stay focused on and complete tasks, and conclude with organization-relevant results. Finally, applicants can show facility with this language by responding to interview questions with short, concise, definitive answers. Doing so not only expedites the interview process, but can also show interviewees' larger order commitment to "getting to the point" and "getting the job done."

The Language of Self-Promotion and Self-Critique. The third language is complicated to articulate; its grammar is highly complex. This is the language of strengths and weaknesses, the language of self-promotion and self-critique. Employers prefer candidates who can easily identify their role in achieving positive organizational results. As a consequence, the ideal candidate profile suggests that employers generally seek bold, self-assured candidates who are able to speak about task-related accomplishments. Meeting this employer preference, interviewees can demonstrate that they know a good outcome when they see one and can pinpoint the strategies that brought about goal achievement. This language blends the assertiveness and task orientation grammars to articulate the strengths interviewees bring to the workplace and how these behaviors promote organizational success. Interviewees must remember, however, that to be effective they must be careful to keep assertiveness from sounding like aggressiveness. Interviewers prefer boldness over bashfulness, yet also appreciate a dose of humility in applicants.

In addition to expecting applicants to demonstrate assertive, job-relevant behavior, employers also want candidates to be in a "continuous improvement" cycle so that changing goals can be met. If applicants are going to engage in this ongoing process of self-study and improvement, they must be able to recognize their mistakes, weaknesses, and challenges, lest they never have a basis for improving or helping the employer's organization evolve. Ideal interviewees can identify a few mistakes or weaknesses, then explain the corrective steps they have taken. Yet, candidates should be aware that "talking this talk" can easily turn into a conversation about failure, examples of inert assertiveness, or ready acceptance of defeat; all of which can seriously undermine one's fluency in all the languages we have addressed thus far. Accordingly, candidates must have a firm grasp of this language's grammar to achieve interviewing success.

Nonverbal Languages

In addition to the spoken languages of employment interviewing, successful job candidates demonstrate their facility with its unspoken languages as well. These candidates recognize that nonverbal languages send loud and clear messages, and they seek to demonstrate to interviewers an understanding of this interview norm. For instance, interviewers want applicants to present themselves as persons who are willing to figure out and follow the rules in order to win the game. Eager to please and impress interviewers, successful job applicants learn and then display the appropriate rule-based normative nonverbal standards (Kirkwood and Ralston, 1999; Ralston and Kirkwood, 1995; 1999). Although there are numerous and complex nonverbal codes, the ideal candidate profile suggests two important languages: professional dress and bodily comportment.

The Language of the Professionally Dressed Body. Employment interviewing takes place in a variety of contexts and places, representing a broad range of formalities. Context notwithstanding, the ideal candidate profile promotes the standard conservative suit for both women and men. Suits must be clean and pressed, and most typically navy or gray. Applicants should wear minimal jewelry and avoid showing body piercings. Men should avoid earrings, facial hair, and white socks. According to O'Hair, O'Rourke, and O'Hair (2000) men should also, "[wear] a gray or blue business suit of a weight suitable for the season, with a white or blue shirt, complemented by a solid, striped, or conservatively patterned necktie" (553). Women should avoid pants or dresses, in favor of skirts, blouses, and blazers. Women should also avoid high or flat heels and runs in their pantyhose. Shoes must be polished, fingernails should be clean and trimmed, and perfume should be minimal. Consider the advice offered by O'Hair, O'Rourke, and O'Hair to female interviewees:

> We recommend a conservative two-piece business suit in gray or blue. A conservatively cut skirt in wool or polywool blend, complemented by a jacket in matching or contrasting colors, is customary. A white or matching-color blouse with a tie, scarf, or accessory pin at the collar establishes a professional look for a woman seeking a professional position. (2000: 553–554).

The Language of the Confident and Engaged Body. Bodily comportment is a powerful way to communicate not only self-confidence, but also engagement with the interview process. Effective interviewees use an erect (not stiff) posture and should appear physically relaxed and at ease. In fact, applicants are often advised to sit leaning slightly forward to show interest in the interviewer. While interviewees should return rather than offer a handshake, it should be willful and with a firm grasp. Interviewees should maintain eye contact with interviewers, but should avoid any prolonged gaze. Of course, successful interviewees smile! The voice should be strong and firm. Taken together, the nonverbal language suggests that applicants must be conscious of what they are communicating nonverbally, using the code effectively to meet employers' expectations of the ideal candidate profile.

Albeit rather complicated to replicate with certainty, the ideal candidate profile may at first seem reasonable. For many interviewees (and many readers of this chapter for that matter), the profile is nothing new and does, in fact, mirror the tactics enacted by successful job applicants. Presumably, the values and behaviors represented in the ideal candidate profile emerge from an employee profile that best 'fits' with organizational values and that demonstrates job-relevant knowledge, skills, and abilities (see Barber, 1998; Schmitt and Chan, 1988). A closer look at the language proficiency interviewees must demonstrate, however, reveals an important story about gender, communication, and power. In effect, the profile sometimes appears to have less to do with candidates' ability to perform given job tasks and more to do with meeting employers' expectations of appropriate interviewee behavior, including gender stereotypes.

Translating the Languages of Employment Interviewing

We now shift attention to how these verbal and nonverbal grammars intersect with gender and interviewing. Toward that goal, we explore the ways in which each of these languages and their prescriptive grammars function to work generally against women and in favor of men. We argue that these languages are spoken more proficiently by persons who adopt traditionally masculine communication styles, and as a consequence, persons who use traditionally feminine communication styles are more likely to be unfairly excluded from job opportunities.[4] Moreover, women who use more masculine styles experience added negative evaluations because they are judged as being too masculine, hence failing to meet interviewer expectations that women should communicate in "feminine" ways. That such bias often takes place despite the conscious intentions of the interviewer is notable, yet this fact does not change the larger cultural effect of gender bias in interviews. In fact, that such profound bias could possibly take place without purposeful intent indicates that this bias is truly embedded in our culture and tells an even more frightening tale about "women's progress" and "gender equality."

Translating the Language of Assertiveness and Competitiveness. The grammars of this language seem antithetical to traditionally feminine communication styles, which are predominately enacted by women. Maltz and Borker (1982) explain that the conversations that boys learn revolve around competition and dominance, whereas girls learn conversation revolving around connection and equality. Girls' play is more likely than that of boys to be about affiliation with equals (playing with dolls, hand-clap games, jumping rope, and slumber parties); boys' play is more likely than that of girls to be about competing and differentiating winners from losers (playing with wrestling characters, racing cars, video games based on annihilation, and football). In addition, whereas the behavior of boys and men tends to center on independence and competition, girls and women tend to center their communication around cooperation. There are women, of course, who are comfortable being competitive and showing assertiveness, but they face two major dilemmas. First, the way women communicate these messages may be through a softer voice, less emphatic or smaller gesturing, a more relaxed response time, or gentler language. These forms of communication can appear to others, especially to those who use more forceful grammars, as something short of assertive, or indeed, passive. Second, women who assert themselves through more forceful forms are often denigrated for being too masculine or too pushy, even though they may use communicative grammars that are identical to that of assertive men. Wood (2000) cites several studies that document these negative evaluations, concluding, "because highly assertive and instrumental communication is socially defined as masculine, women who engage in it may be branded 'iron maidens,' a perception that jeopardizes their acceptance and effectiveness" (256).

Thus, while both females and males may demonstrate competitiveness and assertiveness, females who do so in traditionally masculine ways run the risk of being perceived less positively than their male counterparts. Murphy and Zorn (1996) explain how women can feel caught in this untenable position:

> To display submissiveness is to be weak, and to be weak is not professional. To display strength and power is professional but not feminine, and therefore not approved. Hence the dilemma experienced by many women is manifested in comments such as "He's strong; he's got what it takes; she's a pushy bitch." Women in professional contexts often feel they must choose between being effective women or effective professionals, but they cannot be both simultaneously. (217)

Many women, as well as some men, have difficulty enunciating the language of assertiveness and competitiveness because it feels foreign to how they enact grammar in everyday life. Even when women do speak the language of competitiveness and assertiveness proficiently, they are often heard through the dialect of traditional feminine models. Consequently, women who do so are frequently judged negatively for speaking from too far inside or too far outside that model. To make matters worse, women are criticized for being too overbearing or for "wearing the pants" and trying to be like a man when using more masculine language. Similarly, men are criticized for being too soft and wimpish when they speak in more feminine grammars.

Translating the Language of Task/Results Orientation. A focus on problem solving over understanding, tasks over relationships, and results over processes is a dominant characteristic of the masculine communication model

(Eakins and Eakins, 1978). Feminine models of communication are characterized quite differently. Because women are socialized to be affiliative rather than competitive, they tend to be oriented first toward the process of human interaction and second to outcomes. Theirs is more likely to be a relationship orientation. For women, more often than for men, having a thorough understanding of a problem and how it affects people comes before attempting to solve it (Heim and Golant, 1993). Such an understanding may require the asking of questions to clarify or the seeking of more information, or at least the careful consideration of multiple alternatives and the different consequences for the people affected. Unfortunately, interviewers may view the feminine approach as an inefficient use of valuable time. Ralston and Kirkwood (1995) and Buzzanell (1999) point out that managerial and other dominant groups in control define and restrict the range of valued communicative behaviors permitted during interviews. As a result, interviewers operating from a traditional masculine framework might not provide the latitude necessary for demonstrating the value of a relationship orientation during an interview.

Through training and other methods, interviewees learn about employer expectations and then seek to meet these expectations during interviews (Kirkwood and Ralston, 1999). As a consequence of these and other control mechanisms, interviewees are frequently not allowed the freedom to enact behaviors that fall outside the prescribed parameters directly and indirectly established by employers, such as women candidates' use of masculine grammars. Likewise, asking questions for clarification might be negatively read by interviewers as hedging, as failing to understand simple questions, or as taking control of the interview. Doing so would likely violate employers' taken-for-granted assumptions and would therefore undermine applicants' employment opportunities. Why? These are not the grammars of the ideal applicant profile.

Answering PBDI questions, such as "Tell me about a time when you demonstrated effective leadership," and SI questions, such as "What would you do if your team leader requested a leave of absence in the middle of a critical project?" are likely to elicit from women answers that illustrate a leadership style that emphasizes handling relationships before tasks, or at least simultaneous with tasks. Responding to questions in more feminine grammars, that is, taking time to think through a situation out loud and asking questions to gain a clearer understanding of the situation, might not provide the task-oriented focus that most interviewers expect from ideal candidates. Relationship-oriented language reveals emotional engagement with work and the lives influenced therein. Men are more likely than women to avoid talking about personal feelings or disclosing a sense of affiliation with coworkers (Kramarae, 1981). Not all men want to avoid this talk of course, but as Borisoff contends in chapter 2 of this text, "even if men *want* to reveal their feelings and their emotions, the negative assessment of such behavior would discourage them from doing so" (22). Consequently, applicants who demonstrate proficiency in a feminine style grammar may be viewed as less attractive than applicants who demonstrate more masculine grammar.

Interviewers seeking to match applicants with the ideal candidate profile generally look for clear, succinct, definitive answers to their questions; they seem to prefer a linear progression from question asking to getting to the point. Such a preference is characteristic of masculine styles and reflects a problem-solving, task-oriented approach to communication. Men are more likely to exhibit this approach, particularly in the employment interview. Feminine styles, on the other hand, involve a contextualizing progression from question to answer; thereby reflecting a problem-understanding, relationship approach. Consequently, women are more likely to provide clear but highly detailed answers in their efforts to contextualize their responses to interviewers' questions. Regrettably, women tend to be proficient in a language for which the interview process has little regard.

Translating the Language of Self-Promotion and Self-Critique. Because feminine styles are grounded in collaboration more than competition, in relationships before results, in equality rather than hierarchy (Gilligan, 1982; Heim and Golant, 1993), people who use this style are less likely to identify their accomplishments eagerly. The language of self-promotion, therefore, tends to be more difficult for women to articulate. The grammar requires indicating times when one rose above the rest, when one's results were especially successful, when one's own ideas were highly regarded or particularly insightful. Applicants who use a masculine style, mostly men, are fluent in the language of competitiveness and assertiveness, and have less trouble identifying victories during interviews. Masculine grammar tends to reflect valued hierarchical views of success, leading communicators to speak more clearly about which successful contributions were theirs. Murphy and Zorn (1996) explain, "if men tend to see communication as a competitive tool while women see it more as a way to build connections, then men are more likely than women to broadcast their professional abilities and accomplishments. Men also find it easier to take credit for ideas and jobs well done" (223). Those who use a feminine style will not speak this language as easily because doing so may feel contradictory to collaborative goals. Kacmar (1993) suggests that women are "less comfortable with what they see as boasting. They are more likely to let their work speak for itself" (6).

The collaborative nature and the "we" language of feminine grammar can often make it difficult for women to pinpoint workplace achievements as theirs alone. Women who are more comfortable with self-promotion might well identify their victories and successes in terms of effective collaborations, and for these they must share credit. They may also identify strengths, for example, in terms of how coworker relationships remained intact when the organization was restructured. Given managerial bias in interviewing (Ralston and Kirkwood, 1995), "successes" are likely to be defined by interviewers in terms very different from how many women might define them. Yet, women who do explain their successes in a masculine style risk being read negatively, though perhaps unintentionally, because of their failure to conform to expectations that they will adopt a feminine style. Their assertive behaviors tend to be read as aggressive and "strident" or worse. Murphy and Zorn (1996) report that many women "say they constantly search for ways to convey just the right combination of masculine and feminine signals" (215).

Self-critique is likely to come more easily than does self-promotion for feminine-style communicators. Self-critique is integral to a relationship orientation and a necessary part of collaboration and compromise. On the other hand, identifying one's weaknesses is problematic for competitive, masculine style communicators. As a consequence, interviewer questions that require scrutiny of one's faults are more likely to put interviewees who adopt masculine grammars at a greater disadvantage than interviewees who use more feminine styles. However, men are more likely than women to identify task-oriented problems when discussing weaknesses, thereby mediating the disadvantage of responding to such questions.

Translating the Language of the Professionally Dressed Body. In preparing to write this chapter, we expected that the literature on personal appearance in employment interviewing would clearly identify an ideal candidate profile that prescribed a long list of rules for women's wear and a short list for men's wear. Instead, we found that both lists were relatively short and equal. It seems reasonable that interviewees' fingernails should be clean and trimmed, that they should dress up, and their shoes should be polished. Still, a close examination of taken-for-granted assumptions about women's and men's appearance suggests that even in nonverbal languages, women's proficiency is more likely to be questioned. Aside from the expectation that men should avoid earrings and—even more absurdly for bearded and/or mustached men—facial hair, the terms of this language may be easier to negotiate for men. For example, "minimal jewelry" may be easier for men to translate, since they tend to wear less jewelry then women. Female applicants might have more difficulty discerning what constitutes "minimal" jewelry than their male counterparts, and interviewers (both men and women), may hold very different expectations about appropriate jewelry than do women applicants.

Similarly, while a necktie is unquestionably constricting, pantyhose, pumps, and crossed legs might well be a more complicated costume for moving about the interview stage. The definition of "trimmed" nails is also easier to match for men than for women since women are more likely to have nails at varying lengths. Because many women wear nail polish (and men usually do not) and because most women wear makeup (and most men do not), they are subject to additional critiques about how their own styles play into professionalism, critiques to which men are not subject. Though these differences may seem innocuous, successful interviewees and the employers who would hire them appreciate the power of nonverbal messages. Because nonverbal codes are largely connotative in meaning, it is difficult to measure how interviewers will respond to one's own interpretation of "professional and conservative attire."

Translating the Language of the Confident and Engaged Body. Confidence and engagement would appear to be reasonable expectations for interviewee communication. Yet, problems arise when the person conveying confidence and engagement in one language is interpreted based on the grammar rules of a different language. Women using feminine styles confront such problems when they enter the masculinized culture of employment interviewing. These problems echo the complication women face when they identify their strengths in relationship terms and when they are evaluated by interviewers who use a relatively narrow, on-task accomplishment rule. Why? In part because men tend to speak the language of assertiveness more proficiently or without retribution than women. In addition, because men tend to take up more physical space than women, interviewers may find it easier to read men's posture and comportment as "confident." Interviewers are also more likely to perceive men as relaxed since wearing pants, flat shoes, and open legs more easily conveys relaxation than skirts, pumps, and crossed or tightly closed legs (Hall, 1984).

Assertiveness and physical strength expectations for men are likely to result in handshakes that are more readily interpreted as "willful" and using a "firm grasp." The supposition that interviewees should return, rather than extend a handshake, combined with the fact that women tend to get a "cup the fingers, half handshake" extended to them (Ivy and Backlund, 2000), suggests that interviewers *call forth* handshakes from women that are likely to be read as less confident. Women who use a solid, firm handshake may also be read negatively as too masculine because such nonverbal behavior violates taken-for-granted assumptions about femininity. Moreover, because deep, loud voices are generally perceived as more dominant (Burgoon, Buller, and Woodall, 1989) and men more often have such voices, theirs are more likely to be read as strong and firm; women who actually use deep or loud voices are likely to be read negatively as too masculine. Since men tend to occupy more upper management positions than women, men are also more likely to conduct interviews with applicants, and more likely to control hiring decisions. This likelihood, coupled with men's tendency to avoid the gaze of other men (Hall, 1984), suggests that women may be at an advantage in their use of more direct and consistent eye contact during interviews.

To summarize, a strong argument can be made that the verbal and nonverbal languages of feminine communication styles, predominately spoken by women, can place those who would speak it at a disadvantage in employment interviewing. Specifically, feminine grammar is more easily interpreted as passive or indifferent during interviews. Conversely, women using the languages of masculine communication styles are more easily interpreted as aggressive. Similarly, men who use feminine verbal and nonverbal language styles during interviews are viewed less favorably compared to men who enact traditional masculine grammar.

Summary and Conclusion

This chapter considered the intersection of gender and employment interviewing, where we found the crossroad difficult to navigate with certainty. First, the Federal Employment Practice (FEP) law was briefly discussed. Second, we summarized the research literature on gender bias in employment interviewing. It was at that point that the intersection of gender and interviewing became difficult to negotiate. As you recall, many of the studies contradicted each other about the influence of gender on the process and outcome of employment interviewing. Following the literature summary, we offered three possible explanations for the discordant findings. Fourth, the final section of the chapter took a closer look at the third explanation, discussing the impact of gender stereotypes on employment interviewing.

Clearly, the typical ideal applicant profile expected by so many employers and adopted by most applicants puts those who use a more feminine style at a distinct disadvantage. Our analysis showed that the problem for women is not that they lack proficiency in the languages necessary for effective employment; rather, women demonstrate *high* proficiency in languages which, when evaluated by masculine-style standards, just do not measure up to expected norms for successful job applicants. If women and men are to have equal opportunity in the workplace, they must be afforded equal advantagc in the employment interview. Such advantage will not emerge, as we have argued, from the perpetuation of an "ideal candidate profile" and other organizational norms that devalue feminine communication styles or women who use masculine communication styles. If masculine-style standards continue to privilege men in organizational life, gender equality will not be attained and women's "progress" will be stopped short.

For Further Discussion

1. To what extent do you believe government can legislate the elimination of gender bias in employment interviewing?
2. How could a study be constructed that might reliably assess the effect of gender on employment interview processes and outcomes?
3. Can you identify any specific jobs that tend to be associated with one gender? Do you believe that sex role stereotypes influence who applies and who is hired?
4. Describe the ideal feminine attire for a woman interviewing for a position in sales? On what information do you base the decision?
5. Can you think of an interview situation in which men might use more feminine verbal and nonverbal communication without negative consequences?

6. Imagine that a single woman knows that an interviewer prefers married women as employees. She decides to use what she knows and wears what looks like a wedding band to the interview. What are your reactions?

Endnotes

1 See Wilson (1991) for a complete description of these and other federal regulations.

2 Consult Gilliland (1993) for a comprehensive treatment of procedural and distributive justice as they apply to employment selection.

3 Kirkwood and Ralston (1999) indicate that employment interviews always prompt performances from applicants. The kinds of performance employers' expectations and questions prompt from interviewees can support or undermine successful interviewing.

4 We discuss communication in terms of "feminine" and "masculine" styles. These terms identify communicative behaviors that women generally (and men sometimes) are taught and adopt, and those that men generally (and women sometimes) are taught and adopt, respectively. Not all women and men fit into these neat divisions, and there are probably few people who fit into either category all the time. Nevertheless, as our analysis and the other chapters in this text reveal, women and men do tend to be socialized in markedly different ways. Girls and women tend to be socialized into communicative behaviors culturally defined as "feminine" and boys and men tend to be socialized into communicative behaviors culturally defined as "masculine." This socialization begins in infancy (and perhaps before birth) and continues to be reified through everyday life institutions and discourses, of which education, religion, economics, family, politics, and the workplace are parts.

References

Adler, R. B., and J. M. Elmhorst. 1999. *Communicating at Work* (6th ed.). Boston: McGraw-Hill.

Americans with Disabilities Act of 1990, 42, U.S.C.A. 12101.

Arvey, R. D. 1979. Unfair discrimination in the employment interview: Legal and psychological aspects. *Psychological Bulletin* 86: 736–765.

Arvey, R. D., and J. E. Campion. 1982. The employment interview: A summary and review of the recent research. *Personnel Psychology* 35: 281–322.

Arvey, R. D., M. E. Miller, Gould, and P. Burch. 1987. Interview validity for selecting sales clerks. *Personnel Psychology* 40: 1–12.

Baker, G. P., and P. M. S. Hacker. 1985. *Wittgenstein: Rules Grammar and Necessity.* Cambridge, MA: Blackwell.

Ballard, P. D. 1999. Dress for success. *The Black Collegian* 29(2): 69–70.

Barber, A. E. 1998. *Recruiting Employees: Individual and Organizational Perspectives.* Thousand Oaks, CA: Sage.

Bible, J. 1998. Discrimination in job applications and interviews. *Supervision* 59: 9–11.

Burgoon, J. K., D. B. Buller, and W. G. Woodall. 1989. *Nonverbal Communication: The Unspoken Dialogue.* New York: Harper and Row.

Buttner, E. H., and M. McEnally. 1996. The interactive effort of influence tactic, applicant gender, and type of job on hiring recommendations. *Sex Roles* 34: 581–591.

Buzzanell, P. 1999. Tensions and burdens in employment interviewing processes: Perspectives of non-dominant group applicants. *The Journal of Business Communication* 36: 134–162.

Cable, D. M., and T. A. Judge. 1997. Interviewers' perceptions of person-organization fit and organizational selection decisions. *Journal of Applied Psychology* 82: 546–561.

Campion, J. E., and R. D. Arvey. 1989. Unfair discrimination in the employment interview. In R. W. Eder and G. R. Ferris, eds., *The Employment Interview: Theory, Research, and Practice.* Newbury Park, CA: Sage, 61–73.

Cianni-Surridge, M., and J. J. Horan. 1983. On the wisdom of assertive job-seeking behavior. *Journal of Counseling Psychology* 30: 209–214.

Cohen, S. L., and K. A. Bunker. 1975. Subtle effects of sex role stereotypes on recruiters' hiring decisions. *Journal of Applied Psychology* 60: 566–572.

Damhorst, M. D., and J. A. Reed. 1986. Clothing color and facial expressions: Effect on evaluations of female job applicants. *Social Behavior and Personality* 14: 89–98.

Davis, A. G., and L. A. Penner. 1986. The sex matching heuristic in employment decisions. *Bulletin of the Psychonomic Society* 42: 47–50.

Dipboye, R. L., and J. W. Wiley. 1977. Reactions of college recruiters to interviewee sex and self-presentation style. *Journal of Vocational Behavior* 10: 1–12.

———. 1978. Reactions of male raters to interviewee self-presentation style and sex: Extensions of previous research. *Journal of Vocational Behavior* 13: 192–203.

Drake, J. D. 1997. *The Perfect Interview: How to Get the Job You Really Want* (2nd ed.). New York: AMACOM.

Eagly, A. H., M. G. Makhijani, and B. G. Klonsky. 1992. Gender and the evaluation of leaders: A meta-analysis. *Psychological Bulletin* 111: 3–22.

Eakins, B. W., and R. G. Eakins. 1978. *Sex Differences in Human Communication.* Boston: Houghton Mifflin.

Equal Employment Opportunity Commission (EEOC). 1978. *Uniform Guidelines on Employee Selection Procedures.* Washington, DC: U.S. Government Printing Office.

———. 1981. Pre-employment Inquires and Equal Employment Opportunity. Washington, DC: U.S. Government Printing Office.

———. 1995a. ADA Enforcement Guidance: Pre-employment Disability-related Questions and Medical Examinations. Washington, DC: U.S. Government Printing Office.

———. 1995b. Disability Discrimination. Washington, DC: U.S. Government Printing Office.

Forsythe, S. M. 1990. Effect of applicant's clothing on interviewers' decisions to hire. *Journal of Applied Social Psychology* 20: 1579–1595.

Forsythe, S. M., M. F. Drake, and C. E. Cox. 1985. Influence of applicant's dress on interviewer's selection decisions. *Journal of Applied Psychology* 70: 374–378.

Frey, L. R., B. W. Pearce, M. A. Pollock, L. Artz, and B. O. Murphy. 1996. Looking for justice in all the wrong places: On a communication approach to social justice. *Communication Studies* (47): 110–127.

Futoran, G. C., and R. S. Wyler. 1986. The effects of traits and gender stereotypes on occupational suitability judgments and the recall of judgment-relevant information. *Journal of Experimental Social Psychology* 22: 475–503.

Gallois, C., V. J. Callan, and J. M. Palmer. 1992. The influence of applicant communication style and interviewer characteristics on hiring decisions. *Journal of Applied Social Psychology* 22: 1041–1060.

Gilligan, C. 1982. *In a Different Voice.* Cambridge, MA: Harvard University Press.

Gilliland, S. W. 1993. The perceived fairness of selection systems: An organizational justice perspective. *Academy of Management Review* 4: 694–734.

Glick, P., C. Zion, and C. Nelson. 1988. What mediates sex discrimination in hiring decisions? *Journal of Personality and Social Psychology* 55: 178–186.

Graves, L. M. 1999. Gender bias in interviewers' evaluations of applicants: When and how does it occur? In G. Powell, ed., *Handbook of Gender and Work*. Thousand Oaks, CA: Sage, 145–164.

Graves, L. M., and G. N. Powell. 1995. The effect of sex similarity or recruiters' evaluations of actual applicants: A test of the similarity-attraction paradigm. *Personnel Psychology* 48: 85–98.

———. 1996. Sex similarity, quality of the employment interview and recruiters' evaluation of actual applicants. *Journal of Occupational and Organizational Psychology* 69: 243–261.

Green, P. C. 1996. *Get Hired!: Winning Strategies to Ace the Interview.* Austin, TX: Bard.

Hagevik, S. 1998. Interviewing with assurance. *Journal of Environmental Health* 61(2): 36–37.

Hall, J. A. 1984. *Nonverbal Sexual Differences: Communication Accuracy and Expressive Style.* Baltimore, MA: Johns Hopkins University Press.

Harp, S. S., S. M. Stretch, and D. A. Harp. 1985. The influence of apparel on responses to television news anchorwomen. In M. R. Solomon, ed., *The Psychology of Fashion.* Lexington, MA: D.C. Health, 279–291.

Harris, M. M. 1989. Reconsidering the employment interview: A review of recent literature and suggestions for future research. *Personnel Psychology* 42: 691–726.

Heilman, M. E. 1984. Information as a deterrent against sex discrimination: The effects of applicant sex and information type on preliminary employment decisions. *Organizational Behavior and Human Performance* 33: 174–186.

Heilman, M. E., R. F. Martell, and M. C. Simon. 1988. The vagaries of sex bias: Conditions regulating the undervaluation, equivaluation, and overvaluation of female job applicants. *Organizational Behavior and Human Decision Processes* 41: 98–110.

Heilman, M. E., and L. R. Saruwatari. 1979. When beauty is beastly: The effects of appearance and sex on evaluations of job applicants for managerial and nonmanagerial jobs. *Organizational Behavior and Human Performance* 23: 360–372.

Heim, P., and S. K. Golant. 1993. *Hardball for Women: Winning at the Game of Business.* Santa Cruz, CA: Plume Publishing.

Hite, L. M., and K. S. McDonald. 1995. Gender issues in management development: Implications and research agenda. *Journal of Management Development* 14: 5–15.

Hitt, M. A., and S. H. Barr. 1989. Managerial selection decision models: Examination of configural cue processing. *Journal of Applied Psychology* 74: 53–61.

Ivy, D. K., and P. Backlund. 2000. *Exploring Genderspeak: Personal Effectiveness in Gender Communication.* Boston: McGraw-Hill.

Jenkins, M. C., and T. V. Atkins. 1990. Perceptions of acceptable dress by corporate and non-corporate recruiters. *Journal of Human Behavior and Learning* 7: 38–46.

Kacmar, K. M. 1993. Look at who's talking. *HRMagazine* 38(2): 56–58.

Kacmar, K. M., and W. A. Hochwarter. 1995. The interview as a communication event: An examination of demographic effects on interview outcomes. *The Journal of Business Communication* 32: 207–232.

Kinicki, A. J., and C. A. Lockwood. 1985. The interview process: An examination of factors recruiters use in evaluating job applicants. *Journal of Vocational Behavior* 26: 117–125.

Kirkwood, W. G., and S. M. Ralston. 1996. Ethics and teaching employment interviewing. *Communication Education* 45: 167–179.

———. 1999. Inviting meaningful applicant performances in employment interviews. *The Journal of Business Communication* 36: 55–76.

Koonce, R. 1977. How to ace a job interview. *Training and Development* 51(3): 13.

Kramarae, C. 1981. *Women and Men Speaking: Frameworks for Analysis.* Rowley, MA: Newbury House.

Liden, R. C., and C. K. Parsons. 1986. A field study of job applicant interview perceptions, alternative opportunities, and demographic characteristics. *Personnel Psychology* 39: 109–123.

Lord, M. 1999. Pregnant—and now without a job: Is bias building against expectant mothers? *U.S. News and World Report* 118(3): 66.

Maltz, D., and R. Borker. 1982. A cultural approach to male-female miscommunications. In J. J. Gumperz, ed., *Language and Social Identity.* Cambridge, England: Cambridge University Press.

Marlowe, C. M., S. L. Schneider, and C. E. Nelson. 1996. Gender and attractiveness bias in hiring decisions: Are more experienced managers less biased? *Journal of Applied Psychology* 81: 11–21.

Maurer, S. D., V. Howe, and T. W. Lee. 1992. Organizational recruiting as marketing management: An interdisciplinary study of engineering students. *Personnel Psychology* 45: 807–833.

Meyer, M. F. 1999. Improving job interview skills. *Healthcare Financial Management* 51(9): 2656–2663.

Morrow, P. C. 1990. Physical attractiveness and selection decision making. *Journal of Management* 16: 45–60.

Murphy, B. O., and T. Zorn. 1996. Gendered interaction in professional relationships. In J. Wood, ed., *Gendered Relationships.* Mountain View, CA: Mayfield.

O'Hair, D. H., J. S. O'Rourke, and M. J. O'Hair. 2000. *Business Communication: A Framework for Success.* Cincinnati, OH: South-Western College Publishing.

Perry, E. L. 1994. A prototype matching approach to understanding the role of applicant gender and age in the evaluation of job applicants. *Journal of Applied Social Psychology* 24: 1433–1473.

Perry, E. L., A. Davis-Blake, and C. T. Kulik. 1994. Explaining gender-based selection decisions: A synthesis of contextual and cognitive approaches. *Academy of Management Review* 19: 786–820.

Pingitore, R., B. L. Dugoni, R. S. Tindale, and B. Spring. 1994. Bias against overweight job applicants in a simulated employment interview. *Journal of Applied Psychology* 79: 909–917.

Ralston, S. M. 1988. The effect of race upon personnel selection decisions: A review with recommendations. *Employee Responsibilities and Rights Journal* 1: 215–226.

Ralston, S. M., and W. G. Kirkwood. 1995. Overcoming managerial bias in employment interviews. *Journal of Applied Communication Research* 23: 75–92.

———. 1999. The trouble with applicant impression management. *Journal of Business and Technical Communication* 13: 190–207.

Raza, S. M., and B. N. Carpenter. 1987. A model of hiring decisions in real employment interviews. *Journal of Applied Psychology* 72: 596–603.

Reik, T. 1954. Men and women speak different languages. *Psychoanalysis* 2: 3–15.

Rheem, H. 1999. Equal opportunity for women: The verdict is (still) mixed. *Harvard Business Review* 74(4): 12–14.

Roehling, M. V., J. E. Campion, and R. D. Arvey. 1999. Unfair discrimination issues. In R. W. Eder and M. M. Harris, eds., *The Employment Interview Handbook.* Thousand Oaks, CA: Sage, 49–67.

Rosenstein, J., and M. A. Hit. 1986. Experimental research of race and sex discrimination: The record and prospects. *Journal of Occupational Behavior* 7: 215–226.

Russo, G., and J. Ommeren. 1998. Gender differences in recruitment outcomes. *Bulletin of Economic Research* 50: 155–167.

Rynes, S. L., and B. Gerhart. 1990. Interviewer assessments of applicant "fit": An exploratory investigation. *Personnel Psychology* 43: 13–35.

Schmidt, W. V., and R. N. Conaway. 1999. *Results-oriented Interviewing: Principles, Practices, and Procedures.* Needham Heights, MA: Allyn and Bacon.

Schmitt, N., and D. Chan. 1988. *Personnel Selection: A Theoretical Approach.* Thousand Oaks, CA: Sage.

Society for the Advancement of Education. 2000, January. Initial minutes of job interview are critical. *USA Today,* 128, p. 8.

Stewart, C. J., and W. B. Cash. 2000. *Interviewing: Principles and Practices* (9th ed.). Boston: McGraw-Hill.

Stuart, P. 1992. What does the glass ceiling cost you? *Personnel Journal* 71: 70–79.

Taylor, M. S., and T. J. Bergmann. 1987. Organizational recruitment activities and applicants' reactions at different stages of the recruitment process. *Personnel Psychology* 40: 261–285.

Turban, D. B., and T. W. Dougherty. 1992. Influence of campus recruiting on applicant attraction to firms. *Academy of Management Journal* 35: 739–765.

U.S. Department of Labor. 1990, October. *Facts on Working Women.* Washington, DC: U.S. Government Printing Office.

Van Vianen, A. E., and T. M. Willemsen. 1992. The employment interview: The role of sex stereotypes in the evaluation of male and female job applicants in the Netherlands. *Journal of Applied Social Psychology* 22: 471–491.

Williams, K. B., P. S. Radefeld, J. F. Binning, and J. R. Sudak. 1993. When job candidates are "hard"- versus "easy-to-get": Effects of candidate availability on employment decisions. *Journal of Applied Social Psychology* 23: 169–198.

Wilson, G. L. 1991. Preparing students for responding to illegal selection interview questions. *The Bulletin of the Association for Business Communication* 1: 44–49.

Wood, J. T. 2000. *Gendered Lives: Communication, Gender, and Culture* (4th ed.). Stamford, CT: Wadsworth.

www.collegegrad.com

www.jobsontheweb.com

Yeager, N. M., and L. Hough. 1998. *Power Interviews: Job-winning Tactics from Fortune 500 Recruiters.* New York: John Wiley and Sons.

Zebrowitz, L. A., D. R. Tenebaum, and L. H. Goldstein. 1991. The impact of job applicants' facial maturity, gender, and academic achievement on hiring recommendations. *Journal of Applied Social Psychology* 21: 525–548.

CHAPTER 12

Gender, Race, and Communication in Professional Environments

Brenda J. Allen

POINTS TO BE ADDRESSED

- Gender and communication at work
- Intersections of gender and race
- Stereotypes of black women
- Implications for black professional women
- Recommendations for harmonious communication in professional environments

As this book illustrates, gender matters. Gender affects how we communicate with one another across numerous contexts (e.g., at home, in school, and on the job). In addition to gender, other aspects of identity such as race, class, and sexual orientation, also matter. Furthermore, combinations of identity characteristics (e.g., lower-class Asian-American heterosexual woman or middle-class gay white male) can affect how we interact with others and how others interact with us. However, discussions about gender rarely take any of these factors into account. Yet, if we wish to understand relationships between identity and communication, we need to explore distinctions among women and men, instead of lumping them into two categories.

The author thanks Theodis Hall, human resources manager, for his comments on earlier drafts of this chapter.

One particularly conspicuous aspect of identity is race. Similar to how we detect gender, we discern race based upon physical cues. We make assumptions about a person's race based upon features such as skin color, hair, and facial structure. We (consciously or unconsciously) use the information to decide how to interact with that person. Have you ever met someone whose race you could not immediately figure out? Were you curious? If so, why?

Similar to gender, racial categories carry sociohistorical baggage that affects communication processes. Historically in the United States, members of nondominant racial groups (similar to women in general) often experience discrimination, whereas members of the dominant racial group (similar to men in general) tend to enjoy more privilege and power. Within all racial groups, gender hierarchies often exist. Thus, white men tend to make more money than black men, who tend to earn more than white women, followed by black women (U.S. Department of Labor, 1997).

These issues are especially important in the workplace, where increasing numbers of women of color, minority men, and white women are assuming professional roles. These changes in the complexion of the workplace can cause a variety of conflicts. For instance, members of all groups may use gender/racial stereotypes to interact with one another. Or, persons of color or white women may expect others to discriminate against them. White males may feel threatened and intimidated by the influx of minorities and women (Ipsaro, 1997). White males also may be uncomfortable about interacting with newcomers for fear of being perceived as racist, sexist, insensitive, or patronizing.

On the other hand, changes in professional environments due to increased numbers of people of color and white women can create positive consequences (Conrad and Poole, 1998; Gentile, 1996; Ipsaro, 1997). When people of diverse backgrounds work in harmony, they can generate innovative, fresh ideas and products that are responsive to contemporary society's needs (Conrad and Poole, 1998). As Gentile (1996) notes,

> By opening ourselves and our organizations to the perspectives of individuals and groups who have had less managerial voice in the past, we can step outside the traditional frame of business decision making. We make the inside of our corporations look more like the outside world of customers, competitors, and operating contexts. (xvii)

In addition, we can develop "a more human and stimulating work environment for all" (Gentile, 1996: xiv). Therefore, we need to understand how gender/racial dynamics can affect communication in organizations.

In this chapter, I explore ways that perceptions about gender *and* race can impact interactions in professional settings. I begin with an overview of gender and organizational communication, after which I discuss intersections of gender and race. Next, I describe the history and unique position of African-American women and I explore implications for communication in professional settings. Although this topic is relevant to women and men of all races, I foreground African-American women in order to illuminate specific issues about one group. I conclude with recommendations for how to improve communication practices in professional workplaces. To typify some of the issues, I offer anecdotes about two fictional employees, Marcella Jones, a black[1] woman, and Mark Adams, a white man. As I describe some of their experiences, I do not want to imply that Mark and Marcella represent all white men and all black women. I offer anecdotes about them simply to illustrate some of the dynamics that *might* occur.

> Marcella Jones and Mark Adams recently were hired as senior level managers for AllCo, a software manufacturer. Mark and Marcella have similar educational backgrounds and work experiences. They also have similar work responsibilities. However, they will experience their new jobs differently. Some of their employees, coworkers, and bosses will interact differently with them because Marcella is a black woman and Mark is a white man. Also, since Mark and Marcella have been socialized differently because of their gender and race, they sometimes will exhibit different communication styles and attitudes. In addition, Marcella and Mark may use dissimilar perceptual filters to interpret ways that other people communicate with them.
>
> Although Mark and Marcella manage different divisions, their paths cross at weekly management meetings. All of the other managers at their level are white males except for Ed Johnson, a black male, and John Alvarez, a Hispanic male. Marcella is the only woman senior manager, and the first black woman in the position. A white woman, Ellen Hamlin, preceded her in the position. Marcella and Mark communicate easily with one another, and they quickly become allies. They confer about challenges of being newcomers, and they help each other to learn the ropes by sharing information and insights.

Gender and Communication at Work

Historical gender issues in the United States help to shape gender issues at work (Conrad and Poole, 1998). When we enter the workplace, we bring taken-for-granted Western assumptions about gender roles. For instance, historically society has dictated that women should assume service, caretaker roles, while men should be leaders and providers. Despite progress in gender equity, these viewpoints linger because of sex role spillover in the workplace; in other words, societal expectations about how women and men should behave carry over into the workplace (Gutek, 1985; Ipsaro, 1997). Consequently, women still are segregated into occupations such as administrative support or secretarial positions, while men dominate high-level managerial and executive jobs (Dunn, 1999; Ipsaro, 1997). Men continue to have more power, higher status, and greater prestige than women. In 1990, women held less than 5 percent of senior level management positions. These conditions persist due to: (1) gender role socialization (women and men receive messages about which occupations are "appropriate" for them); (2) hiring discrimination (some employers conform to gender stereotypes when selecting employees); and (3) family constraints (women frequently are responsible for child rearing and household maintenance) (Dunn, 1999).

History also affects standards of communication in organizations. Because white males have tended to own and dominate organizations, most workplaces adhere to white male values (Ipsaro, 1997). Most business structures emulate military models, with rigid hierarchies, in which employees focus on competition, domination, and winning. In addition, "professional" leadership communication equates to masculine modes such as assertion, independence, competitiveness, and confidence, whereas feminine styles such as deference, inclusivity, collaboration, and cooperation are linked to subordinate roles (Parker and ogilvie, 1996).

Moreover, language in organizations tends to be masculine, including recurring references to sports (e.g., being a team player, play to win, score) and the military (battle plan, war zone, plan of attack) (Wood, 2001). Constant use of these types of terms can help to perpetuate a masculine work environment.

Whether consciously or not, we bring our notions of gender roles into the workplace. Consequently, we enact traditional behaviors and attitudes, including stereotypes. We often rely upon stereotypes about women and men to draw conclusions, and to cue our behaviors. Stereotypes of women at work include: sex object, mother, child, and iron maiden. Stereotypes of men are: sturdy oak, fighter, and breadwinner (Wood, 2001).

These stereotypes and expectations can affect the communication climate in an organization. Gender-based stereotypes also can hinder or help an employee's chance to advance. For instance, informal networks often provide information and connections that allow an employee to be evaluated positively and to climb the corporate ladder. Unfortunately, women usually are less involved in these networks (Wood, 2001). Further, they are not as likely to benefit from mentor relationships, as Wood explains: "Men are sometimes reluctant to mentor young women for a variety of reasons; fear of gossip about sexual relations, their assumption that women are less serious than men about careers, or feeling less comfortable with women than with men as colleagues" (265).

In addition, the climate may be hostile when women enter professions traditionally reserved for men. Women may be expected to perform "motherly" services or they may encounter sexual harassment based upon being viewed as a sexual object. Women also may feel pressured to perform like men in professional roles. Men also can face discrimination when they assume roles traditionally reserved for women.

Moreover, as Wood (2001) points out, "men and women may be judged differently for enacting the *same* communication" (255) because others expect them to behave according to gender stereotypes. For instance, since cultural views hold that women ought to be supportive and friendly, if a woman acts otherwise, another person might evaluate her negatively. Similarly, if a man behaves in so-called feminine ways, he may suffer negative repercussions.

These issues offer important insight into gender and communication in organizations. However, they do not differentiate among racial categories.

Rather, they seem to assume that general stereotypes and experiences of Anglo women and men represent those of all women and men. However, we need to consider the intersection of race and gender, because the issues I described above play out differently when we add race, as I discuss next. First, though, let's check in on Marcella and Mark.

> One evening Marcella is in Mark's office showing him how to use new spreadsheet software. Jim Cross, their boss, asks Mark to join him for happy hour after work. Marcella feels slighted. Why didn't he ask her, she wonders? "Is it because I'm black?" Not that she would go. After all, she doesn't want anyone to think that she is coming on to the boss. People might assume that she's a loose black woman who uses her body to get promotions or other special favors. Jim doesn't invite Marcella because he's afraid that she might interpret his behavior as sexual harassment. "You can't be too careful," he rationalizes. For the same reason, he had never socialized with Ellen (Marcella's predecessor) outside of work. Although Mark isn't much of a drinker, he goes along, but he nurses one drink throughout the evening. Jim shares insight about the company and the job. Jim also makes a couple of sexist jokes and does not seem to notice that Mark is uncomfortable. When Jim invites Mark to go golfing with him, Mark agrees without disclosing that he has never been on a golf course. He signs up for evening golf lessons because he sees this as an opportunity to develop his relationship with the boss.

Intersections of Gender and Race

Each of us belongs to social groups that affect our value systems, our social interaction modes, and our perceptions of members of other groups (Jeanquart-Barone, 1993). From various sources, such as family members, peers, teachers, and the media, we come to know who we are (and who we "should" be). These sources transmit varying information and cues to us, depending on our group memberships. Thus, women receive different messages than men. Likewise, members of different racial groups receive particular information. We also develop distinct communication styles: "members of each social group communicate in some ways that aren't shared by people outside that group" (Houston and Wood, 1996: 42). For instance, you may notice similar behaviors among men, and you may see cultural similarities among Asian-Americans. Further, "how any individual acts and thinks is not purely personal, since each of us is situated within and shaped by broader horizons of cultural life that make disparate experiences available to different groups" (Houston and Wood, 1996: 42).

Two particularly notable social groupings are gender and race. In U.S. society, we simultaneously are socialized about our gender and our race. We learn cultural information specific to our gender and specific to our race. We also receive cues about our particular blend of race and gender. And, our experiences will vary accordingly. For instance, an Asian-American female probably will receive different messages about herself in relation to others than a Mexican-American female. Or, a black male may learn different ways of being than a white male. Thus, Marcella may sometimes exhibit traits based upon being African American, or being a woman, or being an African-American woman. Likewise, Mark may behave in ways related to being white, a man, or a white man.

In addition, gender and race play an important role in how people perceive one another, and consequently how they communicate. As Jeanquart-Barone (1993) asserts, "gender and race attributions are the most powerful characteristics in person perception" (3). Moreover, different stereotypes exist for different race-gender designations, for example, white men, Asian-American women, Latinas, and Native American men.

Because of being socialized about oneself and one's social group(s), as well as about members of other groups, when two people interact, interesting dynamics can occur. For instance, Jim Cross, Mark and Marcella's white boss, expects Mark to be like him because they are both white men. Marcella's black male coworker may expect her to be like him because they are both black. Yet, Marcella may filter cues from him based on her stereotypes of black men and her expectation that he will interact with her based on his stereotypes of black women.

In the professional workplace, experiences of white women and members of minority groups will in many ways be similar because of negative stereotypes about work competence (especially in professional roles) and their low status in Western society in general (Conrad and Poole, 1998). Yet, experiences will vary among groups, due to various sociohistorical factors. These factors are particularly relevant for persons who simultaneously occupy two oppressed positions, as do black women (Allen, 1996; 2000b). Next, I delve deeper into these issues by discussing African-American women.

> When Mark tells Marcella about being invited to golf with the boss, she offers to take him out to the driving range. Marcella is an avid golfer, and she welcomes the chance to convert Mark. Marcella also sees a way to try to penetrate the "old boys' network." After a manager's meeting, she makes a casual comment to Jim about a PGA tournament that recently had been held in their town. Surprised, Jim engages her in a long conversation about area courses. Later in the week, he e-mails her an invitation to join him and his wife for a round of golf. Marcella feels relieved. She was not sure how Jim would respond, but she was certain that he would never have approached her.
>
> Mark appreciates Marcella's help. He is concerned, though, about one of his white male coworkers, who sometimes makes crude remarks about Mark's relationship with Marcella. Mark brushes him off, saying that he and Marcella are just colleagues. Mark grows weary sometimes of the constant horseplay and joking that two of his male coworkers engage in, but he hesitates to say anything because they might accuse him of being a wimp. They assume that he has the same opinions and attitudes as they do, but that's not always the case. Usually he just goes along with whatever they

say. They also routinely expect him to stay late when they are completing a project. Mark usually complies even though he prefers to get home in time to help his wife Natalie (who also works full-time) with household chores.

Marcella is acutely aware of being the first black woman in her position. This is not the first time that she is the "first" and/or "only," and she readily accepts the challenge. She wants to succeed not only for herself, but also to demonstrate that minorities, especially black women, can be competent. She takes pride in her appearance, and she walks with her head held high, as her mother and grandmother taught her. Marcella tends to be bottom-line oriented, even as she invites her employees to participate in decision making. She "shoots from the hip." She also does not talk much about her personal life. Some of her employees complain among themselves that she is "uppity." They frequently compare her to Ellen, who was much friendlier. Rumor has it that Marcella got her job only because the CEO wants diversity in the upper ranks, and he gets to count Marcella as a woman and as a minority.

BLACK *AND* WOMAN

Due to numerous historical developments, and because they simultaneously are members of two traditionally disenfranchised groups (African Americans and women), black women occupy a social location that distinguishes them from other women and from black men (see Bell, 1992; Higginbotham and Weber, 1992; hooks, 1989). However, research and writing about women or about African Americans either assumes that the issues for those groups also apply to African-American women or overlooks African-American women altogether (Etter-Lewis, 1993). Although some of their experiences will resemble those of other women or black men, "what is true for African-American men and white women is not invariably true for African-American women" (Etter-Lewis, 1993: xvi). For instance, "due to the legacy of slavery, black women have never had the privilege of being submissive, docile, or fragile. Rarely, if ever, have black women been afforded the feminine characteristics attributed to white women" (Bell, 1992: 369). Rather, black women are taught to be self-reliant, assertive, and independent, and to be able to provide financially for themselves and their families (Bell, 1992; DeFrancisco and Chatham-Carpenter, 2000; Fordham, 1993; Parker and ogilvie, 1996). Unfortunately, other people may distort these characteristics, partially because of stereotypical assumptions based on media representations of black women as well as comparisons to ideal notions of white womanhood. As Ipsaro (1997) observes, "African American women come into today's workplace independent, direct, and self-confident. Because it is unusual that women act this way in almost all cultures, their behaviors frequently are misinterpreted as being aggressive, strong, and radical" (173).

The relatively few studies on black women's communication reveal that they enact distinct behaviors that stem from being black, woman, and black woman. For instance, African Americans tend to be more confrontational and forceful in conversations among themselves than most European Americans (Houston and Wood, 1996). Also, a collaborative way of working characterizes African-American culture in general (Conrad and Poole, 1998). Black women may exhibit leadership styles that blend white masculine traits (autonomy, strength, independence and self-confidence) and feminine traits of being supportive, caring, and considerate (Parker and ogilvie, 1996).

People often associate "directness" with African-American women's communication, though the interpretation is often negative (Houston and Wood, 1996; Ipsaro, 1997; Shuter and Turner, 1997; Weitz and Gordon, 1993). For example, white professional women viewed black women's conflict management styles as more confrontational than white women's (Shuter and Turner, 1997). Similarly, white college students rated black women as more confrontational than white women (Weitz and Gordon, 1993). These and other distinctions about black women hold important implications for understanding professional workplace dynamics.

Unlike white women, who entered the workforce in record numbers in the mid-1900s, African-American women have been a strong and growing presence in the United States labor force from postslavery to the dawn of the new millennium (Allen, 2000a; Jones, 1985). They consistently have comprised about 50 percent of the black labor force. However, they mainly are (and have been) employed in low status and low paying occupations. In 1996, 1.8 million black women worked in service occupations (60 percent were nursing aides, orderlies and attendants, janitors and cleaners, cooks, and maids) (U.S. Department of Labor, 1997). Fortunately, more and more black women are entering higher paying, career-oriented managerial and professional specialty occupations. In the late twentieth century, numerous black women successfully broke barriers to enter occupations traditionally reserved for white males (such as scientists, lawyers, judges, physicians, engineers, CEOs, and politicians), although they still are quite underrepresented (Allen, 2000a). Most professional black women are segregated into traditional female occupations (e.g., teacher, librarian, and social worker) (Parker and ogilvie, 1996). In addition, they are concentrated in the public rather than the private sector (Higginbotham, 1994).

As growing numbers of African-American women enter the workforce (projections say that 9 million black women will be in the workforce by 2005), contemporary organizations increasingly are hiring them for nontraditional, professional roles (e.g., top-level corporate executives or high-ranking administrators). These hires deviate from traditional recruiting practices of seeking an employee who fits the "ideal" profile of a vacant position. In the past, employers usually based their ideals upon gender- and race-based ideas about who "belonged" in which types of jobs. Thus, employers tended to give white men high-level positions, and to relegate black women to subservient roles.

Due to the historical factors listed above, black professional women enter workplace roles where they previously were not welcome (and still might not be). As I noted earlier, these workplaces may operate on white male value systems. These may devalue both feminine and black traits and styles. Moreover, within these contexts, black women may confront negative perceptions associated with being black, with being a woman, or with being a black woman. A high-level black woman executive explains some of the stigmas:

> As a woman, the questions have been: Does she have the strength of will and character to do the job? Will she get pregnant at a time when we need her most? Will she be emotional in a bad situation? Is she going to be a liability to the organization? Then there is the thought that "we don't need to pay her as much as a we would pay a man." As a Black, the questions have been: Is she dependable? Is she intelligent enough to really do the job? You know how loud angry Blacks can be, will she be able to carry herself in such a manner that makes the organization look good? Is she able to speak well, without a lot of slang? (Fernandez, 1993: 259–260)

Often, a black woman is the first and/or only woman, woman of color, or person of color in her professional role. Thus, she often encounters other persons who have not personally interacted with a black woman in a role of authority. Instead, they may be accustomed to black women in subservient roles. Consequently, these people may rely upon stereotypical images or myths about black woman, as I discuss next.

> After the first round of golf with Marcella, Jim invites her a few more times. He is impressed with her game, and he enjoys talking shop with her. She knows her job, and she asks smart questions. Jim realizes that he would never have guessed that Marcella was a golfer. Although he helped to recruit Marcella, and he felt that she was qualified for the job, he didn't know just how intelligent she was. He agreed to hire her because he felt it would look good to have at least one woman in senior management, and it helped that she also is black. Mark joins Marcella and Jim on a couple of occasions, and Jim and Marcella help Mark to improve his game. The first time out with Jim, Mark confessed that he was a novice, but that he didn't want to miss a chance to "schmooze with the boss." Jim admires Mark's honesty and ambition. He also thinks that Mark is doing quite well on the job.
>
> During a managers' meeting, Roy, one of the white male managers, introduced a new vendor to everyone else in the room but Marcella.[2] To be sure that she was not mistaken, Marcella privately and separately asked each manager if he had been introduced. All of them reported that they had. Marcella met with Roy to describe what had happened. She asked Roy to imagine being the only male in an all-female setting, and how he would feel if he was ignored. He seemed genuinely upset at what had happened, and he apologized. He was not even aware that he had overlooked her.
>
> Marcella often feels that some of the managers acknowledge her presence only when they are discussing diversity or support issues. However, Mark and John (another white male) seem to consciously include her in discussions. In addition, Ed, the only black man, sometimes seems to be her ally, although Marcella is not sure how to interpret some of his behaviors.

When the managers decide to sponsor a company picnic, they ask Marcella to coordinate it. Although she loves to organize these types of events (she is chair of the social committee of her sorority), Marcella declines the invitation. She knows from past experience that if she accepts one assignment like this, they will expect her to coordinate similar events. When the managers decide to preview new budget software, Marcella volunteers to oversee the project. Some of them seem reluctant to allow her to assume this major task. Jim suggests that Marcella team up with one of the other managers. Her colleague initially challenges her ideas and tries to take over the project, but soon sees that Marcella is quite competent. After a few testy meetings, they end up working well together.

Stereotypes of Black Women

In professional settings, other employees may not interact with a black woman based strictly upon their expectations of her position. Because of limited or no personal experience with black women in professional roles, people with whom they interact may rely upon myths and stereotypical images of black women to interact with them (Dumas, 1979; Hoke, 1997; Orbe, 1998; Parker and ogilvie, 1996). These stereotypes are deeply embedded in the consciousness of *all* Americans, not just white men and women (Bell, 1992: 374). As Bell (1992) observes, "conditions created by race, gender, and class oppression have had powerful effects on perceptions of black women" (369).

Many of the white people with whom a black woman interacts will have had fewer experiences with blacks than she has had with whites. They will not be accustomed to dealing with black women in positions of authority; power and authority are not common descriptors of African-American women in the workplace (Parker and ogilvie, 1996). Because many whites do not have a "socially cognitive framework based on authentic contacts with black women, they can easily base their perceptions of them on negative stereotypes and assumptions" (Dumas, 1979: 124). However, other minorities, including black women and men, also may stereotype black women.

In subtle and blatant ways, other people may display stereotyping through their communication behaviors (Allen, 1995). As well, black women may (mis)interpret others' behaviors as stereotyping. Next, I describe recurring stereotypes, and I discuss potential repercussions (see Allen, 1996; 2000b for more extensive discussions). Most of these stereotypes are unique to black women, although some of their characteristics overlap stereotypes about white women, other women of color, or minority men.

Beneficiary of Affirmative Action. Organizational members often perceive a black woman (as well as other women and minority men) to be an affirmative action hire, someone recruited strictly to meet policy requirements (Hine, 1997). Sometimes they also view a black woman as a "twofer" because she can be counted for her gender and for her race-ethnicity (Benjamin, 1991). She also may confront an attitude of white male intellectual superiority (over women and over minorities) and its companion belief that blacks and women are intellectually inferior. These false perceptions may prevent others from perceiving black women as competent professionals. They also might generate hostility, distrust, and opposition (Essed, 1991). Others may display these attitudes through such behaviors as constantly challenging a black woman, questioning her authority, interrupting her, or not soliciting her input.

Token. Members of organizations may regard a black woman as a token, someone who represents her social category. Thus, they view her as a symbol rather than an individual. They may evaluate the black woman more closely than they do nontokens, and then generalize to other persons in the same category (Kanter, 1977). For example, a black professional woman shared this story about a conversation with her white supervisor:

> "I hope *you* make it" [said the supervisor]. Emphasis on *you*. And I told my new supervisor right then and there. I stopped her in her tracks and I said, "What do you mean? I detect some sort of implication here regarding the pronoun *you*." (St. John and Feagin, 1997: 193)

The supervisor finally stated that a black person had never "made it" in the role. A black woman senior vice president of a large finance firm explains the impact of this attitude: "When they put you in a job, you feel as if you are carrying the future of any black person or any woman in this role forever" (panelist quoted in Tucker, 1994: 62).

Tokenism also can cause others to distort the token's characteristics to fit stereotypes, thus limiting the roles that the token may undertake (Kanter, 1977). Viewing a black woman as a "servant" or as an expert on race and/or gender relations represents a common example of this mindset. Combined with the perception that the black woman is not competent to perform her job, this attitude may hinder career development (Collins, 1989, 1997; Ilgen and Youtz, 1984). For instance, executives often place blacks in human resources jobs or assign them to cultural attaché roles (e.g., community liaison) as opposed to more powerful positions where they will have opportunities for promotion to high-level jobs (Collins, 1997; Tucker, 1994).

Mammy. Members of organizations often expect black women to be nurturing caretakers, reminiscent of the black woman's role of mammy during slavery: "Whether she likes it or not, the black woman has come to represent the kind of person, a style of life, a set of attitudes and behaviors through which individuals and groups seek to fulfill their own socioemotional needs in organizations" (Dumas, 1979: 123; also see, Hoke, 1997; Mullings, 1994; Omolade, 1994). Consequently, members of the organization may expect her to be a mother confessor, to provide comfort, and to advocate for the oppressed. For instance, Wood (2001) reports that African-American women are more frequently stereotyped into mothering jobs than European American women.

Matriarch. Black women also may face the stereotype of matriarch—an aggressive, overbearing individual. Sociological studies (Frasier, 1939;

Moynihan, 1965) attributed the derisive label of matriarch to a society that devalues powerful women or blacks (Mullings, 1994; Parker and ogilvie, 1996). Similar to the myth of the "Black Lady Over Achiever," this perspective suggests that "successful black women are arrogant, hard, controlling, self-centered, and uppity" (Bell, 1992: 369). Other recurring stereotypes of black women include welfare queen (someone who tries to beat the system) and jezebel (a wanton, promiscuous woman).

In summary, black women's history in the United States predisposes them to experience the compounded effects of gender occupational segregation, gender role stereotypes, and gender discrimination that other women may endure. Due to interactive effects of being a member of two disenfranchised groups, black women in professional roles are likely to face numerous obstacles, including stereotypical perceptions and negative or hostile work environments. These dynamics may influence black women's interactions with others in professional environments, as I explain below.

> After six months, Marcella and Mark feel good about their progress in their new jobs. From past experiences in other jobs, Marcella has learned to identify people who seem to be allies and to ask them for information and guidance. In her first professional job, she hesitated to ask questions because she feared that others would think that she was incompetent, which would reinforce their misperceptions of her as an unqualified black woman who got her job to fill a quota. She made a few mistakes that she might have avoided if she had only asked for help. Kay Masters, her white supervisor in that organization, told Marcella to figure out who supported her and wanted her to advance and to solicit their guidance. "Some of us may want to help you, but we don't want to seem condescending," she said. "So, you have to let us know that you welcome our counsel." Marcella heeded that advice, and she applied it wherever she worked. Kay also told Marcella that no matter what she did, some people would never accept her, whereas others would grow to appreciate her expertise. "Don't let them get to you," she advised. "Just do your best."
>
> Most of Marcella's employees have grown to enjoy working with her. None of them had ever had a black female boss, and they weren't quite sure what to expect. When she first became manager, one of them went over Marcella's head to question one of her decisions. Marcella's boss, Jim, supported Marcella. Marcella confronted the employee to set the record straight; she instructed him to check with her if he ever had any questions. All of her employees agree that Marcella definitely knows her job. They say that she is fair and open to suggestions. They also know that if you ask her opinion or her feedback, she is going to be honest, sometimes painfully so. She works hard for the money, and she expects them to do so as well. However, she is flexible and understanding about family or educational needs. For instance, she allows Dolores, a Hispanic secretary, to leave work 2 hours early each Wednesday to attend a computer class at a technical college. She even found company funds to pay for the class.

Implications for Black Professional Women

Newcomers to organizations typically use formal and informal methods to gather information about their job from a variety of sources. However, a black professional woman may proceed differently and more cautiously than a white male due to her sensitivity to and apprehensions about racial-gender dynamics. Moreover, those who work with her and for her may treat her differently than they might a white male. These differences can be negative or positive. For example, aware that others might use stereotypes to perceive and evaluate her behaviors, a black woman may hesitate to seek information directly, not only because of how others might judge her, but also because she feels responsible for representing other black women. She also may fear that others might offer her misinformation because they want her to fail. Her white coworkers as well as minority males may feel competitive and threatened by her presence because they believe that she will reap benefits that they will not, due to her perceived "twofer" status (Benjamin, 1991).

On the positive side, a black professional woman may enact a direct yet collaborative communication style that others welcome. She may consult with her employees and her coworkers as she makes decisions, and they may support her efforts because they find her approach to be refreshing and productive.

As she learns her new role, a black woman may consider acquiring mentors to help her understand her job. As noted earlier, women in general are less involved in mentor relationships than men. Research shows that black women are disproportionately likely not to have mentors (Benjamin, 1991; Justus, Freitag, and Parker, 1987; Moses, 1989; Wood, 2001). However, Thomas (1989) reports that black women tend to participate in developmental relationships with other women, but rarely with white men. In professional settings, white men usually are best-positioned to mentor black women. Because people tend to initiate relationships with people like themselves, white men and black women might not easily develop mentoring partnerships with one another (Wood, 2001). White males may hesitate to create sharing relationships with black women, in part due to a history of race relations and racial taboos that impact cross-sex/cross-race mentoring relationships (Conrad and Poole, 1998; Thomas, 1989). Black women and white men in mentoring relationships may confront negative consequences, such as being accused of having sexual relations. White coworkers might accuse the white man of being disloyal to other whites (Moses, 1989). Similarly, black people may criticize a black woman for interacting with a white man (Allen, 2000b). Or, the black woman may feel pressure to avoid contact with other blacks to seem loyal to the dominant group (Benjamin, 1991).

Social networks also provide important role information and contacts for newcomers. However, a black woman may have limited access to informal networks because others exclude her or because she isolates herself (Allen, 2000b; Benjamin, 1991; Denton, 1990; Greenhaus, Parasuraman, and Wormley, 1990). Her white colleagues may not invite her to participate, due to outright prejudice or simple misgivings about interacting with an "other" outside of the job context. She may decline because she "interpret[s] invitations to participate in informal relationships as bids to behave according to stereotypes" (Dumas, 1979: 125).

A black woman may choose to draw a distinct line between work and social life (Bell, 1990). Many black women have other obligations (e.g., family responsibilities or community work) that prevent them from spending time on extracurricular activities (e.g., happy hour, or golf or other sports).

In addition, a black woman may be "torn between the expectations and demands born of her mythical image and those that are inherent in her official status and task in the formal organizations" (Dumas, 1979: 123; see also, Allen, 2000b; Omolade, 1994). She may struggle with the dilemma of trying to contest others' stereotyped expectations of her (e.g., to be a "mammy") versus her indoctrinated sense of obligation to be a caretaker, to look out for others (see Collins, 1991). Sometimes black women feel frustrated because "people around them are likely to be insensitive to their needs for sociopsychological support, reassurance, or some relief from the heavy demands on their time and energy" (Dumas, 1979: 124–125; also see Allen, 2000b; Benjamin, 1991). She may waste a lot of energy trying to make sense of interactions, wondering, for example, if a comment was racist, sexist, both, or neither. She also may question herself: is she being paranoid, or too sensitive? In a study about black women executives, Bell (1990) concludes, "they are extremely vigilant in their work environments, and they take pain in not revealing parts of their true selves" (474).

To conclude, black women and those who interact with them in professional settings may suffer the consequences of gender and race expectations and stereotypes. Black women's experiences may differ from those of others with whom they interact. The preceding discussion illuminates some of those distinctions. In the final section of this chapter, I offer recommendations for improving communication among professional employees of all gender-racial backgrounds.

> Mark believes that he will get an outstanding first annual evaluation. His employees have always worked well with and for him, and his unit is doing well. In addition, he and Jim have a great relationship. Mark isn't crazy about the occasional happy hour foray with Jim, since Jim tends to drink a bit too much and get raunchy. Plus, Natalie (Mark's wife) doesn't like him coming home late. But, Mark figures it's for a good cause. Mark really enjoys his friendship with Marcella, although they spend time together only at work and occasionally golfing. He and Marcella have a similar work ethic, and they both are very ambitious.
>
> Although Marcella feels great about the job as she ends her first year, she also feels frustrated and lonely sometimes. She appreciates Mark's friendship, but she's sure he doesn't know half of what she endures because she is a black woman, and she's not comfortable talking with him about it. Most of her employees who seemed to doubt her have come around. Only one or two seems determined to challenge her at every turn. However, she wishes that she could get her peers to be more collab-

orative. It seems that the other managers, with the exception of Mark and John, always want to compete. If they all worked together, all of their units (and the company) would benefit. Instead, most of them seem to be vying for the boss's attention, for selfish reasons. She also cannot understand the other black manager, Ed. A couple of times, he privately shared helpful information with her, yet during managers' meetings, he behaves as competitively as the others. Once, he made a snide remark during the meeting about her being "the female Tiger Woods." Although she enjoys golfing with Jim, she doesn't appreciate the sexist jokes he often tells during meetings. She also wishes that he wouldn't refer to everything using sports metaphors. That language contributes to the sense of competition, she's sure. "Maybe I'm just too sensitive," she thinks.

Recommendations for Harmonious Communication in Professional Environments

Be Aware. To develop harmonious conditions in diverse professional environments, each of us must become more aware of some of the issues that I have raised. First, gender and race matter when people communicate with one another. Of course, other aspects of identity such as age, class, and sexual orientation also make a difference. Second, recognize that racism, sexism, prejudice, and discrimination are not limited to blatant, overt behaviors. They can occur in subtle ways during interpersonal interactions. Third, as Gentile notes, "acknowledge that some identities exact a higher and/or different price for the bearer in a particular societal, historical, or even situational context than others" (xvi). As I hope I have shown, for instance, African-American women's historical experiences have important ramifications for their interactions in professional settings. Fourth, realize that our identities are not static. Rather, we can develop them and make changes as we learn about others and ourselves. Fifth, remember that each of us simultaneously occupies many different social groups. Thus, we should not fixate on any one aspect of someone's identity.

Be Sensitive. In addition to awareness, we should bring certain sensitivities to our attempts to develop more harmonious professional environments. For example, we should understand that although each of us is an individual, we also are members of social groups that other people sometimes treat in predictable, discriminatory ways. Also, as Houston and Wood (1996) recommend, "Understand that you may not understand" (50). Instead of assuming that you will understand someone who is different, begin with the idea that you may not: "this allows you to avoid the mistake of imposing your meanings on others' behaviors and to open yourself to learning about meanings and communication styles that differ from your own" (50). Try to understand, for example, that people of color in professional settings routinely endure subtle and blatant racism; or, that white people sometimes are not aware that their behaviors may seem racist and/or sexist.

Houston and Wood also urge us to respect how others interpret their experiences. For instance, although you may not relate to a Hispanic woman's complaint about how one of her coworkers constantly corrects her when she rolls her 'r's while pronouncing certain words, try to listen respectfully and understand why she feels as she does.

Be Proactive. No matter what race-gender group you belong to, make a personal commitment to make a difference, and be willing to be changed. Everyone must participate in the process and respect everyone else. As Ipsaro (1997) notes:

> White males, who daily become fewer and fewer in the workplace, must be brought into the change process. White females, who inherit some of the same advantages as white males, also must play a significant role in changing the established rules that not only have to do with gender roles, but with race. (143)

Check yourself for stereotyping behaviors. You may sometimes be guilty of stereotyping if you can *easily* fill in the blanks of the following statements: Black men are ____________ . White women are ______________ . Asian-American women are ________________ . In addition, try not to reinforce negative gender-race stereotypes and expectations about other people. For instance, while some minority women and men and white women are affirmative action hires, they undoubtedly are quite qualified to perform their professional roles, because they have had to struggle to advance themselves.

Check your own perceptual filters. If you constantly look for prejudice, discrimination, and "isms," you probably will find them. I know some people of color who measure almost every interaction with a racism yardstick. Although racism and sexism (as well as homophobia and classism) persist in our society, we must be careful not to interpret all experiences as if they are.

We also can be proactive if we show curiosity about others' differences. As Houston and Wood (1996: 51) observe, we can shift from thinking "that's wrong" to "That's interesting—what might I learn here?"

In addition, we should acknowledge differences without totalizing them. Totalizing occurs when we overemphasize one aspect of someone's identity (Wood, 1998). Furthermore, we should respect the validity of varying communication styles. By doing so, we can "grow beyond the perspectives of the groups in which we were originally socialized" (Houston and Wood, 1996: 53).

Formal steps we can take in professional environments include seeking professional help by hiring communication consultants and developing formal mentoring programs that are available to everyone in the organization.

Finally, practice the golden rule. When in doubt during an interaction with someone whose gender and/or race is different from yours, simply think about how you would want her or him to talk with you.

In conclusion, gender *and* race matter. I hope I have shed some light on how and why the intersection of gender and race affects interactions in professional environments. I also hope that my recommendations offer useful direction and insight. If we wish to reap professional as well as personal benefits of diverse perspectives and communication styles in the twenty-first century, we will need to be patient and persistent. With commitment and a sense of adventure, each of us can make a positive difference.

For Further Discussion

1. Which do you believe is a more important aspect of identity in the United States, gender or race? Why?
2. What stereotypes do people use to characterize members of your gender? Of your race? Of your gender-race blend?
3. Are you aware of specific socialization processes related to your particular gender-race identity? Compare your experiences to persons of the other gender designation, and of other racial categories. For instance, if you are a Hispanic male, were you socialized differently than Hispanic females in your family or community? Did you receive different messages about masculinity than males from other races? Or, if you are a white woman, did you learn different behaviors and values than white males and than women from other races?
4. What challenges does Mark face that demonstrate the complexities of gender-race stereotypes? How well do you think Mark is handling these challenges? What else, if anything, might he do?
5. How do Marcella's experiences exemplify issues discussed in this chapter about black women's unique social position? How well do you think Marcella is handling challenges? What else, if anything, might she do?
6. Ed Markson, the only black male manager, seems to fluctuate in his relationship with Marcella. What issues raised in the chapter might help to explain Ed's behavior?
7. Imagine that you are the CEO of AllCo, and you have to choose between Marcella and Mark to promote to division head. Pretend also that both of them have demonstrated equal competence in their jobs. What factors would you consider in making your decision? How would you choose?

Endnotes

[1] I use "African American" and "black" interchangeably.

[2] This is based on an actual experience of an interviewee, described in Ipsaro (1997).

REFERENCES

Allen, B. J. 1995. "Diversity" and organizational communication. *Journal of Applied Communication Research* 23: 143–155

———. 1996. Feminist standpoint theory: A Black woman's (re)view of organizational socialization. *Communication Studies* 47: 257–271.

———. 2000a. Careerscope. *In the Black* 3. Aurora, CO: In the Black Publishing, Ltd., 20–22.

———. 2000b. "Learning the ropes": A black feminist standpoint analysis. In P. Buzzanell, ed., *Rethinking Organizational and Managerial Communication from Feminist Perspectives*. Thousands Oaks, CA: Sage, 177–208.

Bell, E. L. 1990. The bicultural life experience of career-oriented black women. *Journal of Organizational Behavior* 11: 459–477.

———. 1992. Myths, stereotypes and realities of black women: A personal reflection. *The Journal of Applied Behavioral Science* 28: 363–376.

Benjamin, L. 1991. *The Black Elite: Facing the Color Line in the Twilight of the Twentieth Century.* Chicago: Nelson-Hall Publishers.

Collins, P. H. 1991. *Black Feminist Thought: Knowledge, Consciousness, and the Politics of Empowerment.* New York: Routledge.

Collins, S. M. 1989. The marginalization of black executives. *Social Problems* 36: 317–331.

———. 1997. Black mobility in white corporations: Up the corporate ladder but out on a limb. *Social Problems* 44: 55–67.

Conrad, C., and M. S. Poole. 1998. *Strategic Communication: Toward the Twenty-First Century* (4th Ed.). Fort Worth, TX: Harcourt Brace Jovanovich.

DeFrancisco, V. L., and A. Chatham-Carpenter. 2000. Self in community: African American women's views of self-esteem. *The Horward Journal of Communications* 2: 73–92.

Denton, T. C. 1990. Bonding and supportive relationships among black professional women: Rituals of restoration. *Journal of Organizational Behavior* 11: 447–457.

Dumas, R. G. 1979. Dilemmas of black females in leadership. *Journal of Personality and Social Systems* 2: 120–129.

Dunn, D. 1999. Women: The fifty-one percent minority. In A.G. Dworkin and R. J. Dworkin, eds., *The Minority Report: An Introduction to Racial, Ethnic, and Gender Relations.* Orlando, FL: Harcourt Brace Jovanovich, 415–435.

Essed, P. 1991. *Understanding Everyday Racism: An Interdisciplinary Theory.* Newbury Park, CA: Sage.

Etter-Lewis, G. 1993. *My Soul Is My Own: Oral Narratives of African American Women in the Professions.* New York: Routledge.

Fordham, S. 1993. "Those loud black girls": (Black) women, silence, and gender "passing" in the academy. *Anthropology and Education Quarterly* 24: 3–32.

Frasier, E. F. 1939. *The Negro Family in the United States.* Chicago: University of Chicago Press.

Gentile, M. C. 1996. *Differences That Work: Organizational Excellence Through Diversity.* Prospect Heights, IL: Waveland Press.

Greenhaus, J. H., S. Parasuraman, and W. M. Wormley. 1990. Effects of race on organizational experiences, job performance evaluations, and career outcomes. *Academy of Management Journal* 33: 64–86.

Gutek, B. A. 1985. *Sex and the Workplace: The Impact of Sexual Behavior and Harassment on Women, Men, and Organizations.* San Francisco: Jossey-Bass.

Higginbotham, E. 1994. Black professional women: Job ceilings and employment sectors. In M. B. Zinn and B. T. Dill, eds., *Women of Color in U.S. Society.* Philadelphia, PA: Temple University Press, 113–131.

Higginbotham, E., and L. Weber. 1992. Moving up with kin and community: Upward social mobility for black and white women. *Gender and Society* 6: 416–440.

Hine, D. C. 1997. The future of black women in the academy: Reflections on struggle. In L. Benjamin, ed., *Black Women in the Academy: Promises and Perils.* Gainesville: University Press of Florida, 327–339.

Hoke, B. 1997. Women's colleges: The intersection of race, class, and gender. In L. Benjamin, ed., *Black Women in the Academy: Promises and Perils.* Gainesville: University Press of Florida, 291–301.

hooks, B. 1989. *Talking Back: Thinking Feminist, Thinking Black.* Boston: South End Press.

Houston, M., and J. T. Wood. 1996. Difficult dialogues, expanded horizons, communicating across race and class. In J. T. Wood, ed., *Gendered Relationships.* Mountain View, CA: Mayfield Press.

Ilgen, D. R., and M. A. Youtz. 1984. Factors affecting the evaluation and development of minorities in organizations. *Research in Personnel and Resources Management* 4: 307–337.

Ipsaro, A. J. 1997. *White Men, Women and Minorities in the Changing Work Force.* Denver, CO: Meridian Associates.

Jeanquart-Barone, S. 1993. Trust differences between supervisors and subordinates: Examining the role of race and gender. *Sex Roles* 29: 1–11.

Jones, J. 1985. *Labor of Love, Labor of Sorrow: Black Women, Work, and the Family from Slavery to the Present.* NY: Basic Books, Inc.

Justus, J. B., S. Freitag, and L. L. Parker. 1987. *The University of California in the 21st Century: Successful Approaches to Faculty Diversity.* Berkeley: The University of California.

Kanter, R. M. 1977. *Men and Women of the Corporation.* New York: Basic Books.

Moses, Y. T. 1989. *Black Women in Academe: Issues and Strategies.* Washington, DC: Project on the Status and Education of Women: Association of American Colleges.

Moynihan, D. P. 1965. *The Negro Family: The Case for National Action.* Washington, DC: United States Dept. of Labor, Office of Policy Planning and Research.

Mullings, L. 1994. Images, ideology, and women of color. In M. B. Zinn and B. T. Dill, eds., *Women of Color in U.S. Society.* Philadelphia, PA: Temple University Press, 265–289.

Omolade, B. 1994. *The Rising Song of African American Women.* New York: Routledge.

Orbe, M. P. 1998. *Constructing Co-Cultural Theory: An Explication of Culture, Power, and Communication.* Thousand Oaks, CA: Sage.

Parker, P. S., and D. ogilvie. 1996. Gender, culture, and leadership: Toward a culturally distinct model of African-American women executives' leadership strategies. *Leadership Quarterly* 7: 189–214.

St. John, Y., and J. R. Feagin. 1997. Racial masques: Black women and subtle gendered racism. In N. V. Benokraitis, ed., *Subtle Sexism: Current Practice and Prospects for Change.* Thousand Oaks, CA: Sage, 179–200.

Shuter, R., and L. H. Turner. 1997. African American and European American women in the workplace: Perceptions of conflict communication. *Management Communication Quarterly* 11: 74–96.

Thomas, D. A. 1989. Mentoring and irrationality: The role of racial taboos. *Human Resource Management* 28(2): 279–290.

Tucker, S. H. 1994. Black women in corporate America: The inside story. *Black Enterprise* 25(1): 60–66.
U.S. Department of Labor. 1997. Black Women in the Labor Force. Available: http://www.dol.gov/dol/wb/public/wb_pubs/bwlf97.htm.
Weitz, R., and L. Gordon. 1993. Images of black women among Anglo college students. *Sex Roles* 28: 19–34.
Wood, J. T. 1998. *But I Thought You Meant . . . Misunderstandings in Human Communication*. Mountain View, CA: Mayfield Publishing Co.
———. 2001. *Gendered Lives: Communication, Gender, and Culture*. Belmont, CA: Wadsworth.

CHAPTER 13

Communication and Gender in the Classroom

Cheri J. Simonds
Pamela J. Cooper

POINTS TO BE ADDRESSED

- The extent of sexism in curriculum materials
- The extent of sexism in classroom interaction
- The consequences of sexism
- Strategies for eliminating sexism in the classroom

In May Santon's book, *The Small Room* (1961), Harriet Summerson asks Lucy Winters, "Was there ever a life more riddled with self-doubt than that of a female professor?" (29). What is it she doubts? She doubts the dominant forms of knowledge, the privileged ways of knowing and thinking and speaking. Why? Because, as Belenky and her associates (1986) suggest, women have cultivated and valued ways of knowing that have often been denigrated or neglected by the "dominant intellectual ethos of our time." The different voice by which women speak is often devalued in the educational system (Gilligan, 1982).

Women students now account for 55 percent of the total number of students enrolled in colleges in the United States (Almanac, 1999). Yet the dominant model for education is geared toward men. As Belenky and her associates point out, "Conceptions of knowledge and truth that are accepted and articulated today have been shaped throughout history by the male dominated majority" (5). This model stresses objectivity, separateness, competitiveness, and hierarchical structure. In contrast, women learn better in a model of education that emphasizes "connection over separation, understanding and acceptance over assessment, and collaboration over debate" and one that accords "respect to and allows time for the knowledge that emerges from firsthand experiences" (Belenky, Clinchy, Goodberger, and Tarule: 229).

Perhaps the dominant model tenaciously holds on because the dominant sex in the academies is male. Recent figures reported in the 1999 Almanac published by the *Chronicle of Higher Education* indicate that the proportion of women faculty on U.S. campuses remains low. In 1995, only 34 percent of faculty at colleges and universities were women (Almanac). However, consistent with this report, the American Association of University Professors, (AAUP) Committee on the Status of Women (Committee W) indicates that women are employed in the greatest numbers at the lowest ranks, that they are the majority in untenured positions, and that they still are not being compensated equitably. For example, in 1995, women comprised 54 percent of the faculty at the lecturer level; whereas, they comprised only 17 percent of the faculty at the professor level. The 1999 data show that salaries of female professors trail those of male professors, primarily because women have less experience at the higher ranks and generally do not teach in the higher paid disciplines of science, law, and engineering. Because there are a limited number of women in positions of authority, the likelihood that female students will find role models to support their aspirations is reduced (Marshall, 1996).

According to the editors of *Educating the Majority: Women Challenge Tradition in Higher Education* (Pearson, Shavlik, and Touchton, 1989), an enormous, amount of differential treatment, with regard to both the academic and social climate for women still exists in some form at all institutions (Wolpe, 1989). Blair, Brown, and Baxter (1994) argue that the "male paradigm" (characterized by impersonal abstraction, disciplinary territoriality, individuation, and hierarchy) constitutes the central obstacle to female achievement in academia because females are constantly being measured against a male-centered system of logic and morality. However, the circumstances that riddle female professors with self-doubt exist at all levels of education. Regardless of whether we examine the educational system historically, the differences in male/female occupational choices, the content of curriculum, or classroom communication patterns, we find that the educational system helps to mold the future dominant roles of males and channel females into less dominant roles. This sex-role stereotyping results in what has been termed girls' "below stairs" relationship to education (Mahony, 1983; Rubin, 1988). Sex-role stereotyping exists in both the content of educational materials and in classroom interaction patterns. Often this stereotyping is subtle. In this chapter, the extent and types of this sex-role stereotyping, the consequences of this stereotyping, and strategies for change will be examined.

CURRICULUM MATERIALS

Textbooks

As schools are powerful agents of socialization, they teach us about our cultural values, history, and practices. As Wood (2001) points out, "schools teach us who is important and who is not; who influenced the directions of history, science, literature, and social organization . . . and [schools] contribute in major ways to the process of gendering individuals" (221). One way that schools do so is in the biases present in curriculum materials. Sex-role stereotyping in curriculum materials may be very subtle—so subtle, in fact, that we do not notice it at first. For example, more males than females are pictured in textbook illustrations. Researchers examining the most-used elementary textbooks in grades one through six found disturbing results (Weitzman and Rizzo, 1975). For example, in social studies textbooks, only 33 percent of the illustrations included females. In one series designed to teach reading, 102 stories were about boys and only 35 were about girls. Milner (1977) examined elementary and junior high school math and science texts. In these textbooks, females were pictured as Indians, dolls or witches, or as participating in activities such as skipping rope and buying balloons. Males are pictured as sailors, kings, bakers, circus performers, band members, and balloon sellers. The ratio of males pictured to females was 15:1. Nilsen (1987), comparing three decades of science materials, found that artists draw three times as many pictures of males as females. In addition, in the majority of books examined in this study, the word man is used to describe people in general, and few books depict women in scientific careers. Bazler (1989) examined the seven best selling high school science texts and determined only one of the texts provided a balance of pictures of men and women. Calling for a change, Bazler says, "If women do not see women in science, if their teachers are 95 percent men, and if textbooks are predominantly male, they won't go into science unless they're specifically out to break down those barriers" (33).

Such discrepancies present negative images of females and reinforce sex-role stereotyped behavior. Thus, although more females may be taking math and science classes, curriculum materials still tend to reinforce traditional stereotypes.

Numerical discrepancies exist in other content areas as well. When women are discussed in history textbooks, for example, passages frequently include misleading words or phrases that detract from the significance of women and their accomplishments. For example, one text informs readers that no women were members of the Senate in 1972 when, in fact, Margaret Chase Smith served as a senator at that time (Kirby and Julian, 1981).

Generally, stereotypical roles can be found in all types of textbooks. In speech communication textbooks, for example, hypothetical applications of communication skills, such as a man arguing in court and a woman making an announcement at a PTA meeting, perpetuate sex-role stereotypes (see Randall, 1985; Sprague, 1975). Most anthologies dealing with speech communication feature speeches by men (Sprague, 1975). A more recent study of sex representation and gender bias in introductory communication textbooks revealed that while some of the numerical disparities seem to be decreasing (men and women were referenced in similar proportions and gender neutral pronouns were used), men were still portrayed in more traditional, powerful, and dominant roles (Cawyer, Bystrom, Miller, Simonds, O'Brien, and Martin, 1994). These authors suggest that equal representation does not fully address the more subtle forms of bias and that to do so would require revisiting the standards used to address sexism in curriculum materials.

In math textbooks, men are depicted as active, alert, and scientific. Mathematics is typically seen as a masculine activity (Fennema, 1984). Males are more often pictured doing math, and most story problems are about males. Women are depicted as dull and insignificant, and are rarely involved in career situations. In scientific textbooks, males control the action and females watch the action; boys perform experiments, girls clean up. In addition, adult women are almost never presented in scientific roles (Nilsen, 1987).

In economics textbooks, women are most frequently portrayed in stereotypical ways, and their socioeconomic experiences are treated as anomalous or deviant (Feiner and Morgan, 1987). In an analysis of 21 major introductory economics textbooks, the number of pages that make even a passing reference to economic topics salient to women is remarkably small, ranging from 2 to 22. The total pages of the texts ranged from 399 to 968 (Feiner and Morgan, 1987). Feiner and Roberts (1990) suggest that simply expanding the treatment of women in these textbooks would not solve the fundamental problem:

> We argue that two fundamental characteristics of neoclassical economics unavoidably bias its treatment of gender and race: its philosophical premises, including the positive-normative distinction, and the equilibrium structure of its analyses, which are based on deriving economic outcomes from the rational character of constrained individual choice. (161)

In general, despite the adoption of nonsexist guidelines during the past decade, textbook publishers have made relatively few changes to increase the visibility of females and decrease the stereotyping of males and females. For example, in elementary school textbooks, stories about females are only included in one or two books in a series or added to a single grade level (deNys and Wolfe, 1985). The "nonbiased" material is sometimes added to the center or end of a text, without any attempt to integrate it into the overall format of the rest of the book. Peterson (1994) notes how women are now included in separate chapters such as "great women in history" rather than throughout the book. Such practices indicate that women are relegated as "apart from" rather that "a part of" society.

Children's Literature

In addition to textbooks, educators are being encouraged to use other books to supplement basic curriculum (Aiex, 1988; Holmes and Ammon,

1985). A major supplement is children's literature. A plethora of research demonstrates that children's literature reflects and reinforces sex-role stereotypes. Numerical disparities and stereotyped behavior patterns and characteristics reflected in children's literature teach girls to undervalue themselves and teach boys to believe that they must always be stereotypically masculine.

Females are not included in children's books in numbers that reflect their presence in the general population. Several studies have examined how sex roles are treated in books that won the prestigious Caldecott Medal or the Newbery Award (Cooper, 1989; Kolbe and LaVoie, 1981; Weitzman, Eifler, Hokada, and Ross, 1972). From 1967 to 1972, the ratio of male characters to female characters in Caldecott Medal books was 11:1. From 1972 to 1979, the ratio of male characters in Newbery Award books was 18:1. Finally, from 1987 to 1989, the ratio of human male characters to human female characters in Caldecott Medal books was 2:1 and the ratio in Newbery Award winners was 6:1. From 1967 to 1987, only 14 books (out of a total of 97) depicted women working outside the home (see Cooper, 1991b).

Although numerical disparities are decreasing in children's books, the role models presented for children have not become less stereotyped. The three studies cited above also examined the stereotyped behavior patterns and characteristics depicted in children's books. The 1967 to 1972 study showed that when females were illustrated, traditional sex-role characterizations were reinforced: girls were passive, boys were active; girls followed and served others, boys led and rescued others. Adult men and women in these books also were stereotyped: women were depicted as wives and mothers, while men held a variety of occupations. In the years from 1972 to 1987, sex-role stereotypes were still prevalent. From 1967 to 1971, all 18 Caldecott Medal books portrayed traditional sex roles; from 1972 to 1979, 17 out of 19 did; from 1980 to 1987, 22 contained traditional sex-role stereotypes. In an update of her 1989 study, Cooper (1991b) examined the Caldecott and Newbery winners from 1980 to 1990. The ratios remained the same, as did the stereotypical role portrayal.

Stereotyped role portrayal does not occur only in Caldecott and Newbery Medal books. For example, Cooper (1987) examined the sex-role stereotypes in children's books concerning stepfamilies. She examined 42 books available in libraries in the Chicago metropolitan area and found many stereotyped sex roles in these books. Women worked, but in stereotyped occupations such as receptionist, secretary, or nurse. They were relatively passive and focused on their appearance. When women worked outside the home, they neglected their children or became aggressive. Men were depicted as lawyers and doctors who were inept at simple household duties. They were caring and sensitive, but only to a point—when problems were not resolved quickly, they became impatient.

Peterson and Lach (1990) examined picture books listed in the booklist in *The Horn Book* for 1967, 1977, and 1987. These researchers found that although the prevalence of stereotypes had decreased somewhat, the decreases in quantity and kind were not statistically meaningful.

Lee Barton (1984) suggests that the sex-role stereotyping of male characters in children's literature has been greatly ignored. The author analyzed over fifty children's books and found that books that depict a sensitive male role model do exist, but not in great numbers.

The concern with sex role stereotypes in curriculum materials stems from the fact that gender stereotypes influence a variety of cognitive processes, such as recall of material, clustering of learned concepts, inferences drawn from the material, and comprehension (see Martin and Halverson, 1983; Signorella and Liben, 1984). Gender stereotypes also affect readers' perceptions of others' behavior, and their memory for that behavior as well as the inferences they draw from it (Berndt and Heller, 1986). As Peterson and Lach (1990) suggest, "It is clear that gender stereotypes affect not only self-concept, potential for achievement and perceptions of others, but a variety of dimensions of cognitive performance as well" (194). Campbell and Wirtenburg (1980) suggest that the amount of exposure children receive to gender-biased or to bias-free materials influences the effect these materials have—the longer the exposure to gender-biased material, the more gender-stereotyped their attitudes become and the longer these attitudes are retained.

Authors have recently begun to examine ways to read and evaluate children's literature from a feminist perspective (Fox, 1993; Paul, 1998; Trites, 1998). In class one day while engaging in a critical discussion of children's literature, a student of Lisa Paul's asked her, "How did you learn to 'think like that'?" meaning how did she learn to shift from accepting "an imposed version of the text to challenging it" (7). In attempting to answer that question, Paul wrote a book instructing her students how to "read otherways." Some critical advice she gives includes asking some of the following questions: "Whose story is this? Who is named? Who is not? Who is silenced? Who speaks? Who acts? Who is acted upon?" (16). Fox argues that "gender stereotypes in literature prevent the fullness of female human potential from being realized by depriving girls of a range of strong, alternative role models" (84). She also posits that "teachers and writers have the power to change 'gender-appropriate' behavior and attitudes, yet many of us seem blind to the opportunity" (85). Finally, Fox states that "both genders have to be allowed to be as real in literature as they are in life" (88). Therein lies the equity. In keeping with these suggestions, Roberta Trites wrote a book entitled, *Waking Sleeping Beauty: Feminist Voices in Children's Novels* where she provides teachers who work with children's literature the skills to revise gender stereotypes and to replace them with more complete visions of females in children's books. She suggests that teachers who wish to engage in feminist pedagogy should provide children with feminist texts, use nonsexist multicultural texts, validate female voices as clearly as they validate male voices, allow their students to make self-empowering choices, and listen when students voice dissenting opinions.

Classroom Communication Patterns

A review of research indicates that the students face an educational system today that continues to reinforce gender stereotypes in important ways (Orenstein, 1994; Sadker and Sadker, 1994). Despite federal laws and regulations that prohibit sex discrimination in education institutions, inequities still exist (Sadker and Sadker, 1994). For example, in 1992, the American Association of University Women Educational Foundation commissioned a comprehensive review of 1,331 studies of gender and education practices. The result was a report entitled "How Schools Shortchange Girls" (*Newsweek*, 1992) in which evidence was amassed to show that female students continue to receive less attention, less encouragement, and less serious regard than their male peers (as cited in Cooper and Simonds, 1999). Perhaps more disturbing is the report's finding that "girls enter first grade with the same or better skills and ambitions as boys. But, all too often, by the time they finish high school, 'their doubts have crowded out their dreams'" (62). Are we to believe, then, as this study indicates that our current curriculum creates a "downward intellectual mobility cycle in which girls are less likely to reach their potential than boys" (62)?

A review of literature for all educational levels suggests six major ways in which teachers communicate sex-role expectations to students (Hall and Sandler, 1982). First, teachers may call on male students more often than on female students. When female students are asked why they believe teachers call on male students more often, they indicate that teachers either do not expect them to know the answer or do not feel the answer would be correct or worthwhile.

Second, teachers often coach male students to help them work toward a fuller answer. Female students are not coached as often. For example, a teacher is more likely to say, "What do you mean by that?" or "Why do you believe that?" to male students than to female students. Coaching may communicate to males the expectation that, with a little help, they can succeed. The lack of coaching may communicate to females that their ideas are not important enough to probe further or that they are not intellectually capable of succeeding.

Third, teachers wait longer for males than they wait for females to answer a question before going on to another student. This may subtly communicate to females that they are not expected to know the answer and may communicate to males that they are more intellectually competent than their female counterparts. In addition, a male's silence following a question is often perceived as time used formulating an answer, while a female's is perceived as lack of knowledge.

Fourth, female students are more likely to be asked questions that require factual answers ("When was television invented?") and male students are more often asked questions that require critical thinking or personal evaluation ("How do you feel the concept of symbolic interaction affects communication?"). Teachers communicate expectations regarding the intellectual capability of each student—females are capable only of low-level cognitive processes; males are capable of high-level cognitive processes.

Fifth, teachers respond more extensively to male students' comments than to female students' comments. Thus, males receive more reinforcement for their intellectual participation than do females. In this way, a teacher communicates to female students that their comments are not as worthwhile or as interesting as those of male students

Finally, teachers communicate sex-role stereotypes by their use of sexist language. Richmond and Gorham (1988), in their study of current generic-referent usage among 1,529 public school children in grades 3 through 12, found that the masculine generic usage prevailed. In addition, a heavy dependence on masculine referents were associated with self-image. Males used significantly more masculine referents than did females. Males who selected traditionally male careers used more masculine referents than did males who selected a gender nonspecific career. Females selecting stereotypically feminine careers used the most feminine referents.

A great deal of research has explored the communication patterns that exist in the classroom in relation to sex of students and teachers. Generally, we know that differences exist in terms of initiation, discipline, and dominance (Stake and Katz, 1982).

Initiation

Male students initiate more interactions with teachers than female students initiate (Brophy, 1985). In addition, the interactions between male students and teachers last longer (Hall and Sandler, 1982). Teachers call on males more often and give them more positive feedback than they give girls. In addition, males are given more time to talk in class (Keegan, 1989).

Pearson and West (1991) examined 15 college classrooms and found that female students ask fewer questions than male students in courses taught by males. Good and Slavings (1988) charted the types of questions male and female students at various grade levels asked in mathematics and language arts classes. The results suggest that, in advanced secondary mathematics classes, female students ask fewer questions than males. In addition, teachers subtly discouraged female students from participating. Teachers explain how to do things to male students, but they simply do them for female students. Interaction time increases as a teacher explains how to set up lab equipment, work a math problem, or write a thesis sentence. If the teacher is "doing for" the female student, as is often the case, interaction time is decreased.

Teachers have suggested that males are more creative and fun to teach (Sadker and Sadker, 1985). Teachers may communicate this attitude to male students, who, in turn, may be more willing to initiate interactions because they feel more valued in the classroom.

Discipline

Classroom communication patterns differ in terms of how male and female students are disciplined. Criticism of female students focuses on their lack of knowledge or skill; criticism of male students focuses on disruptive behaviors. Male students receive more discipline than female students receive and are more likely to be reprimanded in a harsher and more public manner than female students (Brophy, 1985).

High-achieving male students receive more teacher approval and active instruction; low-achieving male students are likely to receive more criticism. However, high-achieving female students receive less praise than both low and high-achieving male students (Parsons, Heller, and Kaczala, 1980). Thus, although male students receive more disciplinary messages, they also receive more praise, in general, than female students receive, particularly for their intellectual ability. Boys believe they earn higher grades. Girls more often attribute their success to luck (see research reviewed in Cooper, 1991a).

Dominance

Male students often dominate classroom talk. They are given more opportunities to respond in the classroom, and teachers direct more attention (both positive and negative) toward them. In addition, teachers ask male students a higher proportion of product-and-choice questions (questions that require synthesis or analysis), thereby encouraging problem-solving behavior in male students to a greater extent than in female students (Brophy and Good, 1974).

Male students dominate more than just the conversation in the classroom; they also dominate nonverbal aspects of classroom communication (Thorne, 1979). In addition to dominating linguistic space, male students dominate the physical space of the classroom.

Boys may also emphasize their masculine dominance by using girls as a negative reference group. One researcher asked students, "Who would you least wish to be like?" All of the boys named girls (and only girls). The characteristic of girls most vehemently rejected by boys was their apparent marginality in classroom encounters. The term "faceless" was used repeatedly by male students (but by none of the females) to describe their female classmates, and seemed to sum up their feeling that silence robs female students of any claim to individual identity and respect (Stanworth, 1981).

Male students use several strategies to achieve dominance in mixed-sex classrooms. They deny female students' academic abilities, make negative remarks about females' appearances, and overtly resist females' adopting of nontraditional roles. Reay (1990) reports research that demonstrates that when girls' achievement levels were improved, boys became angry and resentful. As Sandler (1991: 6) suggests, "By giving men students the greater share of classroom attention, faculty unknowingly creates a climate that subtly interferes with the development of women students' self-confidence, academic participation and career goals."

Not only do teachers communicate differently with male and female students, but teachers also perceive male and female students differently in both competence and compliance. For example, King (1998) found that teachers graded essays perceived to be written by boys more favorably than the same essays perceived to be written by girls. In addition, studies have shown that males are praised for academic interest and achievement, while females are supported for being quiet and compliant (Fagot, 1984; Lister, 1997; Sadker and Sadker, 1986). Gold, Crombie, and Noble (1987) found that preschool girls whose behavior is in accordance with the compliant good student model are more likely to have their abilities perceived at a high level than girls whose behavior does not fit the model. Evaluations of boys' competence is not affected by teachers' perceptions of their compliance.

Classroom communication patterns differ in terms of how male and female students treat male and female teachers. A growing body of research indicates that male and female students treat female faculty differently than they treat male faculty (Ryan, 1989). Nadler and Nadler (1990), using a questionnaire measure of male and female perceptions of class-related communication behavior, found that male instructors were viewed as engaging in more dominant, controlling behaviors than female instructors. Female instructors were viewed as engaging in more supportive behaviors toward students than were male instructors. In addition, students rate their female instructors more harshly than their male instructors. A woman's voice, clothing, appearance, and form of address can, and often are, used against her (Sandler, 1991). The classroom climate is not only chilly for female students (Hall and Sandler, 1982, 1984), it's chilly for female faculty (Sandler and Hall, 1986).

The perceptions students have of instructors affect student communication in the classroom. Male and female students communicate differently with male and female instructors. When the instructor is male, male student interactions are three times more frequent than female student interactions. When the instructor is female, male and female student interactions are nearly equal (Karp and Yoels, 1976).

Rosenfeld and Jarrard (1985) examined how the perceived sexism of college professors affected classroom climate. They found that students who perceive their male teachers to be highly sexist describe their classes as less supportive and less innovative than those taught by nonsexist male teachers. In a follow-up study (Rosenfeld and Jarrard, 1986), the researchers examined coping mechanisms used by students in classes taught by sexist and nonsexist teachers. Coping mechanisms used by students in sexist male teachers' classes were passive (not doing what the teacher asked, hiding feelings) when students liked the class. If students did not like the class and perceived the male teacher as sexist, students used an active coping mechanism—forming alliances against the teacher. Generally, teachers in disliked classes were perceived as more sexist than teachers in liked classes. Also, male teachers were perceived as more sexist than female teachers.

CONSEQUENCES OF SEX-ROLE STEREOTYPING IN EDUCATION

As the research discussed in this chapter indicates, curriculum materials and classroom interaction patterns influence student sex-role stereotypes and behaviors. The question now becomes, "What is the effect of sex-role stereotyping in education?" Basically, sex-role stereotyping in education affects three areas: (1) the self-concept of students, (2) the curriculum choice of students, and (3) the occupational choice of students.

Self-Concept

When instructors have preconceived gender expectations, they not only reinforce stereotypes, but they influence a student's self-concept as well. Mboya (1995) reports that student self-concepts depend on teacher expectations which, in turn, affect learning. For example, studies indicate that while females students are praised for being quiet and compliant, male students are praised for academic interaction, interest, and achievement (Hall and Sandler, 1982; Sadker and Sadker, 1986; Wood and Lenze, 1991).

Lenney (1977) reviewed the research concerning women's self-confidence in achievement settings and concluded that women's self-confidence is not lower than men's when (1) the task is appropriate for females; (2) the information available on their ability at a specific task is clear and unambiguous; and (3) the emphasis placed on comparison to others and evaluation by others is low. Generally, these three criteria are not met in achievement settings. Thus, women's self-confidence in the educational environment may be low, and this low self-confidence may affect their self-concept.

McLaughlin (1991) reports results of a major research study by the American Association of University Women that found that at age nine, most girls were assertive, confident, and felt good about themselves. But by the time they got to high school, fewer than one third felt that way. Petersen (1987) also found that the achievement of girls declined from seventh to twelfth grades. Leonard and Sigall (1989) report that women's grades, career goals, and esteem decline over the four-year span of college.

In a major study, Earle, Roach, and Fraser (1987) investigated female dropouts and concluded that the majority of female students who drop out are not pregnant, as had previously been assumed. The report, "Female Dropouts: A New Perspective," speculates that current school practices encourage girls to leave school by depressing their overall achievement. For example, studies have shown that teachers talk less to female than to male students, counsel them less, and provide them with fewer directions and rewards. Also, schools provide limited opportunities for students to work cooperatively, though girls may perform better than boys in such situations. A report on girls' lower SAT scores, "Sex Bias in College Admission Tests: Why Women Lose Out" (reported by Carmody, 1987), suggests the long-term impact a lack of math and science background is having—a real dollar loss for females in later life. Females get less prestigious jobs, earn less money, and have fewer leadership opportunities. Male-dominated occupations are higher paying, on average, than those dominated by females.

Curriculum Choice

The sex-role stereotyping in education also affects the course of study students pursue. Traditionally, female students have perceived math and science courses, spatial ability, and problem-solving as male domains (Goldman, 1987). Research examining differences in male/female math and science performance suggests that males are more likely to take higher-level math and science courses and that this is particularly true in physics, trigonometry, and calculus (Benbow and Minor, 1986). The same is true in science. An analysis of 13-year-olds reports no sex differences in science achievement. Yet females continue to move away from the sciences (Lawrenz and Welch, 1983). Thus, although achievement in science and math may not be different, when male and female students are exposed to the same material, female students tend not to take advanced math and science courses.

In terms of the influence of computer usage, several studies indicate that both elementary and secondary students perceive computer use as masculine (Collis, 1985; Collis and Ollila, 1990; Lockheed, 1985; Sanders, 1984). More recent studies confirm that females spend less time with computers than males (Quilling, 1999) and that boys start schooling with more computer knowledge than girls (Sadker, 1999). Hoyles (1988) suggests that while girls and boys might show a similar appreciation of the significance computers might have for their personal futures, boys tend to be more positively disposed than girls toward computers, are more likely than girls to take optional computer courses in school and to report more frequent home use of computers, and tend to dominate the limited computer resources that are available in school. Because educators argue that the computer should not be seen *simply* as an object of knowledge but should be integrated into the school curriculum as a resource to be used in all subjects when appropriate, the use of gender bias becomes extremely crucial. As Hoyles (1988: 32) argues, "If girls are in general less familiar with computers than boys are, or if children strongly identify computers with boys rather than girls, then the increasing use of computers across the school curriculum will have profound effects on the education of girls."

Occupational Choice

The choice of which curriculum to pursue is directly related to occupational choice. For example, math and science skills are critical in determining educational and occupational choices. Studies have shown that as females and males progress through the mathematics and science curriculum, for example, they show little difference in ability, effort, or interest until the adolescent years (National Research Council, 1989; Sadker and Sadker, 1994). As social pressures increase, females tend to exert less interest in entering advanced math and science courses, which progressively limits their future education and, eventually, their career choices (Manning, 1998; National Research Council, 1989). Thus, when female students avoid science and math training, they preclude themselves from considering a wide range of occupations.

According to research cited in Fallon (1990), for the past 35 years, the wage differential between men's and women's salaries has defied eradication. A study conducted by the Women's Research and Education Institute revealed that for full-time female workers in 1988, the median income was 66 percent that of males—only a 1 percent increase over women's median income for the year 1955. Over a lifetime, a woman who holds a graduate degree will earn $1.3 million, while a man with only a high school diploma will earn more, $1.4 million.

It is well established that sex-typed labeling of school subjects is related to students' attitudes and achievement in those subjects (see research reviewed in Collis and Ollila, 1990). Wilder, Mackie, and Cooper (1985) found that students at all grade levels, K through 12, saw writing as more appropriate for females than for males. Research reviewed in an article by Trepanier-Street and her associates (1990) reveals that elementary school boys at all grade levels and girls in grades 1 through 4 include significantly more male characters than female characters in their stories. The male characters are assigned more physical actions, emotions, physical and ability attributes, problem-solver roles, and occupational roles. Girls in the fifth and sixth grades assign more emotions, actions, and attributes to female characters. Examining the creative writing responses of third and sixth graders to either stereotypic (male mechanic and female nurse) or nonstereotypic (female mechanic and male nurse) occupational roles, Trepanier-Street and her associates found that students had the most difficulty maintaining a character in role when the character's gender did not match the occupational gender stereotype. The researchers conclude that gender-stereotypic thinking is "alive and well" at all levels of elementary education. In social studies classes, researchers examined junior and senior high school students' attitudes toward women in politics. Given adolescents' increased exposure to female political role models in the early 1980s, the researchers hypothesized that these students would hold positive attitudes toward women as political candidates. Adolescent girls had very positive and optimistic views of the role of women in politics; adolescent boys had more negative and pessimistic views (Gillespie and Spohn, 1987).

Strategies for Change

Several researchers are suggesting strategies to change the present gender insensitive educational system to a gender sensitive one (see Wood and Lenze, 1991). Suggestions range from urging the inclusion of works by women in U.S. public address courses and as models in public speaking courses (Campbell, 1991) to using collaborative learning (Reay, 1990). As most writers suggest, creating a gender sensitive classroom doesn't involve simply adding information about women to the curriculum. Ideological and pedagogical challenges abound. The "male-as-norm" conceptions of educational purposes, of students, of teachers, of curricula, of pedagogy, indeed of the profession of education, must be closely examined (Leach and Davies, 1990). To see the absence of women as a significant omission means to change civilization, to reform the disciplines, and thereby to change higher education (Gilligan, Lyons, and Hanmer, 1990). Roth (1987), writing on teaching modern art history from a feminist perspective, speaks of her struggle in this endeavor:

> As mentioned earlier, I had found the piecemeal approach of addition (be it adding women artists of photography, American art, fold art, caricature, etc.) did not work. Rather, a wholesale revision of all material was necessary. Key in this is the examination of how gender together with class and race affect all artists, for to discuss the effect of gender only in the case of women artists places us yet again in the role of the "other" (a once-useful term/analytic structure that is now not only outworn but also pernicious). Thus, I am now radically changing the structure of both individual lectures and of entire courses. (23)

Again, we must continue to reinforce that women are "a part of" rather than "apart from" what has been otherwise considered "mainstream" material. The goal, then, is to reach what E. Peterson (1991) describes for the field of speech communication as "Stage Five: Speech Communication Redefined to Include Us All." So, what has to be done to change the present educational system?

Maher and Rathbone (1986) suggest teachers need to be trained in choosing curriculum and classroom management techniques to equalize classroom interaction and teaching styles, particularly collaborative learning styles. Higginbotham (1990) outlines three tasks: (1) gather information about the diversity of female experience, (2) reconceptualize one's discipline in light of gender-based analysis, and (3) structure classroom dynamics that ensure a supportive climate for all students.

Several specific suggestions for accomplishing the goals of authors come to mind. First, a feminist perspective to teaching/learning is needed. Why? Because, as Wood (1989) outlines, feminist pedagogy is good pedagogy because (1) feminism is inclusive so that topics representative of both sexes' experience and concerns are addressed; (2) feminism values diversity so that multiple ways of knowing are accepted and valued; (3) feminism values human relationships so that teaching becomes interactive rather than authoritative; (4) feminism values personal experience so that thoughtful consideration of how ideas/knowledge relate to personal experience is encouraged; (5) feminism emphasizes empowerment, not power, so that students have control over their own learning; and (6) feminism seeks to create change so that learners perceive themselves as agents of change. Such a feminist approach to pedagogy means that the instructor places an emphasis on such things as individual learning styles, variety in teaching strategies, student–student interactions, creating a collaborative learning environment, requesting and reacting to student feedback on course content and pedagogy.

Perhaps the most important aspect of feminine pedagogy is its emphasis on personal knowledge. The story with which each learner comes to the learning needs to be incorporated into the learning. Feminist pedagogy thus puts an emphasis on narrative. As Pagano (1988) suggests:

> The artistic medium of the teacher is the narrative; her teaching is a narrative enactment. When we teach, we tell stories. We tell stories about our disciplines, about the place of these disciplines in the structure of human knowledge. We tell stories about knowledge, about what it is to be a human knower, about how knowledge is made, claimed, and legitimated. The stories that we tell are stories built on other stories; they work to forge continuity between our stories and those of others, to confirm community among ourselves and others, and to initiate others into our communities. In educational theory, we tell stories of teaching, stories that at once reveal, constitute, and confirm the values that give significance to pedagogical acts. (321)

So, too, the stories students tell are important to an understanding of how their personal experience relates (or fails to relate) to the content being discussed. When we deny, as we often do, students their stories, fearing the stories will take us too far afield from our all-important current topic, we deny students their ability to make the content real to their own experience. One of the most extensive lists of behaviors for nonsexist teaching is presented by Hall and Sandler (1982). Because research suggests that the classroom is a "chilly" climate for females, Hall and Sandler make the following recommendations for creating a climate that will encourage females to communicate:

1. Pay particular attention to classroom interaction patterns during the first few weeks of class, as patterns are likely to be established during this period that will often continue throughout the term.
2. Make a specific effort to call directly on females as well as on male students.
3. In addressing the class, use terminology that includes both males and females in the group.
4. Respond to female and to male students in similar ways when they make comparable contributions to class discussion by: (a) crediting comments to their author ("as Jeanne said . . ." and (b) "coaching" for additional information.
5. Intervene in communication patterns among students that may shut out females. For example, if male students pick on each other's points, but ignore an appropriate comment offered by a female, slow the discussion, and pick up on the comment that has been overlooked.

6. Note patterns of interruption to determine if female students are interrupted more than males—either by yourself or by other students. Make a special effort to ensure that all students have the opportunity to finish their comments.
7. Ask females and males qualitatively similar questions—that is, ask students of both sexes critical as well as factual questions.
8. Give male and female students an equal amount of time to respond after asking a question.
9. Give females and males the same opportunity to ask for and receive detailed instructions about the requirements for an assignment.
10. When talking about occupations or professions in class discussion, use language that does not reinforce limited views of male and female roles and career choices.
11. Avoid using the generic "he" whenever possible.
12. Avoid placing professional women in a "special category," for example, "woman" (or worse, "lady") doctor.
13. Make eye contact with females as well as with male students after asking a question to invite a response.
14. Watch for and respond to nonverbal cues that indicate female students' readiness to participate in class, such as leaning forward or making eye contact.
15. Use the same tone in talking with female as with male students (for example, avoid a patronizing or impatient tone when speaking with females, but a tone of interest and attention when talking with males).
16. Finally, eliminate sexist materials from your curriculum. (16)

Conclusion

In light of the research reviewed in this chapter, can we make any claims of improvement toward a gender-fair educational environment? After three decades of researching gender related issues, David Sadker (2000a) surmises that the "'glass wall' continues to keep women from the most lucrative careers and keeps men from entering traditionally female jobs. Men continue to dominate the high pay, high status college majors" (6). He also argues that "gender bias continues to be documented in curricular materials, staffing patterns, and teaching behaviors. . . it is surprising that so many Americans are unaware of the subtle (and not so subtle) barriers that still exist" (6). Fleming (2000) provides a summary of the 1998 Women's Educational Equity Act (WEEA) and reports both encouraging and discouraging news. According to the report, girls seem to be improving in overall proficiency and achievement, are participating more in sports, and are choosing professional career paths; however, bias still exists in the classroom climate and is reflected in lower expectations, gender stereotypes, and male-focused student–teacher interaction patterns. Finally, Sadker (2000b) suggests that "while bias is less problematic today, its influence is no less virulent" (80).

Why is it the female professor, indeed, the female student doubts herself? The answer is obvious. The research reviewed in this chapter demonstrates she has been taught—through curriculum materials and classroom interaction patterns—to doubt her abilities, her goals, her very means of gaining knowledge. As long as strategies for changing the educational environment are not implemented, the question remains, "Was there ever a life more riddled with self-doubt than that of the female in the educational environment?"

For Further Discussion

1. This chapter argues that the dominant model in education is geared toward men because it stresses objectivity, separateness, competitiveness, and hierarchical structure. What are some examples or instances that support this argument? How would the educational enterprise be different if a female paradigm were dominant?
2. How do textbooks and curriculum materials look different today than they did ten or twenty years ago? What still needs to be done to make these materials more equitable?
3. From your experiences, do you perceive that boys and girls are treated differently in school? If so, how? What needs to be done to make sure that boys and girls are treated equally?
4. If you were commissioned to develop a training program for pre-service teachers on gender sensitivity/equality in the classroom, what would that program entail? How would you implement and evaluate that program?

References

Almanac. 27 August 1999. *Chronicle of Higher Education,* 24, 36.

Aiex, N. 1988. Literature based reading instruction. *The Reading Teacher* 41: 458–461.

Bazler, J. 1989, November. Chem text photos discourage women. *NEA Today,* 33.

Barton, L. 1984. What are boys like in books these days? *Learning* 13: 130–131.

Belenky, M., B. Clinchy, N. Goldberger, and J. Tarule. 1986. *Women's Ways of Knowing.* New York: Basic Books.

Benbow, C., and L. Minor. 1986. Mathematically talented males and females and achievement in high school sciences. *American Education Research Journal* 23: 425–436.

Berndt, T. J., and K. A. Heller. 1986. Gender stereotypes and social inferences: A developmental study. *Journal of Personality and Psychology* 50: 889–898.

Blair, C., J. Brown, and L. Baxter. 1994. Disciplining the feminine. *Quarterly Journal of Speech* 4: 383–409.

Brophy, J. 1985. Interactions of male and female students with male and female teachers. In L. C. Wilkinson and C. B. Marrett, eds., *Gender Influence in Classroom Interaction*, Orlando, FL: Academic Press, 115–142.

Brophy, J. E., and T. L. Good. 1974. The influence of the sex of the teacher and student on classroom interaction. In J. Brophy and T. Good, eds., *Teacher-Student Relationships: Causes and Consequences.* New York: Holt, Rinehart and Winston, 199–239.

Campbell, K. 1991. Hearing women's voices. *Communication Education* 40: 33–48.

Campbell, P., and J. Wirtenburg. 1980. How books influence children: What the research shows. *Interracial Books for Children Bulletin* 11: 3–6.

Carmody, D. 17 April 1987. SATs are biased against girls, report by advocacy group says. *The New York Times*, B2.

Cawyer, C., D. Bystrom, J. Miller, C. Simonds, M. O'Brien, and J. Martin. 1994. Communicating gender equity: Representation and portrayal of women and men in introductory communication textbooks. *Communication Studies* 45: 325–331.

Collis, B. 1985. Sex-related differences in attitudes toward computers: Implications for counselors. *The School Counselor* 33(2): 120–130.

Collis, B., and L. Ollila. 1990. The effect of computer use on grade 1 children's gender stereotypes about reading, writing, and computer use. *Journal of Research and Development in Education* 24: 14–20.

Cooper, P. 1987. Sex role stereotypes of stepparents in children's literature. In L. P. Stewart and S. Ting-Toomey, eds., *Communication, Gender, and Sex Roles in Diverse Interaction Contexts.* Norwood, NJ: Ablex, 61–82.

———. 1989. Children's literature: The extent of sexism. In C. Lont and S. Friedley, eds., *Beyond Boundaries: Sex and Gender Diversity in Education.* Fairfax, VA: George Mason University Press, 233–250.

———. 1991a. *Speech Communication for the Classroom Teacher* (4th ed.). Scottsdale, AZ: Gorsuch-Scarisbrick.

———. 1991b, April. Women and power in the Caldecott and Newbery winners, 1980–1990. Paper presented at the meeting of the Central States Communication Association, Chicago.

Cooper, P. J., and C. J. Simonds. 1999. *Communication for the Classroom Teacher* (6th ed.). Needham Heights, MA: Allyn and Bacon.

deNys, M., and L. Wolfe. 1985. Learning her place: Sex bias in the elementary classroom. *Peer Report* 5: 1–10.

Earle, J., V. Roach, and K. Fraser. 1987. *Female Dropouts: A New Perspective.* Alexandria, VA: National Association of State Boards of Education.

Fagot, B. I. 1984. Teacher and peer reactions to boys' and girls' play styles. *Sex Role* 11: 691–702.

Fallon, J. 1990, November. Challenges to women students: Overcoming the barriers. Paper presented at the meeting of the Speech Communication Association, Chicago.

Feiner, S., and B. Morgan. 1987. Women and minorities in introductory economics textbooks: 1974–1984. *Journal of Economic Education* 10: 376–392.

Feiner, S., and B. Roberts. 1990. Hidden by the invisible hand: Neoclassical economic theory and the textbook treatment of race and gender. *Gender and Society* 4: 159–181.

Fennema, E. 1984. Girls, women and mathematics. In E. and M. J. Agers, eds., *Women and Education.* Berkeley, CA: McCutchens Publishers, 137–164.

Fleming, P. M. 2000. Three decades of education progress (and continuing barriers) for women and girls. *Equity and Excellence in Education* 33: 74–79.

Fox, M. 1993. Men who weep, boys who dance: The gender agenda between the lines in children's literature. *Language Arts* 70: 84–88.

Gillespie, D., and C. Spohn. 1987. Adolescents' attitudes toward women in politics: The effect of gender and race. *Gender and Society* 1: 208–218.

Gilligan, C. 1982. *In a Different Voice.* Cambridge, MA: Harvard University Press.

Gilligan, C., W. Lyons, and T. Hanmer. 1990. *Making Connections.* Cambridge, MA: Harvard University Press.

Gold, D., G. Crombie, and S. Noble. 1987. Relations between teachers' judgment of girls' and boys' compliance and intellectual competence. *Sex Roles* 16: 351–358.

Goldman, D. 2 August 1987. Girls and math: Is biology really destiny? *New York Times Educational Life,* 42–46.

Good, T., and R. Slavings. 1988. Male and female student question-asking behavior in elementary and secondary mathematics and language arts classes. *Journal of Research in Childhood Education* 3: 5–23.

Hall, R., and B. Sandler. 1982. *The Classroom Climate: A Chilly One for Women?* Washington, DC: Association of American Colleges Project on the Status and Education of Women.

———. 1984. *Out of the Classroom: A Chilly Campus Climate for Women?* Washington, DC: Association of American Colleges Project on the Status and Education of Women.

Higginbotham, E. 1990. Designing an inclusive curriculum: Bringing all women into the core. *Women's Studies Quarterly* 18: 7–23.

Holmes, B., and R. Ammon. 1985. Teaching content with trade books: A strategy. *Childhood Education* 61: 366–370.

Hoyles, C. 1988. *Girls and Computers: General Issues and Case Studies of Logo in the Mathematics Classroom.* London: University of London.

Karp, D. A., and W. C. Yoels. 1976. The college classroom: Some observations on the meanings of student participation. *Sociology and Social Research* 60: 421–439.

Keegan, P. 6 August 1989. Playing favorites. *The New York Times,* Section 4A, 26.

King, J. 1998. The effects of gender bias and errors in essay grading. *Educational Research Quarterly* 22: 13–21.

Kirby, D. F., and N. B. Julian. 1981. Treatment of women in high school U.S. history textbooks. *Social Studies* 72: 203–207.

Kolbe, R., and J. C. LaVoie. 1981. Sex role stereotyping in preschool children's picture books. *Social Psychology Quarterly* 44: 369–374.

Lawrenz, F. P., and W. W. Welch. 1983. Student perceptions of science classes taught by males and females. *Journal of Research in Science Teaching* 20: 655–662.

Leach, M., and B. Davies. 1990. Crossing the boundaries: Educational thought and gender equity. *Educational Theory* 40: 321–332.

Lenney, E. 1977. Women's self-confidence in achievement settings. *Psychological Bulletin* 84: 1–13.

Leonard, M. M., and B. A. Sigall. 1989. Empowering women student leaders: A leadership development model. In C. S. Pearson, D. L. Shavlik, and J. B. Touchton, eds., *Educating the Majority: Women Challenge Tradition in Higher Education.* New York: ACE/Macmillan, 230–249.

Lister, L. 1997, fall. Among school girls. *Independent School,* 42–45.

Lockheed, M. E. 1986. Women, girls and computers: A first look at the evidence. *Sex Roles* 13(3/4): 115–122.

Maher, F., and C. Rathbone. 1986. Teacher education and feminist theory: Some implications for practice. *American Journal of Education* 94: 214–235.

Mahony, P. 1983. How Alice's chin really came to be pressed against her foot: Sexist processes of interaction in mixed-sex classrooms. *Women's Studies International Forum* 6: 107–115.

Manning, M. 1998. Gender differences in young adolescents' mathematics and science achievement. *Childhood Education* 74: 168–171.

Marshall, C., ed. 1996. *Feminist Critical Policy Analysis: A Perspective from Primary and Secondary Schooling*. Washington, DC: Falmer.

Martin, C. L., and C. F. Halverson. 1983. The effects of sex-typing schemas on young children's memory. *Child Development* 54: 563–574.

Mboya, M. 1995. Gender differences in teachers' behaviors in relation to adolescents' self-concepts. *Psychological Reports* 77: 831–839.

McLaughlin, P. 10 March 1991. Hiding places. *Chicago Tribune*, Section 6, 5.

Miles, J. B. 1999. Technology and gender bias. *Journal of Family and Consumer Sciences* 91(3): 75–76.

Milner, J. 1977. Sex stereotypes in mathematics and science textbooks for elementary and junior high schools: Report of the sex bias in public schools. New York: National Organization for Women.

Nadler, L., and M. Nadler. 1990. Perceptions of sex differences in classroom communication. *Women's Studies in Communication* 13: 46–65.

National Research Council. 1989. Everybody counts: A report to the nation on the future of mathematics education. Washington, DC: National Academy Press.

Newsweek. 24 February 1992. Sexism in the schoolhouse, 62.

Nilsen, A. P. 1987. Three decades of sexism in school science materials. *School Library Journal* 33: 117–122.

Orenstein, P. 1994. *School Girls*. New York: Doubleday.

Pagano, J. 1988. Teaching women. *Educational Theory* 38: 321–339.

Parsons, J. E., K. A. Heller, and C. Kaczala. 1980. The effects of teachers' expectancies and attributions on students' expectancies for success in mathematics. In D. McGuigan, ed., *Women's Lives: New Theory, Research and Policy*. Ann Arbor: University of Michigan Center for Continuing Education of Women, 373–380.

Paul, L. 1998. *Reading Otherways*. Portland, ME: Calendar Islands Publishers.

Pearson, C., D. Shavlik, and J. Touchton. 1989. *Educating the Majority: Women Challenge Tradition in Higher Education*. New York: ACE/Macmillan.

Pearson, J., and R. West. 1991. An initial investigation of the effects of gender on student questions in the classroom: Developing a descriptive base. *Communication Education* 40: 22–32.

Peng, S., and J. Jaffe. 1984. Women who enter male-dominated fields of study in higher education. *American Educational Research Journal* 16: 285–293.

Petersen, A. 1987, September. Those gangly years. *Psychology Today*, 28–34.

Peterson, E. 1991. Moving toward a gender balanced curriculum in basic speech communication courses. *Communication Education* 40: 60–72.

Peterson, K. 7 September 1994. Teen's tales from the classroom. *USA Today*, 1D–2D.

Peterson, S., and M. Lach. 1990. Gender stereotypes in children's books: Their prevalence and influence on cognitive and affective development. *Gender and Education* 2: 185–197.

Quilling, J. I. 1999. Gender, technology, and leadership development. *Journal of Family and Consumer Sciences* 91(3): 70–76.

Randall, P. R. 1985. Sexist language and speech communication texts: Another case of benign neglect. *Communication Education* 34: 128–134.
Reay, D. 1990. Girls' groups as a component of anti-sexist practice–One primary school's experience. *Gender and Education* 2: 37–48.
Richmond, V. P., and J. Gorham. 1988. Language patterns and gender role orientation among students in grades 3–12. *Communication Education* 37: 142–149.
Rosenfeld, L. B., and M. W. Jarrard. 1985. The effects of perceived sexism in female and male college professors on students' descriptions of classroom climate. *Communication Education* 34: 205–213.
———. 1986. Student coping mechanisms in sexist and nonsexist professors' classes. *Communication Education* 35: 157–162.
Roth, M. 1987. Teaching modern art history from a feminist perspective: Challenging conventions, my own and others. *Women's Studies Quarterly* 15: 21–24.
Rubin, N, 1988, June. Math stinks! *Parents*, 132–136, 207–208, 210.
Ryan, M. 1989. Classroom and contexts: The challenge of feminist pedagogy. *Feminist Teacher* 4(2/3): 39–42.
Sadker, D. 1999. Gender equity: Still knocking at the classroom door. *Education Leadership* 56(7): 22–26.
———. 2000a. Myra and me. *Equity and Excellence in Education* 33: 4–7.
———. 2000b. Gender equity: Still knocking at the classroom door. *Equity and Excellence in Education* 33: 80–83.
Sadker, M., and D. Sadker. 1985, March. Sexism in the schoolroom of the '80s. *Psychology Today*, 54–57.
———. 1986. Confronting sexism in the classroom: From grade school to graduate school. *Phi Delta Kappan* 67: 512–515.
———. 1994. *Failing at Fairness: How Our Schools Cheat Girls*. New York: Simon and Schuster.
Sanders, J. S. 1984. The computer: Male, female or androgynous? *The Computing Teacher* 11(8): 31–34.
Sandler, B. 1991. Women faculty at work in the classroom, or why it still hurts to be a woman in labor. *Communication Education* 40: 6–15.
Sandler, B., and R. Hall. 1986. *The Campus Climate Revisited and Chilly for Women Faculty, Administrators, and Graduate Students*. Washington, DC: Project on the Status and Education of Women, Association of American Colleges.
Santon, M. 1961. *The Small Room*. New York: Norton.
Signorella, M. L., and L. S. Liben. 1984. Recall and reconstruction of gender-related pictures: Effects of attitude, task difficulty and age. *Child Development* 55: 393–405.
Sprague, J. A. 1975. The reduction of sexism in speech communication education. *Speech Teacher* 24: 37–45.
Stake, J. E., and J. F. Katz. 1982. Teacher-pupil relationships in the elementary school classroom: Teacher-gender and pupil-gender differences. *American Educational Research Journal* 19: 465–471.
Stanworth, M. 1981. *Gender and Schooling: A Study of Sexual Divisions in the Classroom*. London: Women's Research and Resources Centre.
Thorne, B. 1979. Claiming verbal space: Women, speech and language in college classrooms. Paper presented at the Conference on Educational Environments and the Undergraduate Woman, Wellesley College, Wellesley, MA.
Trepanier-Street, M., J. Romatowski, and S. McNair. 1990. Development of story characters in gender-stereotypic and nonstereotypic occupational roles. *Journal of Early Adolescence* 10: 496–510.

Trites, R. 1998. *Waking Sleeping Beauty: Feminist Voices in Children's Novels.* Iowa City: University of Iowa Press.

Weitzman, L. J., D. Eifler, E. Hokada, and C. Ross. 1972. Sex role socialization in picture books for preschool children. *American Journal of Sociology* 77: 1125–1150.

Weitzman, L. J., and D. Rizzo. 1975. Sex bias in textbooks. *Today's Education* 64(1): 49–52.

Wilder, G., D. Mackie, and J. Cooper. 1985. Gender and computers: Two surveys of computer-related attitudes. *Sex Roles* 13(3/4): 215–223.

Wolpe, A. 1989. *Within School Walls: The Role of Discipline, Sexuality and the Curriculum.* London: Routledge.

Wood, J. 1989. Feminist pedagogy in interpersonal communication courses. Paper presented at the Speech Communication Association, San Francisco.

———. 2001. *Gendered Lives: Communication, Gender, and Culture* (4th ed.). Belmont, CA: Wadsworth.

Wood, J., and L. Lenze. 1991. Strategies to enhance gender sensitivity in communication education. *Communication Education* 40: 16–21.

CHAPTER 14

Women in the Legal Profession
Challenges and Changes

Anna Matias

POINTS TO BE ADDRESSED:

- The entrance of women: Challenging the male paradigm
- Gender bias in law school
- The structure of corporate law firms: Effects on women
- Alternative opportunities and remedies

Over the past four decades, there has been a remarkable increase in the number of women entering the legal field. Presumably, this rise would augur that firms have opened their doors to female practitioners. The question posed in this chapter, however, is whether these doors have been opened widely or if they instead remain partially closed. Consider the following comments that have been reported to us by graduate students and by practitioners in the field.

> From the time I entered college, my goal was to be hired by one of the top corporate firms. I was hired but found early on that the work environment was different for me than for the male associates. Most of the men were married—they had support at home. I found that not only were men who I dated scared off by my credentials, opportunities to network with my male colleagues were all but denied to me. I finally decided to

> move to a smaller firm where I could stand out but also create a life outside of work. (Ellen, a Harvard-educated attorney)

> My sister-in-law has been interviewing for a position in a large firm. She was being interviewed by one of the female associates and was pleased with how the conversation was progressing. The associate, herself married with three children, suddenly learned forward and said, "I know this is an illegal question, but do you plan to have a family?" Thrown by the question, my sister-in-law responded honestly that she hoped to have a family and that this is a priority for her. She left the interview feeling disconcerted and wondering if she should have lied to the interviewer. (Rachel, graduate student)

> My friend is an associate in a mid-size firm. We were discussing how women are making it in the field when he confided in me that there was a tacit policy where he worked: they did not hire women associates who were of childbearing age. They had been burned in the past by women taking maternity leaves and not returning and felt it was too costly to take the risk that others would follow suit. (Josh, graduate student)

These comments suggest a pattern that some areas of the legal field maintain professional climates that are inhospitable to women entering the profession; they are resistant to implementing changes that acknowledge the realities of personal lives—in particular, child care. The purpose of this chapter is to examine the nature of the legal profession and to consider how formal barriers for women entering the field have fallen only to be replaced by informal obstacles. It considers, moreover, the impact of these obstacles on women's careers and provides possible remedies that would expand the professional opportunities for women in law.

The Entrance of Women: Barriers to Challenging the Male Paradigm

In her chapter on "Communicating in Legal Settings," Cindy Rhodes Victor suggests that because the legal setting has a longstanding legacy of male domination, the casebooks that discuss the law, the Socratic method of teaching law, and the practice of litigation, which is adversarial in nature, have contributed to a professional climate in which "women . . . have had to accept male gender culture differences or adopt them as a role-playing to succeed as lawyers" (1993: 157).

This environment cultivates the need to develop what Cynthia A. Irizarry refers to as face. Cultural expectations such as gender and professional image determine a competent or effective public image. In her study of female attorneys' identity management strategies, corrective facework ranks significant in "highly competitive work contexts such as the law where the stress of work, coupled with high performance expectations, may result in conflict requiring the need for corrective facework" (Irizarry, 2000: 2). Even more so, when abstract social norms of gender come into conflict with the normative occupational demands of being a professional, facework management becomes crucial.

In spite of the ostensible barriers to women resulting from the field's long-standing tradition of being a male bastion, over the past four decades the percentage of women entering law school has grown from 4 percent to nearly 50 percent (Decker, 1996; Gaber, 1998; Kende, 1994; Menkel-Meadow, 1994). This statistic suggests a major transformation in the profession. But if we look at the percentage of women practitioners who make up roughly 30 percent of the legal profession (Kende, 1994) and if we consider that women comprise 11–12 percent of the partnership levels in all firms (Decker, 1996), we must question the diminution in the percentage from student to partner status. More than natural attrition seems to be at work here. Studies conducted during the past two decades suggest that discriminatory practices often begin when women enter law school and continue throughout their career. We turn now to the impact these overt and covert practices have on one's professional life.

The Occurrence of Gender Bias in Law School

Feelings of alienation and dissatisfaction with the law school experience reportedly affect a number of students—both male and female (Gaber, 1998). The competitive atmosphere in academic settings, the drive to be in the top echelon within one's class, and the impetus to be tapped by the "right" firm for prime internships and positions contribute to a stressful environment. However, when one is marginalized solely on account of one's biological sex, the psychic and emotional toll is exacerbated. A series of studies conducted during the past two decades suggests that many female students experience the latter treatment—often at the hands of their faculty as well as from fellow male students.

A Florida Task Force survey of law schools, for example, found that 96 percent of third-year female students reported "a variety of remarks and behavior by law professors that were described as demeaning and offensive" (Delfs, 1996: 319). Overt acts were often matched by more subtle ways of making women feel uncomfortable. Studies conducted on Stanford Law School graduates (Taber et al., 1988), on five law schools by Taunya Banks (cited in Delfs, 1996: 321), and at Yale University Law School (cited in Delfs, 1996: 321) revealed that the amount of contributions female students make in the classroom diminishes during their three years in law school. A theme in the reported accounts includes that professors tend not to call on women and may even discount their perspective (Delfs, 1996: 319). When women are (perhaps unintentionally) denied a voice in the classroom, they are simultaneously not being encouraged to hone the very skills requisite for succeeding in a profession that requires speaking up and out.

Similarly, several studies indicate that women of color and from different cultures are targets of discrimination. Gaber (1998: 168) refers to a study at the University of California at Berkeley Law School that concluded, in part, that women from different cultures find it difficult to spend three years as an outsider in a world created by and for the white male insider establishment. According to one of the students interviewed for this study: "I think I've felt race more than gender here but I've definitely felt gender too. . . . It's just so male. It's so regressive, competitive. . . . But as a woman, I think I've definitely felt silenced. Especially being an Asian woman, I feel like I'm not the norm. I feel invisible" (Gaber, 1998: 240). Gaber highlights an incident at Yale University School of Law in 1995 where race was implicated for targeting female students. In this instance, students returned from a break to find anonymous flyers posted in some of the dorms and left in some male students' mailboxes that listed five women in the first-year class as "Total Packages." The flyers described the women in graphic sexual terms, "awarding" them titles such as "Boy-Toy," "Barbie," "Best Potential Wife and Mother," and "Most Exotic/Most Erotic" (176–177). Of the five women identified in the flyer, four were women of color. Not surprisingly, women in this study reportedly felt ostracized.

Regardless of whether gender alone, or coupled with culture and race, causes the discrepant treatment of female law students, the result, according to Weiss and Melling (1988) is "four faces of women's alienation: from ourselves, from the law school community, from the classroom, and from the content of legal education" (quoted in Gaber, 1998: 166–167). Feelings experienced during schooling often accompany women who join private firms. We turn to an examination of how the professional climate and stereotyped assumptions about women attorneys may serve as potent barriers to their success.

THE STRUCTURE OF CORPORATE LAW FIRMS: EFFECTS ON WOMEN

Perhaps the most glaring obstacle facing women in law lies with the private corporate law firm. In law school, academic achievement is primarily based on merit, which establishes who obtains the best interviews and subsequent job opportunities. However, the rules change once one enters the world of corporate law. The authoritative center of the legal profession rests with corporate law firms, and within this structure, the partnership track determines who holds authority, voice, and power.[1]

To establish full authority and to influence the rules in the legal profession, women need to pursue the traditional route leading to the corporate firm and to navigate the partnership track. The firm represents the source of the lawyers' professional authority; thus, the rules governing access to the leading firm's inner circle will determine women's status as lawyers. Yet, women, in particular, face a number of challenges en route to becoming a partner. Several of these challenges are connected to how these firms function; others stem from pervasive stereotypical assumptions about women as lawyers. Regardless of the source, these challenges combine to undermine their success. We examine five factors that create barriers.

1. Hiring and Assigning Women. In the earlier chapter on "Intersections of Gender and Employment Interviewing," it was suggested that women traditionally have encountered difficulty being hired and being promoted in fields that are sex-typed as masculine. Even though the situation has improved somewhat as women continue to enter these fields (e.g., engineering, medicine, business, and law), assumptions about women being sufficiently assertive, competitive, and committed may influence how they are positioned once hired.

In the past, law has been criticized as being an occupationally segregated profession. "As the practice of law has changed in structure and organization, women and minorities find themselves disproportionately located in particular segments of the profession" (Menkel-Meadow, 1994: 627). That is to say, minorities and women are still more likely to practice in the public sector, in small firms, and in solo practice. Although their numbers have increased in large corporate firms, they are predominantly associates.

How women are tracked and allocated assignments accentuates the discrepancy in how male and female attorneys have been treated. Women have traditionally been diverted into less prestigious areas of the firm such as family law, research, trusts and estates, wills, and domestic relations; they receive less desirable case assignments and often are cast in supporting roles in litigation where there is minimal chance for advancement, client exposure, and ultimately, significant pay (Decker, 1996: 518; Farrer, 1997: 552; Kende, 1994: 34).

The above-mentioned tracking perpetuated the assumption that women could not compete successfully with male colleagues. Research findings, however, contradict this notion. Scholars in communication and in related fields contend that individuals often choose career paths that match their personality (Powell, 1993); that when women and men work together they mutually influence each others' communication styles (Aires, 1987; 1996). Most significantly, Carol Watson's (1994) review of studies on negotiating behavior revealed that power may be a more salient indicator in determining outcome than one's sex, leading her to conclude that, "women are not nicer negotiators than men in terms of being more fair-minded or compassionate as some feminist writers should have us believe. . . . Rather, women are likely to accept the rules of interaction as men have written them" (206). Noted sociologist Cynthia Fuchs Epstein has commented with some irony, "For some lawyers the stereotype that women are too frail to be litigators has been replaced with the stereotype that some women are too argumentative not to be litigators" (cited in Farrer, 1997: 555). Increasingly, therefore, the trend to keep women from the forefront of the practice is changing, although this change may be slow, and public perception even slower.

2. Billable Hours. The structure of the practice of law measures success, in part, by billable hours—the number of hours that are billed to a client. Billable hours and the bottom line control evaluation or productivity. Given this method of measurement, it is not surprising that associates claim that every minute is clocked and monitored in the law firm (Menkel-Meadow, 1994: 632). Neither is it surprising that one study referred to in Menkel-Meadow's article (American Bar Association, 1991) claims that over 50 percent of associates bill more than 2,400 hours annually and take less than two weeks of vacation a year.

Decisions about partnerships are inextricably connected to one's record of billable hours. Thus, total commitment to the firm becomes a major ingredient to success. Yet, the ability to balance one's professional and personal obligations is a major challenge. As reflected in two of the comments presented at the beginning of this chapter, this challenge affects women especially. Women who have children may find it impossible to satisfy the professional and personal demands on their time. However, Menkel-Meadow suggests that male associates increasingly have begun to voice concern about this issue: "What began as a 'women's issue'—how inhospitable the large law firm was—has grown into an issue that affects all who work in law firms" (1994: 629).

Ironically, the very issue that has been a major barrier to women in law—child care—may lead to reevaluating uninterrupted time commitment as a major arbiter of success. A recent article on paternity leave suggests that despite passage of the Family and Medical Leave Act of 1993, men in a variety of fields are explicitly or implicitly discouraged from taking leave, particularly for child care, which is still regarded as women's responsibility (Ligos, 2000: G1).[2] Law firms are mentioned specifically as one of the professions that discourages this type of leave. However, one prominent firm, Millbank, Tweed, Hadley & McCloy, was singled out as a firm that "offers both male and female employees a full month of paid leave after the birth of a child" (Ligos, G1). Hopefully, as other firms join in acknowledging women's and men's commitments outside of the workplace, the notion of billable hours will not remain synonymous with uninterrupted performance.

3. Networking. In the legal field, inaccessibility to a network may have serious consequences for an attorney's long-term career growth because it affects the ability to generate business. For female lawyers, the lack of an "old girls' network" to augment the "old boys' network," which, by definition, excludes women, presents an obstacle to becoming a partner.

The law largely deals with property and business, which at present, are managed chiefly by men. In business, in politics, and socially, male lawyers meet more men than women do. Consequently, they have more opportunities to forge professional bonds through casual and informal encounters than their female counterparts. As Farrer puts it, female attorneys do not possess "equal access to the 'good ol' boy' networks, the private clubs, and the traditional business organizations essential to 'making rain' for law firms" (1997: 558). Eighty-five percent of the women attorneys surveyed by the National Law Journal/West Publishing Company in 1989 (as cited in Kende, 1994) indicated that generating new business was more difficult for female lawyers. While a more recent study has not been conducted, a number of judges and commentators more than a decade later resonate this finding.

For women on the partnership track, the lack of networks and mentors becomes even more poignant. To illustrate this point, of two associates being considered for partnership at a law firm, the male may have an advantage simply because his friends, not hers, are running corporations of their own and are able to direct business to the firm (Kende, 1994: 38). If women have less access to the pool of potential contacts, their ability to (indirectly) contribute to the firm's growth will be qualified.

Internal mentoring opportunities may also be limited for women in law. Much has been written to suggest that the professional mentor–mentee relationship has an overall positive effect on individuals' careers (Borisoff, 1998; Kram and Isabella, 1985; Murray, 1991; Roche, 1985).[3] There are two major reasons why women in law may be denied productive mentoring. First, male partners may be ill at ease in assuming the role of mentor—especially to younger female associates—lest their relationship be questioned as other than purely professional in nature. Second, the paucity of senior women to provide mentoring, coupled with those women still struggling to manage their own careers, may deprive new hirees of critical guidance (Farrer, 1997: 558; Kende, 1994: 34).

Regardless of whether a lack of networking or mentoring is the cause, women unable to generate sufficient business are denied the mantle of "rainmaker," a moniker, as the following section suggests, is crucial for success.

4. Rainmakers. Given that the cultivation of new business—rainmaking—is integral to the survival of law firms, the challenge for women to generate new clients poses a serious risk in terms of career longevity and access to the partnership track. Kende references Arthur Goldgaber, a reporter who interviewed several attorneys and judges. A constant theme in their comments is, as suggested in the section above, access to business connections. Typical is the observation by one woman, a partner in a Los Angeles firm:

> "Women do have disadvantages when being judged for promotion to partner that have nothing to do with their ability to handle legal work. For example, women have to work harder than men do at 'rainmaking' because it is easier for men to socialize with potential clients in their spare time. I could never call up a 45-year-old businessman and say, 'Hey, how would you like to go to a football game?' " (quoted in Kende, 1994: 38)

Perceptions about access to clients is one barrier. A potentially greater barrier is clients' perceptions about who can best represent them. According to Victor (1993: 170), "if a client prefers a lawyer with whom he or she feels most comfortable (as opposed to selecting a lawyer on skill and reputation), that client might select a male lawyer if the perception is that women lawyers are not as aggressive, bright, well-connected with the court personnel, or other such stereotypes." If stereotyped assumptions are used as an excuse to deny women (as well as other underrepresented groups) visibility and access to clients, the cycle of erroneous assumptions will continue; these professionals' positions will remain at greater risk of termination.

Altering the logos about women's perceived ability to represent a client requires acknowledging the client's concerns as well as explaining the reasons for the female attorney's participation, specifying why her particular expertise is required, and delineating her role on the case (Decker, 1996; Haste, 1994). "Lawyers of both genders should be sensitive to the gender perceptions and stereotypes their clients might hold, while continuing to work toward eliminating negative stereotypes and replacing them with a non-gender-based appreciation for legal ability and effective representation" (Victor, 1993: 170). Only through such change will the client, and ultimately the firm, best be served.

5. Partner Track and Salary Implications. One of the effects implicated by the inaccessibility to formal and informal networks and the subsequent lack of business contacts is an underrepresentation of women in the law firm partnership track.

Over the past decade, studies by Harvard Law School and the American Bar Association reveal that the partnership rate for men as opposed to women remains about three to one; approximately 8 percent of the partners in the largest 250 law firms are women (Decker, 1996; Kende, 1994). This discrepancy is one of the factors that translates into salary differences.

The literature on wage differentials between women and men in the legal arena is well documented (Gaber, 1998; Kende, 1994), with an average estimate that women earn 60–70 percent of men's salaries; the percentage is even lower when they work in the same firm. Difficult to tease out is the direct source of this disparity because multiple factors, as alluded to in the previous four sections, appear to contribute to these discrepancies. That is, disparate treatment in law school may lead to women being tracked into less lucrative areas of law. Stereotyped assumptions about women's competence also may limit their access to contacts that would assure their success as "rainmakers," often leading them to believe they have to outperform their male colleagues just to make it in the profession. And, perceived roles for women as primary providers of child care often influences their decision to take a leave of absence or scale back their hours. Each of these factors alone, or in combination, all too often results in fewer billable hours and consequently, in less income and in not achieving partnership status.

To this point, the statistics cited have referred primarily to the status of white women in the profession. The field of law erects even more formidable barriers to other women seeking entry into law school and professional assignments. Together, African-American women and men, Latin Americans, Asian-Pacific Islanders, American Indians, and other underrepresented populations make up about 10 percent of the total enrollment in law schools. They comprise significantly less than 10 percent of total bar membership (Menkel-Meadow, 1994: 627). Minority women remain overrepresented in entry-level jobs with the government and are less likely than their white counterparts to find significant posts in private firms (Bowman, 1998/99: 161). A recent article in the American Bar Association Journal, in fact, indicated that only 3 percent of all partners in the largest firms are male and female minorities (in contrast to 8–9 percent for women) (cited in Menkel-Meadow, 1994: 627).

In response to a perceived climate of discrimination, women often respond by feeling that they have to work harder and be more competent than their male counterparts to be their professional equals—behavior indicative of "tokenism" (Tarvis and Wade, 1984). According to Deborah K. Holmes, a law professor, "Women cannot merely match men's performance; in areas where women are traditionally perceived as weak, they must outperform their male colleagues. Women who succeed are more tough, more committed to their careers, and more willing to take risks than their successful male colleagues" (as quoted in Kende, 1994: 35).

In light of these very real challenges, we examine some of the alternative opportunities that women turn to and consider suggested remedies to lessening barriers in the legal profession.[4]

ALTERNATIVE OPPORTUNITIES AND REMEDIES

In 1967, law professor James White published a seminal article entitled "Women in the Law" which was regarded as the first major scholarly attempt to assess women's status in the legal profession. Based on his analysis tracking then recent male and female graduates from various law schools, White (78–79) concluded that:

1. There was a large income differential between men and women. Men consistently earned more than women; the income gap increased over time.
2. There was substantial sex segregation of legal work, with men obtaining positions with large firms and women landing positions primarily with state and local government.
3. Holding all other variables constant, only discrimination based on gender could account for these results.

A series of studies published since White's article suggest a persistent undercurrent of difference. Studies conducted in the 1980s tended to support White's findings. The most compelling of these studies was Jill Abramson and Barbara Franklin's (1986) chronicling of 70 women graduates of Harvard Law School. Interviews with these professionals a decade after graduation revealed a pervasive theme. Initial enthusiasm about their work was followed by a reexamination of their life choices—most particularly, as they approached the age of 35. Not only did they begin to wrestle with issues of workaholism, many of the women also felt that their profession failed to accommodate working mothers. Some voiced concerns that working part-time could jeopardize their positions. Within five to ten years following graduation, many of the women of the Harvard '74 law school graduating class had left private practice because they wanted to devote more time to their personal lives.

Other studies on University of New Mexico Law School graduates (Teitelbaum, Lopez, and Jenkins, 1991) and on University of Michigan law students (Chambers, 1989) found that even though the gap between men and women opting for positions in the public sector was closing, and the ghettoization of private practice was decreasing, women continued to leave private practice to work in other settings (within the first five years of practice) at a rate of two to one; substantial income differentials between men and women persisted. An important additional finding, however, was that feelings of dissatisfaction resonated not only with women practitioners. Men, too, began to articulate their discontent.

Many practicing attorneys, both male and female, privately admit that the practice of law can be a brutal profession, characterized by grueling hours, often repetitive work, relentless competition from one's colleagues, and "golden handcuffs" (Schroer, 1993, B1). The new economy has provided one alternative as attorneys increasingly are lured to the dot-com industry.

At a roundtable discussion, seven in-house lawyers at Texas Internet-related companies discussed their evolving roles and satisfaction working at a dot-com company. The group, comprised of both men and women, cited five major reasons for selecting their career paths: (1) A smaller company enabled them to establish their reputation earlier in their careers, that is, they were able to stand out among their colleagues; (2) in high-tech companies, people function as entrepreneurs, that is, they can generate work without gender-based stereotypes that in other arenas may limit productivity; (3) they have the opportunity to be creative without models steeped in tradition that heretofore privileged one sex over the other; (4) they are able to make direct and meaningful contributions to driving the business without being tethered to billable hours; and (5) they are intellectually challenged by being able to address legal issues that are at the cutting edge of their profession (law.com/business, 2000). Other attorneys who have defected to Internet start-ups echo similar motivations—often citing the allure of a business environment and helping to realize a vision (Kehoe, 1999; McManis, 2000; Stacklin, 2000). Ironically, even though they admit that the hours devoted to work may compare, or even exceed, those of private practice, they derive greater professional satisfaction through making direct contributions to the company; they derive greater personal satisfaction by having more control over their projects. The expansion of the new economy is likely to bring about changes in how the traditional private firms operate. These firms are recognizing that they are in competition with other industries to attract and retain the best and the brightest talent.

Conclusion

Both professional and personal quality-of-life issues are coming under intense scrutiny in the legal profession. Several writers posit concrete recommendations to change the climate (Bowman, 1998/99; Decker, 1996; Menkel-Meadow, 1994). Some of the suggestions, such as parental leaves (without sanctions) and flex-time policies, are directed to both men and women. Other strategies, including formal training for all firm members on women's and men's styles of communication and management, would help to dispel the sex-role and sex-trait stereotypes about women in particular, which are deeply embedded in society. Finally, tactics have been raised to target women's situations directly: a top-down commitment to encourage, to reward, and to retain successful women; support of alternative forms of client entertainment (e.g., theater, musical events, etc.) that would acknowledge a breadth of interests; firm-supported events to attract female clients; and, the creation of concrete and powerful networking and mentoring relationships for women in the firm.

New opportunities for lawyers coupled with the above-mentioned strategies indicate that those in the field are beginning to scrutinize the professional climate. While this chapter has suggested that formal barriers for women entering the field have fallen, informal obstacles remain. We anticipate that as increasing numbers of firms continue to examine and remedy the conditions that have barred women and other underrepresented groups from achieving their potential, the metaphoric door to this field will, over time, be fully opened.

For Further Discussion

1. This chapter focused primarily on women in the private sector of law. Do similar barriers exist in other areas such as, the public sector; small, private firms; and/or academia?
2. Telecommuting has expanded the potential for professionals in a wide range of fields. To what extent is telecommuting possible in the legal field? Are there certain areas, in particular, that would lend themselves to this possibility?
3. Sexual harassment remains a pervasive aspect of workplace settings in all fields. While harassing behavior of staff members by attorneys has been documented repeatedly in the media, to what extent does harassing behavior occur among associates, among partners, and in the courts?
4. Interview men or women who have remained with large, private firms. What aspects of their work environment do they enjoy? Are there aspects they would change? To what extent do quality of life issues remain a challenge?

5. Interview men or women who have left large firms for a different alternative. What influenced their decision and how satisfied are they with the change?
6. The legal field has traditionally been a white, male, and heterosexual environment. Interview practitioners who do not belong to the so-called "dominant" group. How would they characterize the climate where they work? What strategies have they employed to help them succeed in this environment?
7. Are there similar challenges faced by female lawyers in the global arena? Conduct an international study comparing treatment of female lawyers in Latin America, or Asia, for example, against their U.S.-based counterparts.

ENDNOTES

[1] Of the almost 800,000 U.S. lawyers in the last decade of the twentieth century, most still work in small units of solo practice or small law firms. While the percentage of lawyers serving as sole practitioners has decreased considerably in recent decades, still over 60 percent of lawyers practice alone or with a partner (Menkel-Meadow, 1994, 628). For the purposes of this chapter, however, discussion has focused on corporate law, which remains the most lucrative area in the profession.

[2] The Family and Medical Leave Act of 1993 requires any employer with more than fifty employees to grant up to twelve weeks of unpaid leave to a worker who needs to care for a new baby, an adopted child, an ill family member, or to recover from his or her own illness, after which the worker is entitled to return to the same or to an equivalent position.

[3] Literature on mentoring suggests that mentors provide concrete assistance in two major areas. First, mentors help with career functions: serving to coach new hirees, serving as an advocate and protector ("gatekeeper") to new employees, and providing constructive feedback. Second, mentors provide psychosocial assistance: serving as a role model of organizational values; acting as a counselor who listens to, empathizes with, and provides counsel to the new hiree; and, providing confirmation to the mentee to enhance motivation, feelings of acceptance, and respect.

[4] While at this point in time child care may not thwart men's opportunities to make it in many of the large law firms, certainly the time drain, the emphasis on billable hours and on rainmaking affects them as well. Many alternative careers where they can practice their profession are, therefore, particularly attractive to them as well.

REFERENCES

Abramson, J., and B. Franklin. 1986. *Where They Are Now: The Story of the Women of Harvard Law 1974.* New York: Doubleday.

Aires, E. 1987. Gender and communication. In P. Shaver and C. Hendrick, eds., *Sex and Gender.* Newbury Park, CA: Sage, 149–176.

———. 1996. *Men and Women in Interaction: Reconsidering the Differences.* New York: Oxford University Press.

American Bar Association. 1991 *The Report of At the Breaking Point: A National Conference on the Emerging Crisis in the Quality of Lawyers' Health and Lives—It's Impact on Law Firms and Client Services.*

Borisoff, D. 1998, May. Strategies for effective mentoring and for being effectively mentored: A focus on research institutions. *Journal of the Association for Communication Administration* 27: 84–96.

Bowman, C. 1998/99. Biographical essay: Women and the legal profession. *American University Journal of Gender, Social Policy & the Law* 7: 149–175.

Chambers, D. 1989. Accommodation and satisfaction: Women and men lawyers and the balance of work and family. *L. and Social Inquiry* 14: 251, 261 n.49.

Decker, A. 1996. Women in corporate law: Rewriting the rules. *The American University Journal of Gender & the Law* 4: 511–534.

Delfs, E. 1996. Foul play in the courtroom: Persistence, cause and remedies. *Women's Rights Law Reporter* 17: 309–324.

Epstein, C. F. 1993. *Women in Law.* Urbana: University of Illinois Press.

Farrer, N. 1997. Commentary: Of ivory columns and glass ceilings: The impact of the Supreme Court of the United States on the practice of women attorneys in law firms. *St. Mary's Law Journal* 28: 529–572.

Gaber, P. 1998. Just trying to be human in this place: The legal education of twenty women. *Yale Journal of Law and Feminism* 10: 165–275.

Goldgaber, A.1990. Glass ceiling remains for women going for partner. *Los Angeles Business Journal* 33.

Haste, H. 1994. *The Sexual Metaphor: Men, Women, and the Thinking that Makes the Difference.* Cambridge: Harvard University Press.

Irizarry C. A. 2000. *Responding to Face Threatening Criticism: A Qualitative Analysis of Female Attorney's Identity Management Strategies.* Department of Communication Studies, Stetson University. Paper presented at the Eastern Communication Association Annual Convention, Pittsburgh.

Kehoe, L. 15 December 1999. A web head brain drain: Management consultants and lawyers are leading a talent stampede to dot-com start-ups. *Financial Times* (London), 19.

Kende, M. S. 1994. Shattering the glass ceiling: A legal theory for attacking discrimination against women partners. *Hastings Law Journal* 46: 17–83.

Kram, K. E., and L. A. Isabella. 1985. Mentoring alternatives: The role of peer relationships in career development. *Academy of Management Journal* 28: 110–132.

law.com/business. 8 May 2000. *GC.com: Moving at Internet Speed.*

Ligos, M. 31 May 2000. The fear of taking paternity leave. *New York Times*, G1.

McManis, S. 7 January 2000. Associates making legal decisions in favor of dot-coms. *San Francisco Chronicle*, B3.

Menkel-Meadow, C. 1994. Symposium: The future of the legal profession: Culture clash in the quality of life in the law: Changes in the economics, diversification and organization of lawyering. *Case Western Reserve Law Review* 44: 621–662.

Murray, M. 1991. *Beyond the Myths and Magic of Mentoring.* San Francisco: Jossey-Bass.

Powell, G. N. 1993. *Women and Men in Management.* 2nd ed. Newbury Park, CA: Sage.

Roche, G. R. 1985. Much ado about mentors. *Harvard Business Review* 57: 14–28.

Schroer, J. 7 October 1993. Running from the law: Discontented lawyers flee profession. *USA Today*, B1.

Simon, R. J., and K. Gardner. 1981. Career patterns among University of Illinois women law graduates. *Women Law Journal* 67: 19.

Stacklin, J. 13 March 2000. Defecting to dot-coms: Professionals ditching lucrative, comfy careers for chance to fly high in cyberspace. *Crain's Cleveland Business*, 1.

Taber, J., M. T. Grant, M. T. Huser, R. B. Norman, J. R. Sutton, C. C. Wong, L. E. Parker, and C. Picard. 1988. Project: Gender, legal education, and the legal profession: An empirical study of Stanford law students and graduates. *Stanford Law Review* 40: 1209.

Tarvis, C., and C. Wade. 1984. *The Longest War: Sex Differences in Perspective.* 2nd ed. Orlando, FL: Harcourt Brace Jovanovich.

Teitelbaum, L., A. S. Lopez, and J. Jenkins. 1991. Gender, legal education, and legal causes. *J. Legal Education* 41: 443.

Victor, D. 1993. Communicating in legal settings. In L. Arliss and D. Borisoff, eds., *Women and Men Communicating: Challenges and Changes.* Orlando, FL: Harcourt Brace Jovanovich, 152–172.

Watson, C. 1994. Gender differences in negotiating behavior and outcomes: Fact or artifact? In A. Taylor and J. Benstein Miller, eds., *Conflict and Gender.* Cresskill, NJ: Hampton Press, 191–209.

Weiss, C., and L. Melling. 1988. The legal education of twenty women. *Stanford Law Review* 40: 1299, 1363.

White, J. J. 1967. Women in the law. *Michigan Law Review* 65: 1051, 1090.

CHAPTER 15

Communication in Health Care Settings

Elaine Bass Jenks

POINTS TO BE ADDRESSED

- Role expectations of female and male patients
- How the patient's gender affects communication with doctors: Psychosomatic diagnoses
- Role expectations of female and male doctors
- How the doctor's gender affects communication with patients: Insufficient evidence
- Role expectations of female and male nurses
- How the nurse's gender affects communication with doctors and patients: An indirect "game"

Interpersonal interactions in health care settings are, quite literally, critical events. Somewhere amidst the difficult and complicated process of accurately conveying information, interpreting meanings, and creating understanding among doctors, patients, and nurses lies the crucial concern of a patient's well-being and possibly even his or her life. Unlike any other setting, the medical context is one where an individual's health depends directly on the communicative interactions that occur.

Overall, communication practices in medical contexts have been found to be unsatisfactory. For example, patients are accused of not understanding

The author would like to thank William K. Rawlins for reading and commenting on this chapter.

doctors while doctors are accused of not speaking in understandable language (McGee and Cegala, 1998; Shuy, 1983). Patients are blamed for noncompliance with doctors' orders and doctors are blamed for not making their directions clear (Lane, 1983; Smith, Cunningham, and Hale, 1994). Patients are criticized for not participating in decisions concerning their health and doctors are criticized for not allowing patients to participate in these decisions (Ballard-Reisch, 1990; Fisher, 1983).

Introducing gender as an issue in medical interactions invites the inclusion of nurses for consideration as well as doctors and patients. Nurses are vital participants in health care settings, yet they are not included in most health communication studies.

Communication does not occur in isolation, and all identities require an "other" (Laing, 1969: 82). Accordingly, in this chapter, I consider the interactants in health care settings in relational groupings. In exploring the communicative relationship between doctors and patients, I focus first on the gender of the patient and then on the gender of the doctor. Next, I examine the role of the nurse in the doctor–patient relationship. Each of these sections outlines research findings regarding gender patterns in the relationships and then discusses communicative issues raised by the gender patterns.

The momentum to study gender patterns in medical contexts emerged from the women's movement of the 1960s and 1970s, when female patients began speaking out about controlling their bodies, especially concerning the issues of childbirth and contraceptives (Corea, 1977). At the same time, more females were attending medical school (Gray, 1982) and female nurses were beginning to examine their role in the health care process (Vance et al., 1985). The study of the place of women in the health care context continues to expand. In 1990, the National Institutes of Health created the Office of Research on Women's Health (National Institutes of Health, 2000). And in 2000, a comprehensive study, which is "the first-ever report card to assess the overall health of women," in the United States was released (National Women's Law Center, 2000: 1).

Consequently, while the following discussion notes that various issues concerning males exist, this chapter centers primarily on female patients, female doctors, and female nurses.

How the Patient's Gender Affects Communication with Doctors

According to the *1999 Statistical Abstract of the United States,* approximately one-third more female patients than male patients visit doctors every year, with women making three visits to doctors for every two visits males make (U.S. Bureau of the Census, 1999). Females have higher rates of office appointments, more hospital outpatient and emergency department visits, and a greater number of ambulatory surgery procedures than males. While it is clear that there are more female patients and that females make more visits to doctors, it is not immediately apparent why this situation exists.

Gender Patterns

There are four possible reasons why more women visit doctors and do so more frequently than men. The first reason is that, owing to their reproductive roles, women visit doctors as *well* patients more than men (Hausfeld, 1976; Wallen, Waitzkin, and Stoeckle, 1979). Specifically, doctors see women throughout pregnancy as well as to dispense and monitor birth control methods, even though females are usually not ill when carrying children or using contraceptives.

A second reason for women's more frequent visits is that they often manage the health care of others in their families and see doctors as "non-patient clients" (Hausfeld, 1976: 540). Here, females take the responsibility for the health of their children, husbands, and parents (Weisman, 1987). While the first reason offered can be attributed to biological distinctions in the reproductive capabilities of the sexes, this second reason moves into social distinctions between the genders. Society traditionally puts pressure on males to be financially responsible for their children, their wives, and sometimes their parents, but it is women who are expected to be the caretakers of their families and, by extension, to feel guilt for a relative's illness. Hausfeld (1976) mentions not only the traditional claim that mothers often blame themselves for their children's illnesses (Korsch, Gozzi, and Francis, 1968), but also the irony that women are often blamed for their husband's obesity and heart problems because women cook for their families (even though they cook for their families because food preparation is part of the traditional female role in society).

The female role, itself, is a third reason that more women visit doctors more often than men. Specifically, the role of the patient has traditionally been associated more with female attributes than with male characteristics (Gray and Meginnis, 1978). As Corea (1977) writes, "From childhood, a female is encouraged to admit her pain, to freely ask for help and to expect and accept weakness in herself" (81). Patients are expected to be obedient (Entralgo, 1979) and to cooperate with doctors (Parsons, 1951). Overall, it has been deemed more acceptable for women to express suffering and accept assistance than it is for men (Nathanson, 1975). However, by expressing pain and asking for help, women leave themselves open to "learned helplessness," which is the repeated inability to exert influence over one's own situation (Malterud, 1987b). Learned helplessness leads to a condition where one chooses to play the role of the incapable and allows the stronger partner, in this case, the doctor, to take control of the situation.

This focus on the patient role mirroring the female role in society is prevalent in the literature (Bernstein and Kane, 1981; Borges, 1986; Gray and Meginnis, 1978; Hausfeld, 1976; Malterud, 1987b; Nathanson, 1975). The situation is magnified when the patient is an older female. Older female patients may be willing to "play the stereotypical role of an old woman" and list complaints in detail to the doctor (Root, 1987: 155). This emphasis on the female being willing, and in fact encouraged by society, to speak of her symptoms indicates that it is considered appropriate for females of all ages to seek help for illness and passively to accept the doctor's assistance.

The linking of the female role to the patient role emphasizes, by conspicuous omission, that the patient role is not a role expected of men. Thus, it is less appropriate for males to complain of symptoms and receive help than it is for females. While this may allow males to escape the condition of learned helplessness, it may also push males into the potentially dangerous position of not asking for help when it is needed.

The fourth reason for more numerous female medical visits seems on the surface to be a physiological reason, but actually involves a social explanation. That is, more women visit doctors simply because females *are* ill more often than males. However, the reason for this apparent physical distinction is partially social; females become sick because of the stress from fulfilling their female roles in society (Mastekaasa, 2000; Nathanson, 1975). For example, a female might be expected to take care of her family even while she works outside the home. Or a female might be expected to care for her children while also caring for her aging parents. These forms of stress can cause physical illnesses which lead women to visit doctors.

This last reason brings up the most frequently reported issue concerning the female patient. It is well-documented that doctors routinely diagnose females as having more psychosomatic illnesses than males (Bernstein and Kane, 1981; Hausfeld, 1976; Malterud, 1987a, 1987b; Nathanson, 1975; Wallen et al., 1979; Weisman, 1987). Repeatedly, studies have shown that women are prescribed more tranquilizers than men because females are more often identified as having illnesses that begin in their minds, not in their bodies. This tendency is compounded by the assumption that the stress caused by the female role does not actually produce physical illness. The obvious danger of this position was articulated by Corea (1977) who wrote, "Everyone has heard stories of women who complained of blinding headaches, were dismissed with tranquilizer prescriptions, and had strokes two days later. No one knows how often such incidents occur" (79). With greater awareness of gender bias, such instances can be avoided.

Of course stress is also created by the male role in society because men may feel pressure to succeed in their careers and provide for their families. However, society seems to take ill males more seriously than unwell females, particularly because the male role is not linked to the patient role. It might be assumed that if a male complains, he really is sick. Evidence that society focuses on the physiological, not psychological, reasons for male illness is demonstrated by the appropriation of public health money. For example, the 1988 study, which advocated patients taking an aspirin a day to thwart heart attacks, was conducted entirely on males even though men and women die from heart disease at almost equivalent rates (Ames, 1990). Part of the reason NIH created the Office of Research on Women in 1990 was to change this practice and to "ensure that women and minorities and their subpopulations are included in all human subject research" (National Institutes of Health, 2000).

To review, more women visit doctors more often than men because: (1) females make more well-patient visits; (2) females make more nonpatient visits with family members; (3) the female role in society has similar characteristics to the patient or sick role in our culture and women are expected to play these roles; and (4) women actually are more physically ill owing to the stress of maintaining the female role in society.

Communicative Issues

Four communicative issues emerge from the fact that more women visit doctors more frequently than men. The first three relate to the point that females are diagnosed more often than males with psychosomatic illnesses.

First, there is simply no language for "ill-defined" conditions in the medical context (Malterud, 1987a: 206). "Disease" is the term often used to describe physical abnormalities while "illness" is used to refer to the patient's feelings of unwellness and the effects of these feelings. As Malterud (1987a) points out, "Illness that does not result from disease is not as respectable in our society as illness that does" (206). Thus, if there is no clear name of a disease available for an illness, the patient is often diagnosed as suffering from either a psychosomatic disease or from a nondisease. Patients are being told that their illnesses are in their heads or that their illnesses do not really exist at all. And these patients are usually women. Vanderford and Smith's (1996) exploration of the controversy about whether or not silicone breast implants cause physical problems for women is an example of the complexities that surround not having a disease name for illness.

Second, the fact that the patient speaking is a female may also influence how the speaker is heard by the doctor. Bernstein and Kane (1981) found that both male and female patients who mentioned personal problems were judged more quickly to have psychosomatic conditions by doctors than patients who mentioned only medical symptoms. However, this study also found that both expressive and nonexpressive females were diagnosed as having psychosomatic conditions "as though women were *a priori* more emotional than men" (606). Thus, a male had to behave in a "female" manner—that is, more emotionally—to be labeled with a nondisease illness, while all females, both emotional and stoic, were more likely to be labeled with psychosomatic conditions.

Third, how females are allowed to be heard can also influence whether or not a women is diagnosed with a psychosomatic illness. Paget (1983) explored how questions are used by doctors both to request responses to topics and to follow patient replies, which, in turn, leads to meaning construction. Specifically, a doctor reconstructed a patient's fear of recurring cancer into a simple case of nerves. The case was followed over time and the patient was later diagnosed by another doctor, not with nerves, but with cancer of the spine. The control of the conversation through the use of questions by the first doctor led to the construction of the meaning of her illness, which was then acted upon, or in this case, not acted upon, by the doctor. Doctors' control of medical conversations has been reported in studies of both male and female patients (Beisecker, 1990; Cecil, 1998; Coulthard and Ashby, 1975; Fisher, 1983; Shuy, 1983; von Friederichs-Fitzwater, Callahan, Flynn, and Williams, 1991; West, 1983) and this situation may be a function of the asymmetrical relationship between doctors and patients rather than an issue unique to female patients.

The final communicative area concerning female patients focuses on information flow or the explanations women receive from their doctors. Considering the three preceding issues, it might be assumed that females would not receive very much information from their doctors. This assumption is based on the points that women may have symptoms for which there are no scientific names, that women might be perceived as highly emotional, and that women do not control their conversations with doctors.

However, it has been found that female patients regularly receive more information or more explanations than male patients (Adamson, Tschann, Guillon, and Oppenberg, 1989; Hall, Roter, and Katz, 1988; Wallen et al., 1979; Weisman et al., 2000). It has also been found that female patients receive more time with doctors than male patients (Waitzkin, 1984; Wallen et al., 1979). The reason for these trends seems to be that females routinely ask more questions of their doctors than males (Hall, Roter, and Katz, 1988; Waitzkin, 1984; Wallen et al., 1979). Thus, female patients receive more explanations from doctors because they request these explanations. Women may ask more questions because they visit doctors more often and have more practice making queries, and because they feel responsible for understanding the health care concerns of their family members (Wallen et al., 1979).

Interestingly, it was found by Wallen et al. (1979) that females often receive explanations from doctors that are less technical than the questions asked. Doctors were more likely to match the level of technicality used by male patients, but to "undershoot" the level employed by female patients (142). Thus, women may ask more questions and receive more explanations simply because they are not being given sufficient information and must request further explanations from their doctors.

To this point, we have seen that the gender-linked patterns of communication during medical appointments are not without consequences. While little research has focused directly on male patients, female patients are more often diagnosed with psychosomatic illnesses and are more frequently prescribed tranquilizers than men. The question that arises now concerns the individual who makes these diagnoses and who writes these prescriptions. Are doctors who treat female patients differently than male patients more likely to be male or female?

How the Doctor's Gender Affects Communication with Patients

Although there are more female patients than male patients, there are far fewer female doctors than male doctors. As noted above, according to the *1999 Statistical Abstract of the United States*, two-thirds of all patients are women (U.S. Bureau of the Census, 1999). Only one-quarter of doctors in the United States, however, are female. That is, for every twelve patients, eight are female. But for every twelve doctors, just three are women.

Gender Patterns

Women who help cure others have had enormous difficulty being accepted in societies controlled by males for centuries (Corea, 1977; Scully, 1980). It is estimated that nine million individuals were killed for being witches from the late fifteenth century to the early nineteenth century. Most individuals accused of being witches were women, and many were midwives who helped women deliver their babies (Corea, 1977).

While we do not execute female healers any longer, we also do not make it easy for females to become doctors. Women still have difficulty getting into medical school, entering certain specialties, receiving admission to internship and residency programs, and obtaining faculty positions in medical schools (Bickel, 2000; Brundtland, 2000; Corea, 1977) Women doctors gravitate toward the areas most accepting of females—pediatrics (Kate, 1997), psychiatry, public health (Gray, 1982), and primary care (Brundtland, 2000). These specialties have lower mean incomes than surgery where women are "underrepresented" (Bobula, 1980: 827), but female doctors have noted that general surgery is an area they feel is "closed" to them (Heins et al., 1979: 1136; see also Ennker, Schwarz, and Ennker, 1999).

These difficulties are compounded by the fact that females are socialized by society to play female roles and that medical schools socialize individuals differently. Women are socialized to be "caring, soft, gentle, emotional, involved and nurturing" (Gray, 1982: 167). While these qualities may seem ideal for a doctor, it has been noted that medical school takes an approach that is analytical and rational, focusing on curing, not caring (Gray, 1982; Malterud, 1987a). Even though forty percent of the students in U.S. medical schools are now women, "differences between men and women graduates have persisted" (Jones, Arnold, Xu, and Epstein, 2000). These differences include less preparation in the basic sciences for women and more concern expressed by female students about "psychosocial issues" of the health care context (Jones et al., 2000).

The assumption here is that the doctor role is a male role, and therefore, male doctors do not experience the same role conflict when becoming physicians that their male colleagues find. However, doctors of both genders have other tensions to balance. For example, doctors are expected always to be precisely correct in their diagnostic treatment decisions while also accurately judging how individual patients would like to be communicated with during medical appointments (Jenks, 1995). This pressure to be somewhat of a deity where medicine is concerned and simultaneously human when communication is involved is a tension shared by both male and female doctors.

Additionally, female doctors experience the pressure that most females in predominantly male fields share; that is, females may be superb professionals, but they often are not seen as complete women until they marry and have children (Corea, 1977; Gray, 1982; Sibbald, 1999). Thus, female doctors may excel professionally, but because they have "broken sex-role stereotypes to some extent by becoming physicians" (Weisman and Teitelbaum, 1985: 1120), they must also prove their femininity to society by becoming wives and mothers. But by being wives and mothers, female doctors leave themselves open to the criticism of not being dedicated to their field (Corea, 1977). While it is not easy for anyone, male or female, to be a physician, the doctor role and the female role clearly contain contradictory requirements that are difficult to reconcile (Gray, 1982; Steinhauer, 1999; Weisman and Teitelbaum, 1985).

Communicative Issues

If females are socialized differently than males and if women have a more difficult time becoming doctors, it might be assumed that female doctors treat their patients in a different manner, in a more caring way, than male doctors. It has been demonstrated repeatedly that, in general, females and males display differences in the use of verbal communication (Haas, 1979; Kramer, 1977; Maltz and Borker, 1982; Tannen, 1991; Thorne and Henley, 1975) and nonverbal communication (Henley, 1977; Tannen, 1995). It would follow that the same differences would be found between male and female doctors.

This assumption might be stated by the hypothesis, if the doctor is female, then she will communicate in a more nurturing, relational, "female" way. However, the answer to this hypothesis is a resounding, "maybe." Some researchers state there are differences (Heins et al., 1979; Langwell, 1982; Mendez, Shymansky, and Wolraich, 1986; "Women Doctors," 1995), but other researchers have found no differences in the communicative behaviors of male and female doctors (Murphy-Cullen and Larsen, 1984; Skelton and Hobbs, 1999; Weisman and Teitelbaum, 1985; Weisman, Teitelbaum, and Morlock, 1988; Young, 1979). Moreover, others searched for differences in the patient's expectations of male and female doctors instead of the doctor's communicative choices (Comstock, Hooper, Goodwin, and Goodwin, 1982; Paluszny and Poznanski, 1971; Weisman and Teitelbaum, 1985).

Some of the researchers finding differences between male and female doctors have not focused directly on communicative behaviors. For example, in a study on incomes of male and female doctors, it was found that female doctors see fewer patients per hour than male doctors (Langwell, 1982). This number could indicate that female doctors spent more time communicating with patients because they were more concerned with the doctor–patient relationship and possibly more nurturing. Admittedly, since interpersonal communication was not the focus of this study, disparity in appointment lengths does not necessarily indicate more caring communication, though the perception of having enough time with a doctor is important to patients (Jenks, 1989).

Likewise, doctors' attitudes were examined by Heins et al. (1979), and their study found that female doctors are significantly more egalitarian and more sensitive than male doctors. These findings suggest that female doctors may treat patients with more equality and would be more caring, but again, this study looked at attitudes, not communicative behaviors resulting from these attitudes.

Verbal and nonverbal communicative behaviors of male and female doctors were directly examined by Mendez, Shymansky, and Wolraich (1986). This study found that female doctors asked more questions designed to elicit the patient's feelings and made more attempts to restate the patient's feelings in a nonjudgmental manner. Therefore, female doctors "were more prompt in dealing with the affective dimension of the interaction" (Mendez et al., 1986: 441). However, no differences were found in twelve other verbal categories, such as statements designed to elicit a patient's knowledge and comments aimed at explaining medical jargon. Nor were differences found in any nonverbal aspects of communication even though both vocalics and hand gestures were examined.

A summary of studies in the past 15 years on female doctors' interactions with patients ("Women Doctors," 1995) notes that the three differences that have been found in a more than one study are that female doctors spend longer with their patients during office visits, that female doctors are more likely to treat their patients as equals, and that female patients volunteered more information to female doctors.

No differences in male and female communication were found by researchers who studied malpractice claims among obstetrician-gynecologists (Weisman et al., 1988), patient satisfaction with family practice residents (Murphy-Cullen and Larsen, 1984), and symptom disclosure concerning private and nonprivate parts of the body (Young, 1979).

Researchers who have found no differences in the communicative behaviors of male and female doctors caution that perhaps none have been found because the percentage of female doctors is low, even though it is the highest it has ever been. Thus, perhaps differences are not observed because there are just beginning to be enough female doctors to study (Weisman and Teitelbaum, 1985). Additionally, when female doctors are studied, they are usually younger than their male counterparts and distinctions that may be explained by age variations might be mistakenly attributed to gender differences.

Patient expectations of male and female doctors have been the focus of other researchers. Here, instead of studying how doctors communicate with patients, the emphasis is on how patients' expectations affect their interpersonal interactions with doctors. One of the first areas studied was patient acceptance of female doctors, and it was found that experience with female doctors increases patients' satisfaction with female doctors. Basically, this means that patients like the idea of female doctors more after they have been treated by a woman (Weisman and Teitelbaum, 1985).

Another area studied is the preferences of female patients. One study found that female patients were more satisfied with female doctors than male patients and more satisfied than all patients were with male doctors (Comstock et al., 1982). Others have found that female patients prefer female doctors in situations where female doctors are perceived as more "credible" such as obstetrics-gynecology and psychotherapy (Weisman and Teitelbaum, 1985: 1123).

Focusing on psychotherapy, researchers have examined the reactions of patients to the pregnancy of the therapist. It was found that patients reacted differently, and some showed temporary setbacks, but no permanent harm was witnessed during this period (Paluszny and Poznanski, 1971). From the female doctor's perspective, Scully (1980) noted that some female residents reported feeling more patient toward women in labor after experiencing childbirth themselves.

There are some researchers advocating same-sex dyads—with male patients visiting male doctors and female patients seeing female doctors—as the preferred relational pairing in health care settings, or one that is deserving of further study (Kaplan, 1985; Weisman and Teitelbaum, 1985; Young, 1979). However, it should be noted that even if this were shown to be the ideal pairing, with so many female patients and many less female doctors, it may never be a genuine possibility.

Overall, it is unclear why few distinctions have been found between male and female doctors' communicative behaviors. It may be because there have not been enough studies conducted ("Women Doctors," 1995). Or it may be that female doctors have been socialized in medical school in the same manner as male doctors, and thus, have taken on male communicative behaviors in their professional interactions. Female patients *are* treated differently by doctors, but it is not clear if they are treated differently by male doctors alone or by all doctors. The discussion now moves to the place of the nurse in the doctor–patient relationship.

How the Nurse's Gender Affects Communication with Doctors and Patients

Although males have begun to enter the field of nursing, the overwhelming majority (94 percent) of nurses are still female ("Notes from the National Sample Survey of Registered Nurses," 1996). The beginning of the female dominance of nursing dates back to Florence Nightingale (Bullough, 1975; Manthey, 1989). While Nightingale did much to facilitate the training of nurses, she also did much to establish nurses as inferior to doctors (Bullough, 1975).

Prior to Nightingale, nurses often worked independently from doctors, such as the male nurses in Ancient Rome who cared for wounded soldiers on the battlefields (Bullough, 1975) and the female midwives who delivered babies for hundreds of years (Corea, 1977). To allow her nurses to practice with suspicious, nonwelcoming doctors during the Crimean War in the 1850s, Nightingale told her nurses not to give care until "ordered" to do so by a doctor (Bullough, 1975). She saw nurses as "not in control but under control" (Corea, 1977: 58). Nightingale's philosophy of nursing spread from her own nursing school in England to nursing schools in other countries that employed her model (Bullough, 1975).

Hospitals, and the nurses required to staff them, have been affected by military systems, because nurses were needed during wars, and by religious systems, because hospitals were often run by religious orders between wars. Both of these systems are authoritarian organizations in which women traditionally are not the individuals at the top of the hierarchy (Manthey, 1989). It is of little surprise, then, that the main gender issue in the doctor–nurse–patient relationship is power.

Gender Patterns

There are four gender patterns concerning the concept of power in relation to nurses and other individuals in the health care setting. The first, and most prevalent, issue is the imbalance of power between doctors and nurses in relation to the treatment of patients (Allen, Jackson, and Young, 1980; Bacon, 1986; Griffith, Thomas, and Griffith, 1991; Hutchinson, 1982; Kalisch and Kalisch, 1982; Katzman and Roberts, 1988; Kennedy and Garvin, 1981; Ott, Griffith, and Towers, 1989; Tellis-Nayak and Tellis-Nayak, 1984).

The reasons doctors wield more power than nurses are not only historical, but also social. The two professions differ in societal status, with doctors being in the more valued profession. Moreover, doctors and nurses often come from divergent backgrounds, with nurses having middle and lower class upbringings and doctors coming from the upper class (Hutchinson, 1982; Kalisch and Kalisch, 1982). Additionally, because doctors are usually men and nurses are usually women, their obligations beyond the workplace to their families often differ considerably (Hutchinson, 1982). The most important distinction, however, is that doctors and nurses are educated differently, with doctor training focusing on curing while nurse training focuses on caring (Hutchinson, 1982; Kalisch and Kalisch, 1982; Tellis-Nayak and Tellis-Nayak, 1984). The doctor–nurse relationship is discussed in detail throughout a nurse's education, but rarely during a doctor's time in medical school (Bacon, 1986).

These social distinctions in status, background, responsibility, and education have led the nurse to be seen as a helper or "handmaiden" to the doctor rather than a medical professional in her own right (Allen, Jackson, and

Young, 1980; Katzman and Roberts, 1988; Muff, 1982a). The role of the nurse has changed somewhat since Florence Nightingale, particularly in the amount and types of medical responsibilities nurses now carry out. However, the socialization of nurses has not changed along with these increasing responsibilities (Allen, Jackson, and Young, 1980). In fact, nurses' responsibilities have now increased to the point where doctors sometimes bill patients for services nurses provide (Griffith, Thomas, and Griffith, 1991; Ott, Griffith, and Towers, 1989).

The second power issue concerning nurses relates to a nurse–nurse relationship (Ellis and Miller, 1994). Specifically, some nurses are managers in charge of other nurses. There are status distinctions between registered nurses with bachelor's degrees and licensed practical nurses with less education, as well as between nurses and various hospital aides. These groups "do not support each other in struggling for decent pay, training programs and decision-making power" (Corea, 1977: 71). Rather they often strive to assert or hold their respective status by maintaining solidarity with individuals in the same position and challenging the legitimacy of others' roles.

Moreover, nurse managers have the added pressure of being female bosses to their employees. Some authors advise female managers to behave more androgynously to be successful (Camden and Kennedy, 1986; Sargent, 1979) while another warns that it is up to female nurse managers to keep the "humanism" in health care (Fuller, 1979: 770). Nurses in management roles may have difficulty in being females in supervisory positions because the hospital environment is often dominated by the authority of male physicians. The fact that doctors have the "final say" might diminish nurses' credibility in the eyes of the employees they supervise.

The third power issue also concerns a nurse–nurse relationship, but this time the groups are male and female nurses. While only six percent of nurses are male, gender distinctions exist in the profession. Just as the female role and the doctor role have conflicting tensions, so do the male role and the nurse role (Burtt, 1998). Specifically, male nurses are often assumed by society to be effeminate and/or homosexual (Brookfield, Douglas, Shapiro, and Cias, 1982). But within the medical profession, there is evidence that male nurses are valued more highly than female nurses. Studies of tokenism have not shown that male nurses are treated negatively in either nursing school or in practice (Kreps, 1987; Snavely and Fairhurst, 1984). In fact, being male may actually enhance men's status as nurses because males traditionally hold higher status in society (Snavely and Fairhurst, 1984). The most obvious evidence of this is that male nurses are paid better than their female colleagues ("Male Nurses Earn More," 1998). These role and salary differences led one male nurse to label his "minority status" as "pleasurable" (Brookfield et al., 1982: 276).

The fourth power issue concerning nurses exists in the relationship between lay females and nurses. This may seem odd initially because most nurses are female, but the issue here is how nursing is valued by non-nurse females in society. The women's movement has had a "profound influence" on nursing by encouraging action toward the empowerment of nurses (Vance et al., 1985: 33). However, the relationship between women's rights and nursing is not smooth mainly because of the assumption that women should have wanted to become doctors, not nurses, once equal opportunities became available. And nurses today, both male and female, are often asked why they did not attend medical school (Gordon, 1991; Muff, 1982b). Nurses, however, want the work they do to be valued by society even if it is considered "women's" work (Muff, 1982b; Vance et al., 1985). The image of the nurse has not been helped by the mass media who have portrayed nurses not only as doctors' helpers, but also as sex objects or as battle-axes (Muff, 1982a).

In summary, there are four issues of power and gender in nursing relationships. These issues are: (1) the asymmetrical balance of power between doctors and nurses, with doctors holding virtually all control over decisions concerning patients; (2) the difficulties nurse managers face both wielding power and being female; (3) the power imbalance between male and female nurses, particularly over the issue of comparable worth; and (4) the problems nurses face in trying to become more powerful in a society that devalues their profession.

Communicative Issues

The primary communicative issues that stem from these gender issues concern how nurses and doctors speak to each other. In 1967, Stein wrote an influential essay titled "The Doctor–Nurse Game." The "game" is actually a series of indirect communication behaviors that allow the nurse to make recommendations about a patient to a doctor without appearing to be making a recommendation. Additionally, the game allows the doctor to request advice without appearing to be asking for advice. The doctor must not seem to be accepting advice from a nondoctor while the nurse must not appear to be giving medical recommendations. Actually, nurses may not legally offer medical opinions even when called as expert witnesses in lawsuits (Creighton, 1988).

Nurses learn this "game" in their training. They are told not to insult doctors by giving them advice. But paradoxically, nurses are taught that they are valuable assets to doctors, particularly because nurses spend their entire shifts with patients that doctors may see for only minutes. Thus, a nurse may have information about a patient that is unknown to a doctor. Stein (1967) writes that this game reinforces sex-role stereotypes society holds for males and females. And Wheeless, Wheeless, and Riffle (1989) note the persistence of this style of interaction even when other options are introduced.

A nurse can choose to make recommendations or not, but the same is not true for orders from doctors. Nurses must communicatively manage the situation that arises when they disagree with a doctor's order. Bullough (1975) notes that nurses tend to use indirect strategies, or a form of "feminine gamesmanship," to respond to doctors (230). However, Cunningham and Wilcox (1984) found that nurses initially use more indirect strategies if they disagree with an order, but use more direct and forceful communicative behaviors if their initial comments are disregarded. Additionally, a nurse's chosen response is mediated by how serious the consequences of the order will be for the patient as well as how angry the doctor might become (Cunningham and Wilcox, 1984).

This communication issue of "inappropriate orders" (Cunningham and Wilcox, 1984: 764) given to nurses by doctors moves beyond concerns of collegiality into the legal realm. Nurses can be named in lawsuits: (1) if they follow an order they believe is inappropriate and some harm comes to the patient; (2) if they refuse to follow a doctor's order they believe is inappropriate and the patient is harmed by their refusal (Manthey, 1982; Rabinow, 1989); and (3) if they incorrectly follow a doctor's order causing harm to the patient (Creighton, 1989). Thus, more and more nurses are purchasing separate liability insurance to protect themselves from situations their hospitals' policies may not cover in the event of a malpractice suit (Feutz, 1991; Rabinow, 1989). This legal point is actually a communicative issue because a lawsuit would focus on what doctors and nurses say to each other concerning a specific order.

Beyond the question of how nurses give advice to doctors and follow orders from doctors, the asymmetry of the doctor–nurse relationship is communicatively demonstrated in other ways. Doctors routinely call nurses by their first names, but nurses often call doctors by their titles and surnames, particularly in front of patients (Katzman and Roberts, 1988; Tellis-Nayak and Tellis-Nayak, 1984). The imbalance is demonstrated nonverbally as well in the dress of doctors and nurses because nurses usually wear uniforms, but doctors often wear only lab coats over their street clothes. The use of space also reflects the doctor's superior position: doctors have private offices and separate lounges in hospitals, and their space is usually protected by secretaries and nurses; nurses have no private space and often no separate lounge area. Also, the time of doctors is valued more highly than nurses; doctors are salaried or work on a fee-for-service basis, while nurses are hospital employees, paid by the hour and working in shifts (Tellis-Nayak and Tellis-Nayak, 1984).

Nurses' communication relationships with patients have been examined in light of the nonverbal issue of touch. Lane (1989) studied female nurses' beliefs that male patients would be less receptive to touch than female patients; however, the opposite results were found. Male patients found touch more positive than female patients, perhaps because males are not routinely touched in society and enjoyed the experience more. Likewise, perhaps societal views of appropriateness of touch led female nurses to feel more comfortable touching same-sex rather than opposite sex patients (Lane, 1989). Overall, minimal research has addressed gender as a factor in patients' perceptions of nurses (Molzahn and Northcott, 1989).

The communication issues surrounding the asymmetry of the doctor–nurse relationship are more consequential than simply a power struggle between two professions because doctors and nurses are in the business of helping patients. While the issue of nurses questioning doctors' orders may be potentially healthy for patients, the considerable conflict that exists between predominantly male doctors and mainly female nurses is troublesome to patients of all genders.

SUMMARY AND CONCLUSION

The health care setting mirrors society in that those holding the power are usually male while those without power are predominantly female. The medical context also reflects the recent changes in society as individuals have begun to cross traditional sex-role barriers in their career choices. Much more research needs to be done, but the preliminary findings seem to indicate that females take on the behaviors of those in power when moving into the traditionally male area of the medical profession, while males bring their power with them into the mainly female area of nursing.

The only role in the medical context that traditionally is a male role is that of the doctors, and doctors usually communicatively control their relationships with patients and nurses. Male patients are less prevalent than female patients because men do not bear children and do not routinely take responsibility for the health of others. Also, males are not expected by society to display illness or to seek assistance. Male nurses are unusual, perhaps because society labels men in traditionally female roles as effeminate, even though within the medical profession, male nurses are valued highly.

Female patients are diagnosed with psychosomatic illnesses and prescribed tranquilizers more often than males. They also have the responsibility for caring not only for their own but also for their families' health. Female doctors have difficulties becoming physicians and then must balance their femininity with a traditionally male role. Female nurses are medical professionals with little autonomy in relation to doctors, patients, and even other nurses.

Gilligan's (1982) discussion of the "ethic of care" (30) points out the unique relational attributes of females in society. And Gordon (1991) believes females should value this special characteristic and bring their caring, relational attitude with them into the health care setting. Instead of embracing the traditional "marketplace values that have always denigrated care," women should change the contexts they enter (Gordon, 1991: 46).

These gender patterns and communicative issues stir up many questions to which few definitive answers are available. Would everyone—doctors, nurses, and patients—be better off with more "femaleness" in the health care setting? Or does this view simply put more pressure on females to excel in dual roles, that of a medical participant and that of a woman? Is it fair to ask women to bring the caring along with the expertise to the medical context without asking men to bear some of the responsibility? Perhaps if all individuals in the health care setting practice and value caring, as much as they traditionally practice and value curing, patients, doctors, and nurses of both genders would find improved interpersonal interactions.

For Further Discussion

1. What is your experience with individuals in nontraditional gender roles in the health care context? Have you had contact with a female doctor or a male nurse? Did your communication with these individuals differ from your interaction with male doctors and female nurses?
2. Studies of variables such as age (Bergstrom and Nussbaum, 1996), ethnicity (Rubin et al., 1997), and socioeconomic status (Marshall, Smith, and McKeon, 1995) suggest that these factors influence interaction between individuals in the medical context. Do you believe these variables are more or less important than the gender of the participants (Gabbard-Alley, 1995)? What other factors might affect communication in medical settings?
3. How do your gender expectations affect communication with other health care professionals such as pharmacists (Hammond and Lambert, 1994), dentists (Dunning and Lange, 1989), optometrists (Ettinger, 1994), physical therapists, and dietitians (Northouse and Northouse, 1998)? Do you expect these individuals to be male or female? How do you react when their gender does not match your expectations?

References

Adamson, T. E., J. M. Tschann, D. S. Guillion, and A. A. Oppenberg. 1989. Physician communication skills and malpractice claims: A complex relationship. *Western Journal of Medicine* 150: 356–360.

Allen, M. L., D. Jackson, and S. Young. 1980. Closing the communication gap between physicians and nurses in the intensive care unit setting. *Heart and Lung* 9: 836–840.

Ames, K. 17 December 1990. Our bodies, their selves: A bias against women in health research. *Newsweek* 60.

Bacon, L. L. 1986. The nurse-physician relationship: Conflict to collaboration. *Nebraska Nurse* 19: 6–17.

Ballard-Reisch, D. S. 1990. A model of participative decision making for physician-patient interaction. *Health Communication* 2: 91–104.

Beisecker, A. E. 1990. Patient power in doctor-patient communication: What do we know? *Health Communication* 2: 105–122.

Bergstrom, M. J., and J. F. Nussbaum. 1996. Cohort differences in interpersonal conflict: Implications for the older patient-younger care provider interaction. *Health Communication* 8: 233–248.

Bernstein, B., and R. Kane. 1981. Physicians' attitudes toward female patients. *Medical Care* 19: 600–608.

Bickel, J. 2000. Women in academic medicine. *Journal of the American Medical Women's Association* 55 jamwa.amwa-doc.org/vol55/ 55_1_2.htm

Bobula, J. D. 1980. Work patterns, practice characteristics, and incomes of male and female physicians. *Journal of Medical Education* 55: 826–833.

Borges, S. 1986. A feminist critique of scientific ideology: An analysis of two doctor-patient encounters. In S. Fisher and A. D. Todd, eds., *The Social Organization of Doctor-Patient Communication.* Washington, DC: The Center for Applied Linguistics, 26–48.

Brookfield, G., A. Douglas, R. S. Shapiro, and S. J. Cias. 1982. Some thoughts on being a male in nursing. In J. Muff, ed., *Socialization, Sexism, and Stereotyping: Women's Issues in Nursing.* St. Louis: C.V. Mosby, 273–277.

Brundtland, G. H. 2000. Editorial: The woman physician in the year 2000. *Journal of the American Medical Women's Association* 55 jamwa.amwa-doc.org/vol55/55_1_ed.htm

Bullough, B. 1975. Barriers to the nurse practitioner movement: Problems of women in a woman's field. *International Journal of Health Services* 5: 225–233.

Burtt, K. 1998. Male nurses still face bias. *American Journal of Nursing.* http://www.nursingworld.org/ajn/1998/sept/issu098f.htm

Camden, C. T., and C. W. Kennedy. 1986. Manager communicative style and nurse morale. *Human Communication Research* 12: 551–563.

Cecil, D. W. 1998. Relational control patterns in physician-patient clinical encounters: Continuing the conversation. *Health Communication* 10: 125–150.

Comstock, L. M., E. M. Hooper, J. M. Goodwin, and J. S. Goodwin. 1982. Physician behaviors that correlate with patient satisfaction. *Journal of Medical Education* 57: 105–112.

Corea, G. 1977. *The Hidden Malpractice: How American Medicine Treats Women as Patients and Professionals.* New York: William Morrow and Company.

Coulthard, M., and M. Ashby. 1975. Talking with the doctor. *Journal of Communication* 25: 140–147.

Creighton, H. 1988. The nurse as an expert witness. *Nursing Management* 19: 22–23.

———. 1989. Nurse's failure to follow physician's orders. *Nursing Management* 20: 18–22.

Cunningham, M. A., and J. R. Wilcox. 1984. When an M.D. gives an R.N. a harmful order: Modifying a bind. In R. N. Bostrom, ed., *Communication Yearbook* 8. Beverly Hills, CA: Sage, 764–778.

Dunning, D. G., and B. M. Lange. 1989. Male and female dental students' interaction with patients: A test of sex differences. *Health Communication* 1: 155–164.

Ellis, B. H., and K. I. Miller. 1994. Supportive communication among nurses: Effects on commitment, burnout, and retention. *Health Communication* 6: 77–96.

Ennker, I. C., K. Schwarz, and J. Ennker. 1999. The disproportion of female and male surgeons in cardiothoracic surgery. *Thoracic Cardiovascular Surgery* 47: 131–135.

Entralgo, P. L. 1979. What does the word *good* mean in *good patient*? In E. J. Cassel and M. Siegler, eds., *Changing Values in Medicine.* New York: University Publications of America, 127–143.

Ettinger, E. R. 1994. *Professional Communications in Eye Care.* Boston: Butterworth-Heinemann.

Feutz, S. A. 1991. Do you need professional liability insurance? *Nursing* 21: 56–57.

Fisher, S. 1983. Doctor talk/patient talk: How treatment decisions are negotiated in doctor-patient communication. In S. Fisher and A. D. Todd, eds., *The Social Organization of Doctor Patient Communication.* Washington, DC: The Center for Applied Linguistics, 135–157.

Fuller, S. 1979. Humanistic leadership in a pragmatic age. *Nursing Outlook* 27: 770–773.

Gabbard-Alley, A. S. 1995. Health communication and gender: A review and critique. *Health Communication* 7: 35–54.

Gilligan, C. 1982. *In a Different Voice: Psychological Theory and Women's Development.* Cambridge, MA: Harvard University Press.

Gordon, S. 1991. Fearing of caring: The feminist paradox. *American Journal of Nursing* 92: 45–48.

Gray, J. 1982. The effect of the doctor's sex on the doctor-patient relationship. *Journal of the Royal College of General Practitioners* 32: 167–169.

Gray, M. J., and S. Meginnis. 1978. Role of the gynecologist and the emerging woman. *Clinical Obstetrics and Gynecology* 21: 173–181.

Griffith, H. M., N. Thomas, and L. Griffith. 1991. MDs bill for these routine nursing tasks. *American Journal of Nursing* 1: 22–27.

Haas, A. 1979. Male and female spoken language differences: Stereotypes and evidence: *Psychological Bulletin* 86: 616–626.

Hall , J. A., D. L. Roter, and N. R. Katz. 1988. Meta-analysis of correlates of provider behavior in medical encounters. *Medical Care* 26: 657–675.

Hammond, S. L., and B. L. Lambert. 1994. Communicating about medications: Directions for research. *Health Communication* 6: 247–252.

Hausfeld, F. 1976. Women and the doctor-patient relationship. *Australian Family Physician* 5: 534–543.

Heins, M., J. Hendricks, L. Martindale, S. Smock, M. Stein, and J. Jacobs. 1979. Attitudes of women and men physicians. *American Journal of Public Health* 69: 1132–1139.

Henley, N. M. 1977. *Body Politics: Power, Sex, and Nonverbal Communication.* Englewood Cliffs, NJ: Prentice-Hall.

Hutchinson, S. A. 1982. Four perspectives on physicians, nurses, power and games. *Florida Nurse* 30: 9–12.

Jenks, E. B. 1989. An interpersonal perception analysis of doctor-patient communication. Unpublished doctoral dissertation, Department of Speech Communication, Pennsylvania State University.

———. 1995. Symmetry vs. individuality: Perceptions of the doctor-patient relationship. *Journal of the Northwest Communication Association* 23: 39–69.

Jones, B. J., L. Arnold, G. Xu, and L. C. Epstein. 2000. Differences in the preparation and practice of male and female physicians from combined baccalaureate-MD degree programs. *Journal of the American Medical Women's Association* 55 jamwa.amwa-doc-org/vol55/55_1_8.htm

Kalisch, B. J., and P. A. Kalisch. 1982. An analysis of the source of physician-nurse conflict. In J. Muff, ed., *Socialization, Sexism, and Stereotyping: Women's Issues in Nursing.* St. Louis: C.V. Mosby, 221–233.

Kaplan, A. G. 1985. Female or male therapists for women patients: New formulations. *Psychiatry* 48: 111–121.

Kate, N. T. 1997. Dr. mom—not! *American Demographics* 19: 29.

Katzman, E. M., and J. I. Roberts. 1988. Nurse-physician conflicts as barriers to the enactment of nursing roles. *Western Journal of Nursing Research* 10: 576–590.

Kennedy, C. W., and B. J. Garvin. 1981. The effect of status and gender on interpersonal relationships in nursing. *Nursing Forum* 20: 274–287.

Korsch, B. M., E. K. Gozzi, and V. Francis. 1968. Gaps in doctor-patient communication: Doctor-patient interaction and patient satisfaction. *Pediatrics* 42: 855–871.

Kramer, C. 1977. Perceptions of female and male speech. *Language and Speech* 20: 151–161.

Kreps, G. L. 1987. Organizational sexism in health care. In L. P. Stewart and S. Ting-Toomey, eds., *Communication, Gender, and Sex Roles in Diverse Interaction Contexts.* Norwood, NJ: Ablex.

Laing, R. D. 1969. *Self and Others.* New York: Penguin Books.

Lane, P. L. 1989. Nurse-client perceptions: The double standard of touch. *Issues in Mental Health Nursing* 10: 1–13.

Lane, S. D. 1983. Compliance, satisfaction, and physician-patient communication. In R. N. Bostrom, ed., *Communication Yearbook 7.* Beverly Hills, CA: Sage Publications, 772–799.

Langwell, K. M. 1982. Factors affecting the incomes of men and women physicians: Further explorations. *Journal of Human Resources* 17: 261–275.

Male nurses earn more. 1998. *Australian Nursing Journal* 6: 15.

Malterud, K. 1987a. Illness and disease in female patients I. *Scandinavian Journal of Primary Health Care* 5: 205–209.

———. 1987b. Illness and disease in female patients II. *Scandinavian Journal of Primary Health Care* 5: 211–216.

Maltz, D. N., and R. A. Borker. 1982. A cultural approach to male-female miscommunication. In J. J. Gumperz, ed., *Language and Social Identity.* Cambridge: Cambridge University Press, 196–216.

Manthey, M. 1989. Just what are doctors' orders anyway? *Nursing Management* 20: 26–28.

Marshall, A. A., S. W. Smith, and J. K. McKeon. 1995. Persuading low-income women to engage in mammography screening: Source, message, and channel preferences. *Health Communication* 7: 283–300.

Mastekaasa, A. 2000. Parenthood, gender and sickness absence. *Social Science and Medicine* 50: 1827–1843.

McGee, D. S., and D. J. Cegala. 1998. Patient communication skills training for improved communication competence in the primary care medical consultation. *Journal of Applied Communication Research* 26: 412–430.

Mendez, A., J. A. Shymansky, and M. Wolraich. 1986. Verbal and non-verbal behavior of doctors while conveying distressing information. *Medical Education* 20: 437–443.

Molzahn, A. E., and H. C. Northcott. 1989. The social bases of discrepancies in health/illness perceptions. *Journal of Advanced Nursing* 14: 132–140.

Muff, J. 1982a. Handmaiden, battle-ax, whore: An explanation into the fantasies, myths, and stereotypes about nurses. In J. Muff, ed., *Socialization, Sexism, and Stereotyping: Women's Issues in Nursing.* St. Louis: C.V. Mosby, 113–156.

———. 1982b. Why doesn't a smart girl like you go to medical school? The women's movement takes a slap at nursing. In J. Muff, ed., *Socialization, Sexism, and Stereotyping: Women's Issues in Nursing.* St. Louis: C.V. Mosby, 178–185.

Murphy-Cullen, C. L., and L. C. Larsen. 1984. Interaction between the socio-demographic variables of physicians and their patients: Its impact upon patient satisfaction. *Social Science and Medicine* 19: 163–166.

Nathanson, C.A. 1975. Illness and the feminine role: A theoretical review: *Social Science and Medicine* 9: 57–62.

National Institutes of Health, Office of Research on Women's Health. 2000. http://www4.od.nihgov/orwh/

National Women's Law Center, FOCUS on Health and Leadership for Women at the Center for Clinical Epidemiology and Biostatistics, University of Pennsylvania School of Medicine, and The Lewin Group. 2000. *Making the Grade on Women's Health: A National and State-by-State Report Card.* Washington, DC: National Women's Law Center.

Northouse, L. L., and P. G. Northouse. 1998. *Health Communication: Strategies for Health Professionals,* 2nd ed. Stamford, CT: Appleton and Lange.

Notes from the national sample survey of registered nurses. 1996. Division of Nursing, Bureau of Health Professionals, Health Resources and Services Administration. http://bhpr.hrsa.gov/dn/survnote.htm

Ott, B. B., H. Griffith, and J. Towers. 1989. Who gets the money? *American Journal of Nursing* 89: 186–188.

Paget, M. A. 1983. On the work of talk: Studies in misunderstandings. In S. Fisher and A. D. Todd, eds., *The Social Organization of Doctor Patient Communication*. Washington, DC: The Center for Applied Linguistics, 55–74.

Paluszny, M., and E. Poznanski. 1971. Reactions of patients during pregnancy of the psychotherapist. *Child Psychiatry and Human Development* 1: 266–274.

Parsons, T. 1951. *The Social System*. Glencoe, IL: Free Press.

Rabinow, J. 1989. You stand in the eyes of the law. *Nursing* 19: 34–42.

Root, M. J. 1987. Communication barriers between older women and physicians. *Public Health Reports Supplement*, 152–155.

Rubin, D. L., P. Healy, T. C. Gardiner, R. C. Zath, and C. P. Moore. 1997. Nonnative physicians as message sources: Effects of accent and ethnicity on patients' responses to AIDS prevention counseling. *Health Communication* 9: 351–368.

Sargent, A. G. 1979. The androgynous manager. *Supervisor Nurse* 10: 23–30.

Scully, D. 1980. *Men Who Control Women's Health: The Miseducation of Obstetrician-Gynecologists.* Boston: Houghton Mifflin.

Shuy, R. W. 1983. Three types of interference to an effective exchange of information in the medical interview. In S. Fisher and A. D. Todd, eds., *The Social Organization of Doctor Patient Communication*. Washington, DC: The Center for Applied Linguistics, 189–202.

Sibbald, B. 1999. Be careful who you marry, female physicians warned. *Canadian Medical Association Journal* 160: 977.

Skelton, J. R., and F. D. R. Hobbs. 1999. Descriptive study of cooperative language in primary care consultations by male and female doctors. *British Medical Journal* 318: 576–580.

Smith, D. H., K. G. Cunningham, and W. E. Hale. 1994. Communication about medicines: Perceptions of the ambulatory elderly. *Health Communication* 6: 281–296.

Snavely, B. K., and G. T. Fairhurst. 1984. The male nursing student as a token. *Research in Nursing and Health* 7: 287–294.

Stein, L. I. 1967. The doctor-nurse game. *Archives of General Psychiatry* 16: 699–703.

Steinhauer, J. 1 March 1999. For women in medicine, a road to compromise, not perks. *New York Times*, A1.

Tannen, D. 1991. *You Just Don't Understand: Women and Men in Conversation*. New York: Ballantine Books.

Tannen, D. 1995. *Talking 9 to 5: Women and Men in the Workplace: Language, Sex, and Power.* New York: Avon Books.

Tellis-Nayak, M., and V. Tellis-Nayak. 1984. Games that professionals play: The social psychology of physician-nurse interaction. *Social Science and Medicine* 18: 1063–1069.

Thorne, B., and N. Henley. 1975. Difference and dominance: An overview of language, gender, and society. In B. Thorne, and N. Henley, eds., *Language and Sex: Difference and Dominance.* Rowley, MA: Newbury House Publishers, 5–42.

U.S. Bureau of the Census. 1999. *Statistical Abstract of the United States: 1999.* 119th ed. Washington, DC: U.S. Government Printing Office.

Vance , D., S. W. Talbott, A. B. McBride, and D. J. Mason. 1985. Coming of age: The women's movement and nursing. In D. J. Mason and S. W. Talbott, eds., *Political*

Action Handbook for Nurses: Changing the Workplace, Government, Organizations, and Community. Menlo Park, CA: Addison-Wesley, 23–37.

Vanderford, M. L., and D. H. Smith. 1996. *The Silicone Breast Implant Story: Communication and Uncertainty.* Mahwah, NJ: Lawrence Erlbaum Associates.

von Friederichs-Fitzwater, M. M., E. J. Callahan, N. Flynn, and J. Williams. 1991. Relational control in physician-patient encounters. *Health Communication* 3: 17–36.

Waitzkin, H. 1984. Doctor-patient communication: Clinical implications of social scientific research. *Journal of the American Medical Association* 252: 2441–2446.

Wallen, J., H. Waitzkin, and J. D. Stoeckle. 1979. Physician stereotypes about female health and illness: A study of patient's sex and the informative process during medical interviews. *Women and Health* 4: 135–146.

Weisman, C. S. 1987. Communication between women and their health care providers: Research findings and unanswered questions. *Public Health Reports Supplement,* 147–151.

Weisman, C. S., D. E. Rich, J. Rogers, K. G. Crawford, C. E. Grayson, and J. T. Henderson. 2000. Gender and patient satisfaction with primary care: Tuning in to women in quality measurement. *Journal of Women's Health and Gender-Based Medicine* 9: 657–665.

Weisman, C. S., and M. A. Teitelbaum. 1985. Physician gender and the physician patient relationship: Recent evidence and relevant questions. *Social Science and Medicine* 11: 1119–1127.

Weisman, C. S., M. A. Teitelbaum, and L. L. Morlock. 1988. Malpractice claims experience associated with fertility-control services among young obstetrician-gynecologists. *Medical Care* 26: 198–206.

West, C. 1983. "Ask me no questions . . ." An analysis of queries and replies in physician-patient dialogues. In S. Fisher and A. D. Todd, eds., *The Social Organization of Doctor Patient Communication.* Washington, DC: The Center for Applied Linguistics, 75–106.

Wheeless, V. E., L. R. Wheeless, and S. Riffle. 1989. The role of situation, physician communicator style, and hospital rules climate on nurses' decision styles and communication satisfaction. *Health Communication* 1: 189–206.

Women doctors. 1995. *Harvard Women's Health Watch* 2: 1.

Young, J. W. 1979. Symptom disclosure to male and female physicians: Effects of sex, physical attractiveness, and symptom type. *Journal of Behavioral Medicine* 2: 159–169.

CHAPTER 16

Gender and Communication in the Hospitality Industry

Judi Brownell

POINTS TO BE ADDRESSED

- Symbolic/cultural approach to understanding organizational communication
- Impact of culture on gender and communication
- Cultural aspects unique of the hospitality industry
- Gender issues in hospitality organizations
- Communication behaviors and organizational culture: Changing the way men and women interact at work
- Implications of the symbolic/cultural approach to improving the way men and women communicate

Service industries are one of the fastest-growing segments of the U.S. economy. Well over 70 percent of the working population is engaged in some form of service activity, and this number is steadily increasing. There are nearly ten million people in today's hospitality workforce alone; within the coming decades, that figure will continue to increase.

If you think about it, you can probably name several friends or relatives who have worked in service organizations. Perhaps you've even waited tables or delivered pizzas. If not, you've still played a part as a consumer; you've stayed at a hotel, visited a health care professional, or flown in a plane. It's likely, then, that you know something about service organizations already.

This chapter explores gender and communication in one segment of the service industry—hospitality organizations. The hospitality industry includes such businesses as hotels, restaurants, airlines, clubs, resorts, and casinos. We will be observing communication between men and women in these organizations from a particular viewpoint called the symbolic/cultural perspective.

First, the basic assumptions of the symbolic/cultural approach are defined because they reveal important characteristics of hospitality organizations and provide a framework for better understanding how gender affects behavior in the workplace. The unique aspects of the hospitality industry are emphasized and their influence on gender and communication is discussed. Two significant issues related to gender are then explored—sexual harassment and women in management.

Finally, specific communication behaviors and strategies for addressing common problems of communication between men and women are presented. The skills of listening, communicating verbally, and communicating nonverbally are discussed because they can modify an organization's culture toward more effective male–female communication. In closing, we take a look at the implications our discussion has for gender and communication in the hospitality industry.

Approaches to Studying Organizations

Over the years, scholars and researchers have viewed organizational communication and behavior from a number of different perspectives (Bolman and Deal, 1984; Frank and Brownell, 1989). Each perspective provides a slightly different lens, enabling us to focus on specific aspects of communication and behavior. Our job here is to identify the lens best suited to examining communication between men and women at work.

Early classical theorists such as Max Weber (1947) applied mechanistic, highly rational models that emphasized formalized rules, specialization of roles, and organizational structure. If things didn't go well in their organizations, classical theorists might recommend creating another department or restructuring lines of authority. The human relations theorists, pioneered by researchers like Barnard (1938) and Mayo (1933), were interested in human resources issues and in the individual worker. McGregor's (1960) Theory X and Theory Y clearly distinguished classical theories from the newer human relations approaches that took the needs of the individual and the influence of personal and social factors into account. Human relations theorists were concerned with employee satisfaction, morale, and quality of worklife issues. If an organizational communication problem arose, their approach might be to survey workers to implement training programs, or to create additional opportunities for employees to participate in decision-making processes.

Still other researchers were interested in the sets of properties and patterns that make organization possible. Some of the first applications of systems theory to organizational behavior were described by Katz and Kahn (1966) and Miller (1972). These researchers viewed organizations as integrated systems and emphasized the functional relationships among all parts. Any time a problem was identified, its solution would ultimately affect all aspects of the organization.

Each framework highlights certain dimensions of human behavior in organizations, and allows us to see with varying degrees of clarity a particular aspect of organizational life. When our subject is gender and communication, we discover that focusing our lens on yet another approach, the symbolic/cultural perspective, provides the clearest and most revealing view. An understanding of the symbolic/cultural framework is essential to our subsequent discussions of gender and communication.

The Symbolic/Cultural Approach

From a symbolic/cultural perspective, communication makes the existence of an organization possible. Think for a moment about the implications of this statement. The symbolic/cultural approach to studying organizations focuses on the ways in which individuals "make sense" of their experiences and "negotiate meanings" in the process of their daily interactions. It is through communication—symbolic interaction—that organizational meanings are created, maintained, and shared, and organizational values transmitted. Human communication is seen as sense-making activity; it generates a core of basic assumptions that, in turn, influence members' subsequent perceptions and behaviors.

Through the actions of organizational leaders and the daily activities of members, each organization develops a unique culture that influences behavior as it is itself created through employees' interactions. As Louis (1980: 228) explains, culture is the "process of learning the expectations of others and how to act in terms of context-specific assumptions." A portion of those assumptions, as we will see, pertains to gender and communication.

The concept of symbols and symbolic action is also basic to understanding how an organization develops a particular social reality for its members and affirms basic cultural values. You can determine what a symbol means to an organizational member by observing his or her behavior in response to a particular word or gesture. In one instance, a "great waitress" might mean that a woman has provided efficient, courteous service. In another, the implication might be that she has performed related activities as well—brought your little sister crackers or put extra ice in your water. The meaning of a symbol is strongly influenced, then, by the organizational context in which it is used. As Kreps (1990) explains, culture influences

> the attitudes and values of members; the specialized jargons and languages they use; the social and professional rituals they engage in; the company history that is passed on; the company philosophies that are held; legends, stories, and jokes that are told; informal norms and logic used to guide actions; the visions that organizational members have of the organization's future; and the identification of organizational friends and foes. (126–127)

How does all of this relate to gender and communication? In the next section you will discover that notions of what it "means" to be male or female are socially constructed.

Gender and Symbolic Action

Communication creates gender (Pearson, 1985) just as it creates other organizational realities. It is through interactions with others that we learn what it "means," within a particular framework, to be male or female. You may have Asian friends, for instance, who grew up in an environment where appropriate behavior for women was strikingly different from what you experienced in the United States. Consequently, you and your friend may have disagreements about how women should respond in various situations. The symbolic/cultural perspective helps us view more critically our basic assumptions about gender and, further, recognize how these assumptions are created and perpetuated within organizational environments.

Think, for a moment, about your past experiences as a man or woman in organizations. Although women are generally accepted in "soft" professions like marketing and personnel, many employers still have reservations about hiring women in construction, engineering, or other areas traditionally associated with male-linked characteristics such as mathematical ability and physical strength. In spite of many recent changes, it is still unusual to find male secretaries or female maintenance supervisors.

In addition, gender itself may be a significant variable in influencing individual perceptions. Hackett and his colleagues (1991) discovered that women's expectations about new technology, for instance, were significantly more pessimistic than men's. Women did not anticipate as much job improvement and, in fact, expected some aspects of their work to get even worse. His conclusion was that differences in perceptions could be attributed to gender; men and women simply perceived and interpreted the same experience in different ways.

Other studies (Nelsen, 1990; Shinew and Arnold, 1998; Solomon, 1998) examined upper-level hospitality managers' perceptions regarding whether there are gender-based differences that affect women's career progress. The findings are revealing. Nelsen's study, for instance, found:

Men Agreed and Women Disagreed that:

- Female managers are more visible and this increased exposure has a positive effect

- Women network in similar ways to men
- Upward mobility is equal for men and women

Men Disagreed and Women Agreed that:

- Women are perceived as not being tough enough
- Women have a better record of staying with a company
- Women and men use mentors with equal success
- Women rely less on organizational power politics

Kenton (1989) found that it may be that females must indeed work harder than men to achieve equal results. Others (Rowe, 1999) agree, noting that credibility continues to come less easily for women in the workplace.

What is responsible for these perceptual differences? One explanation might be that from their earliest years, men and women have different social experiences that subsequently influence the way they see and interpret the world (Arliss, 1991). As children, boys and girls are reinforced and recognized for different sorts of behavior. While girls who are pretty and clean may receive attention, boys are more often rewarded for their athletic ability and other physical accomplishments. Each gender is provided different types of stimuli and sent different messages about what is valued or appropriate. While some of these messages are changing in ways that de-emphasize the role of gender, important expectations are largely based on preconceived notions and sex-related stereotypes.

In addition to the influence of their parents or significant adults, the media, children's literature, and early peer groups also contribute to the impressions that children form about what it means to belong to a particular gender group. These attitudes continue into adulthood. The literature (Gregg and Johnson, 1990; Konrad and Cannings, 1997; Shinew and Arnold, 1998) suggests that even when women and men have similar educational backgrounds and produce similar products, they have significantly different work-related experiences. Informal networks, the social contacts that often help to define the organization's norms and expectations, remain affected by gender (Herrick, 1999; Peters, 1988; Solomon, 1998). Women often have more difficulty gaining access to career-relevant information because the "old boy network" operates on golf courses and at happy hours as well as in the organization's hallways and cafeterias.

Although the organizational landscape is slowly changing, significant numbers of employees treat colleagues of both genders in a manner consistent with their gender role expectations regardless of the person's organizational role (Gutek, Cohen, and Konrad, 1990). If men have been raised to believe that women need to be protected, or that they should take care of social events, or that they are easily upset, these assumptions will affect how women are treated at work. Later, you will see some vivid examples of this problem as two fictional characters, Sylvia and Cassie, attempt to communicate with their male colleagues.

Even though there are few documented differences between male and female communication behaviors, women experience a different work environment to the extent that stereotypes and biases persist (Rowe, 1999; Solomon, 1999). The stereotype of women as gentle, clean, and nurturing may be in sharp contrast to their role requirements on the job. Yet, the way she is treated cannot help but influence a woman's subsequent behavior as she receives cues regarding what it means to be a woman in that particular workplace.

Because attributing certain characteristics to one gender or another is likely to produce behavior that is based on stereotypes rather than on individual talents and abilities, it is clearly in the best interest of the organization to develop a culture in which expectations are not gender-linked and self-fulfilling prophecies do not have opportunities to grow. As Eliza Doolittle noted in the well-known story of her transformation from uneducated urchin to a well-mannered woman, "I'll always be a flower girl to Professor Higgins, because he treats me like a flower girl and always will." Those who treat her like a lady, however, empower her to behave in a more appropriate and productive manner.

Although perceptions of behavior are often confused with actual behavior, the truth is that our perceptions are our reality. What we believe is what is true: our beliefs influence our subsequent attitudes and behavior. You can see how the symbolic/cultural approach draws attention to some important aspects of gender and communication. We have examined how employees are affected by the values and culture of the organization and how expectations of gender behavior influence our perceptions. Now, let's focus on the specific ways in which the hospitality environment shapes employees' gender-related behavior.

The Service Industry: A Special Culture

A growing body of literature suggests that service industries are unique in several important ways. The nature of service, as discussed earlier, requires that organizational members deal not only with internal communication but also with the expectations and definitions of their publics as well. In the hospitality industry, quality service is often defined by whether or not the provider meets the customer's expectations. Because a portion of the service occurs during a transaction between two individuals, the meanings negotiated during this encounter become particularly significant.

Internal communication in hospitality industries is affected not only by verbal behavior, but by nonverbal communication as well. The next section reviews some of the characteristics that distinguish hospitality organizations and make them challenging environments for gender communication.

SYMBOLS AND ENVIRONMENTAL CHARACTERISTICS OF SERVICE CULTURES

Three elements that affect an organization's work environment include: (1) performance benchmarks, or standards, (2) ongoing, internal systems that determine how business is conducted, and (3) the values and norms that affect how it feels to work in the particular organization. Although performance standards and internal systems may vary from one property or firm to the next, the service industry in general has strong values that guide member behaviors within the service culture (Wood, 1994).

The symbols and the environment inherent in hospitality organizations (both verbal and nonverbal) are strong forces in shaping the way in which men and women communicate. Hospitality implies meeting needs, having a good time, doing whatever it takes to satisfy. Images of the industry include wine glasses and moonlit patios, whirlpools, bathrobes, and breakfast trays. Symbols of romance, of feeling good, of pampering, predominate.

The work environment itself also influences behavior. Many employees work in close proximity to one another. Their shifts are long and irregular, often including evening and nighttime hours. The duties of hospitality workers are likely to take them into settings traditionally associated with sexual behavior—bedrooms, bars, and lounges. In other instances, employees work poolside in a casual, informal atmosphere.

In addition, hospitality employees are often hired, in part, because of out-going personalities and physical attractiveness. Flight attendants, club managers, front desk personnel—all project their organization's image to the public and, in that regard, are likely to be personable and attractive. In many instances their dress accentuates gender differences and sexuality. The combination of work environment and personal characteristics makes hospitality employees' work experience quite unlike any other.

Note, too, that different cultures mix sex and business in different ways (Axtell, 1990). The changing composition of the hospitality workforce brings together men and women with very different experiences and assumptions because of their cultural backgrounds. Awkward situations are likely to develop when initial expectations are highly discrepant. From the symbolic/cultural approach, this means that organizations need strong cultures with clear norms and expectations to socialize new employees and communicate what it means to work for that particular company.

Although all organizations confront internal problems associated with gender and communication, the nature of service industries poses additional challenges. Not only do employees communicate regularly with coworkers, but their customers and guests represent yet another potentially challenging dimension.

Service and Symbolic Action

In addition to providing a framework for viewing organizational members' interactions as well as the physical and symbolic aspects of the workplace, the symbolic/cultural approach also provides insight into the nature of service encounters. There are few more elusive concepts in today's business world than that of effective service. Difficult to measure or describe, "good service" is largely in the eyes of the customer. It has, most specialists agree, little to do with what the provider believes it is and a lot to do with the customers' perceptions and expectations (Davidow and Uttal, 1989). In fact, good service is frequently defined not by any standard of quality, but rather by behavior that exceeds the customer's expectations. You can see the usefulness of the symbolic/cultural approach in understanding how the meaning of service is negotiated. Because of its subjective nature, the most meaningful approaches to studying service organizations are those that emphasize the dynamic aspects of the service encounter.

In hospitality organizations, service can be viewed as emerging from the coordinated efforts of the service employee and the customer; it is the social interaction itself that defines what service means to the guest (Mills and Morris, 1986). At the moment of service, the organization's representative and the specific customer interact to produce the "product" (Worsfold, 1989).

In one sense, then, the customer becomes a "partial employee" (Barrington and Olsen, 1987), affecting the time of demand, the exact nature of the service, and the quality of the service provided. Clearly, such high-contact systems have an unusually large degree of uncertainty within their daily operations and room for interpretations regarding appropriate gender behavior. Just as with internal communication, customers have sets of expectations regarding how they will be treated. These expectations involve patterns of rights, privileges, and obligations between the guest and the service provider. Some of these expectations, to be sure, have to do with gender-related behaviors.

Basic assumptions about the importance of "satisfied customers" often force employees to conform to expectations that may not be in keeping with their understanding of what their job entails. If, for instance, a customer's "meaning" of barmaid includes services that the employee does not feel obligated to provide, problems are likely to result.

A customer ordering a drink, then, will define his or her experience not only by the quality of the beverage, but also by the extent to which the employee meets his or her expectations regarding service behavior. Expectations for women, who have traditionally been perceived as service providers (mother, helper) or sexual objects, may go beyond the organization's definition of what constitutes appropriate action. The patron who has been drinking and invites the waitress to sit on his lap, or the hotel guest who suggests that the maid give him a backrub, demonstrates this discrepancy. As Chase (1978) explains, interactions with the customer make the worker "part of the product" (139). In some cases, this notion can be taken to the extreme.

There is also a degree of discretion on the part of the service provider; some customers are extended far more and varied service than others. Often, service employees have been coached in advance and are prepared to extend more complete or higher quality service to selected guests. It's not uncommon for the front desk manager to insist that when Mr. Warren arrives, he should be "given priority treatment." Even in these cases, however, problems arise when employees are asked for specific services on the basis of their gender in addition to—or instead of—their organizational role.

Employees must also manage what Albrecht and Zemke (1985) have called "moments of truth." Moments of truth are the specific employee decisions or behaviors that have an impact on the customer and his or her impressions of the particular organization. These moments of truth contribute to customers' definitions of what service means in a particular organization. The ways in which employees respond to inappropriate gender-related behaviors, as we will see in a later section, is critical to the success of any given encounter.

In addition to the moment-by-moment decisions that are made as men and women communicate at work, gender poses several more encompassing concerns as well. Among these are issues of sexual harassment and the difficulties women have had securing and maintaining managerial positions. Because of the pervasiveness of these problems, the next section is devoted to a review of these two issues as they pertain to hospitality organizations.

HARASSMENT

As we have seen, the nature of the hospitality workplace, with its high male–female contact and its sex-associated symbols, provides an environment where the potential for sexual harassment is particularly high. In addition to the harm such behavior brings to those directly involved, organizations lose millions of dollars in diminished productivity and expensive litigation (VanDer Wall, 2000).

Recent statistics on sexual harassment indicate that over half of all employees have been exposed to some form of sexual overture from a coworker of the other sex within a two-year time period (Gruber, 1998). Not all women, however, take formal action in such situations. Although sexual harassment claims climbed to over 15,000 in the United States in 1998 (Davis, 1998), and an estimated 10 percent of working women quit a job because of sexual harassment (Gutek, Cohen, and Konrad, 1990), many researchers believe that a large number of offenses go unreported. These findings are striking; yet, Nozar (1990) proposes that sexual harassment in the hospitality industry may exist at twice the rate it does in other types of organizations.

Harassment in the service industry takes place between managers and subordinates and between service personnel and customers or guests; however, the majority of violations occur among colleagues. In her study of harassment in the hospitality industry, Eller (1989) found that over 40 percent of the women she surveyed said they contended with insulting sexual comments; 28 percent reported experiencing insulting looks and gestures and sexual touching. As Eller (1989) emphasizes, in an industry already faced with "rampant turnover, high labor costs, and a diminishing supply of workers" (84), sexual harassment is a serious problem. On a national level, sexual harassment cost U.S. taxpayers over $300 million in a two-year period.

There are a number of reasons why hospitality workers are particularly susceptible to sexual harassment. Most of these have already been discussed as aspects of the service culture. Clearly, there is frequent physical contact among coworkers. Unusual hours, with peak and slack periods, create an environment where harassing behavior is likely to occur. Because sociability and attractiveness are valued and emphasized, attention is drawn to employees' gender identities. In some situations, skimpy uniforms or other aspects of employees' required dress further contributes to the problem.

One study that is particularly relevant to gender communication in the hospitality industry was conducted by Gutek, Cohen, and Konrad (1990). A review of their work raises some interesting and relevant issues. Are you familiar with the phrase, "sexualization of the workplace"? It's the concept Gutek, Cohen, and Konrad (1990) propose for examining gender and communication in organizations. The authors suggest that a simple measure—the amount of contact between individuals—can partially explain gender behavior in organizational settings. A "sexualized" work environment, or one in which there is a great deal of physical contact, is more likely to encourage people of both genders to make sexual overtures. The degree to which a work environment is sexualized also reflects the acceptability of social-sexual behavior (570).

Gutek and her colleagues believe that understanding the sexualization of a workplace is important because of its "pivotal mediating role" (572) in facilitating both sexual harassing and nonharassing behavior. Managers, they believe, can work to desexualize the contact between men and women at work by establishing appropriate standards of language, conduct, and dress. As Gruber (1998) suggests, organizational leaders have a significant influence on the climate in which employees work, and can decrease the level of tolerance for offensive and harassing behavior. Their specific role in shaping organizational practices will be discussed in a later section of this chapter when we examine culture change. For now, let's continue by focusing on the second significant issue pertaining to gender and communication—women in management.

Women in Management

A group of female executives sits around a table. The main topic of conversation is the growing number of women who are leaving excellent corporate careers because they believe gender discrimination will prevent them from obtaining senior positions. Keep in mind that women account for nearly one-half of the graduates of food service management programs and the majority of service employees are women, yet fewer than a third of management positions are filled by women (Gregg and Johnson, 1990).

A study conducted by *Lodging* determined that fewer than 8 percent of the service companies sampled had a woman president (Nelsen, 1990). This statistic is comparable or slightly higher than those provided for U.S. corporations generally. Rowe (1999) reported that only two Fortune 500 companies were headed by women in 1998, and only 10 percent of all Fortune 500 corporate officers were female. There seems to be little question that although women may manage "differently," they are as effective as their male counterparts in accomplishing personal and organizational goals (Baytosh and Kleiner, 1989; Konrad and Cannings, 1997). In fact, some researchers believe that women may be better suited than men to serve as transformational leaders in the twenty-first century (Bass, 1991; Richardson, 1999; Solomon, 1998). Leadership in the decades ahead is likely to be characterized by a variety of social and technical skills, some traditionally male-linked and some female-linked.

Although increasing numbers of women are moving into managerial positions, Powell (1989) states men have not "demonstrated a corresponding interest in the lower-paid, female-dominated" roles like waitperson or housekeeper. In addition, it appears that once women assume managerial roles, there is often a glass ceiling that prevents further upward mobility (Andorka, 1998). Part of the problem may be due to a culture that perpetuates stereotypes and assumptions about women's role and abilities as a manager.

Mary, for instance, has been an assistant manager at a 300-room, full-service hotel for two years. Dick, her boss, has surrounded himself with an all-male clique. The members of the clique advance, often leap-frogging over women like Mary who have impressive qualifications but who may not participate in the same social activities (DeLuca, 1988; DeVoe, 1999; Solomon, 1998). Men have traditionally used informal networks to help move ahead professionally. As more women reach middle management positions, they have found such contacts unavailable to them (DeWine and Casbolt, 1983; Ibarra, 1997). As one author observes, the service industry's challenge is to "open its doors for female executives all the way to the board room—which is still very much an all-male arena" (Marshall, 1989: 19; see also Andorka, 1998). Bernstein (1990) agrees, noting a study where at least four out of five of one thousand corporate executives conceded that "stereotyping and preconceptions by men were blocking women from reaching top management" (51). As Leonard Roberts, chairman and chief executive officer of Shoney's, Inc., said to his chain's top management: "Wake up and smell the coffee. She isn't making it anymore" (as cited in Bernstein 1990: 29).

Another problem women face as a result of their poor representation in upper-level management is the lack of appropriate role models. Laura Hayden, personnel director of Pizza Hut, noted in an interview that role models for women simply aren't there at the corporate level—at least not in the hospitality industry, at least not yet (Peters, 1988). Although women have the option of turning to men as their models and mentors, as Peters explains, "subtle social and sexual pressures can make women feel uncomfortable in these relationships" (128).

Although women in organizations face numerous challenges, the symbolic/cultural approach provides a means of identifying and addressing some of the most pressing issues. The next section of this chapter provides some suggestions for how individuals can influence organizational cultures so that the environments in which they work promote healthy communication between men and women. First, you'll be introduced to Sylvia and Cassie, managers at The Fortune. Then, you'll discover how listening, verbal communication, and nonverbal behavior can be used to modify organizational culture.

Gender and Communication: Modifying Culture

Gender and Communication at The Fortune

The Fortune Hotel, one of several well-established, smaller but exclusive hotels in Chicago, has a long tradition of quality and service. The Fortune's culture is strong, and over 40 percent of its salaried employees have been with the organization for more than 10 years. Ned Goldman, general manager, has made several significant changes within the past five years. One of the most striking was to hire two women managers, Sylvia Thorz and Cassie Brown. Although rumor has it that Ned was under a lot of pressure from his peers in other properties to demonstrate his commitment to equal opportunity, his staff never knew for sure. In any event, the long-standing tradition of an all-male management team had been permanently disrupted.

Clearly, both women were well qualified for their positions. Sylvia, Food and Beverage Manager, received her Bachelor of Science degree in Hotel Administration from the University of Nevada, Las Vegas. Prior to joining The Fortune she had been the Assistant Banquet Sales Manager at the Beverly Wilshire Hotel in Dallas. Soft spoken and somewhat shy, Sylvia nevertheless had proven to be a very capable and employee-centered manager. Her staff loved her because she was so committed to their welfare.

Cassie was hired five years ago as Assistant Manager of Marketing for The Fortune, having earned an MBA from Dartmouth and having spent two years at Lever Brothers, Inc., in their Marketing Department. After years of hard work at The Fortune, she was passed over for a promotion to Director of Public Relations when Sid Adams retired after 38 years at The Fortune. Although Cassie filed no formal grievance, she did speak out and questioned Ned's decision in hiring an old college buddy of his to replace Sid. She criticized The Fortune's corporate philosophy and questioned whether there were any opportunities for women—especially black women—to be successful within such a male-dominated culture. Soon she had a reputation as a troublemaker. Her behavior seemed to strengthen the opinion most of her colleagues shared; women do well as front desk attendants and servers, but keep them out of management!

One of the strongest aspects of The Fortune's culture was its regular meetings, held every Tuesday morning. As the eleven-member management team convened, the sound of jokes and good-natured bantering could be heard down the hall. "Hey, Steve," Jeff Car, the front desk manager, said as he grabbed the arm of The Fortune's new director of finance. "Listen to this." As Jeff turned around he saw Sylvia taking a seat across the room. "Well, maybe I'd better wait on that one. We don't want to offend any of our colleagues—right Sylvia?" The two men laughed as they went back to the table. Sylvia caught Cassie's eye and she shook her head. She could tell it was going to be one of those days, and began fidgeting with her bracelet.

"You have met the better-looking members of our team, haven't you?" Jeff said as he motioned to the women at the table. "Yes," Steve nodded. "I've had the pleasure." "Well, we'll fill you in on what really goes on around here when we hit the 19th hole next Saturday! These girls may look . . ." Jeff was stopped abruptly by the loud thump of Ned's hand hitting the table as he brought the group to order. The meeting was a long one, as usual, drawn out by discussions that wandered from the main issue and by the fact that Ned, although a solid business person, was not a particularly good discussion leader. After over an hour of reports and various debates, Ned pushed back his chair. "All right gentlemen," Ned began. "I know this has been long, but I think we've about come to the end." He looked down for a moment at his agenda. "Hold it," he said with emphasis, "I almost forgot. We've got one last item on the agenda. It's a problem that Sylvia is having with several of her employees. Sylvia, why don't you explain your problem to the rest of us?"

Sylvia could feel herself becoming angry, not only at the way Ned was presenting her situation to the rest of the management team, but also because both times in the past when she had proposed a discussion topic, it had been put at the very end of Ned's agenda. In spite of her anger, she took a deep breath, smiled, and began. "You all know Karen Duncan, one of our most loyal employees. She came in to talk with me last week about a concern she has with the way our guests have been treating the barmaids. Ever since the staff began wearing, ah, those new uniforms, verbal abuse—which they always had to put up with to some extent—has drastically increased. They're just, ah, I don't think they're appropriate. Last week a guest, um, actually pulled Maria Lorenz onto his lap and wouldn't let her up. I guess she was really frightened and refused to work the late-night shift again.

"Anyway, the employees, well, the employees attribute some of the problem to their new uniforms. They think the short, low-cut uniforms invite suggestive comments and more aggressive behavior. And, well," Sylvia looked down at the table but continued, "Karen even suggested that, um, a couple of the F and B assistant managers were giving the women a hard time. So," she rushed on, "I've been asked to discuss this with you and, um, see if we can't propose some action plan."

"I'll give them a little action," Tony, the F and B manager, quipped. Several of his buddies chuckled. "I wish I had problems like that," Jeff commented. "All those cute girls down at the bar won't have anything to do with me—heaven knows I've tried!"

"Okay, okay, guys," Ned said as he raised his hand to quiet the group. "Sylvia needs help, and the least we can do is make some suggestions."

If you want my opinion," Tony said as he leaned back in his chair, "it's the way the girls act toward the guests, not the uniforms. If they want to be treated like professionals, they need to act like professionals. I've seen them strutting around down there in the bar myself. What do they expect? They're dealing with men who are away from home, who have been working hard all day. Those barmaids are just what the doctor ordered.

"In fact," Tony continued, leaning forward in his chair, "Remember Marge? Well, she was one of our best barmaids. Used to sit on the table and laugh at all the bad jokes. When her customers were ready to leave, she'd give them this pink note that said, 'Hurry back now.' She knew how to increase business."

Cassie had been silent, listening to the conversation. She could see that Sylvia was about to cry—or leave the room—and wondered what she could say that would help. She raised her hand. Ned seemed to look past her as he took suggestions from two more managers. Finally Cassie had had enough. "Ned," she said with irritation, "I know you don't care what I think, but I've been trying to present my opinion and I wondered if you could be quiet and listen."

"Right on, Cassie," Mark said with a grin. "Go for it."

"You men are insensitive jerks. What is the matter with you? Sylvia has brought up a very legitimate problem and you guys just think it's funny. What does it take to get your serious attention?"

"More coffee!" Tony said as he stood up. "And more time. I think we've had enough for one meeting. Tell you what, Sylvia. I'll sleep on it." There were a few isolated chuckles from the group and he continued, "and let you know what I think next week."

Others quickly agreed that the meeting had gone on too long already, and Ned offered no resistance. "Fine," Ned said in closing. "See you next Tuesday."

Sylvia and Cassie walked out of the room together. Although they had seemed eager to adjourn, most of the others stood around and shared reactions to the recent hockey game. Although Sylvia and Cassie had both been with The Fortune almost five years, they still felt as if they were the "new kids on the block" when it came to the tight old boy network that had been in existence when they arrived. Golf on Saturdays, bowling Thursday nights, racquetball on noon hours—there was a whole world from which they were excluded. Upset by the events of the meeting and annoyed to discover that no one was really in any hurry to get back to work, Sylvia and Cassie headed for Cassie's office so they could talk in private.

Communication Behavior and Organizational Culture

Sylvia and Cassie were frustrated in their efforts to communicate with their male colleagues. The Fortune's culture is strong; an old boy network has been well established, and the women's efforts to gain credibility will obviously be hard won. The male managers seem friendly, but discounted Sylvia's problems or made them low priorities. Both she and Cassie felt frustrated and resented the attitudes they perceived were keeping them from participating fully in their professional activities. Do you think this situation still exists in many organizations? Unfortunately, it does. Do you think there's hope?

The answer to the second question may depend on how you view the situation. Some consultants or theorists would suggest redesigning the organization's structure. Others would recommend that Ned make a strong policy regarding gender issues. Others may advocate changes in the formal communication systems. Once again, we will take a symbolic/cultural perspective and argue that, indeed, Sylvia and Cassie can modify The Fortune's culture through their own communication behaviors. By gradually leading their colleagues to new interpretations of how "women managers" at The Fortune behave, they can facilitate a change toward more constructive patterns of interaction between men and women.

We know that organizational culture can be modified or changed. Recall that culture is learned or negotiated through communicative events. As a new manager, Steve gained a number of insights from the meeting. One of the strongest may have pertained to what it means to be a woman manager—or employee—at The Fortune. In order to change culture, Sylvia and Cassie must begin to change the way in which other employees think about women managers and, subsequently, the way they act toward women managers.

The most productive way to begin redefining what it means to be a woman manager is through their own communication behaviors. In essence, Sylvia and Cassie need to create new definitions of what gender means in the context of The Fortune. They must change organizational members' assumptions so that their vision of a fair, equitable workplace is realized.

Although changing culture isn't easy, there are actions that Sylvia and Cassie can take to make a difference in their organization's culture. The next section examines three aspects of communication: listening, verbal communication, and nonverbal behavior. Each is discussed as it could be used to modify aspects of The Fortune's culture.

Listening. Individuals who influence their organizations do a great deal of listening. As you discovered earlier, it is through effective listening that new and long-time employees learn the values, assumptions, priorities, and expectations of other organizational members. Only when members align their actions and activities can an organization move forward to accomplish its larger goals.

Active listening, therefore, is important to understand culture accurately. We have discussed how definitions of gender—what it "means" to be "male or female"—are embedded in a culture. It is essential, therefore, that employees first listen in order to determine exactly what definitions currently exist. As we discussed earlier, men and women may hold different views regarding appropriate gender-related behavior. It is possible that men and women may view the same action, but interpret it differently. Therefore, both men and women in organizations must listen carefully to each other so that differences in perceptions are recognized and addressed.

If Sylvia and Cassie listen carefully, they will quickly realize that the men exclude them from conversations and that the nature of these conversations makes it almost impossible for the women to participate. Nonverbal communication, too, is important to observe; nonverbal cues—winks, laughing, holding on to an arm, nudging, and other signs of camaraderie—suggest an "in" group.

The women also notice that Ned put Sylvia's request at the end of his agenda. When he finally raises the issue, his language suggests that "Sylvia has a problem" and that she "needs help" from the others. Sylvia has the impression, from the conversation, that no one takes the problem seriously; in fact, some of the others do not even define the situation she describes as a problem at all.

These women must first make sure that they understand organizational members' perspectives—in this case, the attitudes and assumptions they want to change. Then, they can move on to choosing appropriate verbal and nonverbal communication strategies.

Verbal Behavior. Sylvia and Cassie can begin right away to model the verbal behavior and style they believe will best communicate a professional image to their peers. If they want organizational members to think of women as competent and credible, then they need to examine their own behaviors. What verbal behaviors did each woman demonstrate at the management meeting? Do you think that Sylvia and Cassie demonstrated effective communication skills?

Unfortunately, neither Sylvia nor Cassie made a good impression on the group. First, Sylvia was so passive that her agenda item almost didn't get discussed. When she was asked to describe the situation, her speech was full of nonfluencies and hesitations that reduced the impact of her ideas. In addition, when the group began to get rowdy, she did nothing and let Ned step in to maintain control of the group. Similarly, when Tony suggested the problem was with the barmaids not the guests, she said nothing. It is not surprising that when male managers observe this kind of behavior from one of a very few women managers, they form assumptions that inevitably undermine the women's ability to be effective in the workplace.

Yet Cassie's behavior was no more productive. Although she spoke out, her hostility and anger were inappropriate. By opening with "I know you don't care what I think," she set the stage for an adversarial relationship. Then, rather than assertively stating her position, she resorted to name calling, referring to her colleagues as "insensitive jerks."

Professional women on the job learn to assert themselves in ways that reduce defensive communication. They are concerned with the quality of their relationships and work to develop "collegiality" as well as credibility. They seek opportunities, such as the one Sylvia had, to demonstrate their ability to analyze situations and problem solve. As Sylvia and Cassie change the way they communicate, they will begin to change the impressions their colleagues have of them. Slowly, their peers will begin to make more positive associations regarding what it means to be a woman manager at The Fortune.

Culture is also transmitted through stories like the one Tony told about Marge. If you think about this story in light of the symbolic/cultural perspective, you'll see that it perpetuates a particular framework and communicates to others expectations regarding how a "good" barmaid at The Fortune behaves. If Sylvia and Cassie want to change The Fortune's culture, one way to go about it is to begin telling different stories, stories that illustrate how effective barmaids handle difficult situations. Clearly, the story Sylvia and Cassie would tell may not resemble the one Tony passed along.

In addition to modifying their verbal behavior, Sylvia and Cassie can also use nonverbal communication to establish their credibility and change the men's perceptions about their female colleagues.

Nonverbal Communication. Organizational members send messages through their appearance, their office furnishings, their gestures and posture, their facial expressions, eye contact, touching, and possessions. No wonder the expression "You cannot not communicate" is repeated so frequently.

Often, individuals' nonverbal communication is unintentional and unplanned. Sylvia, for instance, probably didn't realize that by fidgeting with her bracelet she was sending messages about her anxiety and insecurity. It's likely she didn't give much thought to the seat she took at the table, or her eye contact as her glance moved quickly around the room.

Over two decades ago, Dowling (1981) was among those who noted that women in organizations tend simply to do a good job day after day, assuming that their work will be recognized and rewarded. Many of those in higher level management positions got there because they were at the right place at the right time—their career movement was more coincidence than the realization of personal goals. Unlike those who wait patiently for something to happen, individuals who want to improve communication between men and women must take deliberate actions.

Sylvia might also examine her office after the meeting. Has she hung her degrees on the wall? Does the office communicate orderliness and efficiency? Or are there obvious signs of confusion and a mixture of personal and professional items?

Revisiting The Fortune

At the moment, being a woman in management at The Fortune means that male managers probably don't listen to you. It means that you are excluded from important conversations, and that no one really values your ideas. It may also mean that you get the least desirable office, the weekend shifts, and the late lunch breaks. Although Steve came from a work environment where he was supervised by a woman, he is quickly learning that at The Fortune, women managers aren't taken seriously. Although he empathizes with Sylvia and Cassie, he doesn't feel in a position to speak out. After a few months, he may not even notice that they are discounted by their colleagues because he will have become accustomed to "the way things are" at The Fortune.

Culture cannot be changed overnight. By modifying their communication behavior, however, Sylvia and Cassie can move a long way toward gaining equal status in the workplace. First, they must listen carefully to understand fully just how other organizational members interpret their role. Then, by telling different stories and responding in a more appropriate way to the incidents that arise, they can begin to alter the way they are perceived by their peers. Although their male counterparts may now assume that they are somehow less capable, the women are in a position to redefine currently held meanings and modify the beliefs organizational members hold. By intentionally using nonverbal communication to communicate their professionalism and competence, Sylvia and Cassie can begin to change organizational members' understanding of what it means to be a woman manager at The Fortune.

CONCLUSION

You should now be able to use the symbolic/cultural approach to analyze the way men and women communicate in organizations. The symbolic/cultural approach focuses on the meanings of gender that are created through symbolic action, and how these meanings subsequently affect organizational members' behavior. This perspective is particularly appropriate because it suggests that an individual's choice of communication strategy can, over time, have a direct impact on an organization's culture.

Communication between the genders in the hospitality industry is particularly challenging because of several unique aspects of the industry. Irregular hours, close proximity among employees, and guests' expectations all affect gender and communication. Symbols associated with hospitality organizations—bedrooms, bars, and parties—contribute to the difficulties women may have in maintaining a work environment where their professional contributions are recognized and rewarded.

Women are entering the hospitality workforce at an unprecedented rate; greater numbers are also moving into management positions. To be successful in traditionally male-dominated environments, both men and women must learn and practice appropriate communication behaviors. The need for effective listening will increase as men and women negotiate their respective roles and expectations in each organizational context. Those who are able to "listen to their organization's culture" will be in the best position to take appropriate actions and make appropriate decisions.

If an ideal culture is one in which men and women are treated with equity and fairness, then organizational members can best promote this kind of environment by deliberately managing some of the most apparent culture indicators. They can begin to tell stories to new employees that reinforce desirable behaviors and attitudes. They can choose symbols—both verbal and nonverbal—that represent their vision of what the organization should be like. Through their artifacts, actions, and words, men and women in the 1990s can create a workplace characterized by mutual respect and understanding.

For Further Discussion

1. In what ways are other work environments—a second grade classroom, a construction site, a spa, other places you have been—"sexualized"? What effect does this have on communication?
2. Given that harassment has been called a "receiver defined" activity, can the meaning of "harassment" ever be completely shared—especially across cultural boundaries?
3. How are sexual stereotypes changing? How can women—or men—facilitate positive change to overcome outdated or dysfunctional stereotypes?
4. If you were to design a training program to help both men and women establish a healthy, respectful, and productive organizational culture, what topics and skills training would you include?

References

Albrecht, K., and R. Zemke. 1985. *Service America—Doing Business in the New Economy.* Homewood, IL: Dow-Jones Irwin.

Andorka, F. H. 1998. Women gaining leadership roles. *Hotel and Motel Management* 213(16): 54–55.

Arliss, L. 1991. *Gender Communication.* Englewood Cliffs, NJ: Prentice-Hall.

Axtell, R. E. 1990. Culture shock: The "S" word. *Meetings and Conventions* 25(3): 132.

Barnard, C. 1938. *The Functions of the Executive.* Cambridge, MA: Harvard University Press.

Barrington, M. N., and M. Olsen. 1987. Concept of service in the hospitality industry. *International Journal of Hospitality Management* 3(6): 131–138.

Bass, B. M. 1991. From transactional to transformational leadership: Learning to share the vision. *Organizational Dynamics* 19: 19–31.

Baytosh, C. M., and B. H. Kleiner. 1989. Effective business communication for women. *Equal Opportunities International* 8(4): 16–19.

Bernstein, C. 1990. Unified effort vital to women's advancement; Stereotypes remain barrier to the executive suite. *Nations Restaurant News* 24: 29.

Bolman, L. G., and T. E. Deal. 1984. *Modern Approaches to Understanding and Managing Organizations.* San Francisco: Jossey-Bass.

Chase, R. B. 1978. Where does the customer fit in a service operation? *Harvard Business Review* 43: 137–142.

Davidow, W. H., and B. Uttal. 1989. Service companies: Focus or falter. *Harvard Business Review* 4: 77–85.

Davis, H. A. 1998. Sex and the workplace: Part II. *Restaurant Hospitality* 82(8): 130–134.

DeLuca, M. 1988. Female lodging executives dealing with glass ceiling. *Hotel and Motel Management* 203(15): 10.

DeVoe, D. 1999. Gender issues range from salary disparities to harassment. *InfoWorld* 21(44): 78–79.

DeWine, S., and D. Casbolt. 1983. Networking: External communication systems for female organizational members. *The Journal of Business Communication* 20(2): 57–67.

Dowling, C. 1981. *The Cinderella Complex.* New York: Summit Books, Inc.

Eller, M. E. 1989. Sexual harassment. Prevention, not protection. *Cornell Hotel and Restaurant Administration Quarterly* 30(4): 84–89.

Frank, A., and J. Brownell. 1989. *Organizational Communication and Behavior. Communicating for Improved Performance (2+2 = 5).* New York: Holt, Rinehart, and Winston.

Gregg, J. B., and P. M. Johnson. 1990. Perceptions of discrimination among women as managers in hospitality organizations. *FIU Hospitality Review* 8(1): 10–22.

Gruber, J. E. 1998. The impact of male work environments and organizational policies on women's experiences of sexual harassment. *Gender and Society* 12(3): 301–320.

Gutek, B. A., A. G. Cohen, and A. M. Konrad. 1990. Predicting social-sexual behavior at work: A contact hypothesis. *Academy of Management Journal* 33(3): 560–577.

Hackett, E., P. H. Mirvis, and A. L. Sales. 1991. Women's and men's expectations about the effects of new technology at work. *Group and Organization Studies* 16(1): 60–85.

Herrick, J. W. 1999. Office stories and what they tell us about gender in the workplace. *Journal of Business and Technical Communication* 13(3): 274–296.

Ibarra, H. 1997. Paving an alternative route: Gender differences in managerial networks. *Social Psychology Quarterly* 60(1): 91–102.

Katz, D., and R. Kahn. 1966. *The Social Psychology of Organizations.* New York: Wiley.

Kenton, S. B. 1989. Speaker credibility in persuasive business communication: A model which explains gender. *The Journal of Business Communication* 26(2): 143–156.

Konrad, A. M., and K. Cannings. 1997. The effects of gender role congruence and statistical discrimination on managerial advancement. *Human Relations* 50(10): 1305–1328.

Kreps, G. L. 1990. *Organizational Communication: Theory and Practice.* New York: Longman.

Louis, M. R. 1980. Surprise and sense-making: What newcomers experience when entering unfamiliar organizational settings. *Administrative Science Quarterly* 23: 225–251.

Marshall, A. 1989. Women: The best solution to industry's talent shortage. *Hotel and Motel Management* 204(16): 18–19, 48.

Mayo, E. 1933. *The Human Problems of Industrial Civilization.* New York: Macmillan.

McGregor, D. 1960. *The Human Side of Enterprise.* New York: McGraw-Hill.

Miller, J. C. 1972. Living systems: The organization. *Behavioral Science* 17: 1–182.

Mills, P. K., and J. H. Morris. 1986. Clients as "partial" employees of service organizations: Role development in client participation. *Academy of Management Review* 11: 726–735.

Nelsen, B. J. 1990. Perceptions of sexism in F and B oriented corporations. *Lodging* 15(5): 51–52.

Nozar, R. 1990. Winking at sexual harassment demeans lodging. *Hotel and Motel Management* 205(7): 6–7.

Pearson, J. C. 1985. *Gender and Communication.* Dubuque, IA: William C. Brown.

Peters, J. 1988. Bridging the gender gap: RB women's council challenges the status quo. *Restaurant Business* 87(13): 115–131.

Powell, G. N. 1989. Male/female work roles: What kind of future? *Personnel* 66(7): 47–50.

Richardson, H. L. 1999. Women lead in style. *Transportation and Distribution* 40(4): 78–82.

Rowe, M. 1999. When will women hit the top? *Lodging Hospitality* 55(13): 39–42.

Shinew, K. J., and M. L. Arnold. 1998. Gender equity in the leisure services field. *Journal of Leisure Research* 30(2): 177–194.

Solomon, C. M. 1998. Women are still undervalued: Bridge the parity gap. *Workforce* 77(5): 78–86.

VanDer Wall, S. 2000. Internal affairs: The abuse of power, sexual harassment, and hypocrisy in the workplace. *HRMagazine* 45(1): 132–134.

Weber, M. 1947. *The Theory of Social and Economic Organization*, A. Henderson and T. Parsons, trans. New York: Free Press.

Wood, J. T. 1994. *Gendered Lives: Communication, Gender, and Culture.* Belmont, CA: Wadsworth.

Worsfold, P. 1989. A personality profile of the hotel manager. *International Journal of Hospitality Management* (1)8: 51–62.

CHAPTER 17

Women in News
Television and New Media

Marcia Rock
Sheila Stainback
Julie Adams

POINTS TO BE ADDRESSED

- Paternalism in the television news industry
- Obstacles to gender equality in the industry
- Challenges to male dominance
- Women in new media

INITIAL OBSTACLES

The story of women in the media is the story of latent gender prejudice by a male-dominated industry slowly changed by the women in the industry fighting for their rights. Those women were supported by the Women's Movement, the adoption of the word "sex" in the Civil Rights Act, and government pressure to enforce Equal Employment Opportunity policies. It is also the story of the women in the industry becoming aware of the image of women on television and trying to make that image better reflect reality. This chapter will focus on the women who were pioneers in the broadcast news industry, the challenges they faced, and their methods for change; it will also look at women's obstacles to advancement to the highest level and survey the impact of women working in new media.

Women first entered broadcast journalism during World War II when Edward R. Murrow needed radio reporters overseas. The women were hired on an ad hoc basis. Only a few were allowed to narrate their own stories because the male management in New York thought women's voices lacked authority. Few women were offered jobs after the war when the men came home. One exception was Pauline Frederick.

After Frederick graduated from college in the 1930s, she worked for the *Washington Star* interviewing the wives of diplomats. A woman at NBC thought these columns would make good radio features and hired Frederick on a freelance basis. It was the practice of the news media then to have the few women journalists cover "women's" topics like women celebrities, fashion, and food. After the war, Frederick worked for ABC doing stories on the shortage of nylon stockings and how to get a husband, even though she had not managed to do that for herself. Her break came when none of the men wanted to cover the United Nations and she did. ABC would only use her voice, though, if she got an exclusive. Otherwise a man would record the audio track.

When television came along and convention coverage was extremely competitive, ABC hired her to interview the candidates' wives. At that time, how one should look on television was of major import to Frederick:

> One of her concerns was wondering how one was supposed to look on television. The only information she could get out of the network was not to wear black, white, or red. As for makeup, no one had any information at all. So she scurried over to Elizabeth Arden's to ask if they could help. They knew nothing about television either, but outfitted her with a kit of makeup suitable for still photography which they hoped would work. When she got to Philadelphia and the two conventions, she found that not only did she have to do her own makeup and interview the likes of Helen Gahagan Douglas and Mrs. Harold Stassen, but she found she was expected to do their makeup too, and she did. (Sanders and Rock, 1988: 10)

The women who worked behind the scenes during the war and then continued afterwards to build their careers fared a bit better. They did not have to fight the prejudice against the female voice, and because female expectations of success were limited, the women were grateful for being hired at any level. One would think that today the public accepts women's voices and that the old prejudice has been laid to rest. In 1986 the Screen Actor's Guild commissioned a study to rebuke that prejudice still held by advertising agencies who prefer men to women in voice-overs (the off-camera voice in commercials). The study, conducted by McCollum/Spielman, found that "it makes absolutely no difference whether a male or female voice is used as a commercial voice-over." In fact, the data indicated that "women are more effective presenters" (McCollum/Spielman, 1986). This study was conducted by recording two commercials with both female and male voice-overs. The test audience, composed of males and females, was then asked to select a brand for inclusion in a prize market basket. Eleven percent responded to the male voice and 12 percent responded to the female voice for the Listerine product.

Forty-two percent responded to the male voice and 46 percent responded to the female voice in the Nestlé Morsels commercial. This study also found that the respondents were not very much aware of whether the voice was male or female. The study implies that the voice could readily be female rather than the customary male voice. An updated version of this survey was released in 2000 with similar results (Screen Actor's Guild, 1986/2000).

Female reporters' voices are now accepted and female anchors' voices are accepted on local television news, cable news, and network news magazines. It is still being debated whether a woman's voice could hold the nation's attention in the main anchor position on the network news broadcasts, although it is not unusual to see women filling in during the week, as Diane Sawyer has done from time to time on ABC. From 1993 to 1995, Connie Chung was coanchor of what was then called the *CBS Evening News with Dan Rather and Connie Chung*. During that time, Chung covered the historic Israeli-PLO signing ceremony in the Middle East and gained an exclusive interview with Chinese leader Li Peng, five years after the Tienenmen Square massacre. However, Chung was unceremoniously dropped from the coanchor position due to faltering ratings and eventually left CBS to adopt and raise her infant son. Chung joined ABC in 1997 as coanchor and correspondent for the newsmagazine, *20/20* (ABCNews.com). A growing number of women are entering journalism, much more so than men, with a majority of students who graduated with undergraduate degrees in journalism being female—63 percent in 1998 (Becker and Kosicki, 1999).

PATERNALISM

Another attitude that women broadcast journalists faced is paternalism. Male supervisors, with the self-image of father/protector, often feel uncomfortable sending women into dangerous situations or being in dangerous situations with a woman. Correspondent Betsy Aaron believed this was true because there was a lingering fear on the part of management that the death of a female correspondent would be more embarrassing to the network than the loss of a man (Aaron, 1986). One way women worked around this problem was to do feature stories in war zones and dangerous areas.

In the early 1980s, Aaron went overseas to do a story on the plight of Amerasian children. While she was praised for her work, she says it never seemed to earn her the right to go back without having to fight for the opportunity. Despite Aaron's track record of dangerous overseas assignments, Ted Koppel asked if she had her husband's permission to go to Lebanon.

By the 1990s, there were some gains. CNN's chief international correspondent, Christiane Amanpour, has worked in many of the world's hot spots during the 1990s, including Afghanistan, Bosnia-Herzegovina, Iran, Haiti, Algeria, and Rwanda, receiving wide acclaim for her coverage of the conflict in Yugoslavia. Amanpour's work earned CNN its first prestigious DuPont award in 1985. The other networks and cable channels have not hesitated to send women to cover wars and armed conflicts. They include from CBS: Vicki Mabrey and Martha Teichner; from ABC: Sheila McVicar, Gillian Findlay, and Hillary Brown; Rita Cosby from the Fox News Channel; and from NBC News, Katie Couric.

Another problem that women correspondents and producers have in competing with men on international assignments is sustaining a meaningful personal life. Male correspondents, then and now, often have their families with them on a foreign assignment. Their presence provides a refuge and helps make a stressful life bearable. When women began to cover foreign news, few could find that kind of comfort. The women who become foreign correspondents are almost always single (Sanders and Rock, 1988). Amanpour married, though, and became pregnant while covering U.S. action in Kosovo in 1999. Her husband, former U.S. State Department spokesman James Rubin, resigned his position in 2000 to join Amanpour in her London base, to play "Mr. Mom" (*The New York Times*, 2000). When CNN's Eileen O'Connor was based in Moscow for that network, she was not only married to the bureau chief, but became pregnant and gave birth to several children. However, network news outlets during the 1990s, with the exception of CNN, have reduced their commitment to international coverage, and such assignments are no longer prized with their de-emphasis (*Women, Men and Media*, 1997).

FAMILY AND CAREER

Many women prefer local news specifically because it does not require much travel. The hours may be long but it is possible to see your family every day. Network correspondents have to make some difficult choices. Lesley Stahl joined CBS News in 1972 as a Washington-based reporter. She is married and had a daughter while in her late thirties. Caring for her daughter affected her career choices. In 1986 she wouldn't consider a *60 Minutes* assignment, "because I have a child and it would be a sacrifice . . ." (Stahl, 1986). The *60 Minutes* correspondents are on the road about 70 percent of the time. By 1991, Stahl obviously felt ready for the assignment when she replaced another woman, Meredith Viera. Viera was taken off the show because she was pregnant with her second child and wanted another year of part-time work. Viera had just completed two seasons of part-time work to care for her first child, and Don Hewitt, the executive producer of *60 Minutes*, felt that was enough. He had agreed to the part-time arrangement for her first child but he needed a full-time correspondent to replace the retiring Harry Reasoner and could not extend that arrangement for another year (Daley, 1991). Some feminists argued that CBS should consider time-sharing and hire several women for that position, but Hewitt maintained that "the program is built around the idea that viewers would become familiar with five top-flight journalists seen almost every week" (Daley, 1991: C16).

Viera was not fired but was not immediately reassigned either. At age 37, she felt trapped by her predicament: "If I don't have children now, I'm not sure

I can do it later . . . But if I had kids earlier, I'm not sure I could have established myself" (Daley, 1991: C16). Viera's concerns were understandable. Viera has since gone on to what she has called "the perfect job" as a co-host of the mid-morning talk show, *The View*, which not only allows her to see her three children off to school, but also to be home when they return.

White House correspondent Andrea Mitchell, now married to Federal Board chairman Alan Greenspan, has no children. In a 1986 interview, she was not sure the ambitious women of her generation made all the right choices and thought perhaps they were too available to their jobs. But she thinks ambitious women are not treated the same way as ambitious men.

> Sometimes I think women get criticized in subtle and not so subtle ways for being aggressive or ambitious. We're called pushy, bitchy, if we pursue a line of questioning at the White House aggressively. I get dumped on by the press secretary, but if Bill Plante [CBS News] or Sam Donaldson [ABC News] do it, it's OK. It's really a matter of male expectations that we behave in a certain way. (Mitchell, 1986)

The greatest complaint by young women correspondents and producers is their feeling of being out of control. After facing intense competition to get their jobs and after working hard to get promoted, they find themselves having to make difficult choices between their careers and their families. According to a finding by the *The New York Times* in 1986, only 35 to 40 percent of successful women over forty had children as compared to 93 percent of their male colleagues (Basler, 1986: 159).

Local Chicago reporter Renee Ferguson of WMAQ encountered more problems on an interpersonal rather than on an organizational level when she was pregnant and a correspondent for CBS. She did not feel she was as strong a presence in an interview: "When I go on a story I approach people with a certain strength, power that's important to me. I felt more vulnerable while pregnant, less powerful. It changed the way I'd walk into the room." She overcame that and worked as long as she could before taking an early maternity leave because, "People started to cover for me. I felt I was imposing so I left." Ferguson sees a change in attitude toward day-care and maternity leave when more women are in management and can make decisions on company policy and flexible time arrangements (Ferguson, 1986).

Having women in supervisory positions does not necessarily ensure better treatment. Former ABC producer Betsy Rich decided to leave the news business because of her treatment by another woman. She had been on the road for over a week and was told that she would have to go to Washington, D.C., to edit the story. Her senior producer was enraged that Rich refused to go because she wanted to see her child (Rich, 1986; 1988).

Sometimes Rich feels the women's movement put too much pressure on young women to prove that they could have it all. "It sounds strange, but I feel I was sold a bill of goods to come to expect I could have everything" (Rich, 1988).

Fighting for Rights

In the 1970s, the few women in broadcasting faced similar problems to those of women in publishing: pay equity, promotion, and a clear policy on maternity leave. Women at *Newsweek* filed a complaint with the state attorney general's office in 1970, newswomen negotiated changes in their Newspaper Guild contracts in 1972, and the National Organization for Women (NOW) filed a petition with the Federal Communications Commission (FCC) asking that broadcast licensees be required to file affirmative action reports regarding the employment of women in 1970.

In 1969 the FCC agreed to add the word "sex" to various antidiscrimination rulings they already had, and in May 1971 a new requirement was added to the license renewal process: television stations were to file affirmative action plans for women with their application (Sanders and Rock, 1988). Stations had to go beyond merely not discriminating on the basis of race, creed, or sex; they had to take steps to hire women and minorities to remedy the effect of past practices. NOW's strategy for change was to challenge the broadcast licenses of some of the stations in major markets, which were owned and operated by the networks, and thus get the publicity about these issues. NOW claimed that the stations did not act in the "public interest," and thus violated the mandate by the Federal Communications Commission when awarded a television license. Attorney Nancy Stanley outlined the following violations in 1971: under the standards of equal employment opportunity, women on the staffs of the stations were underrepresented, underemployed, and underpaid; the stations' ascertainment process (evaluating the community's programming needs) was incomplete because they did not include women as a significant community group; and the stations violated the Fairness Doctrine, a provision that stated a licensee has an affirmative duty to present contrasting views of an issue in its overall programming, because the role of women in society is a bona fide controversial issue of public importance and licensees were not portraying contrasting views of that role in their overall programming (Stanley, 1971).

NOW challenged stations WRC in Washington, D.C., and WABC in New York City, two network flagship stations whose prominence would draw a lot of media attention. Litigation began in 1972. NOW claimed that WRC had very few women employed in management, technical positions, and sales, and had discriminatory policies on wages and maternity leave. It charged that WABC consistently failed to report serious women's issues and, after studying ABC programs for two years, complained that women were portrayed in disparaging roles.

Neither license renewal challenge was successful, but the four years of litigation brought publicity to NOW's grievances. Change came indirectly as a result of these legal actions. Stations around the country started hiring women and became aware of their female employees' problems. "Consciousness-raising," a new phrase in the language, was forced on the television brass. They began to look around, not only at how their own companies were run, but also at the articulate, able women lawyers facing them across the table. Interestingly, station legal departments became receptive to women, and that was one area where changes took place rather rapidly (Sanders and Rock, 1988).

At the network level, change came more slowly. Women did not have the legal avenue of license renewal challenges because networks are not licensed by the government as are individual television stations. But the networks were covered by a Labor Department ruling that required that such companies draw up affirmative action programs to remedy the underutilization of women. Organizing the women at networks was not easy because the companies were large and encompassed women on all different levels, from secretaries to correspondents. ABC women were organized indirectly through the license challenge of the local ABC station in New York City. NOW charged that Channel 7 had not hired or promoted enough women. The station replied it couldn't find qualified people. Lawyers for the women's group turned to several network women for consultation.

During all this, a female executive at ABC stated that no woman had ever complained about any problems at the network. The ABC women suddenly realized that they needed to speak up, but first they had to get together and find out what was wrong. That's when the women realized that they had no avenue of communication and no place to meet. The first solution was to put notices in the place they all frequented, the lavatory. Eventually the newly formed Women's Action Committee (WAC) got permission to post notices and use board rooms for meetings. Their grievances were generic: women were not given job postings; women had to wait longer in line than men for promotions; they were frustrated because outside men, often younger and with less experience, were brought in for them to train for jobs the women should have had; they faced an unresponsive personnel department; they felt deep disappointment with being stuck in dead-end jobs; and salary discrepancies.

It was common for men to be hired from the outside for the same level job as a woman, but at higher pay. The myth went that a woman didn't "need" the money. Perhaps her husband had a good job, or maybe she was single and didn't need that much. The WAC felt salaries should reflect individual worth, not someone's uninformed speculation on another's needs. When men negotiate salary, no chart is made of their family obligations. How many single women support elderly parents, assist younger siblings in college, or are saving for their old age—or just plain deserve to be paid well? (Sanders and Rock, 1988).

The ABC group had a few triumphs. They got job postings even though many jobs were filled before posting. ABC hired a manager to recruit minorities and women. An informal employee grievance committee procedure was established wherein a woman (or a man for that matter) with a complaint against a boss did not have to face him alone, but could call on a WAC member to accompany the complainant to a meeting with her (or his) superior.

The most difficult attitudinal problem to solve was deep-seated cronyism. Women were not members of the "old boys club," were not on the lunch and golf circuit with them, had not come through the same employment route, and were, therefore, not considered for some of the top jobs. After a protracted series of discussions, management agreed that some kind of sensitivity training was needed.

There were several specific accomplishments by the WAC. In 1972, when it was organized, two women held the title of vice president and only half a dozen women, exclusive of performers, earned more than $20,000 a year. The female portion of the broadcasting division totaled just under 30 percent. By mid-1975, the proportion of women was up to 32 percent and approximately fifty women on the talent payroll earned more than $20,000 a year. There were still only two vice presidents, but there was a female corporate officer and a woman was put on the board of directors. Those gains were not astounding by any means, but were at least in the right direction (Sanders and Rock, 1988).

At CBS, the most militant step taken was over the issue of clothes. In 1970, when pantsuits were the latest vogue, a memo was issued by a middle manager in the news department to the effect that "it is not company policy nor the discretion of the immediate supervisor for female employees to wear slacks during the course of their normal working day. . . ." The women acted swiftly, and the next morning almost all of them appeared in pants. Their action merited coverage in *The New York Times.* The rule was rescinded.

Following the pants revolt in 1970, no organized activity by the women of CBS occurred until 1973. Oddly enough, the women got together as a result of a "policy statement on women" distributed company-wide from the network president. The memo declared that every employee at CBS should receive equal opportunity, that there was a policy of equal pay, and that five part-time women's counselors would be appointed to handle women's "aspirations and gripes." The memo was intended to head off law suits like the one at NBC. Although change came slowly, the numbers improved. In the news division in 1972, only 22 women were in producers' jobs, but by January 1979, there were 40 more. Where there had been three female technicians, the number rose to 15.

While the management of ABC and CBS were by and large conciliatory in the 1970s, NBC was so hostile that legal intervention became necessary. The women at NBC had not initially wanted a lawsuit. One of their grievances was that secretaries were graded according to the standing of the men they worked for. A secretary to a vice president was paid more than a secretary to a lower-level person. No matter how well they did their jobs, secretaries were treated as appendages. Their initial appeals to the human resources department to change this practice were ignored. Money was not the main issue; the women wanted fairness.

At their second meeting with management, the women's grievances went beyond employment; they charged that women's concerns were ignored on the air as well. The men made a counterpresentation charging that the station dealt with women's issues on soap operas: adultery, abortion, rape, homosexuality, and incest. These were certainly sensational subjects and surefire ratings grabbers, but they were not what the women had in mind. The management's definition of "women's issues" underscored for the NBC women's group just how far apart they were from management in the comprehension of the issues (Sanders and Rock, 1988).

Soon after that, with the help of the New York City Human Rights Commission, the 16 NBC women decided to sue. A crucial development helped to conclude the litigation. The case was joined by the Equal Employment Opportunity Commission, which filed its own charges. NBC first tried to settle out of court for $500,000, but the women turned them down. Money, they repeated, was not the whole problem. The settlement finally included a payment of $2 million, but much more was involved.

The bulk of the agreement involved a broad range of affirmative action policies designed to bring more women into previously male-dominated management and technical positions, to improve the salaries and job assignments in the primarily female clerical positions, and to provide a more open, documented personnel system. Twenty thousand dollars a year was set aside for monitoring compliance efforts, to end in 1981.

The work of these women's groups was not always lasting. By 1983 the ABC women organized again, unaware of the group that had preceded them by ten years. The discontent began in the news division where there were nearly 100 correspondents and only 15 of them were women. When they complained to the Washington bureau chief, he basically told them they were lucky to have jobs. By 1985 they appealed to the news division president. Of the 1,100 employees in the news organization at the time, 500 were women. The women's research revealed large wage discrepancies. They said women producers were paid on the average 30 percent less than men. Management expressed disbelief and wanted to know where those numbers had come from. The women pointed out they were reporters and had found a way. The other major issue brought up was sexual harassment. Both were red flags to the network because they spelled possible litigation. The women also wanted a Woman's Advisory Board to serve as a watchdog group and a full-time recruiter to hire qualified women as well as minorities. They wanted job postings and a system of employee evaluations. Instead of bad-mouthing people behind their backs, the women wanted evaluations on a regular basis. Lastly, the women asked for a pay equity study.

The company responded positively to several of those demands. In January 1986, a female news recruiter was hired. Job posting did begin, but top jobs, like senior producer, were not listed. A company salary study revealed discrepancies, but ABC explained that was caused by different hiring patterns. Women tended to rise within the company, restricted by the company policy of a 10 percent limit on raises. Men often came in from high-paying outside jobs. However, the company study resulted in substantial raises for more than 40 producers, 15 of them men. Although this second group was successful in effecting change, by 1988, the women's group was having difficulty arranging any meetings at all with management.

Overall, the networks' nightly newscasts boosted their female staffing between 1988 and 1996 by about a third. The biggest increases came in those areas where the networks' interest was waning: ABC, in foreign bureaus, and at NBC, in election coverage (*Women, Men and Media*, 1997).

On-Camera Pressures

Anchors in local news were experiencing other kinds of pressures that began interfering with their work. Christine Craft was hired as a local news anchor at a then Metromedia-owned station, KMBC-TV, in Kansas City in 1981. She brought a discrimination suit against them in 1983. Her complaint was indicative of the problems on-camera women were having in an industry where news is seen as entertainment.

KMBC had hired a research consulting firm, Media Associates (now known as Audience Research and Development), to find a female anchor who could bring "warmth" and comfort to the news. Media Associates went all over the country taping local talent off the air. They liked Craft because she looked "laid back with California energy." In 1980 KMBC-TV in Kansas City, the 27th-sized market, offered her the anchor job at a salary of $35,000.

Craft was wary of consultants and disliked makeup artists. In her negotiations with Ridge Shannon, news director for KMBC, she stressed the fact that she wanted to be hired for her journalistic abilities and not because her appearance would fit into some consultant's categorization. Although her boss assured her otherwise, when the ratings did not go up management sent in a consultant to "help" her. They "helped" her with her makeup and developed a clothes calendar for her to improve her image. Nine months after she began she was called into news director Shannon's office and told that he was taking her off the anchor position and assigning her as a reporter. Craft's description of his reasons for demoting her was that she was "too old, too unattractive and not deferential enough to men." Shannon later denied making this statement (Craft, 1986: 68).

Craft eventually decided to take her case to court, claiming three things: "sexual discrimination in an advisory capacity," the violation of the Equal Pay Act (her male coanchor was making $52,000), and fraud, because KMBC said they hired her for her journalistic abilities but she was fired for her appearance. A major focus in the trial was on the validity of the kind of research conducted by Media Associates through the use of surveys and focus groups. (Focus groups are small groups of people who experience something together and then are questioned by a trained leader about their immediate reactions.)

In the focus group organized to study Craft's presentational style, the leader began the discussion by asking the group whether the anchorwoman was a "mutt"; he is also reported to have said: "Let's spend thirty seconds destroying Christine Craft," and "if we all chip in we can buy her a ticket back to California" (Craft, 1986). The leader claimed that those remarks were meant to loosen up the group so they wouldn't be afraid to criticize her. The participants in the focus group had not been tested for sexual preference, that is, for whether they liked a man or a woman anchor better. They were tested for what *kind* of woman they wanted to see, whether they preferred a woman with youth, beauty, and a nonaggressive style. Later, the lawyers defending Craft claimed that the method of testing violated Title VII of the Civil Rights Act of 1964 because of the sexual stereotypes encouraged in the testing setup. They said the focus group leader encouraged a negative reaction to Craft's dress and makeup. Most physical appearance requirements are illegal under Title VII. There can be a dress code but not a grooming standard applied more strictly to women than to men (Gielow, 1985: 444). The focus group seemed to demand more from her in terms of appearance than they did from her male coanchor. Based on these evaluations, the news director is reported to have said that "the audience perceived [Craft's] dress, appearance, makeup, and presentation as stumbling blocks" (Craft, 1986: 127). Craft claimed that this kind of reason for demotion was sexual discrimination against women in the category of appearance and demeanor.

The first jury found in favor of Craft on the sex-discrimination and fraud charges and recommended an award of $500,000 in damages. But Judge Stevens threw out the jury's award and ruled that KMBC-TV had not been guilty of sex discrimination in insisting that Craft improve her appearance; it demanded the same of men. Stevens said the only discrimination to be found in the case was the ironic one that, "but for the fact that she is female, [Craft] would not have been hired as a coanchor in December 1980, regardless of her other abilities" (*Broadcasting Magazine*, 1983). Judge Stevens did order a new trial on the fraud charge (that Craft was hired under false pretenses).

The second jury also found in favor of Craft and advised the judge to award her $325,000. Craft's case was eventually dismissed following Metromedia's appeal to the highest court (Sanders and Rock, 1988). Today, Craft is a practicing attorney and radio talk show host at KGO in San Francisco.

It is undeniable that television is an entertainment medium and that one's appearance does affect one's reception by an audience. Most women on television do care whether they look attractive, but they believe this should not be the only criterion by which a female newscaster is judged. Since Craft's case, there have been several suits by female newscasters charging age and/or sex discrimination. In 1994, then 45-year-old veteran anchor Diane Allen resolved her battle with then CBS-owned Philadelphia television station WCAU against which she had made allegations of age and sex discrimination in a federal complaint with the U.S. Equal Employment Opportunity Commission. In her forties, Allen was replaced on the 11 P.M. news by a 32-year old female anchor, and assigned only to the 5:30 P.M. news, when she had been anchoring both newscasts for nearly 18 years; her then coanchor,

Larry Kane, turned 50 while anchoring the later newscast. Allen left WCAU at the end of her contract and then settled her dispute with the station (*Philadelphia Inquirer*, 1994). She became a Republican state senator in New Jersey in 1996. CNN's Patti Paniccia settled her sex discrimination suit in 1996 with that company after she was fired from her correspondent's job following her second pregnancy in two years. Paniccia, who is also an attorney, now teaches Gender and the Law at Pepperdine University.

Veteran anchorwoman Janet Peckinpaugh, at age 48, won an $8.3 million jury verdict in her sex discrimination suit against WFSB-TV of Hartford, Connecticut, a station then owned by Post-Newsweek. Peckinpaugh, who went on to coanchor the 5 P.M. news for rival Hartford station WVIT, reached a confidential settlement with Post-Newsweek (Peckinpaugh, 1999). A jury awarded another longtime anchor, Sara Lee Kessler, $7.3 million in 1999 after she charged her station, WWOR-TV of Secaucus, New Jersey, with discrimination. Kessler, who worked for the station for more than 17 years, charged that her station demoted her from her anchor duties to full-time reporter and forced her to take a disability leave after she injured her tailbone. Interestingly, the jury rejected the then 47-year-old journalist's charges of age, sex, and religious discrimination (Kessler, an Orthodox Jew, requested Friday evenings off to observe the Sabbath). Chris-Craft, owner of the station, has denied all charges (Kessler, 1999). Kessler is currently a health and medical reporter at New Jersey Nightly News (NJNN) at a significantly reduced salary from the estimated $300,000 yearly salary she was making as an anchor at WWOR.

None of these women has been able to match the job or the salary she had in television news prior to her law suit—not even Peckinpaugh who remains an anchor in Hartford, Connecticut. However, these women all hope that their lawsuits send a message to the rest of the news business. Said Paniccia, "I've learned that it's very important to stand up for what you believe in" (Paniccia, 2000a). She's written a handbook for women to protect themselves against sex discrimination (Paniccia, 2000b).

Women in Management

Because there are a limited number of power positions in any system, including television news, questions of promotion are inherently questions of politics. Promotions often come from within and occur among friends. Women have not usually been part of the in-group. Those few women who do advance are often not particularly anxious to help or identify with other women. If women are going to change corporate structures, they will only do so when their numbers increase to a critical mass—then, if so inclined, they can act without fear of being overruled or mustered out.

One obstacle for women is called the "comfort factor," a phrase credited to Professor Richard L. Zweigenhaft of Guilford College in Greensboro,

North Carolina, in the course of a study on executive-suite discrimination in the 1980s in Fortune 500 companies commissioned by the Institute of Human Relations of the American Jewish Committee. His 1984 report, called "Who Gets To The Top?," is based on his interviews of people who graduated from Harvard Business School as far back as the 1960s and includes women, blacks, and Jewish men.

One female with a Harvard MBA from the class of 1975 told him that management now knows the right things to say. She said the problem surfaces when one wants to advance beyond the assistant vice president level. She said,

> Way up at the top, a lot of business gets conducted in non-structured ways, over a golf game, or even in the men's room after a meeting. It's not really the old boy's network, but a lot like that, and women just aren't in it. It's hard for them to get into it because people at that level still are born and raised with the belief that women belong at home. They might make an exception, but they don't do it in general. They don't have the same comfort with women. (Zweigenhaft, 1984: 62)

A 1980 graduate told Zweigenhaft, "They're so used to dealing with women in a teasing sense, or in a non-business sense. Socially, it's still difficult to be a woman in management. Men still perceive you either as their daughter or their mistress. They find it difficult to relate to you as a co-worker" (Zweigenhaft, 1984: 62). In a report issued by the Federal Glass Ceiling Commission in 1995, white male managers' comments supported earlier claims that upper management was willing to accept women and minorities only if they were not too different. As one manager is quoted as saying, "When we find minorities and women who think like we do, we snatch them up" (Federal Glass Ceiling Commission, 1995).

Opinions vary as to why women consistently fill only 20 percent of management jobs in newsrooms, though the numbers are increasing in local news, particularly in news directors' positions (RTNDA, 1999). At the network level, Linda Mason (2000), a CBS News vice president for public affairs, believes, "If you can do the work, you'll get the opportunity. There's no glass ceiling at CBS." Part of her proof: CBS had five female vice presidents in its news division by the millennium, one of the highest numbers of all the networks. NBC News president Andrew Lack said he often hears about the shortage of women available to fill top level jobs, and many other people believe there are more management jobs than women available to fill them. Lack (2000) said he believes one reason women don't seek higher level jobs is because of the nature of the news business. The newsroom, he said, is a collegial place but it's also like a boot camp. Talented people get burned out by the long and unpredictable hours that this labor-intensive business demands, especially in management jobs and at evening news shows.

Susan Zirinsky (2000), another CBS News executive, called evening news production "a steamship" because it goes day to day with breaking news.

When a storm or flu bug hits, most people try to stay home, but the work has just begun in the newsroom. Personal priorities must take a back seat and employees are needed on the job. Senior producers of *The NBC Nightly News* said they carry beepers and are on call 24 hours a day. At ABC's *World News Tonight*, a producer said that one senior producer broke her tailbone and was hospitalized but she continued to work from her hospital bed. The news magazine shows can often offer better hours, but they are still intense. Siobhan Nolan, 31, a former associate producer at ABC's *20/20*, began at that network in 1989 as a college intern and worked her way up by putting in 12-hour days. Nolan (2000) said she knows she has to "pay her dues" and is, therefore, constantly working. She often puts in 10 hours a day and sometimes 90 hours a week; Nolan has often been beeped in the middle of the night.

Many women journalists decide against having children, and Ralph Lowenstein, dean of the University of Florida's College of Journalism, actually recommended that choice in an article published in the Freedom Forum's *Media Studies Journal*. Lowenstein stated, "Women who want to make it in the mass media must take the vow of childlessness" ("A Field Guide . . . ," 1993). Insiders call them "news nuns." Mary Alice O'Rourke, an NBC *Today Show* senior producer who is childless, plans the popular annual feature, "Where in the World Is Matt Lauer" trip, and she often travels for months at a time. "A woman with two children," she said, "wouldn't go for this job" (O'Rourke, 2000). CBS News Productions vice president Margery Baker-Riker, now in her fifties, said most top-ranking women are either childless like herself or waited to have children. Zirinsky was 43 when she adopted her son; NBC News's female solo vice president, Cheryl Gould, had her son at age 42; and Suzy Allen, a coordinating producer at *48 Hours*, said "it's always hard" to juggle work and children. Allen had to spend her daughter's second birthday in China covering the Tienenmen Square riots in 1989. More than ten years later her teenaged daughter didn't remember this, but Allen still feels guilty. "You want to make sure you can do your job well and not expect coworkers to pick up after you," she said. "But I don't want to shortchange my daughter either" (Allen, 2000).

Many women in the younger generation are not willing to wait to have children, nor are they content to be childless. ABC's Siobhan Nolan (2000) said the child care issue is often on her mind, especially when she found out she was pregnant, although she's not that unique among women working in various news organizations. *Nightly News* has an entire bulletin board devoted to "Look who's just arrived"; and four babies were born among the *48 Hours* staff during 1999. Still, Nolan was hesitant to admit that she was expecting a child. She has good role models for career advancement, but few for how to be a working mother in television news. The press, writes Lowenstein in his 1993 *Media Studies Journal* article, doesn't make accommodations for working mothers. Many women quit their jobs and others prefer freelance work or working from home.

The impact of child care on career advancement is highly controversial. Many newsroom executives have commented that child care only slows down, rather that prevents, career advancement. "Talent always helps people rise," said executive producer Neal Shapiro of NBC's *Dateline.* "Part-time employees aren't as visible and it can take longer for their talents to be noticed. They are slowed-up if they stay at home for seven years but they can still get into management." Shapiro has five female producers at *Dateline* who work part-time and several who plan to advance into management when their children are older. In addition, one of his female senior producers works two days a week (Shapiro, 2000). However, many have observed that the issue of child care is far too pervasive throughout society to be the main factor preventing women from advancing in the newsroom. Some women might leave the newsroom because of its rigorous pace, unpredictable schedules, and negative impact on child care, and this lessens the pool of available women to rise to management. But these problems can affect both men and women and don't fully explain why women don't advance into executive jobs.

The executive producer's job of most news broadcasts has always been held by a male. Only one woman in broadcast network news history has been named executive producer of one of the evening newscasts: Emily Rooney was a local news director recruit from WCVB in Boston in 1993 to run *World News Tonight* and was fired after just seven months. "It was a bad fit between me and the network," says Rooney who now hosts a public affairs show in Boston. "I wasn't part of the ABC culture" (Rooney, 2000). By 2000, each network news operation had at least one female vice president and several executive producers, though none were at the helm of the prime, weeknight newscasts.

Evening news programs traditionally have more male senior producers and executive producers. Most of the male senior producers also belong to the same gyms and health clubs and socialize with each other regularly. Even though younger employees are raised with fewer gender-role expectations, Ronnie Steinberg, director of the Women Studies Center at Vanderbilt University, points out that people in charge hire those they are comfortable with and who fit in with them (Steinberg, 2000).

Women in New Media

An April/May 2000 poll by The Pew Research Center for The People and The Press found that 53 percent of Internet users watch some TV news on average days—down from 59 percent in just two years. They are part of a demographic group of more affluent and more well-educated Americans who are moving away from the nightly network news and toward on-line news use in the greatest numbers. The survey also found that for the first time, on-line news users are more likely to believe information on the Web sites of CNN, ABC, CBS, *USA Today* and Fox News than they are from the parent TV and newspaper outlets (Pew, 2000; *USA Today*, 2000). This is good news for online journalism and should be good news for women who enter this world, which does not have a history of gender stereotyping. But some things have not changed. At the larger Web sites belonging to TV networks, women fill 25 percent of senior management jobs, estimated by Lynn Povich, managing editor of MSNBC.com's East Coast division and the company's only female executive. The CEO of CNBC.com is a woman; two men and a woman hold the top jobs at CBS.com; and men hold the two top jobs at ABCNews.com. "Women are the content providers," said Povich, "and men are the managers" (Povich, 2000). According to a February 2000 Price-Waterhouse survey of the New York new-media industry, the average dot-com employee is a 35-year-old white male—and it has been that way from the start.

Jason Chervokas, 35, who cofounded ATNEWYORK.com in 1995, said he wanted his company to change the usual media hierarchy by hiring men and women equally at all levels. "But the irony is," Chervokas said, "it didn't happen, even in the younger generation." ATNEWYORK.com was sold in the spring of 2000 to a large company, and Chervokas said he believes that gender equality is still unlikely. At most large companies, he said, a "new boys network" has formed which replicates the traditional hierarchical structure where men hold the most powerful jobs (Chervokas, 2000). Suzanne Tufts, CEO of the American Women's Economic Development Corp., counsels thousands of businesswomen each year and said, "Thirty years of progress for women hasn't changed the issues as much as people might think" (Tufts, 2000).

Michelle Preli, in her thirties, is typical of new-media journalists. She is young and energetic and was drawn to the field because it was unfamiliar yet interesting. After graduating from Bard College in 1987, Preli worked as an editor for Penthouse magazine but was intrigued by an offer to help Scholastic Online Network launch its Web site. She liked on-line work from the start and, after graduating from Columbia's journalism school in 1994, Preli helped launch NBC's first news Web site. She was promoted from associate producer to producer to senior producer within a few years, and was on staff during the merger that created MSNBC.com. Preli is now senior producer of the "Dateline" Web site at MSNBC.com, and has an office at NBC at Rockefeller Center. Although she might consult with producers of *Dateline*, she largely connects with coworkers via the Internet. Her designer works at Microsoft in Redmond, Washington, and her other assistants are in Secaucus, New Jersey. She said she encounters many of the same gender issues as her journalism peers in broadcast news and, like others, Preli is concerned about the huge drop-off in numbers of women in higher level jobs (Preli, 2000).

Working in new media can still be a grind for journalists, although it is better because they can often work from home, especially on weekends, because job locations are de-centralized. However, those who work for Web sites like MSNBC.com have to be available 24 hours a day to update the site. Preli says she takes her son to day care each morning at 8:00, but her evening hours are unpredictable. Her husband, a freelance photographer, picks up their son each evening because the day care center closes at 6 P.M. Preli posts the new "Dateline" web page every night after her son is in bed.

Salaries are typically much better in new media. Michelle Preli (2000) says she started out making more than her counterparts in traditional media. However, she said she worked for two start-up companies and watched how the numbers of men increased, especially in management, when the company expanded and the salaries rose. Chervokas (2000) of ATNEWYORK.com and Povich (2000) of MSNBC.com agreed that men in management "jump over" from broadcast to new media because they get a promotion and a salary increase in the process. Younger and less experienced men and women also jump over because new media is the latest thing, but, said Povich, they enter at a lower level and are not candidates for management. Chervokas (2000) said women mainly advance in new media if they helped start the company. His company began with two men and they hired a woman, and all three still work together.

As new media companies expand, however, the traditional male/female hierarchy emerges, at least at network news sites. In 1995, Allison Davis helped start NBC News Online (currently MSNBC.com), but when she departed to become an executive with CBS Eye Mark in 1997, it was a man, Steve Johnson, who replaced her. When MSNBC.com was a start-up company, the staff was largely comprised of women. "As it's merged and expanded," said Preli (2000), "the new hires are mostly men." Chervokas (2000) explained that this happens because companies recruit for managers at networks where the pool is largely male. But Preli disagreed that the pool is largely male. She also said that many of the men have less experience than the women who work for them.

CONCLUSION

Women in television news and on-line journalism face a narrow road for advancement with many obstacles. Having a full, personal life is difficult, the "old boys' club" is a powerful networking tool that excludes women, and stereotypes about a woman's abilities are a constant barricade to opportunities. Young women might try to keep their desires hidden, but most are boldly ambitious and comfortable with being that way. In *Waiting for Primetime*, however, Marlene Sanders predicted that the media would become a pink-collar industry as wages declined, and she appears to be right (Sanders and Rock, 1988). Women currently dominate jobs at cable networks and new media start-ups where salaries are also the lowest. Optimists agree that women are on the track to higher level jobs and will advance in the new millennium into top positions. But others see a logjam just below the highest levels that will not end any time soon, as long as any man is available for the top jobs.

FOR FURTHER DISCUSSION

1. Many women and, increasingly some men, have to curtail their careers in news when they become parents. Discuss whether a more

child-friendly work environment might increase the chances for advancement for all. Should newsrooms consider on-site day care centers or stipends for child care?

2. There have been several lawsuits filed by female newscasters charging sex and age discrimination in TV news since the first such suit was filed by Christine Craft in 1986, but many cite the success of Connie Chung, Diane Sawyer, and Barbara Walters as example of women who are in their fifties and older and continue to enjoy success. What are the relative ages of the female and male anchors in your area? Do the oldest women appear to be as old as the oldest men? What has been the history of women in television in your area?
3. With a growing number of women majoring in journalism and mass communication there are more women than men in newsrooms around the country and most departments and schools of journalism prepare students to become reporters in television. Should there be more courses in management to expose students earlier to leadership positions? How might this make a difference in whether women attain the very top jobs in newsrooms?
4. Discuss why men have become less likely to pursue careers in news, even while the very top positions continue to remain primarily open to them.
5. Compare and contrast the information in a local or network newscast to the information contained on its Web site. Is there more information? Can a consumer become as informed by using only a news Web site? How frequently is the Web site updated?
6. There are annual findings that consumers who use news Web sites are also watching network TV news in fewer numbers. Discuss whether this will result in careers in on-line journalism eventually becoming more desirable than those in television. Will more women than men continue to find these jobs attractive and why?
7. Since many journalists will have to file stories for both their TV programs and their Web sites, what kind of skills will be most valued and how might journalists prepare for that? What particular advantages might a man or woman bring to such developments?

REFERENCES

Aaron, B. 14 October 1986. Personal interview with M. Rock.

ABCNews.com. 19 May 2000. Biographical data on Connie Chung.

Allen, S. February 2000. Personal interview with J. Adams.

Baker, M. February 2000. Personal interview with J. Adams.

Basler, B. 7 December 1986. Putting a career on hold. *The New York Times Magazine,* 159.

Becker, L., and J. Kosicki 1999. *Journalism and Mass Communication Educator.* Fall: 5–22.
Chervokas, J. February 2000. Personal interview with J. Adams.
Craft, C. 1986. *Christine Craft. An Anchorwoman's Story.* Santa Barbara, CA: Rhodora/Capra Press. 2000 Update. How young is too old? *AFTRA Magazine*, Fall 1999: 25.
Daley, S. 4 March 1991. Networks, motherhood and careers. *The New York Times,* C16.
Ferguson, R. 8 November 1986. Personal interview with M. Rock.
Federal Glass Ceiling Commission. 1995. "Good For Business: Making Full Use of the Nation's Human Capital." Washington, DC: U.S. Government Printing Office.
A field guide for women in media industries. 1993. *Media Studies Journal* 7(1–2): 81–98.
Gielow, L. S. 1985. Sex discrimination in newscasting. *Michigan Law Review* 84: 443, 444.
Gould, C. November 1999. Personal interview with J. Adams.
Kessler, S. L. 7 April 1999. *The Star-Ledger.*
Lack, A. January 2000. Personal interview with J. Adams.
Mason, L. February 2000. Personal interview with J. Adams.
McCollum/Spielman and Company, Inc. 1986, February. *Topline* (4).
Mitchell, A. 18 November 1986. Personal interview with M. Rock.
The New York Times. 30 April 2000. Albright spokesman ends singular tenure.
Nolan, S. December 1999. Personal interview with J. Adams.
O'Rourke, M. A. December 1999. Personal interview with J. Adams.
Paniccia, P. 2 June 2000a. Personal interview with S. Stainback.
———. 2000b. *Working Smarts for Women.* New York: Ballantine Books.
Peckinpaugh, J. 29 January 1999. *Hartford Courant.*
Pew Research Center for The People and The Press. 16 June 2000. people-press.org
Povich, L. March 2000. Personal interview with J. Adams.
Preli, M. February 2000. Personal interview with J. Adams.
Rooney, E. February 2000. Personal interview with J. Adams.
Rich, B. 20 September 1986. Personal interview with M. Rock.
———. 21 February 1987. Personal interview with M. Rock.
Sanders, M., and M. Rock. 1988. *Waiting for Prime Time. The Women of Television News.* Urbana: University of Illinois Press.
Screen Actor's Guild. 1986/2000. A woman's voice sells as well as a man's on TV, Screen Actor's Guild study shows. 1986. Screen Actor's Guild press release: 16 September/Update May 2000, Vivian Herndon for SAG.
Shapiro, N. February 2000. Personal interview with J. Adams.
Stahl, L. 1986, November 19. Personal interview with M. Rock.
Stanley, N. 1971. Federal communications law and women's rights: Women in the wasteland fight back. *Hastings Law Journal* 23: 15–53.
Steinberg, R. 11 February 2000. Personal interview with J. Adams.
Tufts, S. January and February 2000. Personal interview with J. Adams.
USA Today. 12 June 2000. Net encroaches on TV news.
Women's Media Project and NOW Legal Defense and Education Fund. 1990. Women, men and network news.
Women, Men and Media. 1997. NY: Freedom Forum Media Studies Center.
Zirinsky, S. December 1999. Personal interview with J. Adams.
Zweigenhaft, R. L. 1984. Who gets to the top? Institute of Human Relations, American Jewish Committee.
———. 1998. *Diversity in the Power Elite.* New Haven: Yale University Press.

Index